DATE			
NOV 19 '86			

CHINA AND
THE TAIWAN ISSUE

CHINA AND
THE TAIWAN ISSUE

Edited by

HUNGDAH CHIU

PRAEGER

PRAEGER SPECIAL STUDIES • PRAEGER SCIENTIFIC

Library of Congress Cataloging in Publication Data

Main entry under title:

China and the Taiwan issue.

    Bibliography: p.
    Includes index.
    1. Taiwan--History--Addresses, essays, lectures.
2. United States--Foreign relations--China--Addresses,
essays, lectures. 3. China--Foreign relations--United
States--Addresses, essays, lectures. I. Chiu, Hungdah,
1936-
DS799.5.C467   320.9'51'249   79-14270

Published in 1979 by Praeger Publishers
A Division of Holt, Rinehart and Winston/CBS, Inc.
383 Madison Avenue, New York, New York 10017 U.S.A.

9 038 987654321
Printed in the United States of America

Preface

In 1973 *China and the Question of Taiwan: Documents and Analysis* was published and within two years it was out of print. I was editor of the book, and since then I have received numerous inquiries concerning the revised edition. Because most of the original contributors are unable to revise their chapters for a new edition, I decided to put out a new book in a somewhat different format and with different contributors.

Despite the recent establishment of diplomatic relations between Washington and Peking on January 1, 1979, it is beyond doubt that the Taiwan problem will remain with the United States for many years to come. The present book is an attempt to combine selected original documents to study the historical, economic, political, and legal aspects of the Taiwan problem.

I am grateful to Professor Shao-chuan Leng for his contribution of the Introduction to this book and to Dean Michael Kelly for reducing my teaching load in 1978-79. I also would like to thank Assistant Dean George Regan for his administrative assistance, David Simon for his editorial assistance, Karen Murphy and Shaiw-chei Yin for their research and secretarial assistance, Jyh-pin Fa for compiling the index, and finally LuAnn Young for typing part of the manuscript.

While this book is a collective work, the views expressed in each chapter are those of the respective authors and do not necessarily reflect the views of the editor, other contributors, or any of the many persons I have consulted or received assistance from in its preparation. With respect to the selection of documents, I alone am responsible. All translations of documents not otherwise credited are my own.

Contents

LIST OF TABLES

Table		Page

LIST OF FIGURES

CHINA AND THE TAIWAN ISSUE

1

Introduction

Shao-chuan Leng

In the Nixon-Chou Shanghai Communique, issued on February 28, 1972, the United States and the People's Republic of China (PRC) expressed their wish to "make progress toward the normalization of relations." One major disagreement between the two sides was over the Taiwan issue. Separate positions were set forth in the communique on this question:

> The two sides reviewed the long-standing serious disputes between China and the United States. The Chinese side reaffirmed its position: The Taiwan question is the crucial question obstructing the normalization of relations between China and the United States; the Government of the People's Republic of China is the sole legal government of China; Taiwan is a province of China which has long been returned to the motherland; the liberation of Taiwan is China's internal affair in which no other country has the right to interfere; and all U.S. forces and military installations must be withdrawn from Taiwan. The Chinese government firmly opposes any activities which aim at the creation of "one China, one Taiwan," "one China, two governments," "two Chinas," an "independent Taiwan," or advocate that "the status of Taiwan remains to be determined."

> The U.S. side declared: The United States acknowledges that all Chinese on either side of the Taiwan Strait maintain there is but one China and that Taiwan is a part of China. The United States Government does not challenge that position. It reaffirms its interest in a peaceful settlement of the Taiwan question by the Chinese themselves. With this prospect in mind, it affirms the ultimate objective of the withdrawal of all U.S. forces and military installations from Taiwan. In the meantime, it will progressively reduce its forces and military installations on Taiwan as the tension in the area diminishes.

Thus Peking made its stand clear that "Taiwan is a province of China" and that "liberation of Taiwan is China's internal affair." The American position, however, was stated with some ambiguity. Washington acknowledged that "all Chinese on either side of the Taiwan Strait" accept the concept of one China to include Taiwan[1] and expressed "its interest in a peaceful settlement of the Taiwan question by the Chinese themselves." It did not renounce the Mutual Defense Pact with Taiwan but promised the progressive and ultimate withdrawal of U.S. forces from the island.

Between February 1972 and December 1978 considerable progress was made in improving U.S.-PRC relations, but a number of factors, including domestic politics in both countries, prevented the normalization of their ties. The main problem remained Taiwan. In order to have full diplomatic relations, Peking asked Washington to accept the following three conditions: the severance of U.S. diplomatic ties with Taipei, withdrawal of all American military personnel from Taiwan, and abrogation of the Mutual Defense Treaty with the Nationalist government. Because of U.S. political, economic, moral, legal, and strategic considerations regarding Taiwan, the question facing Washington was, therefore, how to establish formal ties with Peking without "sacrificing" in substance Taiwan's security and close relationships with the United States.

In an effort to resolve the emotion-packed and multidimensional Taiwan issue, a wide spectrum of policy options have been advanced by academicians, ranging from the German model to the Japanese formula.[2] The former would call for Washington to maintain diplomatic relations with both Peking and Taipei as in the case of the divided Germany. The latter would mean the acceptance by the United States of the PRC's three conditions of normalization while keeping only economic, cultural, and other "nonofficial" ties with Taiwan. Between the two poles there were several other formulas and proposals. Suffice to name just two of them as examples. One was the so-called American formula, under which the United States would raise the liaison office in Peking to the status of an embassy and at the same time reduce the embassy in Taipei to a liaison office or to a consular office. The other may be referred to as the British Commonwealth model, under which Washington would establish full diplomatic relations with Peking, recognized as the symbolic center of authority of the Great Chinese Commonwealth with Taiwan (and eventually Hong Kong, too) being its truly self-governing member able to maintain semiofficial ties with the United States. Whatever their respective merits and flaws, the presence of such a diversity of policy suggestions and formulas has underscored the complexities of the Taiwan issues and the difficulties of finding a solution satisfactory to all the parties concerned.

From mid-1978 on, however, a new momentum was developing toward normalization of U.S.-PRC ties, obviously generated by Peking's eagerness to push forward its modernization programs and Washington's desire to play the "China card" in the ongoing poker game with Moscow. Arrangements were made between American and Chinese authorities for the exchange of scientists, scholars, and students, for expansion of trade relations, and for cooperation in oil, agriculture, and other areas of mutual interest. Then on December 15, 1978, President Carter made the dramatic announcement that the United States and the People's Republic of China had agreed to establish full diplomatic relations on January 1, 1979. Under this agreement the United States would end formal diplomatic ties with Taiwan, withdraw remaining American troops from the island, and abrogate the 1954 Mutual Defense Treaty. In return the United States would maintain cultural, commercial, and other unofficial relations with Taiwan and continue to sell Taiwan "selective defensive weaponry" after the expiration of the defense treaty at the end of 1979.[3] While details of future U.S.-Taiwan relations are yet to be worked out, what seems clear is that the Taiwan issue will continue to draw international attention in the years to come.

To put the issue in perspective, a number of important questions must be explored in depth. What was the origin of the Taiwan problem? How close are the island's ties with China seen from the historical and legal standpoints? What are the conditions in Taiwan in terms of political stability and material progress? Are its political and economic systems strong enough to withstand the impact of normalization of U.S.-PRC relations? What has been the PRC's approach to Taiwan? How has the U.S. position evolved over the island? Under what circumstances might Taiwan be forced to undertake certain painful options that could be detrimental to the long-range Chinese interest? What does the future hold for Taiwan in the postnormalization era?

It is to these and other related questions that the present volume addresses itself. The editor and contributors do not pretend to have all the right answers; nor do they perceive any simple and quick solutions to the Taiwan issue. What they attempt to do is to analyze through their expertise the various pertinent questions in as candid and comprehensive manner as possible so readers can have a better understanding of the complexities of the subject.

In Chapter 2 Yu-ming Shaw gives a historical and interpretative account of the evolution of Taiwan from ancient times to 1945, with the focus on the most significant aspects of the island's development in the last three centuries. In particular, the Japanese rule between 1895 and 1945 is given a critical evaluation. While conceding the good progress made under the Japanese in Taiwanese economic and educational development, the author nevertheless points out the high price the Taiwanese people had to pay for this progress as well as the exploitative nature of the Japanese colonial rule on the island. As the people on Taiwan and those on the mainland have the same ethnic origins, cultural tradition, social customs, and spiritual identity, the author concludes that "despite the 50 years of Japanese occupation, the tie between the people of Taiwan and those of mainland, both in terms of cultural affinity and ethnic origin, remains essentially unchanged."

Political development in Taiwan under the Republic of China (ROC) government is treated in Chapter 3 by John F. Copper. In an attempt to ascertain the role or scope of political change in Taiwan and to assess the functional and dysfunctional aspects of this change, the author examines in detail the structure and use of political power, the impact of economic development upon the policy, the nature and extent of social change and its impact upon protest and reform, and the rule of the ROC leader Chiang Ching-kuo. Despite what he calls the "stagnant image" of the ROC's political structure and ideology, Copper argues that substantial change and "democratization" have been taking place in the government, especially at the local levels. Using the behavioralist criteria for political modernization (for example, economic growth; increases in education, literacy, communications and the media; and receptibility to the penetration of outside ideas), he considers Taiwan as indeed "a rapidly changing society" having experienced a high level of political development. In the concluding section of the chapter an effort is also made to tackle the question whether in terms of domestic political change and modernization the ROC on Taiwan will survive the challenge in the next decade.

Chapter 4 discusses economic development in Taiwan. In evaluating Taiwan's economic system, Jan S. Prybyla carefully examines what objectives the system set for itself and how well these targets were reached. With his findings illustrated by 8 figures and 26 tables, he concludes that Taiwan has successfully combined elements of the market economy with governmental planning and has achieved a level of prosperity well above that of most developing non-OPEC countries, including most of Asia. This record is truly remarkable when "seen in the context of Taiwan's initial poverty, absolute natural resource deficiency, formal political isolation, and heavy burden of defense expenditure." On the other hand, the author also sees many difficulties and perils that lurk on the road ahead for Taiwan. One of the main problems is the island's heavy reliance on the outside world for continued goods purchases, investment, technology transfers, and primary energy-raw materials supplies. Any drastic shift in U.S.-Taiwan relations, according to the author, would seriously affect Taiwan's foreign sources of capital, external trade, and domestic economic development; ultimately, perhaps, the island's political stability.

"Taiwan in Peking's Strategy" is the title of Chapter 5, written by King C. Chen. In analyzing the PRC's position on Taiwan the author gives special attention to four basic elements, namely, Chinese nationalism, ideologic perspectives, strategic and energy interests, and factional politics. According to him, the expression of Peking's attitude toward Taiwan takes several forms. In inspiration it uses national sentiment and communist ideology; in operation it adopts united-front strategy and combines tolerance and militancy. At length Chen examines the various instruments, channels, and tactics employed by the PRC to promote the peaceful liberation of the island. His discussion includes the post-normalization appeals made by Peking to Taiwan to starting negotiations and contacts between the two sides leading to the reunification of the country. Since the use of force has never been ruled out by Peking, he also deals with the following two critical questions: under what conditions will the PRC employ armed force? and what is the Chinese capability for such a military operation?

In Chapter 6 Hungdah Chiu, the editor, provides a systematic analysis of the Taiwan question in the context of U.S.-PRC and U.S.-ROC relations. He begins with a description of the origin of the Taiwan question and then proceeds with a detailed survey of the evolution of the questions through the Japanese Peace Conference, the three Taiwan Strait crises, the U.S.-PRC Geneva and Warsaw talks, and the Shanghai Communique and its subsequent development. In the course of his survey, the author also examines the legal status of Taiwan from the perspective of international law. According to him, the PRC's claim to Taiwan is primarily based on the theory of historical irredentism, which, however, must be pitted against another legal principle, the principle of self-determination. The last part of the chapter is devoted to the normalization of U.S.-PRC relations and its impact on Taiwan. Implications of Carter's recent normalization decision are analyzed by Chiu, who stresses the need for an explicit assurance of Taiwan's security and its close economic, cultural, and other ties with the United States. Otherwise, confronted with the problem of survival, he argues, the government and people on Taiwan might be compelled to resort to what the author labels as "secondary" options: to declare independence, go nuclear, or form a relationship with the Soviet Union. None of these options would be a happy choice for Taiwan; nor could any one be a welcome development in the interest of the PRC or the United States. To avert either of such unfortunate eventualities, Chiu suggests several postnormalization steps for the United States to take, through congressional resolutions or otherwise, to boost Taiwan's morale: for example, maintenance of "semiofficial" relations, continuation of adequate arms sales, and preservation of free and uninterrupted flow of goods and services in the area.

In addition to the analytical chapters mentioned above, the book contains an impressive collection of documents and a selected bibliography. Together they constitute an invaluable source of information on Taiwan that will enable readers to draw their own conclusions and/or to carry on further research on the subject.

NOTES

1. Instead of "all Chinese on either side of the strait," according to one observer, the statement should have referred to "the two governments on both sides of the strait," as a large number of Taiwanese and a growing number of mainland Chinese on Taiwan may not accept the "one-China thesis." "Robert A. Scalapino's Prepared Statement, September 20, 1977," U.S. Congress, House, Subcommittee on Asian and Pacific Affairs of the Committee on International Relations, *Normalization of Relations with the People's Republic of China: Practical Implications*, 95th Cong., 1st sess., September–October 1977, p. 34. Others tend to view this U.S. statement as reflecting Washington's move to disengage itself from fostering Taiwanese independence. See, for example, A. Doak Barnett, *China and the Major Powers in East Asia* (Washington, D.C.: Brookings Institution, 1977), pp. 200, 238.

2. For the variety of suggestions, see A. Doak Barnett, *China Policy* (Washington, D.C.: Brookings Institution, 1977); Hungdah Chiu, ed., *Normalizing Relations with the People's Republic of China*, Occasional Papers/Reprint Series in Contemporary Asian

Studies, University of Maryland Law School, No. 2, 1978; Ralph N. Clough, *Island China* (Cambridge, Mass.: Harvard University Press, 1978); Jerome A. Cohen, "A China Policy for the Next Administration," *Foreign Affairs* 55, no. 4 (October 1976): 20–37; Victor H. Li, *De-recognizing Taiwan: The Legal Problems* (Washington, D.C.: Carnegie Endowment for International Peace, 1977); Ramon H. Myers, ed., *Two Chinese States, U.S. Foreign Policy and Interests* (Stanford, Calif.: Hoover Institution Press, 1978); Michel Okenberg and Robert B. Oxnam, eds., *Dragon and Eagle* (New York: Basic Books, 1978); U.S. Congress, House, Special Subcommittee on Investigating the Committee on International Relations, *United States-China Relations: The Process of Normalization of Relations*, 94th Cong., November–December 1975, February 1976; U.S. Congress, House, Subcommittee on Asian and Pacific Affairs, *Normalization of Relations With the PRC*, 95th Cong., September–October 1977; U.S. Congress, Senate, Committee on Foreign Relations, *Taiwan*, 96th Cong., 1979.

3. For a report on Carter's announcement and texts of statements from the United States, China, and Taiwan, see the New York *Times*, December 16, 1978, p. 1 and December 17, p. 22.

2

Modern History of Taiwan:
An Interpretative Account

Yu-ming Shaw

This chapter attempts to assess the historical evolution of Taiwan from a little-known and uncultivated island to one of the most modern and developed areas of the world today. It will emphasize Taiwan's development since the seventeenth century under the control of the Ming (1368-1644) loyalists, the Ch'ing (Manchu, 1644-1911) rulers, and the Japanese conquerors (1895-1945). Since the other chapters of this book will cover the recent developments of Taiwan under the Republic of China (ROC) or Nationalist government, this chapter will not touch on that period (1945 to present).

This chapter will deal only with the most significant and salient aspects of Taiwan's development in the last three centuries. For a more in-depth understanding of the period, the reader should consult some of the lengthier studies mentioned in the bibliographic section of this book.

TAIWAN FROM ANCIENT TIMES TO 1682

Geographically, Taiwan lies 100 miles east of the mainland of China, 695 miles south of the main Japanese islands, and 199 miles north of the Philippines. It is 13,884 square miles in area, about the combined size of the states of Maryland, Delaware, and Rhode Island, or a trifle smaller than Switzerland.[1]

Some geologists and geographers believe that Taiwan was originally connected to the mainland. It is further thought that during the Great Ice Age (Pleistocene Epoch, between 11,000 and 1 million years ago) that Taiwan separated from China due to some geological changes in the present Taiwan Strait area.[2]

Whereas the geological formation of Taiwan is not contested, the earliest discovery or Chinese conquest of the island is not clear, resulting in various contending interpretations. Some historians have cited *Shang-shu*, a Chinese history book that was probably finished in the early third century B.C., to prove that Taiwan had been a tributary to a Chinese state in ancient times. But this is probably more legend than historical fact. Other historians have dated the earliest Chinese influence on Taiwan as occuring much later. They claim that a Chinese military expedition against "I-chou" in the third century by forces of the Wu ruler Sun Ch'üan (reign 222-252) and the expedition against "Liu Ch'iu" in the seventh century by forces of Emperor Yang of the Sui dynasty (589-618) were all in actuality against Taiwan. Therefore they argue that Taiwan had been conquered during these early periods.

If the above two expeditions were indeed the beginnings of the Chinese subjugation of Taiwan, they were only temporary military victories and did not result in Chinese settlement of the island. In terms of sending Chinese immigrants and a Chinese administration to Taiwan and its adjacent P'eng-hu, it had to wait for several centuries. There are documentary evidences indicating that by 1171, P'eng-hu (Pescadores) had become a Chinese military outpost, and at least by 1225 it was administratively incorporated into the Chinese Empire—placed under the jurisdiction of Tsin-kiang County of Ch'üan-chou Prefecture, Fukien Province.[3] As for Taiwan, no massive settlement began until General Cheng Ch'eng-kung (Koxinga, 1624-62) expelled the Dutch from Taiwan in 1661.

Before General Cheng, a Ming loyalist who took control of Taiwan in 1661, Taiwan and P'eng-hu had been under the molestation of both foreign traders and adventurers and Chinese pirates. In 1602, 1609, 1616, and in the late 1620s several Japanese incursions, either by pirates or by the Tokugawa Shogunate forces, were made against P'eng-hu and Taiwan. None of these invasions, however, brought much benefit to Japan.[4]

The Dutch first appeared in the Far East in the late sixteenth century. In 1602 the Dutch East India Company was established to coordinate all the Dutch colonial activities in East and Southeast Asia, including Taiwan. However, the first occupation of the island did not occur until 1622. Since P'eng-hu at the time was deemed much more important to the commerce and security of China's southeast coast, the Ming court decided to expel the Dutch from P'eng-hu, and it succeeded in doing so in 1624. On the other hand, to satisfy the Dutch desire for trade with China, the Ming court agreed to let the Dutch locate on Taiwan and set up trading posts there. Therefore, Taiwan became a Dutch colony for 37 years, interspersed with Spanish rule over its northern part between 1626 and 1642.[5]

During this period Taiwan and P'eng-hu had been havens for the Chinese pirates. They pillaged China's southeast coast but also served as traders between China, Japan, the Philippines, and other Southeast Asian regions. To maximize their gains, these pirates sometimes cooperated with the Chinese government forces to fight against foreign invaders in the area, and at other times they joined the foreign invaders against Peking. Despite their being pirates, they also played the role of pioneers in opening up and developing areas such as Taiwan.[6]

Among the pirates, two were the most famous: Yen Su-ch'i and Cheng Chih-lung, the father of Cheng Ch'eng-kung. Cheng Chih-lung was alleged to have commanded more than a thousand ships and several hundred thousand followers and was a "pirate king" in the South China Sea. However, for a variety of reasons, Cheng finally surrendered to the Ming government in 1628. Cheng can be considered a great frontier developer, as testified by the fact that in 1626 he transported a large number of Chinese migrants to Taiwan, and in 1630 a large Chinese migration to Taiwan took place largely thanks to his suggestion to the governor of Fukien.[7]

When the Dutch established themselves in southern Taiwan in 1624, Taiwan had a Chinese population numbering between 25,000 and 50,000, comprised mostly of Chinese from Fukien and Kwangtung Provinces.[8] In addition to the Chinese settlers there was a larger aborigine population that belonged to the Malayopolysian or Austronesian linguistic family and originally came from the China mainland, Indonesia, and the Philippines.[9]

The Dutch rule of Taiwan was one of colonial exploitation through onerous taxes and commercial mercantilism. The harshness of the taxes is reflected in two tax systems in particular: a poll tax was imposed on any Chinese who was seven years old or older; and the land tax on each *chia* (about 1.64 acres) of cultivated field land—double that levied in the early Ch'ing period.[10] Dutch traders exported Taiwan's sugar, dried venison, and rattan to China, and its sugar and deerskins to Japan.[11] Though the Dutch colonists drew substantial revenue from their exploitation of Taiwan, it is believed that little of this revenue was used for the development of the island.[12]

Because of this economic exploitation and other harsh colonial practices used in subjugating the Chinese people, a major revolt supported by 15,000 participants broke out in 1652. The significance of this revolt was twofold: It was the first Chinese anti-Western revolt in modern times; and it demonstrated a racial cohesiveness and national identity among the Chinese settlers in Taiwan. The revolt, however, was quickly put down by the Dutch, resulting in nearly 9,000 rebels captured or killed.[13]

In fairness, the net result of the Dutch rule in Taiwan was not all that negative. Dutch colonial authorities encouraged and assisted Chinese migration to the island for farming. Land reclamation is estimated to have reached 10,000 chia covering the entire Tainan area and the northern section of the present Kaohsiung County.[14] The Dutch also facilitated the production of sugar and rice, which in subsequent years became two of the most important products of the island.[15] The Dutch even engaged in what would be called "civilizing" activities among the aborigines. They also introduced Protestant Christianity and promoted education.[16]

The Dutch occupation of Taiwan, however, was not looked upon with calm by the Ming government. A Ming official named Ho Kai wrote to the Ming court in 1635 requesting the expulsion of the Dutch from the island. Since his suggestion was made at a time when the Ming dynasty had become too preoccupied with domestic rebellion and Manchu incursion from the north, nothing came out of this suggestion.[17]

In 1644 the Manchus were established in Peking and began the Ch'ing dynasty. The Ch'ing troops advanced to the south to gain control of all China. At that time a prince of the Ming, who was known as Emperor Lung Wu, established himself at Foochow, Fukien Province. His main supporter was the Cheng family. But Cheng Chih-lung was more a political opportunist than a Ming loyalist. So after his defection to the Ch'ing in 1646 and the death of Emperor Lung Wu in the same year, Cheng Ch'eng-kung became one of the few prominent restorationists of the defunct Ming dynasty. Known as Koxinga (Lord with the imperial surname, given to him by Emperor Lung Wu), Cheng Ch'eng-kung soon became a leader of Ming loyalists, and with his military force he became a serious threat to the new Ch'ing government in the southeastern part of China.

Between 1646 and 1660, Cheng Ch'eng-kung launched numerous campaigns against the Ch'ing government, aiming at its overthrow. During the peak of his military career he commanded about 270,000 troops.[18] In 1659 his forces reached the lower Yangtze valley and in August of that year they even knocked at the door of Nanking. But the seige of Nanking was broken by the Ch'ing defending forces and he was forced to retreat to Amoy. Henceforth he was incapable of staging another major campaign against the Ch'ing, so he began to search for a safe place for recuperation and regrouping.

After a year and a half stay in Amoy, Cheng Ch'eng-kung decided to capture Taiwan. With a force consisting of about 25,000 men and 400 ships, he invaded Taiwan in April 1661. But the battle with the Dutch defending forces was no easy victory. Cheng Ch'eng did not wrest control of the whole island from the Dutch until the following February (see Document 1).[19]

From 1662 to 1683 Cheng Ch'eng-kung and his successors ruled Taiwan for 21 years. Cheng Ch'eng-kung died only five months after his victory over the Dutch, but during his brief rule he set up guidelines for the governing of Taiwan that survived his demise. After his death his son, Cheng Ching, took over the reign. With Ch'en Yung-hua as his chief adviser, the Cheng government began to concentrate on the development of Taiwan.

The administrative policies of the Cheng government and its achievements throughout its rule in Taiwan can be summarized as follows: First was the recruitment of Chinese migrants to Taiwan. The Ch'ing government, having long been harassed by the Cheng forces and pirates on the Chinese coast, tried to keep the residents of coastal areas away from the pirates. Therefore, the Ch'ing government from 1656 to 1684 prohibited people living on the coast from engaging in maritime activities, and from 1660 to 1681 it moved coastal residents approximately 10 miles back from the shoreline.[20] In the short run these policies produced great hardships for the Chengs, but eventually they caused many of these dislocated people to secretly move to Taiwan and elsewhere to seek a better life. In addition to encouraging migration to Taiwan, the Cheng government also went to the China coast to recruit soldiers into its army. With the influx of both settlers and soldiers, Taiwan's population increased to about 100,000 by the end of the Cheng rule in 1682.[21]

Second was land development. The Cheng government maintained a "government field" system, and had tenant farmers to till these fields. In addition, an extensive military colonization system was set up. Large numbers of soldiers were assigned to till land or to open up new fields. Sometimes the Cheng government even detached half of its troops to engage in farming.[22]

Third, the introduction of Chinese traditional education and culture into Taiwan was another accomplishment of the Cheng government. In 1666 the first Confucian temple was erected in Tainan and schools began to spring up in various localities. Even the traditional examination system was introduced in Taiwan. Education was also provided to the aborigines, especially those in the northern part of Tainan.[23] These educational endeavors were probably the most crucial factor that forged a cultural and national identity among the Chinese settlers in Taiwan, which has lasted through the vicissitudes of war and foreign control for three centuries.

Fourth, upon its establishment in Taiwan, the Cheng government continued to pursue trade with foreign countries. Cheng Ching allowed all foreign powers to trade with Taiwan. Among them the British were favored, and in 1670 the Cheng government concluded a 20-article commercial agreement with the British, which covered various aspects of the trade between Taiwan and the British. From 1673 to 1683 the Cheng government also allowed the British to maintain a commercial post in Tainan. This liberal trade policy was clearly beneficial to the island economy and was helpful in providing a necessary source for munitions for Cheng's army. Besides the British, Japan also came to be a very important trading partner, with about 50 Chinese ships a year going to Japanese ports. Taiwan's trading network also included the Philippines and various countries or colonies in Southeast Asia.[24]

In 1673–81 three former Ming generals who defected to the Ch'ing—Wu San-kuei (controlled Yunnan Province), Shan Chih-hsi (Kuangtung Province) and Keng Ching-chung (Fukien)—rebelled against the Ch'ing government. Cheng Ching saw this as a golden opportunity to restore the Ming, so he joined their effort to overthrow the Ch'ing and immediately landed his forces at Fukien to begin his military campaign against the Ch'ing. However, after several years of fighting, he was defeated in 1680 and forced to return to Taiwan. He died in 1681, at the age of 39.

TAIWAN UNDER THE CH'ING, 1683–1895

In September 1683, facing an imminent invasion of Taiwan by the Ch'ing forces led by Admiral Shih Lang, the Cheng government abdicated. Their surrender was prompted by both military and political factors. The Ch'ing's smashing military victory over Cheng forces on P'eng-hu in late July 1683 engendered defeatism and defection to the ranks of the Cheng government. The political factors included dissension among top leaders of the Cheng government; the ineffectual and tyrannical administration over the population after the death of Cheng Ching in 1681, which led to faltering mass support for the government; and the alluring terms offered by the Ch'ing peace negotiators.[25] By this victory the Ch'ing government finally eliminated the last significant group of the Ming loyalists. In addition Taiwan came under the rule of the Ch'ing dynasty for 212 years, until 1895.

In terms of assessing the administrative efficiency of the Ch'ing, its rule of Taiwan can be divided into two periods: from 1683 to the 1870s and from the 1870s to 1895. Before 1874 the Ch'ing government carried on a passive attitude toward Taiwan. It tried to maintain only a semblance of law and order and made minimum effort to develop the island. However, after the Japanese invasion of Taiwan in 1874, the Ch'ing government realized that only the energetic development of the island would forestall further foreign incroachment there. Therefore a series of able administrators was sent to Taiwan and many reforms were undertaken. Following is an examination of these aspects of the Ch'ing rule in Taiwan. Political and economic development, social control, and foreign encroachments are treated separately.

Political and Economic Development

When the Ch'ing government launched a military campaign against Taiwan in 1683, it had envisioned no permanent occupation of the island afterward and had no plans for its long-term development. As a matter of fact, several months after the occupation of the island, there were lengthy debates among Ch'ing government officials about what to do with Taiwan. In view of the many troubles caused by the Ming loyalists on the island during the past decades and apprehensive of the administrative difficulties entailed in ruling such a distant island, some court officials suggested abandoning Taiwan. But those officials who had long been involved in the defeat of the Chengs had an entirely different perspective. Admiral Shih Lang fervently argued for Ch'ing rule. In his memorial to the court he reasoned that since Taiwan holds the key to the defense of China's coastal provinces of Kiangsu, Chekiang, Fukien, and Kwangtung, if it is held by foreign powers or by rebel forces, it could be turned into a stronghold and used as a springboard for attacking the mainland. Since Shih's arguments had been amply proven by the recent Cheng challenge to Ch'ing rule and by erstwhile Dutch colonization of Taiwan, his arguments were irrefutable. His ideas thus won the approval of the Imperial court, and the Ch'ing development of Taiwan began soon after these debates.[26]

In 1684 Taiwan was made a prefecture under the jurisdiction of Fukien Province. Taiwan Prefecture consists of three counties (*hsien*): Tainan, Fengshan (today's Kaohsiung and its adjacent areas), and Chu-lo (today's Chia-i area). Taiwan's prefectural status lasted for more than 200 years until Taiwan was made a separate province in 1885.

Ch'ing policy on Chinese migration to Taiwan had always been one of restriction, at least before 1760. Immediately after the Ch'ing's conquest of Taiwan, instead of sending more people to Taiwan to further its development, the former Cheng officials and almost half of the other Chinese settlers were made to move back to the mainland. Soon, however, the need for manpower for Taiwan's development forced the Ch'ing government to loosen its migration policies. In 1684, married males were allowed to go to Taiwan, but there were still two conditions in this new regulation: they had to apply for permission to migrate; and they had to agree to leave their dependents behind. The first requirement had the purpose of weeding out any suspicious characters, while the second amounted to keeping their dependents on the mainland as hostages as a restraint on their behavior in Taiwan. This harsh and inhumane policy was naturally resented by the migrants as well as by those who intended to migrate. To bypass these regulations, illegal migration by whatever means possible became a widespread phenomenon. Invariably they also had to pay or bribe those who made their migration possible.[27] Also, since these illegal migrants had to sail in unsafe boats, many of them perished on the high seas.

The shortsightedness of this restrictive emigration policy was also self-defeating for the Ch'ing authority. With no family moorings and no loved ones on the island, it fostered feelings of restlessness and rootlessness among the migrants. This in turn was conducive to their becoming social or political deviants. The social and political turmoil of the early decades of the Ch'ing rule in Taiwan reflected in the occurrence of a large number of popular uprisings. Between 1684 and 1732 there were ten popular uprisings, with Chu I-kuei's being the largest, involving 40,000 people.[28] At this point the Ch'ing government recognized the error in its migration policy. Therefore, beginning in 1732, those Chinese migrants who had already acquired land and had managed to make a living, and had been law-abiding, were allowed to bring their dependents to Taiwan.

In 1790 Ch'ing policy was further relaxed and from then on single males were also permitted to go to Taiwan. But totally unrestricted migration did not become an official policy until 1875, a decision that in large part was prompted by the Japanese invasion of Taiwan in 1874. The Ch'ing government finally realized that the most effective way to safeguard a frontier region was to populate it.[29]

With the relaxation of the emigration policy, Taiwan's population gradually increased, especially after 1790. As mentioned earlier, Taiwan's population at the time of the Ch'ing conquest (1683) was approximately 100,000. By the 1810s this population increased to 2 million, and by the 1890s it increased to a little over 2.5 million.[30] The total increase in 212 years was 25 times.

To accommodate this growing population, more land had to be opened up and a more efficient agricultural production had to be achieved. In 1680 the reported cultivated area in Taiwan was 18,455 chia; in 1895 it rose to 361,417 chia,[31] an increase of nearly 20 times. This increase in cultivated land fell somewhat behind the increase in population. But this slight gap should not be taken to mean that people's living standards did not improve. The introduction of early-ripening rice in the eighteenth century, the construction of irrigation systems, improvement on traditional farming techniques, the rapid growth of foreign trade, and the buildup of modern technological services after the 1870s not only produced a modest agricultural and economic advancement in Taiwan but also turned the island into one of the most modern and progressive areas in the Ch'ing empire.[32] This economic progress and relative prosperity were certainly among the reasons that attracted mainland Chinese to migrate to Taiwan.

Taiwan's economic development took an upward swing after the midnineteenth century, especially in the production of the three major export items: sugar, tea, and camphor. Between the 1860s and 1890s, tea production and exportation increased 50 times, sugar exportation grew 2.5 times, and camphor 5 times. This boom in foreign trade was also facilitated by the presence of western commercial firms in Taiwan after the 1850s.[33]

Technological development was made possible by a succession of able Ch'ing administrators, such as Shen Pao-chen, Ting Jih-ch'ang, and Liu Mingch'uan, who came to Taiwan after 1870. Among them, Liu Ming ch'uan's contribution was the greatest. They promoted mining and foreign trade, set up telegraph lines, improved transportation both inside Taiwan and with the mainland, established postal and electricity transmission systems, built railways, opened up modern schools, and engaged in land survey and tax reform. By the 1890s Taiwan had become the most modern and progressive province in China.

Besides material progress, Taiwan by the end of the nineteenth century had also achieved a high degree of educational advancement. Both Han Chinese and the aborigines benefited from this. Under the Ch'ing educational system in Taiwan, there were five categories of schools: prefecture and county public schools (*ju-hsüeh*), charitable schools (*i-hsüeh*), community schools (*she-hsüeh*), academies (*shu-yuan*), and learning centers (*shu-fang*). The prefecture and county schools were regular government schools and were gateways to officialdom through the examination system. The charitable schools, either run by the government or by private sectors or by both, offered basic or elementary education to the young but poor students. The community schools were divided into those for the Chinese and those for the aborigines and both performed the same educational function as the charitable schools. Academies played a supplementary role to the government public schools by offering more advanced education. The administration of the academies was in the hands of government officials, but their financial support came mostly from gentry members. The learning centers were entirely privately owned and run, and they offered different levels of education to their students. Besides traditional-style schools, two modern-style schools were also established: a Western Academy (1887) offering modern subjects, such as foreign languages, mathematics, physics, chemistry, in addition to Chinese studies; and a Telegraph Academy (1890).[34]

Social Control and Disorder

There were inner tensions in Taiwan's social structure that made social cohesion difficult if not impossible to attain. In addition to the hostilities between the Han Chinese and their Manchu overlords, there were also regional antagonisms among the non-Manchu people. Not only were there traditional rivalries between the Fukienese and the Hakka, even among the Fukienese there was the competition between those who originated from Ch'uan-chou (northeast of Amoy) and those from Chang-chou (west of Amoy). According to a Japanese census taken in 1926 the major provincial breakdown was: 83.1 percent of the Chinese population hailed from Fukien, 15.6 percent from Kwangtung, and 1.3 percent from other provinces. Of the Fukien migrants, 44.8 percent were from Ch'uan-chou, 35.2 percent from Chang-chou, and 3.1 percent from other localities.[35] Since there is no reason to believe that there was any major demographic change in Taiwan between 1895 and 1926, the provincial composition of Taiwan's Chinese population as indicated in this 1926 census most likely existed before 1895.

Besides regional rivalry, one should also keep in mind that Taiwan was a frontier land in Ch'ing times. The unsettling effects of the abnormal ratio between the sexes, the competition for land, and the search for food certainly whetted the primitive instincts of the migrants. Furthermore, the plethora of various types of social organizations, such as the secret societies, provided residents with vehicles for social and political activism.[36] Therefore, it is no wonder that throughout the Ch'ing period Taiwan was never short of community strife and popular uprisings. According to a recent study, in Ch'ing Taiwan there were altogether 77 outbreaks of community strife. Their major types were: Chang-chou people versus Ch'uan-chou people (22), Fukienese versus Hakkas (24), strife between different surname groups (11), strife among identical surname groups (4), and strife among people of the same occupation (8).[37]

As for popular uprisings, there were 68 cases. Uprisings were largely motivated or triggered by these factors: other Chinese revolts, such as the Taiping rebellion in the 1850s and 1860s (10); government military suppression of the people (10); government corruption and oppression (8); and foreign encroachment or invasion of Taiwan (8).[38] Some of the major uprisings, such as Chu I-kuei's uprising in 1721 and Lin Kung's in 1853, were based on Han Chinese nationalism. Even Lin Shuang-wen's uprising in 1787–88 and Tai Ch'ao-ch'un's in 1862 could also be counted in this category since both uprisings were engineered and executed by the Tien-ti Hui (Heaven and Earth Society), a secret society that had adopted a strong anti-Ch'ing and pro-Ming stand.

Foreign Encroachment in Taiwan

Although Taiwan was separated from the China mainland by 100 miles of water, it did not escape the consequences of foreign intervention that occurred there in the nineteenth century. After the outbreak of the Opium War in 1840, Taiwan was soon affected. According to the Taiwan officials' report, from September 1841 to March 1842 there were British naval dispatches that reached the Taiwan coast and exchanged fire with the garrison forces. In those exchanges, the British lost two ships (*Nerbudda* and *Ann*) and close to 200 of their crew members were captured. All of their invasion attempts were repulsed. After the conclusion of the Nanking Treaty in August 1842, when British authorities demanded the repatriation of these prisoners and found out that they had been executed, the British demanded the punishment of the involved Chinese officials.

According to the British version of the case, these two ships were not military ships and carried no military personnel and were attacked after they had been shipwrecked. Therefore, the Chinese execution of these shipwrecked sailors was an outright act of barbarism. After hearing the British complaints, Emperor Tao-kuang (1821-51) ordered an investigation of the incident, which turned out to be in general agreement with the British version of the case. Because of this report, and also being intimidated by the recent defeat in the Opium War, the emperor ordered the involved Chinese officials be stripped of their duties.[39]

After the Treaty of Nanking the eyes of the foreign powers, out of their desire to further penetrate the Chinese empire, began to turn upon Taiwan more eagerly. After England and France handed China another series of defeats from 1858 to 1860, Taiwan was finally opened up for trade with all Western powers. Among them, England was the most enterprising, setting up consular offices in Tan-shui, Kaohsiung, and Tainan between 1862 and 1866.

Once Taiwan was opened up to foreign trade and settlement, a number of Sino-foreign incidents occurred, somewhat similar to those that occurred on the mainland. These were the "Rover Incident" of 1867-69, which involved the aborigines' slaughter of the shipwrecked crew of the American ship by that same name; the unauthorized penetration into Taiwan's east coast by some British and German merchants in 1868-69; a Chinese riot against the forced entry by the agent of the British Dent and Company into Meng-chia (today's Wan-hua in Taipei) in 1868; the "Gibson Incident" of 1868, caused by foreign resentment of the Chinese monopoly of the camphor trade and by some antimissionary riots in southern Taiwan.[40] But the most important crises in Taiwan's relations with the foreign powers in the nineteenth century were the Japanese invasion of Taiwan in 1874, the French naval attack on Taiwan in 1884 and 1885, and the cession of Taiwan to Japan in 1895.

The first conflagration between China and Japan took place in 1874 over the issue of the Taiwanese aborigines' slaughter of 54 of the 66 shipwrecked Liu

Ch'iu sailors in the winter of 1871. Immediately after this incident, Chinese officials in Taiwan investigated the case and transported the remaining 12 survivors and 45 other survivors from a previous shipwreck to Foochow for their repatriation to Liu Ch'iu. For many years the king of Liu Ch'iu had been paying allegiance to both China and Japan, though China considered Lou Ch'iu its exclusive tributary. Japan decided to use the incident of 1871 as an excuse to annex Liu Ch'iu entirely as its own. Therefore, in 1874 a Japanese punitive expedition, led by Saigo Tsugumichi, was sent to Taiwan and, after suffering heavy casualties, defeated the resisting aborigines.

After having learned of the Japanese invasion of Taiwan, the Ch'ing government despatched Shen Pao-chen to Taiwan for defensive purposes. Shen made four suggestions tos the Ch'ing court with regard to the pending crisis. The government should mobilize international opinion to exert pressure on Japan, equip Chinese defending forces with modern weapons, send more competent officers to Taiwan, and build up communication lines between Taiwan and Fukien. The court approved all of his suggestions and transported more than 10,000 crack troops to Taiwan as reinforcements.[41]

The Japanese action against Taiwan by now had caused displeasure to the Western powers who, for their own interests, did not want to see further Japanese penetration into Taiwan. American minister Benjamin P. Avery, British minister Thomas Wade, and French minister Louis de Geofroy all intervened in one way or another in the matter and tried to bring about a peaceful settlement. In the face of this international pressure, Chinese military preparedness, and because of its high military casualties in the 1874 expedition, Japan finally decided to accept a peace with China, and an agreement was signed in October 1874. Under this agreement China had to accept the Japanese interpretation that its punitive expedition was for the purpose of protecting its subjects from Liu Ch'iu, an interpretation implying Japanese sovereignty over Liu Ch'iu. China also had to pay 500,000 taels of silver (1 tael equal to approximately 1.2 English ounces) to Japan as reparation.[42]

The second crisis in Taiwan's foreign relations in this period was the French naval attack in 1884. In that year war broke out between China and France over the Vietnam (Annam) question, and France decided to capture Taiwan as a step toward China's capitulation. In response the Ch'ing government in June ordered Liu Ming-ch'uan, governor of Fukien Province, to Taiwan to take charge of its defense. Liu arrived in Taiwan on July 16, and the French naval attack on Keelung began on August 5. Though Liu was able to repulse this attack, Keelung finally fell into the French hands in October. In the same month the French also invaded Tansui and declared a blockade along the Taiwan coast. French military action was renewed in the spring of 1885 and started to close in on Taipei. In March the French took P'eng-hu. In the midst of these losses Chinese forces in the Vietnam-kweichow border area scored a victory, and China decided to seek peace with France with the aim of trading Indochina for Taiwan.

This Chinese decision was also prompted by the worry over Japanese moves in Korea. Thus an armistice with France was signed in April 1885. Though Li Hung-chang was later severely criticized for this decision, his decision was probably the best that could have been made under the circumstances.[43]

In 1894 war broke out between China and Japan over the question of Korea, and China was defeated by Japan. In the Peace Treaty of Shimonoseki, signed in April 1895, China agreed, along with other concessions, to cede Taiwan and P'eng-hu to Japan (see Document 2).

When the news of this imminent cession broke out, it triggered a strong wave of protest throughout all of China and Taiwan. In a memorial written in blood and submitted to Peking, the delegates of the Chinese gentry of Taiwan solemnly declared that they would prefer to fight to death than to live under Japanese rule. This helped to stimulate K'ang Yu-wei, the noted late Ch'ing intellectual leader, to lead the famous May protest movement in which more than a thousand Chinese literati participated. They lodged a petition with the Ch'ing court opposing the cession of Taiwan and demanding reforms. But these emotional outbursts could not alter the fate of Taiwan. The Chinese government, bound by treaty obligations, could not offer much help for Taiwan's defense.

Taiwan now had to find other ways to save itself; and Taiwan resistance leaders decided to seek international support. They first appealed to the British government, asking for British military protection. To compensate the British, they offered Britain Taiwan's gold and coal mines, its tea, camphor, and sulphur, and its customs proceeds. Britain declined this request. T'ang Ching-sung, the newly appointed governor of Taiwan, then requested the Chinese government to approach other foreign powers to arrange either for the neutralization of Taiwan or the transformation of Taiwan into an international settlement. This request was rejected for its impracticality. Taiwan also approached the French, the German, and the Russian governments, but all of these actions ended in failure. Even after the ratification of the treaty, T'ang suggested to Peking that Taiwan could be ransomed to foreign powers to pay Japan for the restoration of both the Liaotung peninsula and Taiwan.[44]

After the failure of all earlier actions and in final desperation, the Chinese patriots in Taiwan decided to try the strategy of declaring Taiwan a "republic" under the title of "T'ai-wan Min-chu Kuo" (Taiwan Democratic Republic). By declaring Taiwan a republic, they hoped to win international sympathy and support and force Japan to give up Taiwan. To assuage any suspicions of their loyalty to China, they designated the reign name of the new republic as "Yung-Ch'ing" (Forever Ch'ing), and in their public announcements they never used the term *tu-li* (independence), but *tzu-li* (self-sustaining) or *tzu-chu* (self-governing). Further evidence of their loyalty to China was that T'ang, the president of the republic, offered to continue to serve as the acting governor of Taiwan for the Ch'ing government. In order to impress the foreign powers, T'ang set up a central government consisting of three ministries dealing with civil, military, and foreign affairs. The pretense of the "republic" of Taiwan was also furthered by the establishment of a parliament, though it was convened for only one session.

A Japanese invasion force of 50,000 landed on Taiwan on May 29. The Japanese commanders hoped that they could bring the whole island to its knees in a very short time, but this proved to be overly optimistic. The Taiwanese resistance force under the leadership of men like Liu Yung-fu put up a fight that lasted for five months. The Japanese were therefore forced to fight in a gradual piecemeal fashion until they finally reached Tainan in October.

The reasons for the Chinese defeat were several. Besides lacking foreign support, the rivalries among the resistance leaders, including T'ang Ching-sung, Ch'iu Feng-chia, and Liu Yung-fu, certainly hurt the preparation and execution of the defense plan. An even more crucial factor was the reappearance of the regional and historical antagonism among the Hakka, the Fukienese, the aborigines, and other mainland residents and troops.[45]

The resistance movement was certainly heroic. But the most impressive thing in the whole movement was the outpouring of loyalty by the people on Taiwan toward mainland China. Despite tensions, this manifestation of loyalty testifies to the basic racial, cultural, and political bonds between the Chinese people in Taiwan and their compatriots on the mainland.

Another salient aspect of this movement was that it revealed the intensity of modern nationalism among the Chinese people on Taiwan. One Western scholar made this succinct comment:

> It is clear that the prolonged defense of Taiwan and the establishment of a republic and its vestiges were manifestations of a rising nationalist spirit among the Chinese. The backers of the republic evinced a marked degree of patriotism in their utterances. Furthermore, their resistance effort, conducted in the name of the people and on behalf of China, certainly was indicative of an outgrowth of modern nationalism.[46]

In conclusion, the two-century-long Ch'ing rule in Taiwan was a mixture of success and failure. On the positive side, the Ch'ing government made energetic efforts to develop the island after the 1870s, and it introduced Chinese culture with all of its attendant values and mores into the island. At least these two important contributions deserve our recognition. On the negative side, its obstructionist migration policy, its rather scant investment of personnel and funds into Taiwan before the 1870s, and, of course, its inability to save Taiwan from Japanese annexation in 1895 were certainly deplorable.

But all these negative aspects have to be evaluated within the historical context. Before the nineteenth century the Manchu rulers failed to perceive the great potentialities of the island. Steeped in their fear of Han Chinese nationalism and repeatedly harassed by the Ming loyalists, they could not but treat Taiwan with suspicion and rule it unenthusiastically. Since the nineteenth century, beset with domestic rebellions and foreign encroachments, the Ch'ing government lacked the resources and strength to develop or to defend Taiwan. When it finally realized the importance of Taiwan and began to develop it energetically after the 1870s, it was already too late.

THE JAPANESE RULE OF TAIWAN, 1895-1945

The Chinese armed resistance to the Japanese occupation of Taiwan did not stop after the 1895 resistance movement. From 1895 to 1903 there were still a number of Chinese uprisings against Japanese occupation.[47] While most of these resisters were called "bandits" by the Japanese authorities, there is no doubt that many of them carried on anti-Japanese activities out of a genuine feeling of Chinese nationalism. The pattern of resistance had developed, in the words of a long-time observer of modern Taiwanese history, "what might be called a nineteenth century Vietcong situation."[48] It was not until 1903 that the Japanese Civil Administrator Gotō Shimpei announced that the pacification of Taiwan had been completed.[49]

It was in the midst of these resistance activities that Japan began its rule in Taiwan. This section will first examine the political development and social control of the island under the Japanese from 1895 to 1945; then it will discuss the economic development and the Taiwanese struggle for autonomy during this period.

Political Development and Social Control

In June 1896 the Japanese Diet promulgated Law No. 63, which gave the Japanese governor-general in Taiwan the authority to use administrative orders, in place of the Japanese laws, to rule the island. Since most of the governors-general throughout the colonial period were high-ranking military men, as such they also became the commanders of the Japanese garrison forces in Taiwan. Thus, combining their legal, military, and administrative powers, these Japanese governors-general were virtually absolute rulers on the island. The significance of the promulgation of this special law for Taiwan was twofold. First, although Taiwan had become a part of the Japanese empire, in terms of their relationship with the home government it was still a dependency. Second, by placing the Chinese in Taiwan (hereafter referred to as the Taiwanese) under a different legal category, they could not enjoy equal protection and other legal privileges under the Japanese constitution. In short, Taiwan, both its land and its people, were only the objects of Japanese administration and were not taken as an integral and homogeneous part of the Japanese state.[50]

Law No. 63 was finally replaced with the more liberal Law No. 3 in 1922. Under this new law, Taiwan in principle would be ruled by the Japanese home laws, but on island matters that required special consideration, which were not specifically defined, the administrative orders of the governor-general would still prevail. This "but" proviso substantially nullified the beneficial effects for the Taiwanese under the new law. For instance, the trial and prosecution system, tax regulations, people's rights in local government, matters concerning the economy, the police system, the school system, and criminal statutes would still be under the purview of administrative orders of the governor-general. Furthermore, the application in Taiwan of Japanese laws dealing with those matters that were unrelated to the above-listed categories would be decided on the basis of whether or not such an application would promote the colonial interests of Japan. If not, the Japanese home laws or parts of them would become non-applicable in Taiwan. The tenure of this law lasted to the end of the Japanese period.[51]

Liberalization was prompted by the strong outcry for self-determination among many subjugated peoples of the world after World War I. Japan had joined a postwar world order that was supposed to promote democracy and freedom. Thus Tokyo had to make some changes in its colonial policies in order to present a new liberal image to the world. Therefore, prior to the promulgation of Law No. 3, Tokyo also, in 1919, appointed its first civilian governor-general to Taiwan, Den Kenjirō.[52]

Besides the discrepancy in the application of different laws in Taiwan and Japan, discrimination against Taiwanese in employment was even more obvious. For instance, in 1905, while 41.3 percent of the Japanese population in Taiwan was comprised of government officials and professionals, only 1.8 percent of Taiwanese were in these occupations; in 1920, the figures changed to 37.2 percent for the Japanese and 2.2 percent for the Taiwanese; and in 1930, 45.6 percent for the Japanese and 2.7 percent for the Taiwanese. This situation continued to 1945.[53] Even the salaries for Japanese and Taiwanese workers who were at the same rank were different: the former's salary was at least 50 to 60 percent higher than that of the latter.[54]

Comparing Taiwan's colonial setup with that of Korea, which also fell under Japanese rule in 1910, Taiwan's situation was much worse. According to a famous Japanese scholar, Yanaihara Tadao, at least by 1929, Korean subjects enjoyed numerous benefits that their Taiwanese counterparts did not. For instance, in Korea the governor-general did not command troops; there were elections on the local level; many Koreans could assume high official positions and become prosecutors and judges; no *pao-chia* control (see later) system was implemented; and several Korean-language newspapers were published by Koreans themselves.[55]

In terms of social discrimination, the nature of the education system is also revealing. In education the Japanese in Taiwan, as a recent study so aptly put it, "were less interested in 'the highest and most natural development of the individual' than they were in the highest development in each individual of loyalty to Japan."[56] The discriminatory nature of this educational system can be seen from some statistics. In 1926, in elementary education, while the enrollment of Japanese school-age children was 98.2 percent, the Taiwanese enrollment was only 28.4 percent.[57] In higher girls' schools the Japanese enrollment in 1935 was 72.8 percent, the Taiwanese was only 27.2 percent.[58] Since the Japanese population in Taiwan was generally less than 10 percent of the Taiwanese population,[59] the student ratio between the two populations as shown in the above statistics was certainly not a fair one. In college education the discrepancy was also shocking. From 1928 to 1944, in Taihoku Imperial University (the predecessor of the present National Taiwan University), the total Taiwanese enrollment was 786 as compared with 2,998 Japanese. Discrimination even extended into fields of study selected by students. Taiwanese were induced to study those subjects that were considered not subversive, such as medicine. Therefore, out of those 786 Taiwanese students, 513 majored in medicine.[60]

Discrimination aside, the Japanese educational system in Taiwan did produce some impressive results, especially in elementary education. In 1944, 71.31 percent of Taiwanese school-age children were enrolled in elementary schools, a figure higher than that of many countries in the world then and now.[61] Japanese education for women was another area where progress was made. In the year just cited, 60.94 percent of the Taiwanese school-age girls enrolled in elementary schools.[62] If we compare Japanese educational results with that achieved by other Western colonies in Asia, such as the Philippines, Indochina, the Dutch East Indies, and British Burma and Malaysia, Japanese achievements become readily recognizable. A recent study has convincingly demonstrated that, in terms of educational opportunities provided, the seriousness of purpose in the educational endeavor and the funds and personnel invested, the Japanese model was second only to that of the United States in the Philippines.[63]

But that the Japanese ruled Taiwan with relative stability and progress was not only because of their stringent laws or their effective educational system. Another major contributing factor was their ability to institute tight social control through the implementation of the *pao-chia* system.[64] This system is an age-old Chinese social control system, but it was never put into effective use in Taiwan in Ch'ing times. In order to stamp out Chinese resistance movements that developed during the first few years after their occupation of Taiwan, Japanese authorities decided to revitalize the pao-chia system. Therefore, in 1898 Governor-General Kodama Gentarō promulgated the Hokō Law. Under this law all the Chinese households were grouped into pao and chia, and the number of households in each pao or chia varied according to local circumstances. The pao-chia headmen, under the supervision of local police and the chiefs of the ward (a local administrative unit between the subdistrict level and the township level) were charged with these responsibilities: organizing local militia, keeping a record of the local residents, maintaining roads and bridges, assisting the transportation of government goods, improving local sanitary conditions, collecting taxes, and disseminating information and new techniques of production. By assuming such a variety of responsibilities, the pao-chia system soon became indispensible to local administrators.

There were three particular reasons that the pao-chia system worked so well. First, the Japanese government established an urban and rural township system that closed the gap between the district-level government and the rural communities. Thus the government could maintain a closer relationship with the local communities. It was under this very efficacious township setup that the pao-chia system operated. Second, its work received the full backing from the omnipotent and the omnipresent Japanese police who had always been able to exact obedience from the general populace. Third, it functioned through the application of the rule of collective responsibility. According to this rule, whenever a member of a chia was convicted for a felony, each household headman would be fined for negligence. Also, whenever a member of the chia violated pao-chia rules, which covered almost every aspect of local living, all others in the chia would be punished. The effectiveness and usefulness of the pao-chia system in maintaining local law and order was so impressive that it was not abolished until 1945.

Economic Development

To develop Taiwan's economy, the first requisite was the accumulation of financial resources. During the early years of its rule, the Japanese colonial government succeeded in obtaining these necessary resources through several channels. First, it received financial subsidies from the home government. Between 1896 and 1904 these subsidies amounted to 30.5 million yen. Besides subsidies, during this period the colonial government also issued bonds totalling to 25 million yen, which were purchased by the Japanese investors. Second, through land tax reform, its land tax revenue increased four times between 1896 and 1905, rising from 752,000 yen to nearly 3 million yen.[65] Third, by monopolizing several export industries the Japanese government also increased its income. For instance, the sugar tax revenue in 1902 was only 700,000 yen, but it rose to 5.4 million yen in 1909.[66] With this newly acquired wealth, rapid economic development was furthered.

The two most important export products of Taiwan were sugar and rice, and the growth of their production was substantial. In 1905–06 rice production was 632,000 metric tons, and sugar was 106,000 metric tons. By 1935–39 rice production grew to 1,339,000 metric tons and sugar to 1,090,000 metric tons.[67] These two products became the most important exports to Japan after the Japanese annexation of the island. In the 1900s nearly 20 percent of Taiwan's rice was exported to Japan, constituting 8 percent of Japanese rice imports; but by the late 1930s the figure rose to 48 percent and 36 percent, respectively. As for sugar, in the 1900s nearly 94 percent of Taiwan's sugar was exported to Japan and constituted 13 percent of its sugar imports, but by the late 1930s, while Taiwan still exported about the same percentage of its sugar (93.9 percent), because of the production increase it constituted 92 percent of Japanese sugar import.[68] With the progress made in these two industries as well as other areas, there is no doubt that by the 1920s Taiwan had surpassed the Chinese mainland in both agricultural productivity and people's living standards.

But Taiwan's industrial development was a belated affair. This was largely due to the intention of the Japanese government, for it was trying to build up Taiwan as an agricultural exporting colony and a market to absorb Japanese industrial products.[69] It was not until the late 1930s that the colonial government began to promote industrial development. Electricity, aluminum, textiles, chemicals, and other industries sprang up after the mid-1930s. Though it had a late start, the annual industrial output growth rate during the eight-year period of 1937–45 was about 10 percent.[70]

There were several factors that account for this impressive economic development. Besides the political and social stability provided by a police state, other factors included successful capital accumulation in the 1894–1904 period, the inflow of Japanese technicians, bureaucrats, and managerial personnel into Taiwan, and the heavy government investment in economic development, which annually amounted to roughly 25 percent of its total expenditures.[71]

While it is undeniable that Taiwan under the Japanese rule achieved rapid economic growth, the exploitative aspects of this development should also be recognized. For one thing, big Japanese corporations were all given special rights to monopolize. Therefore they literally controlled the production or export of many products, such as sugar, tea, coal, rice, opium, tobacco, pineapples, and others. They also owned a large percentage of the land and timber in Taiwan.[72] The wealth of these Japanese corporations in Taiwan far surpassed that of their Taiwanese counterparts. A 1929 survey of the total capital value of all the business firms in Taiwan revealed that the Japanese firms represented 76.4 percent of the value and the Taiwanese only 21.89 percent.[73]

Another aspect of this exploitative system was the flow of wealth back to Japan. While exact figures are lacking, the Japanese corporations must have yearly sent back tremendous profits to Japan. Furthermore, the colonial government in the latter period of Japanese rule also made large contributions to the Japanese treasury. From 1936 to 1942 this amounted to 125.5 million yen, and in the last few years of the war in the Pacific (1941–45), it was estimated that each year 100 million yen were sent to Japan from Taiwan to pay for war expenses.[74]

The Taiwanese Struggle for Autonomy

In light of the ruthless Japanese suppression of those Taiwanese rebellions during the first decade of the Japanese rule, Taiwanese leaders as well as the common people realized the futility in staging open armed revolt. Therefore they decided to resort to peaceful means to reform the colonial system. Among leaders pushing reform through persuasion, Lin Hsien-t'ang was probably the most respected. Lin's conversion to political reformism through peaceful agitation was greatly influenced by the famous Chinese scholar-reformer Liang

Ch'i-ch'ao and the Kuomintang (Nationalist party) theoretician T'ai Chi-t'ao.[75]

Because of the limited opportunity of receiving higher education, many Taiwanese students went to Japan for higher education. By the 1910s their number had reached several hundred.[76] Influenced by radical thoughts that were prevalent in Japanese intellectual circles and by the revolutionary movement of Dr. Sun Yat-sen, they initiated political action to improve the situation in Taiwan. Their anger over the Japanese harsh treatment of their compatriots in Taiwan was also shared by some enlightened Japanese statesmen and elites. Among them, Itagaki Taisuke (1837-1919), a senior Japanese statesman, was the most sympathetic. In 1914 he paid two visits to Taiwan and tried to set up a Taiwan Assimilation Society (Taiwan dōka kai) to promote equal relations between the Taiwanese and the Japanese in Taiwan. Largely due to his efforts, the society was established in December of that year and it immediately attracted more than 3,000 members. But the Japanese colonial authorities could not tolerate such an organization and promptly dissolved it a month after its founding.[77] Another effort made by some Taiwanese leaders at this time was the founding of the Taichung First Middle School in 1914, which became the first middle school that was started by and for Taiwanese.[78]

At the end of World War I (1914-18) the influence of Wilsonian idealism and its call for self-determination for subjugated peoples in the world created a great wave of resentment against Japanese colonialism among the Taiwanese leaders, especially those Taiwanese students in Japan. Further inspired by the Korean independence movement of March 1919 and the Chinese May Fourth Movement of 1919, these students decided to engage in more active political work. By now they had outgrown the idea of "assimilation" and had become believers in the principle of self-determination. It was in this context that the first major Taiwanese student organization was founded in January 1920 under the name of Hsin-min Hui (New Citizens' Society). The purpose of this society was "to study all matters in Taiwan that need reform so as to achieve cultural advancement." The membership of the society in the beginning was about 100. Though this society lasted only ten years, it was considered as the mother organization for all subsequent Taiwanese political organizations that were founded in both Japan and Taiwan. Six months after its founding, the first issue of *T'ai-wan ch'ing-nien* (Taiwan Youth) was published.[79] This magazine and its successors had a life span of nearly a quarter of a century; its last successor was finally closed by the Japanese colonial government in 1944.[80]

The first political action of the New Citizens' Society was to demand the revocation of Law No. 63 discussed before. But they soon realized the impracticality of this demand in view of the strong opposition of the Japanese colonial government and the fact that in November 1920 the Japanese Diet had extended Law No. 63 indefinitely.[81] So they changed their strategy and demanded the establishment of a parliament in Taiwan chosen through open elections. In January 1921 they presented a petition to the Japanese Diet in which they pointed out that the central responsibilities of the proposed parliament were to participate in the enactment of laws applicable to Taiwan and to prepare a budget for Taiwan. They hoped to use this parliament to take away the special legislative power from the Japanese governor-general. However, nothing came out of this first petition.[82]

The following year they presented their second petition to the Diet, accompanied by a lengthy statement to argue their case. In this statement they challenged the efficacy of the Japanese policy of assimilation in Taiwan, a policy that was now being actively espoused by the Japanese authorities in Taiwan. They cited the failures of many colonial powers in trying to assimilate their colonial subjects. Their list of failures included the French in Algeria and Indochina, the Germans in the French Alsace and Lorraine, and the Russians in the Ukraine. They pointed out that the only successful case was the British handling of the Irish, by allowing the establishment of the Irish Free State in 1922. Therefore they requested the revocation of the policy of assimilation and the establishment of a Taiwanese parliament as a preparatory step leading to self-rule.[83]

From 1921 until 1934 altogether 15 petitions were presented, but none got positive results. In some of the petitions various injustices suffered by the Taiwanese were enumerated. The lists of injustices included the absence of any appeal process for redressing of wrongs caused by administrative orders, the harshness of the rule of collective responsibility, various regulations imposed against the study of Chinese language and culture, the lack of educational opportunities for the Taiwanese, the government's toleration of the continued use of opium by people, the Japanese monopolization of the sugar industry, discriminatory travel regulations, the imposition of the pao-chia system on the Taiwanese and not on the Japanese living in Taiwan, and others.[84]

Throughout this agitation movement Japanese authorities employed various countermeasures. They indicted and imprisoned the movement leaders; organized the so-called patronized gentry (*goyō shinshi*) to make counterattack; and even used government-controlled newspapers to attack the movement and defame its leaders. To the Japanese authorities this movement was simply a stepping-stone for Taiwan's eventual separation from Japan and was therefore unacceptable.[85]

The parliament petition movement was more or less directed at the Japanese Diet and the colonial authorities in Taiwan. After its repeated failure, movement leaders realized the importance of turning the Taiwanese population into a cohesive and aware society through cultural enlightenment. In other words, making a "revolution from inside." They believed that unless the people's level of cultural development was upgraded, no common identity could be formed and no joint action could be taken. It was for this purpose that movement leaders decided to establish the Taiwan Cultural Association (Taiwan bunka kyōkai).[86]

The Cultural Association was established in October 1921 in Taipei, and its initial membership reached more than 1,000. The various activities sponsored by this association included publishing newsletters, arranging symposiums, opening up summer schools, sponsoring public lectures, staging plays, and showing movies. Of these activities, the symposiums, the summer schools, and the public lecture sessions were the most important. In the symposiums they covered topics such as Taiwan and Western history, legal matters, sanitation, Chinese learning, and economics. Between 1924 and 1926 three summer schools opened. With an enrollment of between 60 and 100 in each session, students studied various liberal arts subjects. The public lecture sessions were led by Chiang Wei-sui, Lin Hsien-t'ang, and Ts'ai P'ei-huo. Between 1923 and 1926 about 800 lectures in total were given, with an aggregate audience of about 270,000. But of the 800 lectures, 60 were stopped by the Japanese police present who claimed the lectures were too subversive. Also the association opened up two book stores, and its leaders set up the Great Eastern Trust Company (Ta-tung hsin-t'o kung-ssu) in 1926 with a total capital investment of 2.5 million yen. Soon, however, political division appeared in the association and caused its split in 1926.[87]

By the 1920s a host of Taiwanese youth had become leftist-oriented, turning into socialists, anarchists, and even communists. These Taiwanese radicals mainly consisted of two groups. One was made up of those in Japan who had been influenced by the radical thoughts of the Japanese socialists, such as Yamakawa Kikue and Yamakawa Hitoshi, particularly the latter's *Shokumin Seisakakuka no Taiwan* (Taiwan under colonial policy), which was an indictment of the Japanese colonial rule in Taiwan. The leader of this group was Lien Wên-ch'ing.[88] The other group of radicals included those who had gone to China for education especially after the May Fourth Movement of 1919. Living and working in the midst of the Kuomintang (KMT)-Communist collaboration during the period 1924–27, some of these Taiwanese fell under the spell of the ideology and leadership of the Chinese Communist party (CCP), while many others joined the KMT. Once KMT-CCP collaboration ended and the KMT began to hunt down those who had connections with the Communists, the Taiwanese leftists decided to return to Taiwan. But before they did so they founded the Taiwanese Communist party in Shanghai in 1928 and established a close relationship with the CCP and the Japanese Communist party. The leader of the Taiwan Communist party was Hsieh Hsüeh-hung, a female who had received her communist upbringing in Moscow and Shanghai.[89]

To Taiwanese Communists, political reformism through peaceful agitation, such as the parliament petition movement, was useless. What they wanted for Taiwan was a revolution through class struggle to bring out total political, economic, and social liberation of the Taiwanese people. Therefore they paid special attention to the indoctrination and mobilization of the peasants and the workers.

The immediate task for these returned radicals was to find an organization

through which to reach the masses. Since of the Taiwanese political organizations that existed at the time the Cultural Association was the largest and the
most respected, they decided to join it. But because of their leftist ideas and
their preference for political radicalism, they inevitably came into conflict with
the conservatives in the association. A clash occurred at the sixth annual con-
vention of the association held in 1926 and the next year the radicals gained
control of the association.[90]

In the same year the radical leader Lien Wên-ch'ing issued a report entitled
"Taiwan in 1927," which provided the ideological underpinnings for the new
Cultural Association. As can be expected, this report denounced the conserva-
tives' reformism and espoused class struggle through the peasant and worker
classes. The new association then began to start a series of radical activities.[91]
But soon this new association also split. Lien Wên-ch'ing, because of his
"Yamakawaism," which emphasized the importance of developing mass organizations as opposed to establishing a Leninist vanguard party, also ran into
conflict with a rival group led by Wan Min-ch'uan, who had the support of the
Taiwan Communist party and its dominated Taiwan Peasant Union (Taiwan
nōmin kumiai). With this support Wang's faction won out in the rivalry; Wen was
later expelled from the Cultural Association. From then on the association was
completely dominated by the Taiwan Communist party. This association was
finally suppressed by the Japanese police in 1932 and subsequently faded
away.[92]

Conservative Taiwanese leaders could not give up their political struggle
after their departure from the Cultural Association in January 1927. Six months
later they formed the Taiwan People's party (Taiwan minshūtō) in Taichung. In
its charter the goals of the party were announced as follows: "to enhance the
Taiwanese people's political status, to strengthen their economic base, and to
improve their social life." Significantly, this charter specifically denied that the
party harbor any nationalistic aims, for it believed any "internecine" struggle
(implying a struggle between the Taiwanese and the Japanese) on the island
would not serve the interests of the Taiwanese people. Lest such a denial might
appear to be too appeasing to the Japanese, the charter quickly added that if the
political, economic, and social progress of the Taiwanese people suffers any
obstruction, the party would employ all legal means to "struggle to the bitter
end." It is reported that this insertion of the sentence denying harboring any
nationalistic goals by the party was the result of pressure from the Japanese
police. Without this sentence the party would have been banned.[93]

According to the party platform, its main demands were local self-government; freedom of assembly, association, and speech; bilingual education; equal
educational opportunities for the Taiwanese; the abolishment of the pao-chia
system; police reform; the removal of exploitative and monopoly economic
practices; and the promotion of women's rights. With regard to doing political
work among the people, the platform emphasized that the party would take in
all social classes, including the peasants and the workers. In other words, it

would be politics for all the people, not just the the peasants and the workers.[94]

Examining the activities sponsored by the People's party after its founding demonstrates that it had faithfully carried out what was professed in the party platform. In addition, the party also opposed Japanese imperialism in China. For instance, after KMT (Nationalist) troops took over Peking in June 1927, the party in August sent a telegram to various Japanese parties and their leaders and major Japanese newspapers, criticizing Japanese obstruction of the Nationalist effort to solve the Manchurian problem and to abrogate the unequal treaties.[95] The party also attacked the Japanese government's slow and ineffective policy dealing with the opium-smoking problem in Taiwan. In January 1930 it even telegraphed the League of Nations for its assistance in forcing the Japanese government to take more effective action against opium smoking. When an investigating team from the League finally arrived in Taiwan, it embarrassed colonial authorities. This appeal to international intervention later became one of the major causes for the dissolution of the party by the Japanese authorities in 1931.[96]

The leadership of the People's party was in the Chiang Wei-shui group. By the time of the third party congress, held in 1929, the party had become more leftist-oriented and conservatives, such as Lin Hsien-t'ang and Ts'ai P'ei-huo, had already lost out in a power struggle. In response, the Lin Hsien-t'ang group decided to form another political organization to continue political reformism. Thus the Alliance for Taiwan Local Autonomy (Taiwan chihōjichi renmei) was established in August 1930.

In comparison with the previous organizations founded by the conservatives, this new organization had several special features. First, its membership was open even to their previous detractors, such as the so-called patronized gentry and the Japanese, as long as they supported the aims of the organization. Second, its activities were largely limited to those that would promote local autonomy; therefore, many of their other larger political and economic grievances were set aside. Third, it involved itself in local elections and succeeded in having some of its sponsored candidates elected. As for their demands for local autonomy, the purpose was that all local residents, be they Taiwanese or Japanese, should be allowed to elect their representatives, who in turn would be given the right to decide on local financial matters. Even with such a low profile and such modest demands, the alliance was still closed in 1936 by agents of the Japanese militarists in Taiwan, who by then pretty much dominated the island.[97]

Taiwan's resistance against Japanese rule was not limited to the social and political elites. Many peasants also challenged Japanese rule. The grievances of the Taiwanese peasants were many; among them the large holdings and unjust acquisition of land by large Japanese business corporations; the Japanese monopoly on the sugar, banana, and rice industries; and the special treatment given to the retired Japanese officials in land ownership were the most serious. To remove these injustices, peasants began to get organized. From 1925 to 1928 the Taiwan Peasant Union grew from 13 members to 25,000 strong, with an islandwide organization. By 1928 it had 4 regional offices and 26 local chapters. Despite the genuineness of their grievances and their fervent protests, most of their demands were either rejected or only partially satisfied.

The final demise of the Taiwan Peasant Union was caused by its alignment with the Taiwan Communist party. According to the Japanese police report, the Communists had penetrated the union at its first founding and soon took over its control. Therefore, the Japanese police in February 1929 made an islandwide search of all the offices of the union and of the houses of its members. In this search many of the union leaders were arrested. After this suppressive act the union became defunct.[98]

TAIWAN AND THE CHINESE NATIONALIST REVOLUTION

China's defeat by Japan in the war of 1894 was indeed a turning point in the modern Chinese revolutionary movement. It is no exaggeration to say that before this defeat almost all Chinese were for peaceful reform, but after this, many began to follow a revolutionary path. The clearest evidence of this drastic turn to revolution was the founding of the Hsin-Chung Hui (China revival society) in November 1894 by Dr. Sun Tat-sen, which was also the beginning of the Chinese Nationalist revolution.*

Ever since then the recovery of Taiwan became one of the aims of the Nationalist revolution. Between 1900 and 1918 Dr. Sun went to Taiwan three times. His first visit there was for the preparation for the Hui-chou uprising in that year.[99] Many Taiwanese had become Sun's followers and they joined many of the revolutionary uprisings against the Ch'ing, including the famous Yellow Flower Mound (Huang-hua Kang) uprising in 1911,[100] which preceded the Wuchang Uprising in October 1911 that finally toppled the Ch'ing dynasty.

After the founding of the Chinese Republic in 1912, the impact of the Nationalist revolution inspired many Taiwanese to stage anti-Japanese revolts. Among them, the revolt started by Lo Fu-hsing in 1913 was the most famous. In the poem he composed before his decapitation he capped the first few lines of the poem with characters that read: "Sun Yat-sen saves the Republic of China" (Chung-hua Min-kuo Sun Yat-sen chiu).[101] The Taiwanese people's respect for Dr. Sun was indeed deep. When Sun passed away in March 1925, a large memorial service was held in Taipei with thousands of mourners in attendance, and the *Taiwan People's Daily* (Taiwan Min-pao) published an editorial under

---

*The close influence of the 1894 war on the founding of the Hsin-Chung Hui can be seen from the fact that in its founding declaration it stated: "The recent military defeat and national humiliation has made our neighboring country [Japan] to despise our great China."

the title, "Shouldn't We Taiwanese Cry for the Death of Mr. Sun?"[102] Also, when Sun's body was entombed in June 1929, the Taiwan People's party sent a delegation to attend the ceremony, at the risk of reprisal by Japanese police.[103]

Throughout the first decades of the twentieth century many political organizations were established by Taiwanese revolutionary workers and youths on the mainland. Their organizations in Tokyo, Peking, Shanghai, Amoy, Kwangchow, and other places supported the Chinese Nationalist revolution and opposed Japanese colonial rule. Especially after the Manchurian Incident of September 1931, which resulted in Japanese occupation of all Chinese Manchuria, they began to form political parties.[104] For instance, in 1932 a Taiwan Democratic party (T'ai-wan min-chu tang) was organized under the leadership of Liu Pang-han. The genuine revolutionary spirit of this party can be seen from the fact that six of its leaders in 1933 went to the Yellow Flower Mound in Kwangchow to swear their dedication to Chinese nationalism and their opposition to Japanese imperialism. The demise of the party finally came in 1934 when several of its leaders were captured by some Japanese detectives and were brought back to Taiwan, where they were all given long prison terms.[105]

After China and Japan went to war in July 1937, many Taiwanese patriots also came back to China to fight for its survival. They founded six political organizations in South China during the early period of the war: the Taiwan People's Revolutionary Alliance (T'ai-wan min-tsu ko-ming tsung t'ung-meng), the Taiwan Revolutionary party (T'ai-wan ko-ming tang), the Taiwan Youth Revolutionary party (Ta'ai-wan ch'ing-nien ko-ming tang), the Taiwan Independence Revolutionary party (T'ai-wan tu-li ko-ming tang), the Taiwan Nationalist party (T'ai-wan kuo-ming tang), and the Taiwan Recovery Corps (T'ai-wan kuang-fu t'uan).[106]

To coordinate these diverse Taiwanese organizations, the Organization Department of the Kuomintang decided to group them into a single party. With their approval, the Taiwan Revolutionary Alliance (T'ai-wan ko-ming t'ung-meng hui) was inaugurated in Chungking in February 1941. The aim (tsung-chih) of the new party was set forth with these words: "The Alliance, under the leadership of the Chinese Kuomintang, will defeat Japanese imperialism, recover Taiwan, and assist the fatherland to construct a new China under the Three People's Principles." The new party soon set up eight chapters in China's south and southeast regions.[107]

In the early 1940s there had been some foreign discussions about the postwar status of Taiwan, and one suggestion was that Taiwan should be placed under joint international control. This prompted the Taiwan Revolutionary Alliance to issue a strong statement denouncing such a suggestion and to vow its determination to recover Taiwan from Japanese rule.[108]

Besides this alliance, the Kuomintang in the meantime had also begun to organize its own Taiwan party branch to prepare for postwar party work in Taiwan. In 1943 the Taiwan Party Chapter was formally established and set up its party headquarters in Chang-chou, Fukien, which later moved to Yung-an, the provisional capital of Fukien Province. According to a party report then issued, there were 25 secret party posts in Taiwan. After the Japanese surrender, this party chapter was enlarged and became the Taiwan Provincial Party of the KMT. Among the Taiwanese party leaders who were active in party affairs during this period, Ch'iu Nien-t'ai and Hsieh Tung-min were the most famous, and the latter became the vice-president of the Republic of China in 1978.[109]

During the Sino-Japanese War of 1937–45, some Taiwanese also participated in actual military action against the Japanese forces on the Chinese mainland. For example, a small band of 184 Taiwanese youths, led by several Taiwanese graduates of the Chinese Whampoa Military Academy, which was the foremost military academy in China, organized themselves into an anti-Japanese volunteer group. At their request, the Political Department of the Military Affairs Commission of the Nationalist Government formally designated their group as Taiwanese Volunteer Company (T'ai-wan i-ung tui) and placed it under the direction of the Third War Zone Headquarters of the Nationalist Army.

In 1943 this Taiwanese company was ordered to move into Fukien and set up its station at Lung-yen. The major military action undertaken by this company took place in the same year, making three attacks against Japanese-controlled Amoy from June to July. The significance of this company is certainly not in the number of its volunteers, nor in the results of its military operations, but in its symbolic value, which revealed the support of the Taiwanese people in China's war against Japan.[110]

RESTORATION TO THE REPUBLIC OF CHINA

Soon after Japan started all-out aggression against China in 1937, Generalissimo Chiang Kai-shek announced at the Provisional National Congress of the Kuomintang on April 1, 1938, the determination of the Republic of China to recover Taiwan after the war.[111] On December 9, 1941, the Republic of China government formally declared war against Japan and abrogated all treaties between China and Japan, including the 1895 Treaty of Shimonoseki.[112] At the same time Foreign Minister T. V. Soong explicitly stated in a press conference that "after the war, the Republic of China is determined to recover Penghu, Taiwan and the four northeastern provinces [Manchuria] ."[113]

In November 1943 President Chiang Kai-shek met at Cairo with President Franklin D. Roosevelt of the United States and Prime Minister Winston Churchill of Great Britain. On December 1, 1943, they released a communique, later known as the Cairo Declaration, signed on November 26, pledging, among other things, the return of Taiwan and P'eng-hu to the Republic of China (see Document 3). The Potsdam Proclamation of July 26, 1945, declared that "the terms of the Cairo Declaration shall be carried out."[114] This was accepted by Japan in its instrument of surrender executed on September 2, 1945.[115] On October 25, 1945, Taiwan was formally restored to the Republic of China and has been administered as a part of the Republic of China's territory ever since.

The three-century history of Taiwan demonstrates that the fate of Taiwan is closely related to the developments in mainland China. The Taiwan question has played an important role in the rise of modern Chinese nationalism. Despite 50 years of Japanese occupation, the tie between the people of Taiwan and those of mainland China, both in terms of ethnic origin and cultural identification, remains essentially unchanged.

NOTES

1. Chiao-min Hsieh, *Taiwan-ilha Formosa: A Geography in Perspective* (Washington, D.C.: Butterworths, 1964), p. 3. Also see Chiao-min Hsieh, "The Physical Setting of Taiwan," in *Taiwan in Modern Times*, ed. Paul K. T. Sih (New York: St. John's University Press, 1973), p. 1.

2. Hsieh, *Taiwan-ilha Formosa*, Chapter 1; Hsieh, "The Physical Setting of Taiwan," pp. 2–4.

3. For the early history of Taiwan and the Chinese penetration into P'eng-hu, see Kuo T'ing-yee, *T'ai-wan shih-shih kai-shuo* (General history of Taiwan) (Taipei: Cheng-chung Book Co., 1965), pp. 1–8. See also Wen-hsiung Hsu, "Chinese Colonization of Taiwan," Ph.D. dissertation, University of Chicago, 1975, pp. 15–24; and Fang Hao, "Looking at the Chinese Sovereignty over Taiwan and Penghu from Some Historical Documents," in *Chung-yüan wen-hua yü T'ai-wan* (Chinese Culture and Taiwan) (Taipei: Taipei Historical Commission, 1971), pp. 355–79.

4. Hsu, "Chinese Colonization," pp. 44–45.

5. Ibid., pp. 54–57, 77–78.

6. Kuo, *General history*, pp. 13–17.

7. Ibid., p. 16.

8. Hsu, "Chinese Colonization," pp. 70–71.

9. Ibid., pp. 11–12.

10. Ibid., p. 62.

11. Ibid., p. 60.

12. Ibid., p. 62.

13. Ibid., p. 63.

14. Ibid., p. 74.

15. Ibid., pp. 74–75.

16. Ibid., pp. 75–77; Kuo, *General history*, pp. 29–33.

17. Kuo, *General history*, p. 25.

18. Hsu, "Chinese Colonization," p. 83.

19. Kuo, *General history*, pp. 49–55.

20. Hsu, "Chinese Colonization," pp. 92–96, 291.

21. Ibid., p. 97.

22. Ibid., pp. 98–99.

23. Kuo, *General history*, pp. 64–65.

24. Ibid., pp. 68–75.

25. Ibid., pp. 75–90.

26. Ibid., pp. 91–94.

27. Hsu, "Chinese Colonization," pp. 126–32.

28. Ibid., pp. 598–99, 536.

29. Ibid., pp. 290–99.

30. Ibid., p. 148.

31. Ibid.

32. Ramon H. Myers, "Taiwan under Ch'ing Imperial Rule, 1684–1985: The Traditional Society," *Journal of the Institute of Chinese Studies of the Chinese University of Hong Kong* 5, no. 2 (1972): 438–45; Kuo, *General history*, pp. 195–205; Hsu, "Chinese Colonization," pp. 198–99; James W. Davidson, *The Island of Formosa: Historical View from 1430 to 1900* (New York: Macmillan, 1903), Chapter XVII.

33. Ramon H. Myers, "Taiwan under Ch'ing Imperial Rule: The Traditional Economy," *Journal of the Institute of Chinese Studies of the Chinese University of Hong Kong* 5, no. 2 (1972): 375–77.

34. Kuo, *General history*, pp. 178–209. On Taiwan's educational system and its various educational institutions, see Wang Ch'i-tsung, "On literary academies and learning centers in Ch'ing Taiwan," in *Chiang-i hui-pien* (A collection of instructional materials) (Taipei: Taiwan Historical Study Society, 1977), Chapter 7.

35. Hsu, "Chinese Colonization," p. 591.

36. Ibid., pp. 413–56.

37. Ibid., p. 498.

38. Ibid., p. 528.

39. Chan Lien, "Taiwan in China's External Relations, 1683–1874," in Sih, *Taiwan in Modern Times*, pp. 89–101; Sophia Su-fei Yen, *Taiwan in China's Foreign Relations, 1836–1874* (Hamden, Conn.: The Shoe String Press, 1965), pp. 26–47. There is still reasonable ground to question the veracity of both the British claim of the "innocent" nature of its two ships and the findings of the Chinese investigation of the incident. On these two points, see Chan Lien, "Taiwan in China's External Relations," in Sih, *Taiwan in Modern Times*, pp. 97–101.

40. Chan Lien, ibid., pp. 113–34.

41. Kuo, *General history*, p. 158.

42. Sophia Su-fei Yen, *Taiwan in China's Foreign Relations*, pp. 281–284.

43. Kuo, *General history*, pp. 169–77.

44. Ibid., pp. 219–25.

45. Harry J. Lamley, "A Short-lived Republic and War, 1895: Taiwan's Resistance against Japan," in Sih, *Taiwan in Modern Times*, pp. 272–304.

46. Cited in Ting-yee Kuo, "History of Taiwan," in *China and the Question of Taiwan: Documents and Analysis*, ed. Hungdah Chiu (New York: Praeger, 1973), pp. 18–19. Also see Harry J. Lamley, "The 1895 Taiwan Republic: A Significant Episode in Modern Chinese History," *Journal of Asian Studies* 27, no. 4 (August, 1968): 761.

47. Kuo, *General history*, pp. 233–36.

48. George H. Kerr, *Formosa: Licensed Revolution and the Home Rule Movement, 1895–1945* (Honolulu: The University Press of Hawaii, 1974), p. 31.

49. Ibid., pp. 65–68.

50. Huang Ching-chia, *Jih-chü shih-ch'i chih T'ai-wan chih-min-ti fa-chih yü chih-min t'ung-chih* (Taiwan colonial legal system and colonial rule under the Japanese occupation) (Taipei: privately published, 1960), pp. 47–60.

51. Ibid., pp. 84–90

52. Edward I-te Chen, "Formosan Political Movements under Japanese Colonial Rule, 1914–1937," *Journal of Asian Studies* 31, no. 3 (May 1972): 481.

53. George W. Barclay, *Colonial Development and Population in Taiwan* (Princeton, N.J.: Princeton University Press, 1954), pp. 66–7; Huang, *Taiwan colonial legal system*, pp. 230–31.

54. Huang, *Taiwan colonial legal system*, p. 230.

55. Ibid., p. 218.

56. E. Patricia Tsurumi, *Japanese Colonial Education in Taiwan, 1895–1945* (Cambridge, Mass.: Harvard University Press, 1977), p. 213.

57. Ts'ai P'ei-huo et al., eds., *T'ai-wan min-tsu yün-tung shih* (The history of Taiwanese nationalist movement) (Taipei: Tsu-li-wan-pao-ts'ung-shu-pien-chi-wei-yuan-hui, 1971), p. 40.

58. Ibid., p. 42.

59. Ibid.

60. Tsurumi, *Japanese Colonial Education in Taiwan*, p. 254.

61. Ibid., p. 148.

62. Ibid.

63. Ibid., pp. 224-28.

64. The discussion on the Japanese implementation of the pao-chia system in Taiwan is based on Ching-chih Chen, "The Japanese Adaptation of the *Pao-Chia* System in Taiwan, 1895-1945," in *Journal of Asian Studies* 34, no. 2 (February 1975): 391-416.

65. Samuel P. S. Ho., "The Economic Development of Colonial Taiwan: Evidence and Interpretation," in *Journal of Asian Studies* 34, no. 2 (February 1975): 435.

66. Ramon H. Meyers, "The Economic Development of Taiwan," in Chiu, *China and the Question of Taiwan*, p. 35.

67. Ho, "The Economic Development of Colonial Taiwan," p. 428.

68. Ibid.

69. Huang, *Taiwan colonial legal system*, pp. 40-46.

70. Meyers, "The Economic Development of Taiwan," pp. 40-41.

71. Ho, "The Economic Development of Colonial Taiwan," pp. 437-38.

72. Huang, *Taiwan colonial legal system*, pp. 235-42; Ts'ai P'ei-huo, *History of Taiwanese nationalist movement*, pp. 399-415, 493-524.

73. Huang, *Taiwan colonial legal system*, p. 236.

74. Ibid., pp. 44-46.

75. Ts'ai P'ei-huo, *History of Taiwanese nationalist movement*, pp. 1-14; Chen, "Formosan Political Movement," p. 479.

76. Ts'ai P'ei-huo, *History of Taiwanese nationalist movement*, p. 75.

77. Ibid., pp. 15-35.

78. Ibid., pp. 35-52.

79. Ibid., pp. 80-87.

80. Ibid., pp. 543-71.

81. Ibid., pp. 107-8; Tsurumi, *Japanese Colonial Education in Taiwan*, pp. 185-86.

82. Ts'ai P'ei-huo, *History of Taiwanese nationalist movement*, pp. 108-21.

83. Ibid., pp. 110-16.

84. Ibid., pp. 117-19.

85. Ibid., pp. 159-74, 308-16.

86. Ibid., pp. 281-86.

87. Ibid., pp. 287-349.

88. Ibid., pp. 349-53; Tsurumi, *Japanese Colonial Education in Taiwan*, pp. 203-09.

89. Tsurumi, *Japanese Colonial Education in Taiwan*, pp. 208-10.

90. Ts'ai P'ei-huo, *History of Taiwanese nationalist movement*, pp. 337-49.

91. Ibid., pp. 349-50.

92. Ibid., pp. 350-53; Tsurumi, *Japanese Colonial Education in Taiwan*, pp. 207-08.

93. Ts'ai P'ei-huo, *History of Taiwanese nationalist movement*, pp. 355-66.

94. Ibid., pp. 366-69.

95. Ibid., p. 388.

96. Ibid., pp. 399-415.

97. Ibid., pp. 422-91.

98. Ibid., pp. 493-542; Edgar Wickberg, "The Taiwan Peasant Movement, 1923-1932: Chinese Rural Radicalism under Japanese Development Programs," *Pacific Affairs* 48, no. 4 (January 1976): 558-82.

99. Li Yün-han, *Kuo-min ko-ming yü T'ai-wan kuang-fu ti li-shih yüan-yüan* (The

historical relationship between the Nationalist revolution and the recovery of Taiwan) (Taipei: Yü-shi shu-tien, 1971), pp. 17-22, 44-48, 52-55.

100. Ibid., pp. 1-29.
101. Ibid., p. 35.
102. Ibid., pp. 55-62.
103. Ts'ai P'ei-huo, *History of Taiwanese nationalist movement*, p. 399.
104. Li Yün-han, *The historical relationship*, pp. 67-92.
105. Ibid., pp. 91-92.
106. Ibid., pp. 98-99.
107. Ibid., pp. 99-109.
108. Ibid., pp. 109-12.
109. Ibid., pp. 120-25.
110. Ibid., pp. 112-20.
111. Lin Hsiung-hsing and Huang Wang-cheng, eds., *T'ai-wan sheng t'ung-chih kao* (Draft history of Taiwan), Vol. 10, *Kuang-fu chih* (History of restoration) (Taipei: T'aiwan sheng wen-hsien wei-yüan hui, 1954), p. 2.
112. Chiu, *China and the Question of Taiwan*, p. 204.
113. Lin and Huang, *Draft history of Taiwan*, Vol. 10, p. 2.
114. Chiu, *China and the Question of Taiwan*, pp. 208-09.
115. Ibid., pp. 209-10.

3

Political Development in Taiwan

John Franklin Copper

If one were to take a public opinion poll in almost any Western country, or even query their intellectual classes, one would be impressed by the fact that the majority view is that there has been astonishingly little political change in the territory under the control of the government of the Republic of China (Taiwan, the Pescadores Islands, and the "Offshore Islands" of Quemoy and Matsu) and among its 17 million inhabitants.* Rather the response would be

---

*It is necessary to point out in the way of background information that the large majority of the population under the control of the ROC live on the island of Taiwan. The population of the Pescadores is about 120,000 and all of the offshore islands about 75,000 (excluding the military). About 2 percent of the population, called aborigines, are related to the Malay people of Southeast Asia. The rest of the population hail from China, but there are distinctions based upon the time of migration to Taiwan and the area of China from where they came. Slightly over 85 percent of the population, those called Taiwanese, came from China from several generations to several centuries ago. Most of these came from Fukien Province just across the Taiwan Strait and speak the Fukien dialect of Chinese. There is a historical cleavage in this group between those who came from the Changchou area west of Amoy and those from the Chuanchou area northeast of Amoy. This separation was more meaningful in the past than it is today, but differences are still noticeable and can be observed in politics, where the former group is much more active. Another group of Taiwanese hail from Kwangtung Province and speak a dialect called Hakka, which is generally incomprehensible by the other Taiwanese. They constitute about 13 percent of the population. In some parts of Taiwan there are serious frictions between Hakka Taiwanese and Fukien Taiwanese. The remaining 15 percent of the population is comprised of "Mainlander" Chinese who came to Taiwan with Chiang Kai-shek in 1949 when the Nationalists were defeated on the mainland. They hail from various parts of China and speak a variety of dialects, depending upon the part of China where they were born, though all speak Mandarin. There are a great number of cleavages among this group. Even as late as 1970 the Central Committee of the ruling Nationalist party was comprised primarily (60 percent) of persons from three provinces: Chekiang, Kiangsu, and Hunan. Mainlanders from northern China are almost excluded from government positions, especially those from Manchuria, an area that remained outside of Nationalist control in the 1930s and whose leaders were accused of cooperating with the communists.

that the Republic of China is a regime that has resisted change, and that little has happened in Taiwan politically despite the rapid economic and corollary social development that the nation has experienced in the last two to three decades. In fact, many regard the ROC as outstanding for its qualities of being able to resist political modernization in the midst of economic and social change and a vastly altered international environment.[1] Many reasons can be cited to explain why this is commonly espoused.

First, in terms of both the structure and the operation of the government in Taiwan there has been little change. The basic framework of government has not been altered in any significant way since before the regime moved to Taiwan in 1949. The five branches of the government remain, as does the single-party system; and political power is still monopolized by the Kuomintang or the Nationalist party. Provisions in the constitution that provide for changes in that document and for the means to institute democracy and implement human rights have been circumvented by temporary emergency provisions and martial law, which has been in effect for the approximately 30 years since the government moved to Taipei.

Second, not only has the structure of the government not changed, neither has the ROC's political ideology or the attitudes of most of those who hold top seats of power. Its political ideology is based upon Sun Yat-sen's San Min Chu Yi (Three Principles of the People), which have remained virtually unrevised since he formalized them in the 1920s. Meanwhile the regime claims to be the sole repository of Chinese culture and tradition. And it still takes an adamant anticommunist stand on global issues as it did during the period of intense struggle between East and West in the 1950s.

Third, as further evidence for resistance to change, many observers point to the fact that the death of Chiang Kai-shek produced no visible political change in Taiwan, not even debate regarding the future without him, and that Chiang was succeeded by his son—after the fashion of succession in imperial China. What appears to have happened is that another dynasty has been established and Chiang Ching-kuo will rule in the manner and style of his father.

In addition to the above, what change that has occurred has not garnered much attention from the rest of the world. For example, Taiwan's land reform program—one of the world's most successful—never got the attention it deserved from planners in other countries or even Western scholars and now is largely forgotten. Meanwhile the People's Republic of China flaunts a competing model of political, economic, and social development that is new and revolutionary. Its land reform attracts world acclaim even though it was a failure. Hence, even where the ROC should be regarded as a model of economic and social progress it has gotten little acclaim.

This phenomenon is in part a result of the fact that the West draws attention to Peking because it has long been regarded an enemy. Also, mainland China was closed to most Western observers for so long. Now it is at the forefront of detente, and that is exciting. Conversely the ROC is often labeled as "reactionary" as a form of rationalization by those governments that voted for Taipei's expulsion from the United Nations, or that have given diplomatic recognition recently to the PRC. Many of them perceive that Taiwan's days are numbered and they would prefer to feel that this is Taipei's fault (for being resistant to change and inflexible).

The image that the ROC polity is ossified and its leaders resistant to change, however, cannot go unchallenged. The streamlining of the decision-making processes that economic development has brought is very evident upon even superficial examination. Political corruption, still endemic in most of Asia, is less prevalent in Taiwan than in many Western countries. In recent years the average age of those in government had decreased significantly, and the role of the military has diminished. And whereas the basic ideological tenets of the ROC have not changed, the emphasis has: there is more pragmatism and less regard for ideology in the abstract. Then, albeit social progress in some realms has been tempered by the government's conservatism, surveys show considerable change in citizens' views and aspirations, while one of the most important domestic problems in terms of the future of the country—the differences between Main-lander Chinese and Taiwanese—is rapidly diminishing in importance.

Finally, while Chiang Ching-kuo has indeed followed in his father's foot-steps in many ways, particularly in his style, he has in subtle ways revolution-ized politics in Taiwan and has started new trends that reflect that Taiwan is adjusting functionally to problems both internal and external. He has put more Taiwanese and young people in important positions in the government; he has made the government more honest and responsive to the public; and he has enhanced the influence of civilians in government.

In answer to the critic who may reply that these things are merely facade, or are of minimal importance, one can simply cite some statistics that usually— some say inevitably—relate to political change and modernization. Most obvious is Taiwan's economic growth. It is hard to conceive of a nation with close to the world's best record in terms of economic growth not engineering political change in advance to make that growth possible, or experiencing political change as a result of economic progress. Similarly it seems unfathomable that the sharp rise in the number of educated people has not had manifold and political effects. It is also hard to believe that the large number of citizens who go abroad for study and the many foreigners who reside in the Republic of China or visit the country as tourists have had no impact. Finally the rapid urbanization of the population, and until recently a high birth rate accompanied by markedly longer life ex-pectancy, must be considered. All of these factors have produced political change; it is only a matter of asking how much.

The important questions to be asked then are: What is the lag between economic and social change and change in both of these realms and political change? There does seem to be one. But is it bigger than in other countries? Is political modernization occurring at a sufficiently rapid rate to accommodate other changes, or is the political system impeding change to the point that it will endanger the government's ability to maintain control at some time in the future? Will this in turn threaten the nation? Is political change taking place in such a way that the government can resolve the problem of its legitimacy to the rest of the world? In other words, is the progress in democracy and human rights sufficient so that the ROC can claim global support for its continued right to exist in the face of Peking's claims that Taiwan is a part of China? Will the government be able to adjust to internal antagonisms: for example, those who demand Taiwanese independence or self-government without the Chinese who came from the mainland in 1949, and the "diehards" in the party and government who resist any concessions to the Taiwanese majority and who want to keep them out of positions of political power on the grounds that they do not sufficiently understand the Communist threat? Or will Taiwan become another Rhodesia?

With these questions in mind the author in the following pages will consider the following: changes that have taken place in the structure and use of political authority in Taiwan; the impact of rapid economic development upon the ROC polity; the nature and scope of social change and its impact upon protest and reform; and the rule of the ROC's new leader, Chiang Ching-kuo. In all of these sections there is one common theme objective: ascertaining the rate or scope of political change while assessing the functional and dysfunctional aspects of this change in the context of Taiwan's modernization and the legitimacy of its government, present and future. In the concluding section efforts will be made to sum up and give some final answers to the question whether the ROC, or Taiwan, will survive as a nation-state into the next decade.

POLITICAL STRUCTURE AND POWER

The charge has often been leveled at the government of the ROC that, together with a few old "party hacks" who came from the mainland in 1949, the president has monopolized political power in Taiwan, and that there has been no change in the hierarchy of political authority in the last 30 years. Furthermore, they contend that this situation is now being perpetuated in the rule of his son Chiang Ching-kuo. In order to ascertain whether this is true or not it is necessary to examine in more detail the governmental structure and the loci of political power in Taiwan. In the course of this effort it is hoped the reader will be able to formulate studied opinions on the issue of functional changes in decision-making authority in Taiwan. Particular attention should be directed toward the question of whether revolutionary changes are now needed, in view of Taiwan's diplomatic isolation and President Carter's acknowledgement that Taiwan is part of China, to insure Taiwan's survival as an independent political entity or whether the necessary changes have been or are being made.

The ROC government finds its formal political authority in the 1947 Constitution, clearly a document espousing liberal or progressive economic and social provisions while guaranteeing human rights.[2] There is a division of powers into five branches of government with paramount political power vested in the popularly elected National Assembly, which is granted the powers of initiative, referendum, election, and recall. The Constitution also enumerates various human rights and freedoms similar to the U.S. Bill of Rights. For example, it contains provision for freedom of speech, academic instruction, writing, and publication. It also provides that a person has the right to voice his opinion on matters of public interest before a representative body and that any person may appeal a decision made by a county or municipal government organ by filing a complaint with a higher governmental body. Elections are held based on universal suffrage and secret ballot, with provisions for those who are illiterate to vote. The right to vote is extended to anyone over age 20 and the right to run for office is given to anyone age 23 or more.

Except for a special emergency provision in the Constitution that provides that all freedoms and rights may be restricted by law "for reasons of averting an imminent crisis, maintaining social order, or advancing the general welfare," the Constitution is indeed a progressive one. However, based on this section in the Constitution a set of restrictive laws known as the "Temporary Provisions Effective During the Period of Communist Rebellion" or just the "Temporary Provisions" was adopted by the National Assembly in 1948. Via these Temporary Provisions the president declared martial law. In 1954, five years after the ROC government had set itself up on Taiwan and the "hot" part of the civil war had ended, the National Assembly met and extended the president's emergency powers, including the right to keep martial law. In 1967 the National Assembly gave the president further powers that enabled him to fill elective offices that became vacant and could not be chosen because of the government's location on Taiwan and the fact that the rest of China was not under ROC control.

Inasmuch as martial law nullifies or at least reduces the significance of most of the provisions of the Constitution that provide for fundamental human rights and freedoms as well as democratic practices, the Temporary Provisions are frequently chided by those who feel that human rights and democracy should be given more attention. It is fairly certain that these provisions will remain in force in the forseeable future. In 1977 Premier Chiang Ching-kuo asked the cabinet to review the continued need for martial law in the context of pending hearings in the U.S. Congress on human rights in Taiwan, but he subsequently rejected any change.[3] Immediately after the United States recognized the PRC and derecognized the ROC in December 1978, provisions of the martial laws that had been relaxed were again put into force.

On the other hand it must be remembered that the ROC government had been under the constant threat of communist infiltration and subversion since it moved to Taiwan, and twice, in 1954 and 1958, it was faced with armed invasion. It should also be kept in mind that Peking has repeatedly vowed to "liberate" Taiwan "by military force if necessary" and has by its own admission sent saboteurs and other agents to Taiwan. Finally the ROC government has since 1971 faced the problem of a steady erosion of its diplomatic influence and the steady loss of diplomatic recognition by other nations. This has to some degree threatened the government's legitimacy and thus its authority. Thus the continuance of martial law must be seen in a situation where the government is aware of outside criticisms but has weighed this against the risks. It should also be noted that although there is opposition to the Temporary Provisions, this is not as intense as it might seem, while many support them as both necessary and desirable.

In 1975, for example, a special section of the martial law provisions was invoked in order to deal with the problem of a marked increase in crime, especially violent crime. Criminal defendants in cases where violence was used were sent to military courts and the offenders dealt with quickly and efficiently, usually ending with the firing squad. Even though some of the cases where the death penalty was imposed entailed only petty robbery, public reaction clearly supported the government.* Moreover, high officials noted that a majority of U.S. military personnel and tourists in Taiwan had made favorable comments about the efficient justice that made it possible to walk in any part of Taipei at night without fear, quite in contrast to most large cities in the United States.

Political power in the ROC resides chiefly in the hands of the president, the head of the party (Nationalist party or Kuomingtang), and the military.† It is manipulated or implemented through the five branches of government (or yuan) and the National Assembly they control—although the latter in theory is elected by the people and grants the president his political power. (See Figure 3.1 for a diagram of the ROC government organization.) Chiang Kai-shek until his death in 1975 held all of the important seats of power, and this is true of his son Chiang Ching-kuo at the present time—though there has been some shifting of positions and seats of power since the elder Chiang's death, which will be discussed in later pages.

The National Assembly, which, according to the Constitution, represents the people and therefore could be thought of as the bastion of democracy, is in reality little more than a sounding board. Since the body is designated to have a representative from every 500,000 persons (including Chinese on the mainland) as well as delegates from occupational groups, racial minorities, and the overseas

---

*A news reporter in Taiwan did a survey with a number of taxi drivers at the time and the overwhelming majority supported the harsh penalties that were being meted out under martial law. Although their responses should not be seen as necessarily typical, the author asked a number of people informally about the use of martial law in this way and most of them agreed with government policy. Most of those who disagreed noted that it should not have been applied to one case where a theft using violence did not involve the use of any weapon and the thief got only NT$20, or the equivalent of U.S.$.50.

†The president and the premier have generally not been important at the same time, though this did occur during the transition of Chiang Ching-kuo to power.

FIGURE 3.1
ROC Government Organization (at end of 1975)

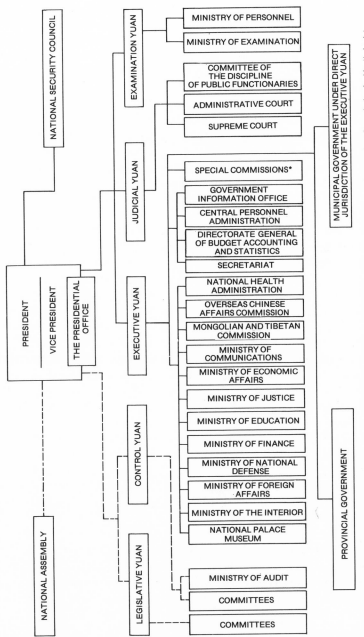

*Economic Planning Council, National Science Council, Atomic Energy Council, Administrative Research and Evaluation Commission, Commission for Youth Assistance and Guidance, Vocational Assistance for Retired Servicemen, Coordination Council for North American Affairs (functional substitute for former ROC Embassy and consulates in U.S.).

Source: *China Yearbook 1976* (Taipei: China Publishing Co.), p. 86.

Chinese, and now has less than 100 representatives from Taiwan Province, it does not in reality represent a voting electorate. After the government moved to Taiwan in 1949, elections, which were to be held at six-year intervals, became impossible and delegates remained in their positions by an interpretation of the Council of Grand Justice of the Judicial Yuan (though in 1969 and 1972 elections were held to elect 69 additional delegates from Taiwan to the Assembly*).[4]

The office of the president, an elected position according to the formal structure of the Constitution (by the National Assembly), is in reality independent of the Assembly and for that matter any other branch or organ of government. The president, except for the period 1975–78, has controlled the Legislative Yuan and other organs of the government through his leadership of the Nationalist party and has ruled the country with almost plenipotentiary powers. In 1975, when President Chiang Kai-shek passed away, Vice-President Yen Chia-kan became president. For the next three years the vast powers of the president resided in the hands of Chiang Ching-kuo who was premier and who became chairman of the KMT after his father's death. The younger Chiang as former defense minister also held sway over the military. In view of his power bases in the party and the military as well as his position as premier, plus the fact that President Yen had been clearly a figurehead when he was vice-president, Chiang Ching-kuo's leadership of the country was not seriously challenged. In May 1978 he was accordingly elected president, replacing C. K. Yen who had already announced his retirement.

Three of the branches of the government—the executive, legislative, and judicial—are similar to their counterparts in Western political systems. The Examination and Control Yuans are a carryover of Chinese tradition. The Examination Yuan is responsible for giving exams for governments jobs and serves as a personnel agency. Members of this yuan are appointed by the president (with the consent of the Control Yuan) and they reflect his wishes. The Control Yuan nominally holds the powers of consent, impeachment, censure, and auditing. Its members are elected indirectly by each provincial assembly and overseas Chinese representatives. Clearly neither the Examination Yuan nor the Control Yuan exercises any political power independent of the president or the Kuomintang but rather are manipulated from above.

The Legislative Yuan and the Judicial Yuan are similar to the two branches of government described in the previous paragraph in that they exert little or no authority independent of the president, premier, or party. The Legislative Yuan, according to formal procedures, decides on budgetary matters, passes bills on war, peace, treaties, and martial law, directs the Executive Yuan to alter policies

---

*Only 1,204 members of this body, including the 69 Taiwanese, were present in March 1978 to vote for Chiang Ching-kuo's nomination to the presidency.

it does not agree with (by a two-thirds majority), and initiates constitutional amendments. It meets twice a year in two- to three-month sessions. The Legislative Yuan, however, like the Control Yuan, is composed of members elected from all of China's provinces, municipalities, border areas, minority groups, and overseas Chinese, and for this reason it does not justly represent the people of Taiwan. It also has suffered from old age and attrition. In 1948, 760 legislators were elected, but by 1966 only 457 were taking their seats in regular sessions. The problem of attrition was overcome to some extent by a special election in Taipei that brought in 11 new members to serve "indefinite terms" and the creation of 52 new three-year seats in 1972. Notwithstanding, the Legislative Yuan does not reflect public opinion in Taiwan; nor has it become an active and important part of the government.

The Judicial Yuan interprets the Constitution as well as all laws, adjudicates civil, criminal, and administrative suits, and is responsible for the discipline and punishment of government officials. Members of the Judicial Yuan are appointed by the president (with the approval of the Control Yuan) and thus reflect the thinking of the president and the party with little or no interpretation or dissent.

The Executive Yuan, in contrast to the other four branches of government, however, is not simply a rubber stamping agency. It is an administrative branch of government and one that carries out or executes policy, in theory made by the Legislative Yuan but in reality made by the KMT or itself with party approval. The head of the Executive Yuan is the premier, who is appointed by the president with the consent of the Legislative Yuan. He presides over the ministries, commissions, ministers without portfolio, and a large administrative staff, as well as the Government Information Office, Director General of Budgets, Office of Accounts and Statistics, and other smaller or temporary agencies. The ministries are: interior, foreign affairs, national defense, finance, education, justice, economic affairs, and communications. Two committees have cabinet status: the Overseas Chinese Affairs and Mongolian and Tibetan Affairs. There are also several important commissions with subcabinet status such as the National Science Council and the Research, Review and Evaluation Commission. The ministries and commissions generate policy internally and are important and efficient organs of government that are generally responsive to current problems. Hence, while officials of the Executive Yuan are not chosen by a democratic process, the Executive Yuan has been very sensitive to public opinion and to the needs of the country and its citizens. And it is here that business leaders, civic and other organizations, and even private citizens communicate with the government.

Below the national government organization are the provincial, county, and municipal governments. Outside of their jurisdiction the offshore islands of Quemoy and Matsu are governed by the Ministry of Defense and thus are administratively under the Executive Yuan, as is the city of Taipei since July 1967 when it was declared a special municipality to bring the temporary capital under the control of the central government. This was done nominally so that Taipei could keep its own tax revenue and thus improve city services sorely needed due to the population growth of the city. The decision, however, also made the mayorship of Taipei an appointed position and ended political campaigns for the mayorship, which accentuated dissension between Mainland and Taiwanese Chinese.

The provincial government, whose capital is 100 miles southwest of Taipei, rules over 16 counties plus the larger cities that are classified as municipalities—with the exception of Taipei (since 1967) and Kaohsiung (since January 1, 1979). According to the Constitution, the governor of Taiwan, who heads the provincial government, is elected along with members of the Provincial Council. The position of governor now, however, is an appointed position—by the president from a list of nominees furnished by the Executive Yuan. Notwithstanding the incorporation of some important positions of local government by the central government, political participation has increased as is reflected in the elections for Provincial Assembly seats, and Taiwanese hold a majority of these four-year elective jobs as well as the positions of speaker and deputy speaker. The Provincial Assembly has broad legislative powers, though the central government has been careful not to allow this body too much power. In short, the top leadership has allowed the Assembly enough prerogatives to prevent an image of Mainland Chinese dominance in provincial affairs, but it has maintained sufficient control to prevent the growth of native Taiwanese nationalism.*

The next tier under the provincial government is comprised of the county and municipal governments. County governments are run by county magistrates and a popularly elected assembly; municipal governments are headed by a mayor who works with an assembly or council. Neither the municipal nor the county-elected bodies can be dissolved by higher authority, though both are under the supervision of the Provincial government. In 1964 more than 1,500 candidates (including 230 women) filed for 907 seats. In 1977, 1,600 offices were contested, though a small amount of the increase came from consolidating local and provincial elections.[5]

Both provincial and local elections bring out the voters in large numbers. And voter turnout has been increasing: in 1964 over 76 percent voted; in 1977, 80 percent.[6] It is an interesting phenomenon, especially in contrast to most Western countries, that the voter turnout in local elections is higher than in national elections. This, of course, reflects the fact that there is more participation and thus more democracy at the level of local government in Taiwan. In

---

*Two young American Ph.D.s hold the positions of chairman of the Research, Review, and Evaluation Commission and deputy foreign minister. When Chiang Ching-kuo became premier in 1972 he appointed Taiwanese to six out of the eighteen cabinet-level posts in the Executive Yuan, though only two or three of these are generally thought of as important positions.

fact, when Taiwan's political system is criticized by Westerners for being undemocratic, the response is often that this is true of national, not local, government, and that democracy is more meaningful at the local level because issues are more personal and less complicated. Some Taiwanese even contend that local elections in Taiwan are more democratic than in most Western countries, because the newness of the democratic process has fostered an intense interest in government as well as a positive attitude toward politics even compared to Western countries. Also, they note there are few entrenched local bosses and a large number of independent candidates supported by "grass roots" movements, while there is less transience among the voting electorate, which does not force candidates to appeal to the public through a political party or the media as in most Western democracies. Democracy at the local level is also enhanced by the growth of a host of farmers' organizations, businessmen's groups, and so on, that generally function as professional or public service organizations rather than lobbies.[7] In short, there is a high level of interest as well as participation in local politics in Taiwan and strong positive feelings toward government at that level.[8]

Paralleling or shadowing governmental organization at all levels is the KMT. Thus understanding the Nationalist party's structure and its influence on politics at all levels is a sine qua non for understanding the political processes in Taiwan. The organization structure of the KMT is hierarchical or like a pyramid, starting at the bottom with local units of 15 or less members, up to subdistrict, district, county, provincial, and finally national headquarters. Each level above the local groups has a central committee and an advisory committee. Committees at the bottom or lower levels are elected by party members; at higher levels they are elected by party congresses. The Provincial Congress meets every two years and the National Congress meets every five years. The Central Committee of the National Congress meets every year and makes decisions that are generally approved pro forma by the latter. Real power, however, lies in the Standing Committee of the Central Committee, which makes policy when the latter is not in session. This committee is headed by the director-general of the party, who is given his authority by the Party Congress and thus has veto power over Central Committee actions. Chiang Kai-shek held this post from 1938 to his death in 1975; his son, Chiang Ching-kuo, holds the post now. Inasmuch as the KMT is tightly controlled from the top and because it is the only political party of importance, heading the party may be said to constitute running the nation.* If one judges the progress toward establishing a democratic system in Taiwan by the KMT's rules or decision-making procedures, or by the growth of opposing

---

*There are two other political parties, the Chinese Youth party and the Democratic Socialist party, both of which had their beginnings on the mainland and continue to function. However, they remain small parties and generally insignificant in terms of their prospects to win an election or to solidify public opinion or votes on important issues.

political parties, then one's conclusion must be a negative one. On the other hand, the majority of non-Western countries have one-party systems and in most where democratic procedures have been put into practice, this has happened within the party, more than through the growth of opposition parties.

The KMT, which was a party of Mainland Chinese and dominated by members from three provinces in east China when the ROC moved to Taiwan in 1949, has expanded its membership and now is fairly representative of Taiwan's population. Although it has not regularly published the size of its membership, in November 1976 it was reported that its rolls had increased from 910,000 in 1969 to 1.5 million.[9] Thus the party would qualify under the definition of "mass party." At this time 48 new members were elected to the Central Committee, bringing the total to 130, of which 16 were Taiwanese and 13 were women. The powerful Standing Committee was also increased in size to 22; two new members were Taiwanese, raising the total to five. The average age of the Standing Committee members has been steadily decreased. Although Taiwanese, who constitute a majority of the population, still do not control the party they do constitute from 60 to 70 percent of its membership and a number are in the top decision-making echelons.[10] Moreover, the representation of the military has diminished while the number of women has increased. All of this reflects a trend toward fairer representation and may indicate that more democratic procedures in decision making and electing top leaders may soon emerge.

Recent elections also suggest increased political party competition in that more candidates have run as independents. In the November 1977 election the KMT won an unprecedently low figure of 85 percent of the elective offices, with almost all of the rest going to independents.[11] President Carter's human rights campaign undoubtedly encouraged independent candidates, though this was an already growing trend. If present trends continue one might speculate that the ROC's political system will evolve into a "one-party-plus-independents" system.

By way of summary, neither the Constitution nor the structure of political authority has changed significantly in Taiwan since the ROC moved there in 1949. Political power remains concentrated at the top, and while there has been a considerable decentralization of governmental functions, ultimate authority is still held by a small select group plus one individual. And while there are provisions in the Constitution and in the law for the implementation of democratic practices and civil rights, this has been and remains circumvented by martial law and the Temporary Provisions. Improvements that have taken place in civil rights have largely been granted by the top and, as we will see in a later section, are qualified. On the other hand, there is a great deal of democracy practiced in local government, and municipal and county governments have expanded in terms of both functions and influence much faster than the national government, especially in the past few years—quite in contrast to political systems elsewhere. What democratization (modernization and streamlining of the political system would probably be better criteria) that has taken place in the national government has taken the form of reform or change by decree and is change in substance rather than organizational, ideological, or image change. Finally, much of the reform and improvement in government efficiency and responsiveness has been the work of one person—Chiang Ching-kuo.

In short, one can say then that political modernization in Taiwan has occurred not by changing the structure of the system but rather by other means. Reform from within has been accomplished by creating ministries and commissions that are more responsive to public, civic organization and interest group demand and are more representative of the Taiwanese and the youth. The central government has delegated power to local officials and has cautiously given increased prerogatives to local government. Here political participation is intense and the system works as democratically as in most Western countries. The KMT has changed very little in terms of organization or structure, though the party membership is now a majority of Taiwanese. Meanwhile, older members of the party leadership are often ignored by the new president or their influence circumvented by making decisions in the Executive Yuan without party concurrence. This, plus the increasing number of independent candidates in recent elections, seems to indicate that there is promise to reform the party and this may soon affect its top leadership.

ECONOMIC DEVELOPMENT AND POLITICAL CHANGE

Among students of political development it is axiomatic that economic development is an important factor in political modernization. It is likewise true that political development fosters economic growth. In other words there is a reciprocal correlation or symbiotic relationship between the two. Nevertheless there are many who contend that Taiwan has experienced rapid economic growth without resultant political change or modernization.* In the next few pages an attempt will be made to explain this seeming contradiction and assess the ways that economic growth has produced political change or vice versa, the extent of this change, and what problems the ROC faces in both maintaining economic growth while insuring that political development keeps pace with economic development. Again the author has in mind a problem of overriding importance: the regime's legitimacy and its ability to resist efforts by Peking to force the ROC to negotiate the incorporation of its territory into the People's Republic. Clearly ROC leaders endeavor to use economic growth to compensate for their setbacks on the international scene, particularly their loss of the China seat in the United Nations and U.S. diplomatic ties, while rapid economic growth reduces the seriousness of domestic political problems at a particularly crucial time.

---

*It is important to note, however, that even the most ardent critics of the ROC admit that its economic growth has been phenomenal.

The specific questions that need to be answered are: Has economic development been accomplished because of a more efficient political system free of corruption and red tape? How has economic growth affected political change? Has economic growth created a demand for open and democratic political institution as most liberals in the West believe should be or is inevitably the case? Can economic growth stave off efforts by the Taiwanese to revolt against the government that they perceive is monopolized by Mainland Chinese? Will prosperity inevitably create greater political demands and revolutionary expectations? What has been the political impact of increasing personal incomes and wealth, and within what time frame can we expect pollution and environmental problems to become serious issues that the regime must cope with? Will a movement develop, as has been the case in developed Western countries, to slow down economic growth? If so, when? Finally, to what extent is the government planning "forced" rapid economic development for the next few years in order to serve as a means of meeting the crisis yet to come in terms of its future as a self-governing entity?

Before answering these questions it is necessary to look at the scope of Taiwan's economic growth and its by-products over the past three decades.* Before World War II Taiwan's economic development under Japan's management surpassed that of any other nation in Asia, except Japan, and was well ahead of any part of China. During the war allied bombing destroyed Taiwan's oil storage and military installations, though overall damage was not extensive and the economy was not severely hurt by the war. The repatriation of the Japanese colonial government, and likewise managers of the economy, however, did have an impact, as did the fact that they were replaced by less than competent administrators from China, who were under orders of the Nationalist Chinese military to provide supplies for the army to prosecute the war against the Communists on the mainland. It was in this context that economic growth came to a standstill, deterioration occurred, and an indigenous revolt against Nationalist Chinese rule occurred on February 28, 1947. The revolt was put down by military force and little was done to relieve economic problems. Then in 1949, when the Nationalist armies were defeated on the mainland, the ROC government and military fled to Taiwan. The sudden influx of more than 1.5 million people caused another shock to the economy.[12]

It wasn't until the early 1950s that Taiwan began to experience economic recovery with industrial production reaching prewar levels in 1953. The two major factors in stimulating economic growth in the initial period were the land reform and rent reduction programs and U.S. economic assistance. From 1953

---

*Taiwan's economic development is treated in detail in Chapter 4 of this volume and will be summarized here only in an effort to relate economic development to political modernization.

to 1966 national income increased fivefold, with individual salaries increasing almost commensurately.[13] Personal investment was moderately high during this period, particularly in industry—a product of the government buying land from the landlords to give to the peasants in return for stocks in government-owned enterprises, together with encouragement it gave to the populace to invest in industry. Thus, industry that accounted for only 17 percent of the net domestic product in 1953, compared to agriculture which was 40 percent, by 1966 accounted for nearly 30 percent of the domestic product and exceeded the contribution of agriculture.[14]

Through the early part of the 1960s Taiwan's economic growth rate measured in increases in gross national product (GNP) was close to 10 percent and in the late 1960s and early 1970s it exceeded 10 percent—surpassed in Asia only by Japan. Per capita income increases lagged behind GNP growth as a result of continuing high levels of investment but were nevertheless impressive. The economy was hit hard by the oil crisis in 1973, yet the Republic of China was the first oil-importing nation in Asia to show signs of recovery; and it was the most successful in restoring high-level growth. In 1976 Taiwan's economic growth in constant dollars exceeded 11.5 percent, and in 1977, despite two extremely destructive typhoons, it went over the 8 percent mark. In 1977 average per capita income in Taiwan passed the U.S. $1,000 mark.[15] In 1978 Taiwan's national economic growth measured in the increase in GNP was 13 percent and per capita income reached U.S. $1,200.[16] Taiwan is not blessed with large quantities of good farmland and has few natural resources, yet its economic growth has put it among the top few nations of the world, a fact that is nothing less than impressive. And this occurred during a period of rapid population growth (unlike Japan for example) and the cutoff of American aid after 1965.

To return then to the questions asked above, one can begin with the hypothesis that, considering the magnitude of Taiwan's economic growth juxtaposed beside serious handicaps to growth such as overpopulation and a lack of natural resources, rapid growth could not have occurred in a setting of corruption and bureaucracy as existed in the Nationalist Chinese government when it was on the mainland. And this is the case. The shocks caused by the loss of the mainland and communist preparations underway to "liberate" Taiwan in late 1949 and early 1950 prompted the ROC government to institute quick reform. The Korean War gave the Nationalist Chinese a period of repite so that they could implement their plans. One of the first political decisions after the ROC moved to Taiwan was to reorganize the party to make it more efficient and responsive to the needs of economic stability and growth. In the realm of economic management the first moves were the land reform and rural reconstruction programs, which, though facilitated by the fact that the Japanese had evacuated a sizable amount of land and the Nationalists owed nothing to the local Taiwanese landlord class, were also the product of understanding the problems of inequitable land tenure and a well-planned program for change. The success of land reform increased agricultural production and facilitated better relations between the local Taiwanese and the newly arrived mainland Chinese. This was followed by a very well-thought-out Four-Year Plan that emphasized agricultural growth and small industry. The government aided development significantly by building dams to supply cheap electricity, financing fertilizer plants, and by channeling investment into light manufacturing enterprises. Other four-year plans followed and were marked by efforts to further reduce the red tape involved in obtaining business and building licenses, setting up a more streamlined tax system, and giving incentives to entrepreneurs and foreign investors.[17]

The argument that the government played a passive or unimportant role in economic development is clearly a naive one. Corruption and bureaucratic procedures were visibly and openly purged by the top leadership in the 1950s and such efforts have been continued since then. During the 1950s specific steps were taken by the government to create better relations with business leaders, while people from the business community found a demand for their talents in government.* Likewise technocrats and officials with economic or business experience were given higher preferences in government jobs. In this connection one should also be reminded of the fact that the size of government in Taiwan during this time did not decrease, rather it increased.[18] This indicates that the government's policy has not been one of laissez faire, but rather one of designing policies to help promote commerce. Some specific examples illustrate this point: From the 1950s business licenses were granted freely or niggardly based upon such factors as the exportability of the product, the need for foreign exchange to buy the product or related products, capital requirements, and technical feasibility. Some licenses were not granted at all, such as for producing vegetable oil, flour, and so on—areas where there were already too many such producers. Beginning in the 1960s the government based many of its decisions in granting new factory licenses on the self-manufactured content of the product. This reduced unemployment markedly. In the meantime the government passed the Statute for Encouragement of Foreign Investment, which provided for a five-year tax holiday for foreign investors, plus a 15 percent tax ceiling after the five-year period. In 1965 another law provided for the establishment of export-processing zones where foreign companies could import and export tariff-free and through very simplified procedures. To date three zones have been established, in Kaohsiung, Nantse, and Taichung. At nearly the same time, in 1967, the government granted tax rebates to local manufacturing companies that exported their products—including 6,000 items. Interest rates were adjusted throughout this period to the advantage of businessmen, and in some cases the government arranged low-interest loans to certain businesses.[19]

The government continued to control and tune the economy. The oil crisis and inflation hit the Taiwan economy hard in 1973, but because of prompt

---

*During the 1960s an increasing number of government officials had prior experience in business and formal education in economics and commerce, while those with a military background decreased markedly as did the number with solely bureaucratic experience.

action the effect was short-lived. By 1975 Taiwan's economic managers had price rises pretty much under control and had engineered a return to high growth again—notably faster than Japan, South Korea, and other rapid growth economies—and without damaging relations with their trading partners.[20]

Two other areas that indicate successful government management of the economy, and which by themselves deserve attention, are unemployment and foreign trade. The rate of unemployment in most societies is generally considered a factor of government planning, or the lack of it, or at least in Western societies the government is blamed for unemployment. Taiwan's unemployment rate is extremely low: the highest since 1973 was 2.87 percent in January 1975 and the lowest was 1.0 percent in January 1977.[21] In fact, unemployment has been so low that some industries have had difficulties hiring workers, one factor that has accounted for the rapid rise in workers' wages and lessening disparities in income.

Beginning in the 1960s Taiwan's exports increased at a rate of over 20 percent annually and from 1965 to 1973 grew at the astonishing rate of 33 percent yearly.[22] This occurred in large part because of the central government's negotiating or helping businessmen attain foreign trade deals and its efforts in modernizing custom facilities and import and export regulations. Inasmuch as foreign trade for more than two decades has exceeded the rate of growth of the gross national product, it may be concluded that the government was more efficient in helping business than business was itself.

In relation to its high level of economic growth it should be noted that the ROC government has perceived, undoubtedly correctly so, that Taiwan must attract foreign investment and technology if it is to continue to sustain rapid economic growth. Foreign investment also serves a political need: it maintains ties with nations that have broken diplomatic relations with the ROC and have recognized the People's Republic of China. It also guarantees foreign commitment to Taiwan's independence. Realizing the fact that the United States is politically the most important country to the ROC, the government has made every effort to get American investment.[23] Up to 1977 it had attracted $600 million in private investment, most of it in the 1970s. Thirty to forty large U.S. corporations are now doing business in Taiwan, and the list generally includes those with the most political influence in the United States. Meanwhile the ROC has borrowed from the United States via both bank loans to public corporations and individual or business investment in private enterprises. One source put total U.S. investment in Taiwan in 1978 at over $5 billion.[24] Japan is second in importance, followed by the overseas Chinese. Japan's investment, notably, is primarily in small businesses—money not easily recoverable in the event of a political crisis. Overseas Chinese investment is enticed chiefly from countries that support the ROC diplomatically. In order to continue to attract foreign investment the government has loosened currency restrictions and now lets local investors take money out of the country.

Thus in the realm of economic management the ROC government has made three major accomplishments. In the 1950s it fostered rapid economic growth that healed the wounds of the 1947 Taiwanese revolt, while at the same time overcoming the image of being corrupt and inefficient. These two points deserve some special explanation. Since Taiwanese constitute the majority of the business community, the government's probusiness and economic expansionist policies have benefited them in particular and have made them approve if not actively support the government.* Second, the fact that Taiwan's economic growth was not unmanaged demonstrates that the government apparatus has been streamlined and is receptive to the needs of the society—at least the business community. It also mirrors efficiency in government, which, as we will see in the next section, is the most important standard of good government to the people of Taiwan. Third, the government by increasing trade and foreign investment was able to insure foreign interest in Taiwan's survival and at the same time attract praise to the government for its intelligent policies that promoted rapid growth. Foreign investment also allowed for even faster growth than was otherwise possible. It is a noteworthy point that though the government experienced a crisis in 1971 when it was expelled from the United Nations, applications for exit visas after increasing for several months decreased markedly the following year.[25] Also, demands on the government for drastic action to cope with the loss of diplomatic ties were minimal. The same appears to be true following the U.S. decision to recognize Peking in December 1978. Large numbers of Taiwanese businessmen made monetary donations to the government and almost all U.S. banks and businessmen in Taiwan announced that they would stay.[26] This seems to indicate that economic growth may have compensated for diplomatic setbacks.

Meanwhile economic opportunities continue to attract ROC citizens back from abroad. Chinese who return from abroad to make residence in Taiwan, in addition to the foreign businessmen in Taiwan and visiting tourists, help publicize the fact that the standard of living of the average person in the PRC is much below that of Taiwan (approximately one-half to one-third measured by per capita income) and it enlists confidence in the government for making this possible. It also evokes confidence in future growth and political stability. It is no doubt partly because of Taiwan's rapid economic growth that virtually no one in Taiwan, even after U.S. derecognition, suggested joining with People's China.†

---

*Evidence for this can be found in the fact that almost none of the dissidents in Taiwan are from the business community and no business organization has been an important supporter of democratic reform. It is also an interesting point that one often meets Taiwanese businessmen who don't like mainlander Chinese but who strongly favor the government and its policies and even oppose bringing Taiwanese into the government because they might alter the government's probusiness policies.

†It is an interesting point that even the strongest opponents of the ROC government and the most adamant pro-PRC advocates have never argued that a free election or plebiscite in Taiwan would indicate a preference for the PRC. Most of them admit that the population opposes "reversion" for chiefly economic reasons.

Although there was, and still is, some criticism of government policies that allegedly cater too much to foreign investors, to the point that there has been some domestic opposition to excessive foreign economic influence, the fact that incomes have increased commensurate with rapid economic growth minimizes these charges. Per capita income has risen almost as fast as GNP, averaging over 9 percent yearly from 1953 to 1975 and 9.57 percent and 5.86 percent in 1976 and 1977, respectively. This has given the population increased buying power while fostering the rapid growth of consumerism.[27] And not only has the average person in Taiwan had much more to spend, the lower income portion of the population have increased their incomes much faster than the middle and high income groups. Between 1953 and 1961 the lower fortieth percentile increased their incomes nearly three times as fast as the top 20 percent.[28] In fact Taiwan's phenomenal economic growth, while based on the capitalist model, has avoided the problem of growth being accompanied by income disparities, and income distribution in Taiwan is now reported to be more equitable than in either Japan or the United States.[29]

This rapid leveling or equalizing of incomes has, as we will see in the next section, broken many of the barriers between provincial and other groups in Taiwan and has closed the rural-urban gap and the disparity between rich and poor areas. It has also promoted the rapid development of a materialist culture, more than the fast rate of economic development alone would accomplish. And it has also done much to integrate the society in Taiwan, a factor that contributes to building better political institutions. On the other hand, as we will see, materialism and the other societal changes induced by economic growth have not created an intense demand for democracy. This is borne out by the obvious absence of demands by Taiwanese businessmen for democratic institutions and their concern with efficiency and responsiveness in government without regard to political ideology or principles. This conflicts with some liberal thinkers who view economic growth as a necessary cause for the growth of democratic institutions.

This then leads us to a related and at the same time crucial question: Will the ROC be able to insure future economic growth of an order that will maintain confidence in the government and prevent any attraction on the part of its citizens to the People's Republic? Put another way, what are the obstacles to future economic growth? And will continued rapid economic growth insure political stability? In terms of managing economic growth of a high order, while attracting foreign investment, increasing economic equality, and keeping unemployment low, the ROC government clearly deserves high marks. And there is no reason to think Taiwan's economic planners cannot continue their good work in the future. Managing the recent problem of a faltering textile industry and dealing with the problem of revaluing the currency suggests continued government deftness in coping with economic problems.

In reference to the above questions it is also necessary to point out that the government has in recent years taken a more active part in the economy than during the 1950s and the 1960s and one way it has done this is through the so-called ten big projects. These projects involve infrastructure building and the construction of large industries such as ship building and steel production, where private investment is insufficient.[30] When these projects were started, skeptics felt that they would cause inflation, might cause a drain on the country's foreign exchange reserves, would provoke labor shortages to the detriment of the private sector, and would not be economically profitable. Inasmuch as these predictions have proven wrong, with the fact that the projects have helped maintain a high growth rate and high levels of employment, they must be seen to reflect sound government planning. It should be added that their completion dates were set ahead when Taiwan was expelled from the United Nations and thus they served as a timely means of keeping employment and growth at high levels during a critical period. Some now say that the projects run the risk of overstimulating the economy, but this is most likely the planners' intention in that Taiwan faces continued political crisis and must keep its economy in high gear to sustain employment, trade, and foreign investment for the reasons already mentioned. Thus the projects have proven both economically and politically sound and new projects on the drawing board will probably be so in the future.

There is some evidence of a movement in Taiwan to slow down economic growth or pursue more "rational" growth. Air and water pollution are already serious and portend to become critical problems in the future.[31] On the other hand there are very few who advocate slowing down economic growth. Therefore, to date environmentalists have had very little impact on economic planning or economic growth. The government, by paying lip service to the problem, can probably avoid taking any actions that might dampen Taiwan's economic growth for at least a few years—a time frame that seems to be crucial in terms of the government continuing to use economic progress to augment its prestige and legitimacy and ultimate survival.

It seems unlikely that any movement will develop in the immediate future to restrict economic growth. It has given the people of Taiwan material possessions they have longed for and they are proud of their accomplishments. It is also seen by the populace as a means whereby Taiwan can maintain its independence, which insures certain freedoms and a way of life that the overwhelming majority cherished. On the other hand, Taiwan is one of the most densely populated nations on earth and the bad effects of rapid economic growth will probably be realized much sooner than in most other nations due to the crowding of the cities and a rapidly growing materialistic mentality. The development of technology-intensive industry and the growth of service industries and more emphasis on cultural achievements in the near future will no doubt help relieve these problems. So will the fact that growth and economic success are seen as related to the survival of the nation and to any hope of future cultural achievements where in many societies these are viewed as contradictory aims.

SOCIAL CHANGE AND POLITICAL MODERNIZATION

Rapid economic growth makes social change inevitable in almost any society or culture. The same is true of increasing access to education by large segments of the society, the importation of new ideas from outside, and materialism—all of which appear to be strongly influencing the society in Taiwan at the present time. To comprehend the rapid social change that is going on in Taiwan one needs only to observe the number of people who see Western movies, their Western dress and buying habits, the decline in population growth, the number of tourists who visit each year, and the breakdown of traditional class barriers.[32] Such manifold and deep-seated change can have vast stabilizing or destabilizing effects on the political system. It can promote political modernization, or it can create serious problems for the decision makers in power. In Taiwan social change is clearly having both effects.

The questions that appear to be most important and that will be entertained in the following pages are: To what extent has economic development created a materialist culture that espouses values that contradict the government's pursuit of stability and its efforts to conserve Chinese culture? And is the latter important? How has the growth of mass education affected political outlooks, and could this present a problem to the regime? In both cases is there an impetus to create democratic institutions and ideals faster than the government is prepared to give up many of its authoritarian practices? Has there occurred a significant rise in crime as a result of social change and is this a threat to political harmony and the government's image? Did the expulsion from the United Nations give rise to an intellectual movement that might make threatening demands on the government, and what is the future of that movement? Finally, does the Taiwanese Independence Movement threaten the government and what is its future?

First let us look at the impact of economic development. Some data on the impact of increases in the standard of living need to be examined to comprehend the scope of its impact. The average yearly per capita income in Taiwan in 1952 was $148; in 1972 it was $1,079. During this same period the average daily caloric intake of the residents of Taiwan rose from 2,078 to 2,770, while the consumption of protein increased over 50 percent from 49 grams per day to 77. During this period the average life span increased from 58 years to over 71. In the realm of material comforts during this period the percentage of households with electricity increased from 35.4 percent to virtually all, or 99.7 percent, while the number of households with T.V. sets increased from zero to 94.5 percent.[33] Citing further evidence, the number of radios increased 13 times during the period 1953-62, making it possible for virtually anyone in Taiwan who wanted a radio to have one. The same thing followed with T.V. sets, and to a lesser extent with telephones, which increased in number by more than 500 percent in the ten years after 1965.[34] Most homes now have refrigerators, ovens, and a variety of kitchen and other appliances. Air conditioners are also commonplace. Most families also have a motorcycle or car. All of this suggests that consumerism, or materialism, has become a way of life in Taiwan. What are its effects?

Because of mass consumption the disparities between social class and other groups in Taiwan are rapidly disappearing. Although Chinese recently coming from the mainland still have an edge over Taiwanese in per capita income, the gap is quickly closing. The rural areas of Taiwan are poorer than urban areas and certain districts are richer than others, but these differences are rapidly diminishing. Other disparities in material wealth and possessions are also evaporating. This has given rise to a materialistic culture and with it secular and detached attitudes. Reflecting these trends a number of attitude surveys conducted in recent years indicate that there is little difference in perceptions on most issues (including political attitudes, confidence in the government, and so on) between the Taiwanese and Mainland Chinese and among other groups on Taiwan, except for recent immigrants.[35] If one thinks in terms of Taiwan's continued independent existence in the context of social problems that might cause instability or opposition to the government and that might in turn weaken Taiwan's unity, these are certainly positive trends.

On the other hand, materialism has also loosened almost all bonds in the society and has created a variety of problems such as a generation gap, juvenile crime, and other such problems. This may cause difficulties for the government in the future, if other problems simultaneously become acute. At present, however, the main product of materialism in terms of social effects—in addition to those specific changes already mentioned—is the fostering of an atomization or individual self-dependence. If Taiwan follows the development patterns of other societies this will give the government more responsibilities and hence increased prerogatives. It will also make the citizenry more government dependent, and although not more satisfied with government certainly less likely to try to overthrow or change it.

This is not, however, to say that present social trends are contributory to democracy. Surveys, for example, show that notwithstanding the high voter turnout at the polls there is a declining interest in politics on the part of Taiwan's citizenry. One survey conducted in the early 1970s recorded that only 18 percent of students talk with their peers about politics once a week, and that only 24 percent of law students who are old enough to vote have actually voted. What is more, 93 percent responded that respect for elders is a "most important virtue," while only 13 percent agreed that majority rule, periodic elections, the protection of dissent, and more than one political party are important characteristics of democracy.[36] One could argue, and a number of Western scholars have, that the explanation is simply that democracy is developing slowly in Taiwan. On the other hand, Taiwan seems to be going in the direction of Japan, more than the United States or Western Europe, where many authoritarian practices are not regarded as undemocratic and where individualism is considered less necessary (and sometimes even undesirable) to the growth of democracy. It may also be true that whereas certain facets of Western democracy have or are now taking hold, it is uncertain whether many others will or not because of Taiwan's citizens' negative attitudes toward many aspects of American democracy and Western culture.

One writer suggests that the people in Taiwan are not being taught democracy, and that what democracy the citizens of the ROC have seen has to a large extent given them expectations that have not been and cannot be fulfilled; therefore their enthusiam for democratic values has diminished in some important ways.[37] Others suggest that the complexities produced by urbanization, technology, and so on are producing the same trends in Taiwan as in the West, namely the feeling that the society is too complicated for democracy. Indeed material comforts and higher standards of living have fostered more concern with a "meaningful life," which includes such amenities as leisure time and artistic pleasure but has not produced any obvious attitudes or perceptions toward the government that can be categorically positive or negative.

The rising standard of living in Taiwan in contrast to producing new political attitudes directly, however, has made possible extremely rapid rises in the level of education, and this in turn has affected social change as well as attitudes toward politics. The importance of this can be comprehended only after seeing the scope of the broadening of education in Taiwan. From 1954 to 1974 the percentage of the population in secondary schools increased almost five times and the percentage in institutions of higher learning increased nearly twelve times. Three times as many persons were working on advanced degrees in 1974 as received degrees during the entire preceding ten years. At present more than one-fourth of the population in Taiwan is students—more than in England.[38] Moreover, whereas at one time one-quarter of Taiwan's university graduates went abroad and few returned, now less than 8 percent leave and several times as many as once returned now come back.[39] It is also a new phenomenon for there to be a high level of unemployment among the higher educated while some factories have difficulties hiring workers.[40] This suggests potential intellectual disenchantment and unrest. Taiwan's educated thus might be expected to serve as a bastion of support or opposition to government or make certain demands for political change that the government may be compelled to meet or reject with force.

Another recent survey indicates that whereas there has been and continues to be a high regard for education, the gap in education level between Mainland Chinese and Taiwanese is still large, with Mainlanders (who are about 15 percent of the population) constituting 40 percent of the enrollment in the best universities.[41] This is juxtaposed beside the fact that both groups perceive that having an education is more advantageous to a Taiwanese than to a Mainlander, and that there is a larger portion of Taiwanese than their ratio of the population given government jobs. While there is still discrimination against Mainlanders in business (which is largely Taiwanese controlled), this suggests that there could be considerable disenchantment among young, educated

Mainlanders. This is borne out by a number of observers who have talked to young Mainlanders in Taiwan in recent years.* There is even evidence that some among this group may constitute opposition to the government.† At this juncture, however, the top ruling hierarchy of the government does not seem to have cause for fear and may even see this as an advantage in that it would distract support from the Taiwanese Independence Movement and discourage Taiwanese from opposing the government that they see as granting them favorable treatment.

Still another survey of the higher educated in Taiwan indicates a low level of concern for national security compared to the less educated or average citizen.[42] It is no doubt correct to assume that this suggests that future high defense expenditures may not have as much public support as in the past and there may even develop opposition to a large defense burden. This seems to agree with the observation often made that there has long been a decline in support for the "return to the mainland" policy. Although this contradicted by the reaction of Taiwan people to U.S. derecognition, for example, they voluntarily donated U.S. $50 million to the national defense fund within two months, in the future most citizens may not be willing to fight or pay for what it costs to remain independent. On the other hand, this may simply suggest that they do not perceive a serious threat and may change their attitudes when and if a threat arises.

Another gap in terms of the educated population's outlook and government policy, and this is perhaps ironic, is that the more educated people do not give a high priority to equality as compared to those with an average level of education.[43] This may reflect the fact that they perceive that the government's income leveling policy has gone too far or that the government bureaucracy has become too impersonal and doesn't give due recognition to the value of education. It is interesting that whereas this is a widely espoused position of the educated, activist intellectuals in Taiwan frequently complain of the "ravages of capitalism" and the evils of economic inequality. The conclusion would seem to be warranted that the activists do not have a strong base of support on these charges at least and that the government may have already given the country as much equality, and perhaps more, than it wants. Two other differences indicated by survey research between the more and less educated that may be significant, but which at the same time are difficult to draw conclusions from, are that more education produces more interest in politics, but a lower voter turnout, and that

---

*I have, in fact, noticed this myself when talking to young Mainlanders during recent visits to Taiwan and consider it a recent phenomenon.

†It is worthy of note that a number of those arrested in Taiwan in recent years for sedition and other political crimes are Mainlanders, whereas in the past this was quite unusual.

higher education increases the probability of supporting the KMT platform as opposed to independent candidates.[44]

This brings us to the problem of dissent and political opposition in Taiwan. With the exception of the Taiwanese Independence Movement there has been little organized public dissent or protest by ROC citizens—that is until 1971. Prior to that date a few political candidates would occasionally take a "Taiwanese" line in campaigning or would criticize the KMT for autocratic practices and human rights violations. Generally, however, they did not pass certain bounds and when they did they were "visited" by the police or were arrested. At times outspokenness would transcend the understood boundaries for a while, but this would be followed by a crackdown to serve as a warning to future mavericks or radicals. In 1971, however, two events occurred that changed this. First, the Senkaku Islands (Tiao Yu Tai in Chinese), 100 miles north of Taiwan, were promised to Japan along with Okinawa as part of the U.S. reversion agreement with Tokyo. These small, uninhabited islands were mentioned in early Chinese records, thus giving China a historical basis for a claim on them even though they were under Japanese sovereignty prior to World War II. In 1969 it was reported that there might be oil undersea near the Senkakus and the reversion of Okinawa (which included the Senkakus) to Japan gave Tokyo claim to the oil. Meanwhile, geological evidence had indicated that the islands were not part of the Ryukyu chain but were rather part of China's continental shelf. The second event was the ROC's expulsion from the United Nations. This was a blow to the ROC government's prestige, particularly in view of its uncompromising anticommunism and its unwillingness to do anything to prevent or soften this diplomatic setback and instead predicted incorrectly that UN members would "come to their senses." Both events evoked intellectual concern and thus a protest movement.

To what extent the movement to claim the Senkaku Islands was spontaneous is uncertain. In any case the government, rather than trying to stop the movement, organized its own demonstrations by gathering groups of college students to march in Taipei and protest at the U.S. and Japanese embassies. Demonstrations of sufficient size to attract attention were also held in the United States and Hong Kong, though the ROC soon put the lid on when it appeared that Peking may be able to infiltrate the demonstrations abroad.[45] The movement soon fizzled out and little has been heard about the issue since. It did, however, set a precedent of open protest in Taiwan and it may have compounded the seriousness of what soon followed.[46]

Shortly thereafter, when Taipei was expelled from the United Nations, a number of intellectuals formed study groups to discuss the problem of the ROC's deteriorating world position and methods to cope with Taiwan's image, including the problem of a government that was "weak, unaware of current problems, too old," and so on. Sometimes criticism was couched in even stronger language such as "reactionary, authoritarian, undemocratic, and self-serving." During this time a number of journals or magazines started publishing articles dealing with contemporary issues, especially problems that related to Taiwan's new predicament. Most notable of these was the *Taiwan Political Review*. However, the movement, which at first showed some signs of unity of purpose and spirit, soon began to split apart. Some leading members of the movement began to call for expression on issues that were either unrealistic or had no support among the masses. For example, a number of members of the movement called for reducing antagonisms between Taiwanese and Mainlander Chinese. This may have been a good idea, but it was clearly something that the movement could not accomplish. Some members also criticized the government for placing too much stress on economic growth and for allowing foreign exploitation and economic inequalities. Since economic growth had widespread support and since Taiwan's development was quite outstanding for producing a minimum of inequality, this tended to discredit the movement. Finally, personalities became an issue and the movement floundered.[47]

To what extent the top hierarchy of the government was responsible for the failure of the intellectual movement is uncertain. There were certainly other causes than those just mentioned. However, one other factor that did serious damage to the movement, though this was probably important only after the movement was already on the skids, was the fact that, beginning in 1972, Chiang Ching-kuo appointed a number of young, American-educated Ph.D.s to important positions in the government—but none that had been or were leaders in the intellectual movement.

In any event in the last several years the thrust of dissent has once again focused on independent political candidates who take a stand against the KMT and official government policy. But this has not gotten out of hand and it may be seen by the top hierarchy of the government as a way of allowing more dissent (to please liberals in the United States and elsewhere) yet not allow it to go too far. Judging from what independent candidates have said in recent years, the government is able to tolerate charges of corruption and undemocratic practices, election fixing (when there is some substance to the comments), government policy on a wide range of domestic (especially local) issues, and the age of government officials. Even human rights can be discussed openly within certain limits. On the other hand, the top hierarchy of the government will not tolerate criticism that may be construed to mean changing or overthrowing the system, anything that might be procommunist or suggest negotiating with Peking, or anything aimed directly at individuals in the top leadership hierarchy. Similarly it will not tolerate Taiwanese who run strictly as Taiwanese or who advocate Taiwanese independence.

In the late months of 1977 leading up to the elections in November a marked trend toward more leniency can be perceived. A number of independent candidates openly charged KMT candidates with violations of electioneering practices and the police with interfering in the election. Some criticism was leveled at the KMT itself—though not specifically its top leaders—for allowing corruption and dishonesty. Comments were also made by independent candidates about the KMT being too conservative and controlled by the old and feeble-minded. The highlight of the campaign was a riot in Chungli, a suburb of Taipei. Young independent Taiwanese candidates had criticized the KMT for allowing ballot tampering and police interference in elections. In this context a disturbance flared when officials invalidated some votes. It then escalated into the gathering of a crowd of 10,000 and rioting that culminated in the burning of six police cars. The police did not intervene, as they had apparently been instructed not to. The incident was clearly anti-KMT and marked the first mass violence in Taiwan for 30 years.[48]

On the other hand, the government after 1975 started taking a hard stand on crime, cracking down on violent crime in response to complaints of motor-cycle gangs that terrorized people in the Taipei area, an increase in bodily crimes, and a number of violent crimes that became sensationalized, such as the gang rape of a noted Taipei singer. Contrary to past practice, some cases were sent to military courts under martial law provisions and stern sentences were meted out quickly. Although some protested that the sudden crackdown on crime was being used as a warning to potential dissenters, which is probably true, the move had the sympathy of the majority and did prove effective in reversing the rising crime rate and preserving Taipei's record as the safest city in the world of over 1 million population.[49] In recent years the government has also main-tained its guard against overt threats to its rule under the guise of vigilance against communist infiltrators and spies. In January 1978 a military court sentenced a group of three Taiwanese and three Mainlanders to stiff sentences up to life in prison for writing threatening letters to foreign businessmen and planning to kidnap the director of the United States Information Agency in Taipei and blow up his office along with a U.S.-owned hotel.[50] The government also caught and sentenced the individual responsible for sending several letter bombs in October 1976, one of which injured the governor of Taiwan. In late 1975 the *Taiwan Political Review* was banned and not long later one of its edi-tors was sentenced to jail for sedition.[51] In September 1978 the Taiwan *Daily News* was brought under government pressure by pro-government Taiwanese businessmen; the apparent reason was that it had given too much attention to opposition within the Provincial Assembly[52]

These above-cited incidences of crackdown were probably more an effort to keep the lid on protest and keep the crime rate from escalating rather than eliminate dissent and opposition completely. However, they also served as a signal to potential opponents of the government that there were limits to what the government would tolerate. In any case they were balanced by an unprece-dented statement by Chiang Ching-kuo in December 1976 that since 1949 the government had convicted 254 persons on charges of sedition and that only one had been sentenced to death, and that there had been only 33 such convictions in 1976. Chiang went on to say that he would be glad to cooperate with an inter-national organization that wanted to review human rights in the ROC. He also issued orders to Taiwan's police organizations, especially the Taiwan Garrison

Command, which handles sedition cases, to use more orthodox investigating and enforcement techniques, and judging from their behavior this was carried out.[53]

The Taiwanese Independence Movement (TIM) constitutes another sort of opposition to the ROC government: one not active in Taiwan, but organized abroad. The main centers of activity abroad are in the United States and Japan, areas where there are sizable numbers of Taiwanese with foreign citizenship. The organization has been active in both countries for some time and advocates a Taiwan ruled by Taiwanese and the overthrow by force if necessary—and it is generally assumed by members that it is necessary—of the ROC government. Some would also expel Mainland Chinese from the island. During the 1960s the TIM got considerable publicity when the United States and Japan seemed to be moving toward a two-China policy, and also because of support allegedly given by the ruling Liberal Democratic party in Japan and the Central Intelligence Agency in the United States. Two incidents particularly gave the TIM notoriety: the escape of a TIM leader from Taiwan in 1968, after he had been released from prison and was under surveillance, and the attempt made on Chiang Ching-kuo's life by two of its members in New York in April 1970.

Beginning in 1971, however, the TIM began to decline in importance, particularly in terms of the publicity it got abroad. A number of factors and events account for this decline.[54] First, the movement is quite different (in addition to there being two main competing movements in Japan and factions in the United States) in the two countries where it has the largest following, with mostly older members in Japan (many members of the former aristocracy under Japanese colonial rule) as opposed to primarily a student membership in the United States. Second, the movements in the United States and Japan split over the Senkaku Islands issue in early 1971 with the Japan-based group opposing any protest. Third, the TIM suffered a major shock when President Nixon signed the Shanghai Communique in 1972, which said that there was only one China, since it was widely assumed that the United States was moving toward a two-China policy, meaning one China and one Taiwan. Soon after this, Tokyo recognized Peking and members of the ruling party in Japan as well as businessmen became cautious about their support of the TIM. Added to this the United States in 1971 failed to support the independence movement in Bangladesh (or anywhere else of importance) and was thus seen to give a lower priority to the cause of self-determination. The CIA then got involved in serious public relations problems that weakened the agency and put constraints on its covert activities (assuming this was important because it had supported the TIM or at least its membership thought so). Finally, a number of American intellectuals who wanted to ingratiate themselves with the Peking government abandoned the TIM. Perhaps more important than all of these reasons, many Taiwanese came to the realization that the Mainlander-dominated KMT might make a deal with Peking if they tried to overthrow the government and that they must cooperate with the Mainlanders if Taiwan were to survive efforts by Peking to "incorporate" it. In short the majority of Taiwanese came to perceive that they were in the same boat with the Mainlanders vis-a-vis resisting the People's Republic's efforts to force the United States and the international community to forsake Taiwan, and that this was the biggest threat that they faced.

For these reasons the Taiwanese Independence Movement has not been as active in recent years, and though it does not publish its membership rolls, membership figures are no doubt down. In any case, at present it has little hope of attaining its goals as an independent Taiwan Republic. On the other hand, some independent Taiwanese politicians in Taiwan secretly hope that the TIM will survive as it makes the KMT more understanding of their more "moderate" demands and puts the KMT "diehards" (those who resist Taiwanese participation in the party) in the same category as the "extremists" in the TIM who want to rid Taiwan of Mainland Chinese.

At the time of this writing it is difficult to assure what impact U.S. derecognition will have on social change in Taiwan. Initial evidence suggests that it will further alleviate the differences between Taiwanese and Mainlanders and will foster greater unity aimed at preserving Taiwan's independence. Clearly all groups seem to be burying their differences and have become acutely aware of their future. This will undoubtedly affect many social trends in the near future.

THE RULE OF CHIANG CHING-KUO

An analysis of political change in Taiwan would not be complete without an assessment of the man at the helm and the person responsible for most of the changes that have transpired both politically as well as economically in Taiwan in recent years. It is likewise important to understand President Chiang Ching-kuo's attitudes, perspectives, and goals to know the direction that political change will take in the future. It is generally felt uncontestable that the present and immediate future are in this man's hands and further that whether Taiwan will survive as an independent political entity is uncertain but will be decided in this decade in his lifetime.

Although Chiang Ching-kuo is the unquestioned leader of the ROC, very little is known about him. No complete biography has been written about him and by his order the press does not report on his personal life. In short, he is very much an enigma. What is written about him consists primarily of public records, stories about his relationship to his father, and things he has written himself about his life in the Soviet Union.[55]

Chiang Ching-kuo was born in 1910 when his father was age 20. His mother was a village girl who was married to Chiang Kai-shek when he was young—a decision made by the two families.[56] He went to elementary and high school in Shanghai and at the age of 16 decided to go to the Soviet Union for further education, but before he did he joined the KMT. In 1927 he asked to return to China, but because of his father's turn against the communists this request was denied. He subsequently joined the Red Army as an enlisted man, and based on his outstanding performance was sent to a Soviet military school.

However, Chiang was sympathetic to Trotsky and because of his anti-Stalinist attitudes he was removed from school and sent to work as a manual laborer in an electrical plant. Subsequently his opposition to the head of the Chinese communist movement got him sent to Siberia. However, following the formation of a "united front" between the KMT and the communists and the rapprochement between China and the Soviet Union in 1936 in the face of Japanese expansionism, he was allowed to go back to China. He returned after 12 years and with a wife and two children.

Once in China his father put him through an intense period of study and indoctrination following which he gave him control of the Southern part of Kiangsi Province, a region that was not under Japanese threat. There he proved loyal to his father and an efficient administrator as well as a good leader. During these years he also had frequent contacts with U.S. military officers and with other foreigners.

In 1949, when the Nationalists fled to Taiwan, Chiang Ching-kuo was put in charge of the General Political Department of the Ministry of Defense. At the same time he also organized the China Youth Corps, in his words, to prevent what had happened on the mainland where the communists had gained control of the minds of the youth—which he himself had experienced for a time.[57] And he also took responsibility for the repatriation of Chinese troops from Korea who did not want to return to the People's Republic.

In ensuing years Chiang Ching-kuo, who became known to foreigners as CCK, occupied increasingly important positions. In 1958 he was appointed vice-minister of defense; in 1965 he was minister of defense; in 1969 he rose to the rank of vice premier; and in 1972 he became premier.

The appointment of Chiang Ching-Kuo to the premiership paralleled his father's deteriorating health, which meant that he was virtually running the government and the KMT. From his position as premier CCK initiated a number of reforms that were to have far-reaching impact on politics in Taiwan. More precisely he was responsible for increasing the tempo of political change as well as the direction of that change. The most important areas where he instituted reform were: appointing more Taiwanese and more young people to positions in the central government and the party; cracking down on corruption; widely promulgating information about the running of the government and the proper functions of the various parts of the government; presenting an image of government's interest in the common man; giving added importance to economic development, notably through the ten large projects; and reducing the size of the army.

Chiang Ching-kuo had probably perceived for a long time that the Taiwanese were not well represented in the ROC government and that their support was needed for new government programs to succeed, as well as to insure the ultimate survival of the ROC. The fact that the ROC was expelled from the United Nations in 1971, thus undermining its credibility both at home and abroad, plus the fact that the next year CCK was premier, enabled him to

oppose the diehards in the party and government who resisted Taiwanese participation on the grounds that they were not sufficiently experienced in dealing
with communism.

In view of Chiang's progressive moves to get Taiwanese into the government, it is puzzling to many foreigners why he didn't abandon the "return to the
mainland" policy, declare Taiwan's independence, and apply for UN membership under the name Republic of Taiwan, or why he didn't openly announce
that he would invite the Soviet Union to protect Taiwan in the event that the
United States pulled out and broke the defense pact. Chiang probably perceived
that Taiwan did not need to take such drastic steps to survive and those solutions might be counterproductive.[58] He realized that Taiwanese had to be given
positions of responsibility in the government; but he also realized that political
power was largely in the hands of conservative Mainlanders and most of those at
the top were opposed to making concessions that he had already made. Thus he
might lose control of the party by going too far too fast. Maintaining the return
to the mainland policy and his anticommunist stance placated the older members of the KMT while justifying martial law and thus strict control over the
population, which he probably perceived as necessary during this time of crisis.
It also was a signal to Taiwanese that their demands for proportional representation and thus immediate control of the government would be rejected. It also
had the effect of quelling any suspicion on the part of the Taiwanese that the
government might negotiate with the communists rather than gradually turn
over political power to the Taiwanese. Specific rejection of the "Russian option"
allayed any suspicion about CCK because of his 12 years in the Soviet Union and
his Russian wife. In any case it was not a desirable option in terms of Taiwan's
economic and political system. And if the Americans needed warning, they
would think of this themselves.

Chiang Ching-kuo was also cognizant of the charges leveled against the
ROC government that it was inflexible, out of touch with reality, and resistant
to change because it was full of and controlled by old men. Thus he picked a
number of young people for important positions, most notably American-
trained Ph.D.s. They offered a number of advantages. By being foreign-trained
they would have a different outlook and would be more supportive of change,
but they would also lack a local base of support. Moreover he could pick capable
men, whom he knew, based upon their connections and activities abroad, who
did not support revolutionary change but rather progress. Finally, placing young
people in positions of importance and by associating with young people much of
the time Chiang gave the impression that he was aware of more than just immediate problems and could steer Taiwan on a course whereby it had a future.
Whether this was also done as a means of undermining the intellectual movement
in Taiwan that began to flourish after Taipei was expelled from the United
Nations is uncertain. There were also rumors that Chiang had a secret understanding with the intellectuals and supported them.[59] The decision was probably
made from an administrative and pragmatic point of view: the best talent was

abroad, it should be attracted back to Taiwan, and using it would help improve relations with the United States while giving the populace some confidence that the government was ready for the future.

Related to Ching Ching-kuo's effort to get more Taiwanese and younger talent into the government was his drive to present an image of a government concerned with the masses. Chiang has been accused of cultivating the foreign press, by taking frequent trips to areas outside of Taipei, especially rural areas, and talking informally with the lower and middle class "common" people. While this may be true, the reason may also be that Chiang spent much of his life with common people and his experience in the Soviet Union probably taught him a lesson he has not forgotten about what life is like in rural areas. Many who have observed him closely say that he feels at home among the people and truly enjoys talking to them and making their problems his own. Whatever his reasons, Chiang has been very successful in making the government appear to be "for the people."

Related to his efforts to promote a concern for the common people is the fact that as soon as he became premier, Chiang immediately demanded the widespread publication of the functions and responsibilities of various organs of the government. This included putting government operations, names, addresses, and so on, in the newspapers and elsewhere. It also involved writing job descriptions.[60] This made it possible for citizens to know where to go for solutions to their problems. It also made it possible for the public to know when a government official was overstepping his authority or behaving improperly, and thus served as a control on improper or irresponsible actions by government officials.

Of special importance in his efforts to reform the government by giving it a new image and making it more responsive to the people, Chiang instituted a widespread campaign to wipe out corruption. The first step was to warn everybody in the government that they also were subject to the law and that the premier expected hard work and honesty and would punish corruption. Subsequently he acted. Soon he had overseen the arrest and imprisonment of his own relatives, members of the feared Taiwan Garrison Command, and numerous wealthy businessmen.[61] As soon as the word was out, Chiang also expressed the feeling that he did not like government officials giving lavish parties, getting wedding gifts, and so on, and compliance came very quickly. Chiang Ching-kuo himself has been a good model. He still resides in an unassuming house in an ordinary part of town and spurns ostentatiousness and luxury. He works long hours and expects others to demonstrate their worth through hard work and accomplishments and not surround themselves with the unnecessary expensive accoutrements of high office.

In his concern for economic growth, which the president apparently feels is the key to Taiwan's strength and its future, the ten big projects have played a special role. Chiang Ching-kuo was largely responsible for their approval and he has taken a special interest in them. In fact the projects have sometimes been labeled "CCK's Ten Projects." His background as an engineer and his special concern with Taiwan's economic growth probably account for his preoccupation with the projects. He argued in the beginning against those who said that Taiwan could not afford them and that it would place too much of a burden on Taiwan's foreign exchange position and would require more skilled labor than could be supplied considering the growing demands of industry.[62] Now most of the criticism had been quieted, even though the shipbuilding industry has run into hard times and the future profits of the steel mill and petrochemical industry are uncertain. Most of the projects have been completed ahead of schedule and their vital role in guaranteeing continued economic growth is clear. It has been said that in recent years Chiang has asked for weekly reports on the projects and that his enthusiasm for these projects has provided the impetus for 12 new projects.

Finally Chiang Ching-kuo has been responsible for reducing the size of Taiwan's army. Long persuaded to do so by American advisors, Chiang has been the moving force behind trimming and modernizing the military, which included cutting the size of a 600,000-man standing army by nearly 20 percent while increasing the size of the reserves and upgrading training and weapons procurement.[63] By making these changes the military is now better prepared to defend Taiwan and manpower has been released to increase industrial productivity and alleviate the problem of a scarcity of labor. Ching's argument was that the army was too small for an offensive against the mainland and that overthrowing the communist government on the mainland was for the most part a political task anyway. His decision no doubt helped his image among top American decision makers, but it also reflected wisdom and an understanding of realities, even though it may have cost him some friendship in his own military.

In 1975, shortly after his father died, Chiang Ching-kuo became head of the party. From his positions of premier (or head of the Executive Yuan) and head of the KMT, plus the influences he still maintains in the military, Chiang was clearly in command—even though following provisions in the Constitution, C. K. Yen, who was vice-president, became president. It was reported that there was some opposition to Ching taking the reins of the party and thus consolidating his power, and it was even rumored that diehards in the party who didn't like his appointment of Taiwanese to important posts and other of his reforms opposed him.* Whether or not this is true will probably never be known. In any event Chiang Ching-kuo won without an open fight.

Without his father present to veto any of his moves or the danger of those close to his father trying to use his father's name to block his programs, Chiang Ching-kuo was more free to push the reforms that he had already started. And

---

*This view is in large part based on rumor and conjecture. However, some evidence for this comes from the fact that the vote taken by the party to elect CCK president in 1978 was not unanimous.

this he did. One of his first moves was to enlist even more Taiwanese and young people into the KMT Central Committee and its important decision-making center, the Standing Committee. Other progressive reforms followed, though most were simply a continuation of changes already started.

In early 1978, prior to the upcoming March elections, C. K. Yen announced his retirement as president and recommended that Chiang Ching-kuo was the person that the party should nominate for the job. That recommendation was carried out. Thus in March CCK became president without contest. Although the party's decision seemed nearly unanimous, there were reports that a number of octogenarian members of the party continued to oppose his reforms and thus did not support him as a candidate for the presidency. The protest centered on the fact that Chiang Ching-kuo had nominated a Taiwanese as his vice-president.

At present there is no opposition to Chiang's rule and he is fully in control of ruling the country. Some have criticized him as inheriting power from his father and have said that he lacks charisma and is not a good administrator. It is true that he inherited political power from his father; but at the same time he had to prove himself to his father and to the party and the country as well. Whether he lacks charisma or not is largely a matter of personal view and opinion. And even if he is not an administrative genius he seems to have proven his ability to choose people who are. Most important he seems to have foresight and knows what problems must be overcome and in what direction the nation must go to survive. Also he has had the courage to push through reforms that have been unpopular with many of the top leaders of the party.

The big question concerning Chiang's rule is his health and who will succeed him. Chiang has had diabetes for a long time and is known to have some additional health problems including a liver ailment. He is now 69 years old. Some even speculated in the past whether he would outlive his father. On the other hand, Ching follows a strict diet and exercise program and none of his physical problems shows any sign of worsening.

The question of who follows Chiang Ching-kuo is an open one. His children have shown neither abilities nor interests in politics, so it is clear that leadership of the ROC will not remain in his family. The vice-president may be able to rise to the presidency, but this would be only temporary. Hsieh Tung-ming is older than CCK and has no base of support in the party, military, or elsewhere. He is considered a figurehead and a concession to the Taiwanese by those in government, and to a large extent he is regarded the same way by the Taiwanese. Chiang Ching-kuo has not suggested anyone else who might rule Taiwan in the future, probably to avoid any speculation and fear about his health. Hopefully he will be able to remain in power long enough to groom a successor, who, judging from his accomplishments, would have to be someone who can continue with the reforms he has instituted and continue to bridge the gap between Taiwanese and Mainlander Chinese. If Chiang passes from the scene soon there will undoubtedly be a power struggle and competition among those in control of the party, the government, and the military. Such a struggle could produce instability and possibilities for Peking to take advantage of the situation.

CONCLUSIONS

The image that Taiwan is stagnant in terms of political change is far from the truth. Using the behavioralist approach to political change whereby modernization follows economic growth, increases in education, literacy, improved communications facilities, more consumerism and secularism, and the degree to which the society is penetrated by outside ideas, Taiwan has the foundations at least for a high level of political development. Compared to the PRC—a nation with less than half the per capita income, literacy, and urbanization, less than one-tenth the number of newspapers per capita, and only a tiny fraction of the T.V. sets per capita—the stimuli for political modernization are much more present in the ROC. Across the board, the factors that cause·political change are much more present in Taiwan than in People's China.

When comparing the two countries in other realms one notes that the PRC has experienced in recent years efforts by local leaders to exert autonomy from Peking, intense social and political instability, and even leadership crises. In the PRC the problem of factionalism in the party and the "red versus expert" controversy seems to be lasting and perhaps constitutes irresolvable problems. Such do not exist in the ROC. In Taiwan there have been no efforts by local leaders to challenge the center, except to request a little more autonomy and democracy. There is no "red versus expert" controversy, unless one wants to perceive the changing role of higher education as giving rise to a similar but clearly less serious problem. Certainly it is not a source of conflict as severe as exists on the mainland. And the ROC political leadership is stable as evidenced by the succession of Chiang Ching-kuo—achieved very smoothly and without having destabilizing effects on the society.

To the uninitiated observer, however, it appears that vast political development has been generated in the PRC while little or no change has occurred in the ROC. This image is fostered from looking at superficialities and what the leaders say they want to do or are going to do, while ignoring the real factors that underlie political modernization. ROC leaders have consistently opposed change in almost everything they say. After all they are the preservers of Chinese tradition. Just exactly the opposite situation prevails in the PRC: change for change's sake. But when looking at substance instead of rhetoric it becomes clear that Taiwan is a much more rapidly changing society and political modernization of the lasting kind is taking place at a much more rapid pace.

To cite just a few examples, the ROC government has demonstrated that it has the capabilities to engineer and manage economic growth. On the mainland, Chinese leaders are still experimenting, and their overall record is not good. Bureaucracy is a problem in Taiwan, but not as serious as in People's China.

Education and technology have expanded to a degree in Taiwan that makes the PRC appear backward. Secular attitudes and individualism are present in Taiwan to a degree unknown in China. Elections are with little doubt more meaningful in Taiwan than in the PRC, and if public opinion polls could be taken, mass approval of and support for the government would indicate a much more popular and responsive government in Taiwan. Personal freedom and human rights are also much more prevalent in Taiwan.

Another reason that political development hasn't been noticed in Taiwan is that too much attention is given to political institutions and organizations that haven't remained important as appearances would suggest. A number of ROC political institutions haven't modernized. What has happened is that they have simply become relics of the past and no longer have much influence on political decision making. For example, the naive observer is often led to believe that the Executive Yuan and the Legislative Yuan or the Control Yuna have equal power. Nothing could be further from the truth. Rather than changing the organizational structure of government, top leaders in Taiwan simply use much of the system as a rubber stamp. The same thing is done in other societies including the PRC. The difference is that Westerners recognize the branches of government (except the Examination and Control Yuans) as counterparts of their own system and see that they are not functional, whereas the rubber-stamp organs of government in the PRC are seen as exactly that without expectations that they should be anything else.

Finally there is the issue of democracy and human rights. Westerners assume that a country headed by a Christian (Chiang Kai-shek was a Christian, although it is uncertain whether his son is or not), allied with the West, and receiving large quantities of U.S. aid (true until 1964) should establish democratic institutions, have free elections, and respect human rights. Americans also expect even more of the ROC since it is regarded as a historic ally and a nation closer to the United States than most other Asian nations. The populace of Taiwan, however, was not steeped in democratic traditions. Many Mainlanders, especially those in government, were brought up in the Confucian tradition—which has a democratic foundation yet is very different from Western democracy. The Taiwanese have not governed themselves and are not accustomed to doing so. From 1895 to 1945 Taiwan was a part of the Japanese Empire and was ruled by a Japanese colonial government, and no attempt was made to teach democracy or even self-rule. Furthermore both Taiwanese and Mainland Chinese see much that they consider less than desirable about Western democracy and Western culture. Perhaps most important, they perceive hypocrisy and decadence. With few exceptions Western policies toward China as well as Taiwan were based upon commercial profit and exploitation. The Chinese have also been more aware than others of the waxing and waning of the West; they are more conscious of history. Today most people in Taiwan do not see democracy as necessarily the wave of the future, and they often associate democracy with hippies, drugs, and anarchy. They are very suspicious of the kind of freedoms that allow such social ills to develop. Also they have lived through years of weak and inefficient government and a drug problem the proportions of which the West has never known.

Westerners also fail to realize that the Chinese people are very pragmatic. This can be seen clearly when studying the role of the overseas Chinese, wherever they reside. And Westerners seldom criticize the overseas Chinese for not getting involved in local politics; in fact, they applaud it. But when people in Taiwan say that they are not interested in politics or they don't feel it important not to be able to criticize their leaders on a personal level, Westerners fail to understand. Americans especially fail to comprehend their greater concern with economic growth, security, and national survival rather than with tidy political procedures and institutions.

On the other hand, there is still good reason to apply Western standards to Taiwan's political modernization. After all the West will play a vital role in deciding whether the ROC survives or not, whether it evolves into an independent, autonomous government of Taiwan or is absorbed by the PRC. Westerners, and the rest of the world for that matter, don't give much thought to the question of whether the people in Taiwan want incorporation or not, or the blood bath and loss of human rights that would result if Peking incorporates Taiwan. Rather they are concerned with whether Taiwan deserves its independence and whether self-determination is appropriate. Thus Taiwan must be attentive to the views of the international community. Perhaps Chiang Ching-kuo has already realized this. He is cultivating an image of concern for the peasants and the common man. And he has convinced them. There is little doubt that Chiang and his government have mass support.

In short the ROC government is now trying to publicize the modernization that has occurred in Taiwan in the past two to three decades rather than hiding it. This underscores Taiwan's nationhood status in the context of U.S. derecognition and a deteriorating diplomatic role in world affairs. And it is a race for time. It has to make the world know that Taiwan has joined the ranks of the modern nations and that its government, economy, society, and culture are different from those of the People's Republic to the point that regarding Taiwan as part of the PRC makes little sense. Only in this way can it preserve Taiwan's phenomenal progress and at the same time give its 17 million people their right to choose their own destiny.

NOTES

1. A studied and fairly detailed expression of this view can be found in Neil H. Jacoby, *U.S. Aid to Taiwan: A Study of Foreign Aid, Self-Help and Development* (New York: Praeger Publishers, 1966). This view can also be gleaned from a number of articles written in the *Far Eastern Economic Review*. For example, see their recent issues of the *Asia Yearbook*.

2. For a discussion of the Constitution and the decision-making structure in the Republic of China, see Frederick H. Chafee et al., *Area Handbook for the Republic of China* (Washington, D.C.: U.S. Government Printing Office, 1969), Chapter 12; and Richard L. Walker, "Taiwan's Movement into Political Modernity, 1945–72," in *Taiwan in Modern Times*, ed. Paul K. T. Sih (New York: St. John's University Press, 1973), pp. 359–96.

3. "Taiwan Continuously Easing its Curbs on Dissenters," New York *Times*, June 27, 1977, p. 9.

4. *Keesing's Contemporary Archives*, Vol. 24, April 28, 1978, p. 28951.

5. Melinda Liu, "Mustering a Little Opposition," *Far Eastern Economic Review* 98, no. 42 (October 21, 1977): 24.

6. Gerald McBeath, "Taiwan in 1977: Holding the Reins," *Asian Survey* 18, no. 1 (January 1978): 26.

7. In 1976, for example, there were 6,404 civic organizations in Taiwan and 4,534 farmers' organizations (including many small branches of larger organizations that are quite autonomous). See *Statistical Data Book of Interior, 1977*, pp. 216, 220.

8. This is true in spite of the fact that national leaders espouse democratic ideals more than do local politicians and often see local practices as undemocratic. See Arthur J. Lerman, "National Elite and Local Politician in Taiwan," *American Political Science Review* 71, no. 4 (December 1977): 1406–22.

9. Melinda Liu, "Chiang Lays it on the Old Line," *Far Eastern Economic Review* 94, 49 (December 3, 1976): 18.

10. "Rioting Mars Election in Taiwan," New York *Times*, November 21, 1977, p. 4, cites the figure 60 percent. *Far Eastern Economic Review*, December 3, 1976, p. 19, says 70 percent. The latter, on August 8, 1975, states that it may be as high as 80 percent. The percentage would vary according to the definition of Taiwanese. Usually this includes only those with parents born in Taiwan. It is clear, however, that Taiwanese constitute well over half of the KMT's membership and this figure is increasing.

11. "Rioting Mars Election in Taiwan." This point will be elaborated on more in following pages.

12. For a good synopsis of Taiwan's economic heritage and the problems faced in the late 1940s and early 1950s, see Anthony Y. C. Koo, "Economic Development of Taiwan," in Sih, *Taiwan in Modern Times*, pp. 397–433.

13. Ibid., p. 416.

14. See Kung-chia Yeh, "Economic Growth: An Overview," in *Growth, Distribution and Social Change: Essays on the Economy of the Republic of China*, ed. Yuan-li Wu and Kung-chia Yeh (Baltimore: University of Maryland Law School Occasional Papers/Reprint Series in Contemporary Asian Studies, Number 3, 1978), p. 24.

15. *Asia 1976 Yearbook* (Hong Kong: Far Eastern Economic Review, 1976), p. 296; *Asia 1978 Yearbook* (Hong Kong: Far Eastern Economic Review, 1978), p. 317.

16. Diane Ying, "Taiwan's Real Growth Rate Expected to Quicken in 2nd Half, U.S. Report Says," *Asian Wall Street Journal*, September 29, 1978, p. 3.

17. Koo, "Economic Development in Taiwan," in Sih, *Taiwan in Modern Times*, pp. 415–29.

18. In 1971, 27.4 percent of all employed persons worked for the government, showing consistent increase over previous years. See Yung Wei, "Taiwan: A Modernizing Chinese Society," in Sih, *Taiwan in Modern Times*, p. 497.

19. Ching-Yuan Lin, *Industrialization in Taiwan, 1946–52* (New York: Praeger Publishers, 1973), p. 81.

20. Yuan-li Wu and Kung-chia Yeh, "Taiwan's External Economic Relations," in Wu and Yeh, *Growth, Distribution and Social Change*, p. 193.

21. *Statistical Data Book of Interior, 1977*, p. 300.

22. Wu and Yeh, "Taiwan's External Economic Relations," p. 173.

23. This author has argued elsewhere that Taipei has sought more U.S. investment

than is necessary and has dropped restrictions on currency outflow in order to increase American investment—for political reasons. See John F. Copper, "Taiwan's Strategy and America's China Policy," *Orbis* 21, no. 2 (Summer 1966): 261–75.

24. Jocelyn Ericson, "Taiwan's Growing Confidence," *Far Eastern Economic Review* 102, no. 46 (November 17, 1978): p. 71.

25. *Statistical Data Book of Interior, 1977*, p. 300.

26. See *News from China* (daily news report from Taipei provided by the Chinese Information Service), December 20, 1978.

27. Yuan-li Wu, "Income Distribution in the Process of Economic Growth in Taiwan," in Wu and Yeh, *Growth, Distribution and Social Change*, p. 76.

28. Ibid.

29. Ibid. Also see Fox Butterworth, "Taiwan Bridges the Income Gap While Maintaining High Growth," *New York Times*, April 12, 1977, p. 25; and Dennis L. Chen, "Distributional Equality and Economic Growth: The Case of Taiwan," *Economic Development and Cultural Change* 26, no. 1 (October 1977). The New York *Times* states that there is now a more equal distribution of income in Taiwan than in either the United States or Japan.

30. For details on the "ten big projects," see "The Ten Major Construction Projects: Taiwan Government Sets National Priorities in Key Industrial Sectors," *Asian Wall Street Journal*, July 13, 1978, p. 8.

31. See the last part of Chapter 4 for a description of environmental problems in Taiwan. The problems are also discussed in this author's contribution to a forthcoming volume; see John F. Copper, "Taiwan's Energy Situation," *National Energy Profiles*, ed. Kenneth R. Stunkel (New York: Praeger Publishers, 1979).

32. In 1977, 236,000 tourists visited Taiwan, an increase of 23.03 percent over the previous year. Over 16,000 foreigners claimed residence in Taiwan, not including U.S. military personnel. See *Statistical Data Book of Interior, 1977*, p. 207, and *National Conditions* (Taipei: Statistical Bureau of Executive Yuan, 1977), p. 5.

33. All of the above statistics come from *National Conditions*, Winter 1977.

34. *Encyclopedia Britannica 1977 Yearbook*, p. 498.

35. See Richard W. Wilson, "A Comparison of Political Attitudes of Taiwanese Children and Mainlander Children on Taiwan," *Asian Survey* 8, no. 12 (December 1968): 988–1000; and Sheldon Appleton, "Taiwanese and Mainlanders on Taiwan: A Survey of Student Attitudes," *China Quarterly*, no. 44 (October–December 1970), pp. 38–65.

36. For further details, see Sheldon Appleton, "The Prospects for Student Activism on Taiwan," in *Taiwan's Future*, ed. Yung-huan Jo (Hong Kong: Union Research Institute, 1974), pp. 52–62.

37. Arthur Jay Lerman, "Taiwan's Local Socio-Political Conditions and Taiwan's Future," in Jo, *Taiwan's Future*, p. 43.

38. Sheldon Appleton, "The Social and Political Impact of Education in Taiwan," *Asian Survey* 12, no. 8 (August 1976): p. 703; Ralph N. Clough, *Island China* (Cambridge, Mass.: Harvard University Press, 1978), p. 71.

39. Appleton, "The Prospects for Student Activism on Taiwan," p. 57.

40. See Frank J. Young, "Problems of Manpower Development in Taiwan," *Asian Survey* 16, no. 8 (August 1976): 721–28.

41. These figures are from the Ministry of Education and are cited in Appleton, "The Social and Political Impact of Education in Taiwan."

42. Appleton, "The Social and Political Impact of Education in Taiwan," pp. 711–12.

43. Ibid., p. 711.

44. Yung Wei, "Political Development in the Republic of China on Taiwan: Analysis and Projections," in Jo, *Taiwan's Future*, p. 21.

45. For further details, see John F. Copper, "The Fishing Islands Controversy," *Asia Quarterly*, no. 3 (1972), pp. 217–26.

46. See Mab Huang, *Intellectual Ferment for Political Reforms in Taiwan, 1971-73* (Ann Arbor: University of Michigan Press, 1976).

47. For further details, see Ibid.

48. See "Rioting Mars an Election in Taiwan," p. 4.

49. See William Armbruster, "Paying the Price of Dissent," *Far Eastern Economic Review* 92, no. 17 (March 5, 1976): 10.

50. *Facts on File* 38, no. 1941 (January 20, 1978): 35.

51. William Armbruster, "Editor Goes Down with his Journal," *Far Eastern Economic Review* 94, no. 47 (November 19, 1977): 19.

52. Bill Kazer, "The Medium Gets the Message," *Far Eastern Economic Review* 104, no. 35 (September 22, 1978): 22.

53. According to some observers this has been true for four or five years. See Douglas H. Mendel, Jr., "Domestic Politics in Taiwan," in *The Taiwan Issue*, ed. Jack F. Williams (East Lansing, Mich.: East Asia Series/Occasional Paper No. 5, May 1976), pp. 7-14.

54. For background details, see Douglas H. Mendel, Jr., "The Formosan Nationalist Movement in Crisis," in Jo, *Taiwan's Future*, pp. 144-60.

55. One of these sources is Chiang's *My Days in Soviet Russia*, which provides more information about the new president's early life than other sources.

56. Many of the details that follow come from Tillman Durdin, "Chiang Ching-kuo and Taiwan: A Profile," *Orbis* 18, no. 4 (Winter 1975): 1023-42; and Tillman Durdin, "Chiang Ching-kuo's Taiwan," *Pacific Community* 7, no. 1 (October 1975): 92-117.

57. F. A. Lumley, *The Republic of China under Chiang Kai-shek: Taiwan Today* (London: Barrie and Jenkins, 1976), p. 11.

58. The officially stated reason is that no ROC would under any circumstances negotiate with the communists. For further details on this point, see Edwin F. Faulner, Jr., "Chiang Ching-kuo: Asia, Taiwan and the Man," *Asia Mail* 2, no. 8 (May 1978): 10.

59. See Huang, *Intellectual Ferment*, p. 73.

60. See Lumley, *The Republic of China under Chiang Kai-shek*, p. 12.

61. Ibid.

62. *President C.K. Chiang: Man of the People* (Taipei: China Publishing Company, 1978), p. 15.

63. Lumley, *The Republic of China under Chiang Kai-shek*, p. 12. For a recent analysis of Taiwan's new weapons, see Melinda Liu, "Taiwan's Defenses: Going it Alone," *Far Eastern Economic Review* 102, no. 43 (October 27, 1978): 17-20.

4

Economic Development in Taiwan

Jan S. Prybyla

Any economic system is a coordinated, internally consistent collection of man-made institutions (arrangements among people) the purpose of which is to aid in the selection of individual and social objectives ("preferences"), which primarily deal with material welfare, and to allocate natural, human, and produced resources toward the realization of the chosen objectives.

Graphically the basic components of an economic system are represented in Figure 4.1* In the pages that follow I shall deal only with the Republic of China in Taiwan's societal objectives in terms of their achievement or otherwise. Because of space limitations, discussion of Taiwan's economic institutions—the anatomy and physiology of the decision-making process—must be deferred to another time and place. Unfortunately this important and fascinating subject has been neglected in published studies of Taiwan's economy. Some discussion of the island's natural, human, and capital resource base is included in the analysis of Taiwan's objectives, and in the next section.

RESOURCES AND INSTITUTIONS: AN OVERVIEW

The land area of Taiwan is 36,000 square kilometers or 13,900 square miles. In comparative terms Taiwan is about the same size as the Netherlands or the states of Vermont and Connecticut combined. At its longest the island is 250 miles north to south and 90 miles east to west. During the half century of

---

*Notice in Figure 4.1 that the interaction of resources, institutions, and objectives is a two-way process. The choice of objectives and the institutional structure of an economy have at least as important an influence on the supply and quality of resources as the other way around.

FIGURE 4.1

Economic System

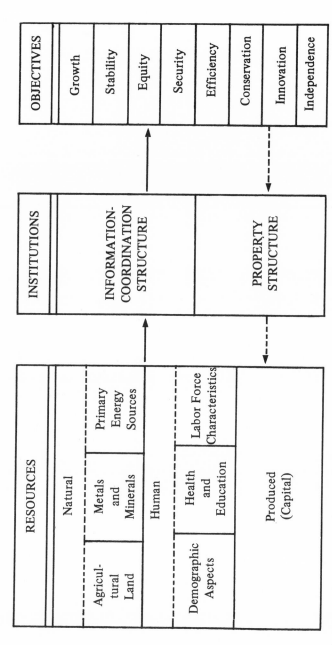

Source: Compiled by the author.

occupation of the island by the Japanese (1895-1945) substantial economic progress was made, so that when the province was returned to China at the conclusion of World War II, its overall level of economic development was higher than that of the mainland. Despite this developmental edge, economic conditions on the island were poor and the task of moving the economy forward was staggering.

Taiwan, as we shall have occasion to see, has been successful in achieving the economic objectives it set for itself. Indeed, it has become something of an institutional model for those in Asia and elsewhere who do not like the communist alternative. Taiwan has successfully combined elements of the market economy with governmental planning of both the indicative and imperative kinds, and it has achieved a level of prosperity that is the envy of most of Asia. In the face of repeated external political setbacks, government policy has emphasized the domestic economy, vigorous pursuit of foreign trade, and a pragmatic, entrepreneurial approach to developmental problems still confronting the country. Numerous difficulties and perils lurk on the road ahead. The Chinese on Taiwan are the first to acknowledge their existence. But underlying this recognition there is a determination and confidence in the future that do not ring false. In the space of three decades, Taiwan has brought into being a middle class society that has neither the arrogance nor the fawning of social extremes.

OBJECTIVES

Objectives are the preferences of participants in an economic system that are achieved by the effective application to them of relatively scarce resources of land, labor, and capital.

In evaluating a system's social objectives, two basic norms of evaluation may be used: the norm of the system's effective participants, or the norm set for the system by the outside observer. I shall evaluate Taiwan's societal objectives according to the first norm. In other words, I shall try to identify what objectives the system set for itself and how well these targets were reached. Thus functional and analytical approach will hopefully give the reader a clear notion of the distance traveled by Taiwan on the road to economic development. Whenever possible, comparative data are given for the mainland (People's Republic of China).

ECONOMIC GROWTH AND FOREIGN TRADE

Economic growth is the capacity of an economy to increase the stock of wealth (goods and services) over time.* Economists seek to express growth in

---

*The wealth to be increased may be actual or potential. Actual wealth consists of the stock of goods and services that are currently produced and marketed within the system.

quantified form, which, while it serves a useful purpose in giving a general idea of the dynamics of an economy, is deficient in many respects. We cannot enter here into the methodological shortcomings of the major growth indicators beyond the warning that these measures leave out some important constituents of growth, which do not readily lend themselves to quantification, while at the same time they include many things that, while statistically quantifiable are harmful in a broader human perspective.

Among the conventional growth indicators are the following: total and per capita product (gross national product [GNP], gross domestic product [GDP], and national income); total and per capita output of the product's major source components: agriculture, industry, services, internal and external trade; factor productivity; consumption; saving; and investment. Because of space limitations, we cannot consider all of these indicators with the detailed attention they deserve. We shall, however, examine some of them with enough care to convey a general idea of the growth performance of the Taiwanese economy since 1952.*

Rapid economic growth in the sense just mentioned has been a top societal objective of Taiwan since the early 1950s. It has been rivaled only by the objective of stability, which we shall consider subsequently.

Total and Per Capita Real GNP and Real National Income

Table 4.1 shows the evolution of Taiwan's real GNP from 1952 through 1977 (the figure for 1977 is preliminary). The data are not adjusted for gain or loss due to changes in the terms of trade. The period 1952-77 is divided into three subperiods: 1952-60, 1961-70, and 1971-77, which, as we shall see later, broadly correspond to three significant reorientations in economic policy.

Table 4.2 shows the average annual growth rate of real GNP in the whole period 1952-77 and each of the three subperiods. Data for the PRC are included for comparison.

The figures in Tables 4.1 and 4.2 reveal two things: spectacular growth of total real GNP between 1952 and 1977—a sevenfold increase in 26 years; and very high annual rates of product growth, fairly consistently sustained over the entire period with the exception of 1974-75, which was a period of world market recession generated by the oil crisis. The annual rates of GNP growth during the entire period as well as during each of the three subperiods compare favorably with the rates registered over comparably long periods by the faster

---

Potential wealth consists of known but currently unused resource stocks. The nonuse of such resources is due to a combination of existing cost-price structures and currently usable technological knowledge.

*The year 1952 has been chosen because it marks the end of the period of postwar reconstruction and the beginning of long-term economic planning in Taiwan, as well as on the mainland.

TABLE 4.1

Real Gross National Product, 1952–77
(in constant prices of 1971)[a]

Period	Amount (NT $ Million)	Index (1952 = 100)	Growth Rate (percent)
1952	57,795	100.0	10.9
1953	62,582	108.3	8.3
1954	68,022	117.7	8.7
1955	73,270	126.8	7.7
1956	77,149	133.5	5.3
1957	82,461	142.7	6.9
1958	87,184	150.9	5.7
1959	93,278	161.4	7.0
1960	98,523	170.5	5.6
1961	104,974	181.6	6.6
1962	112,622	194.9	7.3
1963	122,262	211.5	8.6
1964	136,197	235.7	11.4
1965	150,342	260.1	10.4
1966	162,058	280.4	7.8
1967	178,790	309.4	10.3
1968	194,648	336.8	8.9
1969	211,341	365.7	8.6
1970	234,161	405.2	10.8
1971	261,346	452.4	11.6
1972	292,693	506.4	12.0
1973	327,588	566.8	11.9
1974	329,560	570.2	0.6
1975	337,540	584.0	2.4
1976	376,477	651.4	11.5
1977 (prel.)	406,896	704.0	8.1

[a]GNP figures not adjusted for gain or loss due to changed terms of trade.

[b]U.S.$1 = New Taiwan (NT) $38.

Sources: SYROC 1977, p. 2; *TSDB 1975*, p. 19; *NC* Winter 1975, Winter 1976, Spring 1978, p. 8. (See Notes Section for full source titles.)

TABLE 4.2

Comparative Average Annual Growth Rates of Real Gross National Product (percent)

Period	Taiwan	PRC
1952–60	7.3	7.1
1961–70	9.3	6.3
1971–77	8.3	5.9[a]
1952–77	8.4	6.5[b]

[a]1971–76.
[b]1952–76.
Sources: Taiwan: Derived from Table 4.1. PRC: Derived from Central Intelligence Agency, *China: Economic Indicators* (October 1977), p. 3.

growing economies: developed and non-OPEC developing, market-oriented and command-oriented alike. The rate of 8.4 percent for the whole period is better than that experienced by other Asian countries with the exception of Japan.[1] It is better than the rate for the People's Republic of China. Taiwan's fastest growth was registered during the years 1964–73 when the annual growth rate of real GNP was 10.4 percent. The period of highest GNP growth rates for Communist China (not counting the period of reconstruction 1949–51) was 1952–57. During that time the average annual growth rate of real GNP was better than 7 percent.

Table 4.3 shows real GNP per capita and Table 4.4 the average annual growth rates of per capita real GNP. In 1952 real GNP per head was U.S.$188. In 1977 it was U.S.$637, or about 3.33 times the 1952 level. Comparable figures for the PRC are: 1952, U.S.$153; 1976, U.S.$340 (both figures in 1976 dollars), an increase of roughly 2.20 times. In 1952 per capita GNP in Communist China was four-fifths the Taiwan figure.[2] In 1977 it was just over half the Taiwan figure. The slippage was due almost entirely to the PRC's comparatively slower growth of product during the intervening years. The reason for the discrepancy between a sevenfold increase in Taiwan's real GNP and a little better than a threefold increase in Taiwan's per capita real GNP is, of course, the relatively rapid increase of population, especially between 1952 and 1961. The rate of natural population increase fell for the first time under 2 percent only in 1972. In 1976 it bounced back to 2.1 percent. Table 4.5 shows the evolution of the natural increase rate since 1950 in Taiwan and on the mainland. The Taiwan population, which at the end of 1952 totaled 8.1 million, reached 16.8 million at the end of 1977. Although there is some disagreement on this subject, the overall consensus seems to be that a rapid growth of population has a retarding effect on growth of per capita income. A family planning program has been

TABLE 4.3

Real Gross National Product Per Capita, 1952 and 1977 (constant prices of 1971)*

Year	Amount (NT$)	Index (1952 = 100)
1952	7,135	100.0
1977	24,220	339.5

*Not adjusted for gain or loss due to changed terms of trade.
Sources: SYROC 1977, p. 2; *TSDB 1975*, p. 19; *NC* Winter 1975, Winter 1976, Spring 1978, pp. 1, 8.

TABLE 4.4

Average Annual Growth Rates of Per Capita Real Gross National Product (based on constant prices of 1971)*

Period	Annual Growth Rate (percent)
1953–77	5.1
1953–60	3.1
1970–77	5.8
1971–77	6.2

*Not adjusted for gain or loss due to changed terms of trade.
Sources: SYROC 1977, p. 2; *TSDB 1975*, p. 19; *NC* Winter 1975, Winter 1976, Spring 1978, pp. 1, 8.

initiated in Taiwan, but its effectiveness—in light of the recent upsurge in the birth rate—remains uncertain.*

---

*In 1978 about U.S.$2 million was to be spent on the family planning program that consists essentially of three things: provision of birth control information; appeals addressed to women in the 20–29 years age brackets to space out their children; and supply of contraceptives. Abortion is prohibited by law. The effect of the program is apparently quite minimal on married couples under 19 years of age. Many families, especially in the countryside, continue to have children until the birth of a boy. Several explanations have been offered for the rise in the birth rate in 1976. The high natural increase rates of 1957–60 (average

TABLE 4.5

Average Annual Rates of Population Growth,
Taiwan and PRC

	Annual Rate (percent)	
Period	Taiwan (actual)	PRC (estimates)
1950–63*	3.4	2.2
1964–71	2.4	2.3
1972–76	1.9	2.4
1977 (est.)	2.0	2.4
1981 (planned)	1.8	<1.0

*1954–63 for the PRC. The annual rate for Taiwan 1954–63 was 3.4 per cent.
Sources: Taiwan: *SYROC 1977*, p. 2; *FCR*, December 1977, pp. 51–52. PRC: U.S. Department of Commerce, Bureau of Economic Analysis, Foreign Demographic Analysis Division (FDAD), in Leo A. Orleans, "China's Population: Can the Contradictions be Resolved?" in *China: A Reassessment of the Economy* (Washington, D.C.: U.S. Government Printing Office, 1975), p. 75. Of the various Western estimates, the FDAD rates are among the higher.

A rate of 5.1 percent per annum in the growth of per capita GNP over 25 years is very respectable; in fact, it is better than the record of most developing non-OPEC countries. The absolute level of U.S.$637 per capita real GNP is still far below Japan but well above the level of most developing non-OPEC countries, including such Asian neighbors as South Korea, the Philippines, Malaysia, Thailand, Indonesia, the PRC, India, Pakistan, and Burma.

Taiwan's per capita real national income (1971 constant prices) in 1952 was U.S.$154, and U.S.$570 in 1977 (U.S.$1,079 in current prices).

There cannot be any doubt that the objective of growth in terms of real gross national product and national income (total and per capita) has been achieved. While the contribution of American aid to Taiwan's product growth was certainly important in the early years, after 1965 growth proceeded at accelerated rates without foreign aid.

Agricultural Growth

A problem facing Taiwan is how to feed—and feed better over time—a rapidly growing population out of a very limited land area. Of the island's total

---

annual rate of 3.3 percent) showed up in the mid-1970s in large numbers of teenagers whose responsiveness to birth control propaganda was not very marked. Also, 1976 was the year of the dragon, a propitious year according to tradition to be born in.

land area of 36,000 square kilometers, a quarter is arable land, roughly half of it suitable for growing paddy rice. The bulk of arable land is located on the western side of the island. It has been estimated that because of industrial and urban expansion, some 4,000 hectares of farmland are lost every year. Table 4.6 shows Taiwan's land:population ratio. The availability of land per capita of agricultural population is roughly the same in Taiwan and the PRC.

The growth of agricultural output in Taiwan is shown in Table 4.7. The average annual growth rate (1953-77) of farm products output (as defined in Table 4.7) was 3.3 percent; forestry products grew at 2.6 percent per annum; fisheries (1953-76) at 8.8 percent; and livestock at 7.7 percent. Between 1953 and 1977 the general index of agricultural production rose at an average annual rate of 4.4 percent. Estimages of the growth of agricultural production in the PRC vary. There is, however, fair agreement that from 1953 through 1977 the average annual growth rate of farm products output (mostly grains) was just under 3 percent—below Taiwan, but not by much.

Because of the rapid natural population increase, the per capita growth of farm output has been much more moderate. Over the whole period 1953-77 the average annual per capita growth of farm output was only a little better than 0.5 percent, and just under 2 percent per year for total agricultural output (forestry, fisheries, and livestock included). The per capita annual growth of farm output in Taiwan was probably not much different from what it was in the same 25-year period, assuming the annual rate of growth of just under 3 percent to be near the mark and the annual rate of population growth for the PRC to have been about the same as that for Taiwan over the period. In other words, in both Taiwan and mainland China farm output (as defined in Table 4.7) from 1953 through 1977 was ahead of population growth, but only marginally so. Taiwan's average annual rate of growth for the whole agricultural output was comfortably ahead of the rate of population growth (4.4 percent as against 2.7 percent for population).*

Rates of growth varied for different categories of farm products. The fastest growth was registered by fruits, vegetables, and mushrooms. Their growth was spurred by a rapidly expanding export potential (for example, for canned mushrooms, bamboo shoots, asparagus, tomatoes, pineapples)† as well as by relatively high income elasticities of domestic demand.

---

*Although hard data are difficult to come by, it is likely that overall agricultural output growth in the PRC during the period 1953-77 also kept ahead of population growth by a fairly comfortable margin. Significant expansion has taken place in forestry, fishing, and the pig population.

†Taking 1971 = 100, mushroom production in 1961 was 4.8. It reached a high of 149 in 1972 and fell to 90.5 in 1976. The fluctuations are due partly to international price swings, partly to protectionist measures taken by the United States and the European Economic Community. In 12 years (1964-76) the export value of Taiwan canned mushrooms more than tripled.

TABLE 4.6

Land and Population, 1952 and 1976

Year	Total (end of year) Population (million)	Agricultural Population*		Cultivated Land		Cultivated Land per Capita of Population (hectares)	Cultivated Land per Capita of Agricultural Population (hectares)
		Total (million)	As Percentage of Total Population	Total (1,000 hectares)	As Percentage of Total Land Area		
1952	8.1	4.3	53	876	24	0.11	0.20
1976	16.5	5.6	34	920	25	0.06	0.16

Note: In 1974 cultivated land per capita of agricultural population in the PRC was 0.14–0.16 hectares, depending on assumptions about population growth. In 1952 the relevant figure had been 0.22 hectares.

*Those living on farms. All agricultural population, not just those exclusively engaged in agricultural employments. Those engaged in agricultural employments (farm, forestry, livestock, hunting, and fishing) numbered 1.8 million in 1964 and 1.6 million in 1976. In 1964 agricultural employment represented 49 percent of total employment in all occupations; in 1976 it represented 28.9 percent.

Sources: TSDB 1975, pp. 49–50; *SYROC 1977*, pp. 6, 48–49, 96.

TABLE 4.7

Annual Growth Rates of Agricultural Production, 1953–77

(percent)

Period	Farming Products[a]	Forestry[b]	Fisheries[c]	Livestock	General Index
1953	8.4	2.0	2.7	23.8	9.5
1954	0.7	5.6	19.5	1.8	2.2
1955	-1.4	5.3	15.4	3.8	0.6
1956	8.5	-5.5	7.3	6.7	7.6
1957	5.7	15.9	10.3	11.8	7.2
1958	5.6	14.4	2.6	12.2	6.7
1959	-0.3	28.1	6.6	-0.8	1.7
1960	1.6	3.7	4.1	-3.4	1.3
1961	7.4	14.1	15.0	10.7	8.8
1962	1.3	2.5	3.9	8.5	2.6
1963	-1.3	-0.4	7.6	2.5	0.1
1964	12.5	23.6	8.8	6.2	12.0
1965	8.1	2.1	4.0	2.8	6.6
1966	1.4	-7.8	14.8	10.9	3.1
1967	4.1	1.8	13.1	14.2	6.3
1968	4.1	5.4	25.2	7.1	6.7
1969	-4.0	-5.7	9.2	7.2	-0.7
1970	4.8	4.7	4.5	9.8	5.6
1971	0.1	4.5	4.9	1.7	1.3
1972	1.1	-6.3	7.1	7.9	2.4
1973	1.0	-5.5	11.7	17.9	5.5
1974	5.4	-7.6	-4.7	-7.6	0.5
1975	-2.7	-8.7	9.6	-6.6	-2.0
1976	7.1	-3.2	7.7	29.2	10.7
1977	2.1	-18.9	—	13.5	4.7

[a]Covers common crops (rice, other dry land food crops such as sweet potatoes), special crops (for example, tea, sugarcane), fruits, vegetables, and mushrooms.

[b]Covers timber, firewood, charcoal wood, and bamboo.

[c]Covers deep sea, inshore, coastal, and culture fishery.

Sources: TSDB 1975, p. 52; *SYROC 1977*, pp. 90–91; *NC*, Spring 1978, p. 2.

Taiwan's rate of self-sufficiency in food crops (ratio of domestic production to domestic consumption in 1976 was 87 percent, down from 93 percent in 1961. It should be noted, however, that the self-sufficiency rate varies considerably among the major food crops. The cereal processing industries (for example, flour and baked goods, soybean products, edible oil, beer, chocolate products), which produce almost exclusively for the domestic market, rely very heavily on imported raw materials. On the other hand, food processing industries that produce mainly for export (for example, canned foods of all kinds) obtain the bulk of their raw materials from domestic sources. Table 4.8 shows the output of selected agricultural products in 1952 and 1976 in Taiwan.

Given the more or less fixed arable land area (some reclamation of tidal land has taken place) the very creditable increase in agricultural output must have been due to multiple cropping and intercropping and an increase in factor productivity. It should be noted that successful multiple cropping and intercropping presuppose progress as regards improved plant strains, chemicalization, pest control, irrigation, drainage, and efficiency of work organization. Table 4.9 gives the multiple cropping index for Taiwan and the PRC. Most farmland in Taiwan yields two or three crops a year: out of some 920 hectares of arable land, well over 520,000 hectares consist of double cropping fields.

Chi-ming Hou has demonstrated that from 1946 through 1970 total agricultural factor productivity in Taiwan increased at an average annual rate of 1.7 percent, but at a decreasing rate averaging 2.4 percent a year over the period.[3] Average annual rates of increase in the productivity of land and labor were about the same, both attributable in large measure to increases in capital and modern current inputs (especially chemical fertilizer), a process known as the intersectoral transformation of agriculture.[4] The average annual rate of increase of fixed rural capital construction from 1946 through 1970 was 3.8 percent; 7 percent per annum from from 1969 through 1976. The average annual rate of increase of fertilizer application from 1946 through 1976 was 10.6 percent. Factor productivity increased at a decreasing rate, probably because of diminishing returns to a practically fixed land area, institutional problems (smallness of the average family farm), and perhaps secular deterioration in the quality of agricultural labor because of migration of the younger, able-bodied, better educated people to the cities. Agricultural employment (forestry and fishing included) was the same in 1976 as in 1966 (1.6 million) despite the fact that its share of total employment dropped during the period from 43 percent to 28 percent. The increase in factor productivity as a decreasing rate continued in the period 1970-77, with the rate of decrease accelerating somewhat.

To maintain the agricultural growth rate in the future it will be necessary to contain the pressure of diminishing returns by resolving simultaneously several policy problems, including the continuing parcelization of farmland and migration of talent from the countryside. (Between 1971 and 1975 the net labor transfer rate in agriculture [rate of labor outflow minus rate of labor inflow] was -5.58 percent.) By contrast, the PRC policy for many years, but especially

TABLE 4.8

Output of Selected Agricultural Products, 1952 and 1976

	Output 1,000 Metric Tons	
Product	1952	1976
Rice	1,570	2,712
Wheat	17	1
Barley	0.9	0.7
Corn	7	114
Sugar cane	4,800	8,728
Sweet potatoes	2,090	1,851
Sorghum	1	10
Soybeans	15	53
Tobacco	9	26
Peanuts	69	89
Potatoes	0.3	44
Cotton	1	0.1
Eggs (hen)	60	89
Milk	1	45
Pigs (thousand head)	2,611	3,676
Poultry (thousand head)	9,954	38,479
of which:		
Ducks (thousand head)	2,912	8,051
Chickens (thousand head)	5,593	28,355
Cattle (thousand head)*	383	253
Goat and sheep (thousand head)	181	211
Horses	0.3	0.1
Bananas	107	213
Citrus fruits	28	384
Grapes	0.02	1
Pineapples	63	279
Plums	5	21
Papayas	2	33
Pears	negl.	93
Bamboo shoots	negl.	162
Asparagus	negl.	94
Cabbage	88	188
Head cabbage	negl.	213
Tomatoes	8	199
Watermelons	27	250
Fish catches	122	811
of which:		
Deep sea catches	19	325
Timber (thousand cubic meters)	449	824

*Including water buffaloes.

negl. = negligible.

Source: SYROC 1977, pp. 97-109.

TABLE 4.9

Multiple Cropping Index, Taiwan and PRC, 1952 and 1975

Year	Taiwan	PRC
1952	172	131
1975	181	185
Highest	190 (actual)*	250–300 (planned)

Note: MCI = $\dfrac{\text{Crop (sown) area}}{\text{Cultivated (arable) area}}$

*In 1966.
Sources: Taiwan: *TSDB 1976*, p. 52; PRC: H. B. Henle, *Report on China's Agriculture* (Rome: FAO, 1974), p. 91. The *Report* was withdrawn from circulation shortly after publication at the request of the PRC representatives.

after 1968, had been to prevent "spontaneous" outmigration from the countryside. In fact, under the *hsia-hsiang* movement more than 20 million educated urban youths have been resettled in rural areas since 1968. Table 4.10 shows the average annual increases in the yields of principal crops in Taiwan.

Industrial Growth

Industrialization has proceeded rapidly, especially after the mid-1960s (see Table 4.11), more rapidly than in the PRC (see Table 4.12). From 1952 through 1977 the general index of industrial production rose 28 times (1952 = 100; 1977 = 2,873). The rapidity of Taiwan's industrial growth is remarkable not only by comparison with currently developing economies but also with the historical experiences of presently developed, highly industrialized economies. Kung-chia Yeh shows that whereas Taiwan in the space of two decades increased industry's share of net national product (NNP) by 18 percentage points, industry's share of NNP in Britain rose by 11 percentage points in 40 years (1801-41*).[5] Moreover, whereas the process of industrialization in Taiwan was

---

*Britain's industrialization (1801-1841), it should be noted, took place in what was, at best, a surrounding world scientific and technological desert. British industry was overwhelmingly a product of British scientific thought and knack for putting scientific breakthroughs to industrial uses, ultimately benefiting the individual citizen in tangible ways. Japan, Taiwan, and others had plenty to borrow from. They could, and did, and still do elaborate on borrowed knowledge. This saves time. Without in any way diminishing the achievement, Taiwan's rapid economic progress must be seen in a comparative historical setting. Taiwan, like Japan before it, has been good at borrowing and adapting. Whether it will be equally proficient in innovating on the foundation of borrowed adaptation remains to be seen.

TABLE 4.10

Average Annual Increase in Yields of Principal Crops, 1953–74

Crop	Percent Increase
Brown rice	2.1
Sweet potatoes	2.5
Wheat	3.5
Soybeans	4.3
Peanuts	3.1
Cotton	4.2
Jute	0.9
Tea	4.2
Bananas	5.3
Pineapples	3.6
Citrus fruits	2.9
Sugarcane	2.7
Sugar	1.2
Brown sugar	5.4
Citronella	0.8
Mushrooms*	8.9
Watermelon	4.9

*1965–74.

Source: TSDB 1975, pp. 53–57.

Note: Estimated average annual increases in yields of selected crops in the PRC, 1953–74, are as follows:

rice	2.0	soybeans	1.6
wheat	4.3	peanuts	0.4
coarse grains	2.7	rape seed	0
tubers	0.5	cottonseed	5.8
cotton	5.8		

Calculated from *PRC Agricultural Situation, Review of 1977 and Outlook for 1978* (Washington, D.C.: U.S. Department of Agriculture, ESCS, May 1978), pp. 29, 30, 32, 33.

carried out without adverse effects on agriculture (agricultural modernization preceded industrialization), British agriculture, despite its prior modernization, fell victim very quickly to the profound structural transformation of the economy that accompanied industrialization. From 1878/82 to 1923/27 (a period of 45 years) industry's share of Japan's NNP rose by 22 percentage points. Measured by industry's share of total output, among Asian countries Taiwan in the mid-1970s was second only to Japan in the degree of industrialization.

The rapid growth of industrial output in Taiwan was due to two major factors: expansion of industrial employment and rise in industrial labor productivity, especially the latter. In 1966, 850,000 persons were employed in industry

TABLE 4.11

Index of Industrial Production, 1952–77, Selected Years
(1971 = 100)

	Index Number			
Year	General*	Mining	Manu-facturing	Electricity, Gas, Water
1952	7.3	35.4	6.1	11.4
1957	12.7	44.9	11.7	16.6
1962	22.1	75.8	19.7	30.9
1967	45.7	95.8	42.4	54.8
1972	121.0	104.6	121.7	116.3
1977	209.9	154.1	207.9	197.1

*Includes construction of buildings. Average annual growth rate 1953–77 was 27.6 percent.
Sources: *TSDB 1975*, p. 70; *NC*, Winter 1977, pp. 13–14.

(mining and quarrying, manufacturing, construction, public utilities); in 1976 the number was 2.1 million. Fast employment growth occurred in manufacturing: from 1966 through 1976 manufacturing employment expanded 1.5 times. The construction industry increased its labor force also by about 1.5 times during the period. It should be noted that the relatively significant labor inflow into manufacturing during the period 1966–76 was fed for the most part by new entrants into the labor force rather than by intersectoral labor transfers. While lacking in practical experience, the bulk of entrants into the industrial labor force was intellectually superior in terms of formal educational training.

Table 4.13 shows the evolution since 1972 of direct labor productivity in manufacturing, a subsector that accounted in 1977 for almost 30 percent of total employment and roughly 80 percent of industrial employment. Table 4.13 also shows the evolution of monthly earnings in manufacturing during the same period.

It wil be seen from Table 4.13 that in the period 1972–76 the rate of increase in monthly earnings in manufacturing exceeded by a substantial margin the rate of increase in labor productivity. During the period average hours of work in manufacturing remained about the same, that is, 8.8 hours per day.[6] The increase of average manufacturing wages since 1972 at rates outstripping increases in labor productivity was due in part to pressures exerted on the wage level by labor shortages, especially at the junior-middle and vocational school levels. Combined with rising consumer expectations and a more relaxed internal political climate, these pressures were hard to resist. In the setting of a still pre-dominantly labor-intensive industrial structure, money wage hikes that outrun

TABLE 4.12

Average Annual Growth Rates of Industrial Production in Taiwan and PRC (percent)

Period	Taiwan		PRC	
	General Index[a]	Manufacturing	Period	General Index[b]
1953–77	14.6	15.5	1952–75	10
1953–57	11.9	14.3	1952–57	16
1957–65	13.0	12.0	1957–65	9
1965–70	18.5	20.0	1965–70	10
1970–76	19.7	16.2	1970–76	8

[a]Includes construction of buildings.
[b]Excludes construction activity.

Sources: Taiwan: *TSDB 1975*, p. 71; *NC*, Winter 1977, p. 13. PRC: Central Intelligence Agency, *China: Economic Indicators* (October 1977), p. 3. See also R. M. Field, "Civilian Industrial Production in the PRC: 1949–74," in *China: A Reassessment of the Economy* (Washington, D.C.: U.S. Government Printing Office, 1975), p. 150, and *China: Gross Value of Industrial Output, 1965–77* (CIA, National Foreign Assessment Center, Research Paper, June 1978).

TABLE 4.13

Direct Labor Productivity and Monthly Earnings
in Manufacturing, 1972–76

Year	Index of DLP (1973 = 100)[a]	Monthly Earnings (NT$)	Monthly Earnings Index (1973 = 100)
1972[b]	96.46	1,323	92.00
1973	100.00	2,525	100.00
1974	104.80	3,389	134.22
1975	121.46	4,029	159.56
1976	141.92	4,572	181.07

[a]Average for calendar year.
[b]Average July–December.
Source: SYROC 1977, pp. 420, 424.

by significant margins increases in labor productivity contribute to cost-push inflationary pressures and tend to lower the international price competitiveness of Taiwan's export products. By the same token they raise important questions regarding future industrialization strategies: labor-intensive, "light" industrialization versus capital- and skill-intensive, largely "heavy" industrialization.

The structure of industrial output has changed significantly since 1952. In its broadest sense the change reflects the shift of resources from lower to higher productivity employments. It is also the outcome of changing developmental policies. In the 1950s and early 1960s Taiwan pursued a policy of import substitution industrialization benefiting primarily the "infant" textile, chemical fertilizer, and cement industries. The textile industry with forward linkages to the apparel industry and backward linkages to petrochemicals received special protection. In the early and mid-1960s the import substitution policy gave way to a policy of export promotion (or export-led industrialization) involving progressively higher-grade textiles, processed foods, fishery, and wood products. In the late 1960s and early 1970s export-led industrialization came to include products of the chemical industries (chemicals, plastics, man-made fibers), electronic equipment (for example, television sets), general machinery, and household durables (sewing machines, electric fans, refrigerators, air conditioners). Around that time, especially in the early and mid-1970s, a significant policy reorientation took place. Export-led industrialization had thus far been dominated by labor-intensive light industries despite the progressive incursion of "heavy" industrial output (chemicals, metal products, machinery), which itself was produced in a relatively labor-intensive way. The policy reorientation of the early 1970s comprised three major decisions: a decision to upgrade the quality of industrial products (this had already occurred in textiles and some synthetic fibers and was thenceforth to be generalized); a decision to increasingly stress the development of heavy industry, the most forceful expression of which was found in the so-called Ten Major Construction Projects initiated in 1972 and involving, among others, the development of nuclear power and the construction of an integrated steel mill, shipyard, and petrochemical complex at Kaoshiung. Implicit in this development is a third decision: to gradually shift industry toward more capital- and technology-intensive branches (including precision manufacturing). Naturally, these three decisions, involving as they do a commitment of vast resources, are not without their critics who point to more urgent priorities (for example, low-cost housing). Despite many unknowns and fairly high risks, the policy decision, like its predecessors, appears well founded and, in view of rising labor costs and other considerations, well timed.

Table 4.14 shows the structural transformation of Taiwan's manufacturing industry between 1952 and 1976 (comparative data for the PRC are included).

The four main subsectors of industry presently undergoing intensive development are petrochemicals, machinery, electronics, and energy exploration. Output of plastics and resins, which was 24,000 metric tons in 1963, rose to 405,000 metric tons in 1976. Manufacture of television receivers, which began in 1964 (31,000 sets), reached 4.9 million sets in 1977—all but 500,000 of them black and white. The output of radio receivers rose from 25,000 in 1963 to 7.4 million in 1977. A total of 25 exploratory wells are scheduled for drilling in search of oil and natural gas (15 of the projects are offshore; 11 in the Taiwan Strait).

Foreign Trade

The strategy of export-led industrialization (or an "outward-looking" strategy as Wu and Yeh describe it in contrast to the "inward-looking" strategy of earlier years) that was adopted by the ROC government after 1959 presupposes vigorous expansion of foreign trade, particularly export promotion. While under the strategy of import substitution (1952-59) exports grew at an annual average rate of only about 4 percent, over 1959-65 the rate accelerated to an annual 22 percent and a remarkable 33 percent a year from 1965 to 1973.[7] Table 4.15 gives some relevant data regarding the growth of Taiwan's foreign trade. On a per capita basis the value of total foreign trade, exports, and imports in 1952 and 1976 may be seen from Table 4.16, for both Taiwan and PRC.

The rapid expansion of exports after 1959 was due to a combination of favorable world market circumstances and appropriate domestic policies initiated by the government on Taiwan to take advantage of these circumstances. The policies included a de facto devaluation of the currency through a bold foreign exchange reform (1958); specific measures taken to promote exports

TABLE 4.14

Gross Value Added in Manufacturing Industry by Subsectors,
1952–76, Selected Years
(percent)

Year	Light Industry[a]	Heavy Industry[b]	Total Manufacturing Industry[c]
1952	75.5	21.4	100.0
1962	65.7	33.3	100.0
1972	44.9	51.7	100.0
1976	45.2	51.3	100.0

[a]Manufacture of food, beverages, and tobacco; textile, wearing apparel, and leather industries; wood and wood products, including furniture; paper and paper products, printing and publishing.

[b]Manufacture of chemicals and chemical products, petroleum, coal, rubber, and plastic products; nonmetallic mineral products, except products of coal and petroleum; basic metal products; fabricated metal products, machinery, and equipment.

[c]Includes other manufacturing industries not easily classifiable as light or heavy.

Source: Derived from *SYROC 1977*, pp. 450–51.

Note: For rough comparison, the following estimates for the PRC are of interest (percent, based on values in 1952 yuan):

Year	Light Industry	Heavy Industry	All Industry
1952	64.4	35.6	100.0
1974	38.3	61.7	100.0

Calculated from R. M. Field, *China: A Reassessment of the Economy* (Washington, D.C.: 1975), pp. 168, 170.

(low-cost export loans, subsidies, government-sponsored export insurance, foreign exchange concessions to exporters, foreign market research carried out by government organizations); a reform in the direction of greater liberalization of the tariff structure and simplification or removal of direct import controls; and encouragement of foreign investments, which included tax holidays for new foreign investments, corporate income tax incentives, deferred payment of import duties on plant and equipment required by exporting industries, and the establishment (in 1965) of export processing zones—a combination of free trade zones and industrial parks with prebuilt factory buildings, developed infrastructure, minimum bureaucratic red tape, and generous tax incentives to overseas investors.

The important role of exports in Taiwan's growth process may be seen from the following data. In 1952 the share of exports in GDP was 9 percent; by

TABLE 4.15

Indexes of Foreign Trade, 1961–77
(1971 = 100)

Year	Value Index		Quantum Index		Unit Value Index	
	Exports	Imports	Exports	Imports	Exports	Imports
1961	9.78	17.44	12.11	20.63	80.72	80.53
1962	10.93	16.46	13.79	20.70	79.28	79.53
1963	16.62	19.59	17.08	23.91	97.30	81.91
1964	21.73	23.21	22.46	27.28	96.76	85.06
1965	22.51	30.15	25.59	43.62	87.98	87.09
1966	26.84	33.75	30.75	36.63	87.31	87.09
1967	32.07	43.70	35.70	47.09	89.85	92.80
1968	39.50	48.99	43.79	53.07	90.22	92.30
1969	52.53	65.77	55.85	71.22	94.05	92.34
1970	71.50	82.65	73.59	87.80	97.16	94.13
1971	100.00	100.00	100.00	100.00	100.00	100.00
1972	145.98	136.32	134.29	121.60	108.70	112.10
1973	209.47	196.21	162.28	142.13	129.08	138.05
1974	262.10	356.87	155.15	175.99	168.93	202.78
1975	243.98	303.96	153.45	156.40	159.00	194.35
1976	387.19	388.38	237.83	199.74	162.80	194.44
1977	431.03	438.00	256.09	207.43	173.17	210.00

Sources: SYROC 1977, p. 392; *MBSROC*, April 1978, pp. 11–12.

TABLE 4.16

Taiwan and PRC: Foreign Trade, Exports, Imports Per Capita, 1952 and 1976 (U.S.$ at current prices)

Year	Total Trade		Exports		Imports	
	Taiwan	PRC	Taiwan	PRC	Taiwan	PRC
1952	38	3	15	1	23	2
1976	1,085	14	570	8	515	6

Sources: Taiwan: *TSDB, 1975*, p. 173; *SYROC 1977*, pp. 2, 391. PRC: CIA, *China: Economic Indicators* (October 1977), p. 1; *China: A Reassessment of the Economy* (Washington, D.C.: U.S. Government Printing Office, 1975), p. 75; CIA, *China: International Trade 1976–77* (November 1977), p. 10.

TABLE 4.17

Structure of Foreign Trade by Major Commodity Categories, 1961–76 (percent)

Year	Exports			Imports		
	Primary Commodities[a]	Manufactured Goods[b]	Total[c]	Primary Commodities[a]	Manufactured Goods[b]	Total[c]
1961	63.4	36.6	100.0	46.0	53.6	100.0
1962	53.8	46.2	100.0	44.9	54.1	100.0
1963	61.1	38.8	100.0	51.3	48.3	100.0
1964	61.7	38.3	100.0	47.5	52.1	100.0
1965	58.3	41.7	100.0	40.5	59.2	100.0
1966	49.4	50.6	100.0	39.4	60.3	100.0
1967	42.3	57.6	100.0	35.5	64.2	100.0
1968	35.4	64.5	100.0	37.8	62.1	100.0
1969	29.9	70.1	100.0	34.2	65.6	100.0
1970	23.2	76.8	100.0	34.6	65.1	100.0
1971	20.2	79.9	100.0	34.2	65.4	100.0
1972	17.9	82.1	100.0	36.9	62.7	100.0
1973	16.1	83.9	100.0	34.8	64.9	100.0
1974	15.8	84.2	100.0	37.5	61.9	100.0
1975	18.6	81.4	100.0	39.8	59.8	100.0
1976	14.9	85.0	100.0	40.7	58.8	100.0

[a]Food and beverages, raw materials, fuels.
[b]Chemical products, machinery and transport equipment, other manufactured goods.
[c]Total may not add up to components because of rounding.
Source: SYROC 1977, pp. 388–89.

1965 it had risen to 17 percent; in 1976 it was 51.7 percent (all percentage shares are based on GDP at purchasers' values in constant 1971 prices). Wu and Yeh have shown that the increase in the incremental ratio of exports to GDP has been even more significant, revealing the rising importance of exports to output expansion.[8]

The rapid growth of Taiwan's foreign trade in the 1960s and 1970s was accompanied by a spectacular structural transformation of that trade, particularly of exports. This transformation—corresponding to changes in the makeup of the domestic, export-geared economy—is illustrated by Table 4.17. Between 1952 and 1958 manufactured goods averaged 12 percent of total exports, compared with 64 percent over 1961-76. The most important change on the import side has been the sharp absolute and relative rise in the cost of imported oil after 1973. Fuel imports (mostly crude petroleum), which in 1973 accounted for just over 4 percent of total imports, had risen to over 17 percent of imports by 1976. In the early 1950s oil represented about one-fifth of Taiwan's total primary commercial energy supply; at the present time it accounts for roughly 70 percent of that supply. All the oil that fuels Taiwan's industry and almost all industrial raw materials have to be imported. Guaranteeing the security of fuel and materials supply is a most significant and urgent preoccupation of the government, requiring diplomatic virtuosity of an exceptional order.

The reorientation of exports toward manufactured goods with a relatively high technological content will probably have to be soon supplemented by exports of services. Some technical advice to friendly countries in Africa and Latin America is currently exported and the tourist industry is being given high priority. However, because of diplomatic reverses the number of technical assistance personnel dispatched abroad has declined from the relatively high levels of the mid-1950s through mid-1960s as has the number of foreigners trained in Taiwan. The tourist industry is booming (see Table 4.18) and the expansion is expected to continue.

Another problem that will have to be tackled concerns the need to diversify export markets and supply sources. The geographic pattern of Taiwan's trade reveals relatively heavy dependence on the United States for exports and on Japan for imports. This is not a very satisfactory situation. Taiwanese exports are meeting with increasingly stiff resistance, not to say resentment, in some quarters of the United States and the European Common Market, with concurrent domestic producer appeals for protection against alleged Taiwanese "dumping." Table 4.19 shows Taiwan's and the PRC's foreign trade with the United States and Japan in selected years. Reliance on Japan for a significant proportion of vital imports raises cost questions in the setting of an appreciating yen and an NT dollar pegged to a falling U.S. dollar. The NT dollar was appreciated by 5.26 percent against the U.S. dollar in July 1978.

In sum, the rapid growth of Taiwan's external commerce may be attributed to a number of factors that include the diligence of Taiwan's workers, good governmental economic planning and management, political stability, large-

TABLE 4.18

Taiwan Tourism, 1956–90

Year	Number of Visitors	Growth Rate (percent)	Tourist Receipts (U.S. $)	Spending per Person per Day (U.S. $)	Average Length of Stay (days)
1956	14,974	—	936,000	25.00	2.50
1957	18,159	21.3	1,135,000	25.00	2.50
1958	16,709	8.0	1,044,000	25.00	2.50
1959	19,328	15.7	1,208,000	25.00	2.50
1960	23,636	22.3	1,477,000	25.00	2.50
1961	42,205	78.6	2,638,000	25.00	2.50
1962	52,304	23.9	3,269,000	25.00	2.50
1963	72,024	37.7	7,202,000	25.00	4.00
1964	95,481	32.6	10,345,000	27.50	3.94
1965	133,666	40.0	18,245,000	37.50	3.64
1966	182,948	36.9	30,353,000	35.30	4.70
1967	253,248	38.4	42,016,000	—	—
1968	301,770	19.2	53,271,000	31.58	5.59
1969	371,473	23.1	56,055,000	33.10	4.56
1970	472,452	27.2	81,720,000	35.59	4.86
1971	539,755	14.2	110,000,000	44.22	4.61
1972	580,033	7.5	128,707,000	48.45	4.58
1973	824,393	42.1	245,882,000	64.98	4.59
1974	819,821	0.6	278,402,000	76.83	4.42
1975	853,140	4.1	359,358,000	66.86	6.30
1976	1,008,126	18.2	466,077,000	68.90	6.71
1977	1,110,182	10.1	502,000,000	68.93	6.56
1978 (est)	1,243,000	12.0			
1980 (plan)	1,488,000*	9.1			
1990 (plan)	2,928,000*	5.7			

Note: Official PRC reports show total tourist traffic on the mainland in 1977 totaling just under 100,000 visitors.

*Compared with previous year (plan).

Source: K. H. Chu, "Development and Investment Potential in Recreation in Taiwan, ROC," *ER*, May–June 1978, pp. 10, 11.

TABLE 4.19

Taiwan and PRC: Trade with the United States and Japan, 1952
and 1976 (percent of total exports and imports, respectively,
based on current values)

Year	Taiwan		PRC	
	United States	Japan	United States	Japan
	Exports to:			
1952	4	53	negl.	
1976*	41	12	3	18
	Imports from:			
1952	22	45	0	
1976*	22	33	2.5	29

*Taiwan: January–July 1978.
negl. = negligible.
Sources: Taiwan: *SYROC 1975*, pp. 138–45; *SYROC 1977*, pp. 382–83; Chinese Information Service, New York, *News from China*, August 8, 1978. PRC: CIA, *China International Trade 1976–77* (November 1977), pp. 9–10.

scale investments by foreigners and overseas Chinese, and the "seed money" of U.S. aid, which amounted to roughly $1.5 billion from 1949 through July 1965 (when it was terminated). Taiwan faces some difficult foreign trade problems, most of them centering on the need for product, market, and supply source diversification.

ECONOMIC STABILITY

The objective of stability means the avoidance of periodic fluctuations in output, employment, and the general level of prices. These are socially undesirable because they increase the uncertainty inherent in the economic decision-making process, spontaneously redistribute income and wealth among different social classes, and generally undermine the legitimacy of a system.

Output

The output stability record for Taiwan has been very good until the recession of 1974–75. By 1976 the disturbance had been by and large corrected (Figures 4.2, 4.3, and 4.4). It may be noted that output stability in Taiwan has been superior to what was achieved during the same period in the PRC. After the

FIGURE 4.2

Real Gross National Product, 1950–77
(1952 = 100)

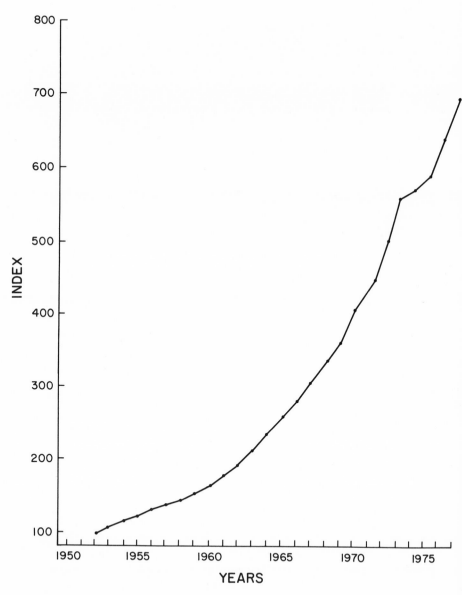

Source: *TSDB 1978*, p. 23.

FIGURE 4.3

Index of Agricultural Production, 1952–77

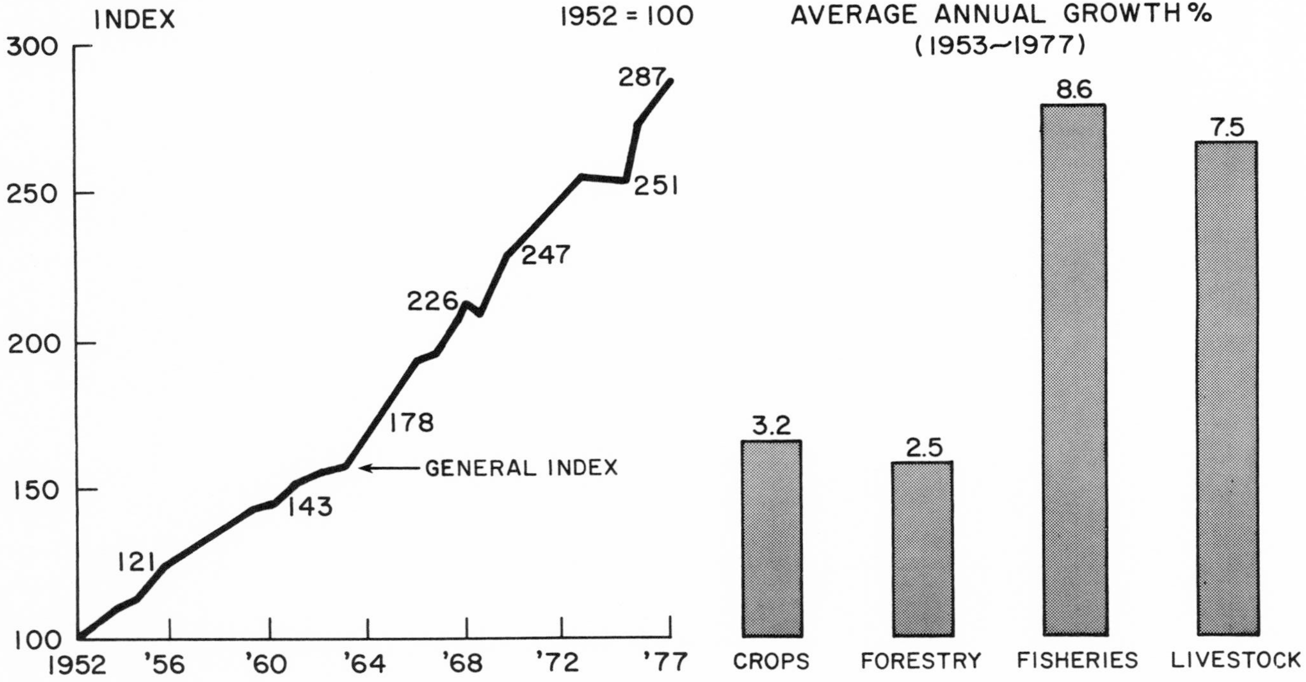

AVERAGE ANNUAL GROWTH %
(1953–1977)

LIVESTOCK 7.5
FISHERIES 8.6
FORESTRY 2.5
CROPS 3.2

INDEX   1952 = 100

300
250
200
150
100

287
251
247
226
178
143
121

GENERAL INDEX

1952 '56 '60 '64 '68 '72 '77

Source: EDROC, p. 8.

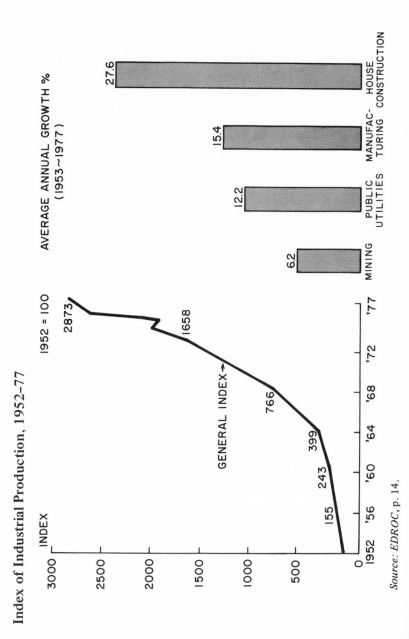

FIGURE 4.4

Index of Industrial Production, 1952–77

Source: EDROC, p. 14.

104

FIGURE 4.5

Foreign Trade, 1952–77

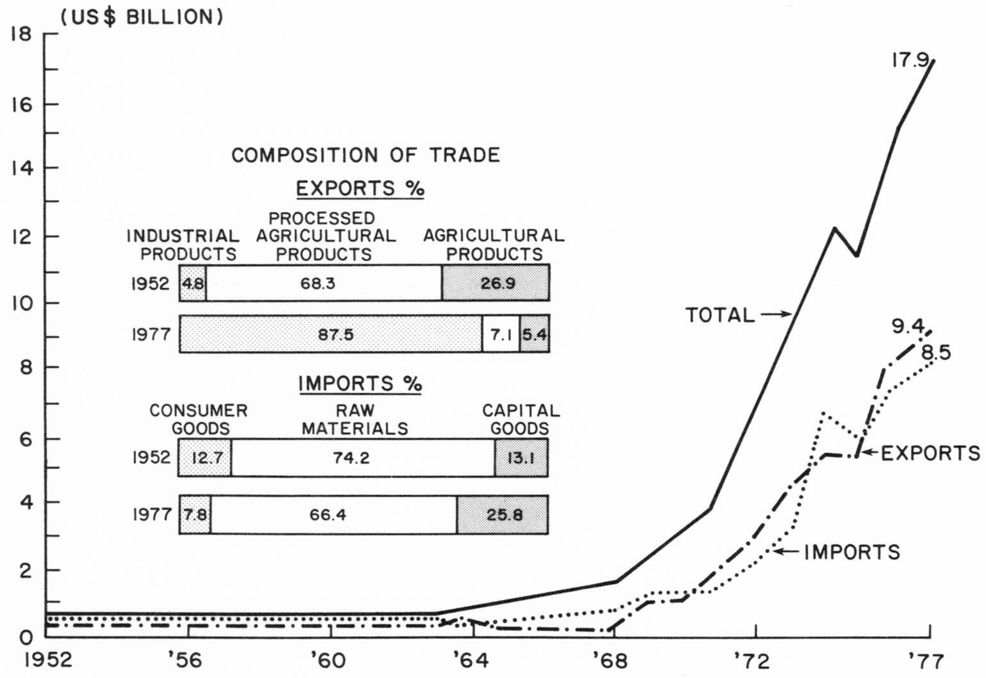

(US $ BILLION)

COMPOSITION OF TRADE

EXPORTS %

INDUSTRIAL PRODUCTS	PROCESSED AGRICULTURAL PRODUCTS	AGRICULTURAL PRODUCTS
1952 4.8	68.3	26.9
1977	87.5	7.1 5.4

IMPORTS %

CONSUMER GOODS	RAW MATERIALS	CAPITAL GOODS
1952 12.7	74.2	13.1
1977 7.8	66.4	25.8

TOTAL

17.9

EXPORTS
9.4, 8.5

IMPORTS

1952 '56 '60 '64 '68 '72 '77

Source: EDROC, p. 21.

early 1960s, despite fluctuations in world markets, the expansion of Taiwan's foreign trade has been not only rapid but remarkably smooth (Figure 4.5).

Employment

Taiwan's employment record since the early 1960s has been remarkably good (see Table 4.20). The only sizable and, as it turned out, temporary unemployment among certain categories of workers in some export-oriented branches of industry occurred in 1974–75 as a consequence of the energy crisis and world recession. But even in the midst of unemployment there were specific labor shortages, especially for unskilled and lower-skilled female labor. Some analysts believe that the labor shortage is due in large measure to inadequate level and structure of incentives. In 1976 about 200,000 potential workers under 40 years of age expressed readiness to enter the labor force if wages were raised.

In the PRC full employment has been the rule. However, visual evidence and official press references point to the existence of substantial underemployment in certain sectors of the economy.

TABLE 4.20

Average Annual Unemployment Rate, 1963–77

Year	Rate (percent)
1963*	5.2
1964	4.3
1965	3.3
1966	3.1
1967	2.3
1968	1.7
1969	1.9
1970	1.7
1971	1.7
1972	1.5
1973	1.3
1974	1.5
1975	2.4
1976	1.5
1977	1.3

Note: Unemployment figures prior to 1963 are not available since the labor force survey had not been conducted at that time.

*October 1963.

Sources: Statistical Bureau, *DGBAS*, Executive Yuan, Republic of China; and *NC* (various years).

Prices

The major upward push on domestic prices in Taiwan came in the early 1970s, especially between 1973 and 1974. Until that time inflationary pressures had been kept fairly well under control and the overall price stability record was respectable for a market-oriented economy sensitive to international trade and price movements (see Table 4.21, which includes selected comparative data for the PRC). Since that time the situation has given rise to considerable apprehension. In the first quarter of 1978 the consumer price index rose at an annual rate of 6.75 percent compared with the same period of 1975, but the wholesale price index rose at an annual rate of only 1.44 percent. However the relative stability of the wholesale index was believed to have been temporary: The rapid appreciation in the value of the Japanese yen was bound to affect prices that Taiwan pays for a third of its imports, and the rise in international prices of steel, cotton, foodstuffs, and capital goods also put pressure on the wholesale price level. In the last few years, it will be recalled, manufacturing wages increased at about 20 percent per year. The inflationary trade surplus has resulted in foreign exchange reserves passing the U.S.$5 billion level. Among the steps taken by the authorities to slow down the inflationary spiral are the easing of some import restrictions, the lowering of selected import duties, encouragement of purchases from the United States, and reduction of purchases from Japan. Powerful domestic counterforces are also at work. The Taiwan Power Company, under pressure from interest payments on its loans, was scheduled to hike its rates in 1978, coinciding with substantial wage raises for government employees.

It should be noted that the overall relative stability of the price level conceals some sharp price rises in particular areas. Some of these have grievous impact on those at the lower end of the pay scale. Costs of medical care, for example, have been rising fast, as have the costs of housing, nondurable consumer goods including food, and transportation. In Taipei City the index of medical and personal care (1971 = 100) rose to 212 in 1976, while the housing index reached 151. The general index of services in Taipei City in 1976 was 181 (1971 = 100). For Taiwan as a whole, retail food prices in 1977 rose by about 8.5 percent over 1976, as did transporation and communications charges. Medical costs rose by about 7 percent, as did the costs of education and entertainment. (Both of these increased very much faster in Taipei City.) As any consumer who has experienced inflation knows, official consumer goods price indexes have a way of understating inflation's erosion of the family budget; and Taiwan's statistics are no exception. Instability of the general price level is, I think, one of the more serious threats facing Taiwan's economy.

It should be remarked that in the PRC, where prices are set and rigidly controlled by the authorities, price indexes are poor indicators of inflationary pressures. Such pressures do exist and manifest themselves in periodic goods shortages, queues, worker and consumer unrest, and black markets.

TABLE 4.21

Index of Wholesale and Retail Prices in Taiwan and PRC, 1952-77 (1952 = 100)

Year	Taiwan		PRC	
	Wholesale	Retail	Wholesale	Retail
1952	100.00	100.00	100.0	100.0
1953	108.76	118.79		
1954	111.34	120.77		
1955	127.02	132.74		
1956	143.15	146.69		
1957	153.49	157.73	100.0	98.2
1958	155.63	159.74		
1959	171.62	176.62	101.3	102.2
1960	195.90	209.21		
1961	202.23	225.60		
1962	208.39	230.93		
1963	221.85	235.96	117.1	124.2
1964	227.33	235.54		
1965	216.77	235.39		
1966	219.97	240.13	101.1	114.5
1967	225.52	248.18		
1968	232.21	267.75		
1969	231.67	281.32		
1970	237.96	291.35		
1971	238.27	299.56	100.4	100.8
1972	248.89	302.52		
1973	305.79	333.77		
1974	429.85	492.47		
1975	408.06	517.94		
1976	419.36	530.85		
1977	436.77	564.19		

Sources: Taiwan: TSDB 1975, p. 157; MES, January 1978, February 1978, p. 4. PRC: Calculated from Ten Great Years (Peking, 1960), pp. 170-73; Bank of China, Hong Kong (1959); Ta Kung Pao, Hong Kong, December 4, 1964; H. V. Henle, Report on China's Agriculture (Rome: FAO, 1974), p. 38.

EQUITY, OR ECONOMIC JUSTICE

Equity is taken to mean "economic justice"—that is, "fairness" as regards the distribution of income. Fairness or economic justice in this sense means reduction of inequalities of income distribution, preferably in the setting of a rising general income level, in other words, in the context of economic growth.*

The equity objective has important social, political, and psychological ramifications, many of which elude quantification and can be dealt with only cursorily here.[9] Compressing income spreads, especially where these are very wide, tends to cut across and lower social barriers among groups of people ("class differences"), reduce political tensions, and raise the income earners' satisfaction from what they perceive to be greater involvement in the shaping of their working and leisure environments. In short, distributive justice tends to promote economic democracy and, perhaps, political democracy as well.

Equity of income distribution in the environment of growth has been, and remains to this day, one of the more important social objectives of Taiwan. There are several basic techniques with the help of which overall distributive justice may be measured. The major techniques are lowest:highest income ratio, decile and quintile analysis (graphically), the Lorenz curve, and Gini coefficients.

In decile and quintile analysis the surveyed population (usually household units) is ranked by groups of 10 percent (deciles) or groups of 20 percent (quintiles), beginning with the lowest income decile/quintile up to the highest. Each decile/quintile population group is then assigned the percentage of the total population income received. The technique can be used in various ways. For example, the lowest and highest deciles/quintiles may be compared to throw light on the relative position of the poorest and richest groups in the population, an exercise in comparison not without significance for the longer-term political legitimacy of the system. According to one study of Taiwan, the ratio of average per family income of the lowest to the highest quintile was 1:15 in 1952, and 1:4 in 1976 (see Figure 4.6).[10] The results of Y. L. Wu's careful analysis over the period 1952-72 are given in Table 4.22.

The Lorenz curve is a graphic technique derived from decile analysis. It plots the cumulative percentage of actual income earners against the actual cumulative share of income they receive. Perfectly equal income distribution is

---

*In a more comprehensive sense, equity additionally means fairness in the distribution of power, that is, of the ability to influence the behavior of others, and fairness in the distribution of opportunity at the start among the system's participants as individuals or decision-making groupings. In some economic systems, money income is a poor measure of actual total power exercised by individuals or groups within the system. Equity in the narrower sense used in the text should strictly speaking include fairness (that is, reduction of inequalities) in the distribution of wealth (stocks of assets). In view of all this, it should be noted that our analysis of income distribution trends in Taiwan addresses itself to only part of the overall equity problem—an important part, but not the totality of the problem.

FIGURE 4.6

Comparative Ratio of Family Income, 1952–76

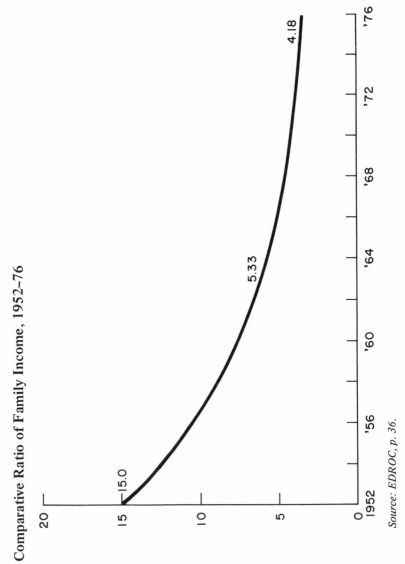

Source: EDROC, p. 36.

TABLE 4.22

Changes in Income Distribution in Taiwan, 1953–72, Selected Years

Distribution in Quintiles	1953	1961	1964	1972
Lowest quintile of all households	3.0	4.5	7.7	8.6
Second quintile	8.3	9.7	12.6	13.1
Middle quintile	9.1	14.0	16.6	17.0
Fourth quintile	18.2	19.8	22.1	22.2
Highest quintile	61.4	52.0	41.0	39.1
Second highest 15 percent	28.8	26.4	24.8	24.8
Top 5 percent	32.6	25.6	16.2	14.3
Gini coefficient	0.56	0.46	0.33	0.30
Ratio of income share				
Top 10 percent to bottom 10 percent	30.4	19.3	8.6	6.8
Top 20 percent to bottom 20 percent	20.5	11.6	5.3	4.6
Index of decile inequality	0.46	0.37	0.26	0.24

Source: Y. L. Wu, "Income Distribution in the Process of Economic Growth in Taiwan," in *Growth, Distribution, and Social Change*, ed. Y. L. Wu and H. C. Yeh (Baltimore: School of Law, University of Maryland, 1978), p. 77.

represented by a 45° line drawn from the origin 0,0 to 100,100 (see Figure 4.7). The maximum theoretical inequality of income distribution is given by the area of the triangle bounded by the X axis, the Y axis, and the 45° line. The area between the 45° line and the Lorenz curve gives the actual inequality of income distribution. The nearer the Lorenz curve to the 45° line, the less the inequality of actual income distribution. The Lorenz curve for Taiwan has, in fact, moved in the direction of the 45° line since the early 1960s. The Gini coefficient (see Table 4.22) is the ratio of the area of actual inequality to the area of maximum theoretical inequality. The coefficient can vary from 0 (total absolute equality) to 1 (total absolute inequality), that is, the smaller the coefficient the "more equal" the distribution of income and vice versa.

Equity of income distribution also concerns the distributive shares accruing to workers in different sectors of the economy, especially those in agriculture and industry. The available evidence indicates that between 1964 and 1972 the average income rose for both farm and nonfarm families, but much faster for the latter. Thus during this period the degree of inequality between average farm and nonfarm family incomes grew. Average income per farm family in 1964 was NT$32,013, rising to NT$49,090 (an increase of 53.3 percent), while nonfarm family income rose from NT$32,740 in 1964 to NT$64,497 in 1972 (an increase of 97 percent). Moreover, the degree of equality increased more for nonfarm than for farm families during the period. In 1964 the Gini coefficient for farm families was 0.315; in 1972 it had fallen to 0.291. For non-

FIGURE 4.7

Lorenz Curve

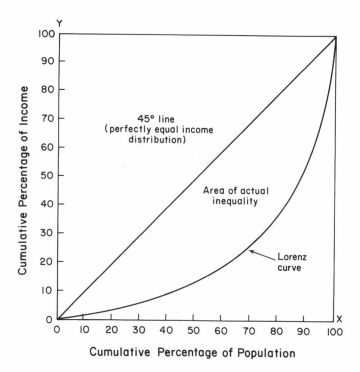

Source: Compiled by the author.

farm families the coefficient fell more: from 0.336 in 1964 to 0.288 in 1972.[11] The trend toward greater distribution inequality within the farm sector than in the nonfarm sector is undesirable and appropriate measures will have to be taken to arrest it. Apart from broader sociopolitical issues, the disparity accelerates labor migration from rural areas (by 1990 nearly 80 percent of Taiwan's population is expected to live in urban agglomerations) and creates labor shortages in specific branches of agriculture, some of which are very lucrative for the economy as a whole. For example, the deep sea fishing industry is expected to bring in an increase of NT$40 billion by 1981, with exports earning about NT$500 million. The industry, however, is beset by labor shortages. Few young men want to become fishermen: compared with urban industrial employment, the pay is low, the risks are high, work is demanding and dull, and insurance coverage is inadequate.

To sum up: the equity objective, insofar as it concerns the narrowing down of income differentials within the system to politically acceptable and socially "fair" dimensions (also ones that do not adversely affect the productivity of the workforce and investor incentives), as been achieved.[12] A much larger income than two decades ago is being shared more evenly, a situation not commonly encountered in developing market-oriented economies. Differences between farm and nonfarm incomes persist and show a tendency to widen. The movement toward lesser income disparities has been more rapid in the nonfarm sector than in the farm sector. The last two trends are socially undesirable and politically dangerous.

Data on PRC income distribution are sparse (exclusively of the lowest: highest income ratio variety). My own investigations suggest—at least until October 1976—a long-term trend toward compression of basic income spreads.[13] However, the spreads remain significant, especially between the earnings of most commune peasants and those of skilled workers and technicians in the modern industrial sector.

SOCIAL SECURITY AND ECONOMIC GROWTH

Security means protection by society of participants in the economic system against various risks. Two major categories of risks may be distinguished: those due to physical causes (illness, physical disabilities, accidents, natural calamities), and those due to adjustments in or malfunctioning of the social mechanism (for example, structural or cyclical unemployment). The problem of personal security becomes particularly acute in times of rapid, strategic adjustments of economic institutions in the process of growth. Some systems—socialist ones as well as market-oriented, "welfare state" systems—place the objective of security against socially generated risks high on the scale of social objectives. Taiwan has proceeded more slowly as far as the subobjective of socially generated risks is concerned, but it has made substantial progress in lessening the impact on the individual of physical risks *sensu stricto*.

Much progress has been made in improving the health of the population through better diet (see Tables 4.23 and 4.24; Table 4.23 includes comparative data for the PRC). The physical availability (as distinct from financial accessibility) of medical care facilities and personnel compares favorably with that of some economically more advanced societies. In 1976 there were 1,437 people per physician (including practitioners of traditional Chinese medicine). Communicable diseases are combatted through massive immunization programs. For example, each year since 1962, following an outbreak of paracholera, nearly 11 million people have been vaccinated against the disease. Table 4.25 shows the incidence of communicable diseases. Malaria, which in the 1940s affected over a million people each year, has been eradicated and the incidence of tuberculosis has been reduced from 280 cases per 100,000 of the population in the late 1940s to less than a tenth of that figure today. Medical services are supplied by both the private and public sectors, mainly the former. In 1976 there were 8,700 hospitals equipped with 32,500 beds (or about 500 of the population per bed).

Drug addiction exists, but apparently is not a serious problem at present. According to data published by the Ministry of the Interior (*SDBI*, 1977) in

TABLE 4.23

Taiwan and PRC: Some Indicators of Physical Welfare, 1952 and 1976

| | Taiwan | | | PRC | | |
	1952	1976	1976/1952	Early 1950s	1976	1976/1952
Daily per capita intake of calories (number)	2,078	2,771	1.33	1,800	2,200	1.33
Daily per capita intake of animal origin as						
percent of total daily calorie intake	12	16	1.33	n.a.	8	—
Net milk supplies per capita per day (grams)	1	12	12.00	n.a.	n.a.	—
Net meat supplies per capita per day	46	87	1.89	n.a.	n.a.	—
Protein consumption per capita per day (grams)	49	76	1.55	45	64	1.42

n.a. = not available.
Sources: Taiwan: SYROC 1977, p. 413. PRC: V. Smil, "Food in China," Current History, September 1978, p. 82.

TABLE 4.24

Taiwan: Average Weight and Height of Schoolchildren
Ages 6 through 18, 1964 and 1975

| Age (years) | Academic Year | | | |
| | 1964 | | 1975 | |
	Weight (kg)	Height (cm)	Weight (kg)	Height (cm)
	Boys			
6	19.00	110.10	19.78	114.98
12	31.05	140.45	35.80	144.07
15	46.50	160.65	51.35	163.39
18	53.00	166.70	57.26	167.87
	Girls			
6	17.85	110.80	18.97	113.95
12	32.95	144.05	36.17	145.63
15	44.85	154.95	47.38	155.65
18	47.40	156.95	49.23	156.97

Source: ROC Ministry of Education survey reported in *FCR*, August 1977, p. 54.

1976 some 260 narcotics users and 104 dealers were apprehended. Drug-related offenses are subject to stiff sentences; use of marijuana (classified as a hard drug), morphine, or heroin is punished with jail terms ranging from three to seven years. Addiction to LSD and pentazocine and glue-sniffing have spread among teenagers. There is one publicly run narcotics clinic that treats exclusively addicts referred to it by the public prosecutor's office. After cure, patients must serve out their jail terms. Conviction on narcotics traffic is subject to severe penalties that include life imprisonment and death.

Health problems due to emotional stress are on the increase. Between 1968 and 1975 the number of attempted suicides rose tenfold. The divorce figure has remained constant over the years at around 0.5 per 1,000 of the population. However, marital disputes and family problems are among the main reasons given for attempted suicides. Emotional stress is cited as the leading cause of the rising number of senior high school dropouts and is a contributor to juvenile delinquency in the cities. As traditional family bonds weaken and break down and new ethical restraints are slow to crystallize and gain adherence, disorientation among the young spreads, while appropriate remedial measures are difficult to find. The instinctive and understandable reaction of the authorities is to seek correctives in a combination of strict laws and return to China's millenial

TABLE 4.25

Incidence of Communicable Diseases, 1952–76, Selected Years

	1952	1962	1972	1976
Total				
C[a]	1,148	950	171	167
D[b]	248	76	5	5
Cholera[c]				
C	–	383	–	–
D	–	24	–	–
Dysentery				
C	180	57	28	13
D	21	5	4	4
Typhoid[d]				
C	217	55	65	130
D	21	–	–	1
Smallpox				
C	39	–	–	–
D	–	–	–	–
Epidemic Cerebrospinal				
Meningitis				
C	60	9	2	1
D	9	2	1	–
Diphtheria				
C	548	446	76	23
D	95	45	–	–
Scarlet fever				
C	2	–	–	–
D	–	–	–	–
Rabies				
C	102	–	–	–
D	102	–	–	–

[a]C = cases.
[b]D = deaths.
[c]1962 outbreak of paracholera.
[d]Including paratyphoid.
Source: SYROC 1977, pp. 530–31.

past: to try to breathe new life into Confucian behavioral prescriptions, rejuvenated a bit by the infusion of Sun Yat-sen's Three Principles of the People. There is also youthful dissent and alienation of a different order, which has little to do with common street crime. Taiwan's future as an increasingly democratic and tolerant society hinges to a crucial extent, I think, on the ability of the leaders to give Taiwan's millions of healthy and well-educated young people a sense of meaningful participation in the affairs of the Republic.

Social insurance in Taiwan is in its infancy. There is no unemployment insurance, for example. In periods of unemployment, those out of work rely primarily on family support and personal savings. Much the same is true of medical expenses, which, for most people, have to be covered out of current earnings plus family savings. While medical facilities and personnel are available, institutionalized means of payment (in the form of publicly sponsored medical insurance schemes) are, by and large, lacking. In part because of the overwhelming preoccupation with growth, the intention to remain internationally cost competitive, and the government's care not to discourage foreign private investors, there has been extreme caution in enacting legislation concerned with protecting the workers' welfare and regulating overtime. Labor costs in Taiwan, it is argued, are already higher than in South Korea, with which Taiwan competes in world markets.

Thus, under the heading of security, the showing to date has been mixed. Great progress has been made in improving diets and controlling communicable diseases. This, plus a better standard of public hygiene, has resulted in a reduction of the death rate (both sexes) from 9.9 per 1,000 of population in 1952 to 4.7 per 1,000 in 1976. The death rate per 1,000 of infants under 1 year of age (both sexes), which was 37.2 in 1952, fell to 12.9 in 1976. Expectation of life at birth for men was 56.5 years in 1952 and 68.8 years in 1976; for women the relevant figures were 60.7 and 73.7 years—among the longer average life expectancies in the world. As old diseases were brought under control, new—more "modern"—afflictions have emerged. The provision of social security has been lagging behind the achievement of other objectives. When it comes to risks induced by the process of adaptation or malfunctioning of market-related social institutions, the individual household in Taiwan has to fend pretty much for itself.[14]

An instance that comes to mind is the problem of low-cost publicly sponsored housing. Because of the rapid migration of people from the countryside to the cities, a housing shortage for low-income people was bound to arise. Taiwan's residential construction statistics are impressive. However, the guidelines for the building industry are mostly related to the purchaser's ability to pay the going—and rapidly rising—market price for housing. Thus the supply of housing for upper-middle and high income earners has been tolerably good, while the needs of lower income recipients have been handled less satisfactorily.[15]

ECONOMIC EFFICIENCY, CONSERVATION, AND INNOVATION

The objective of efficiency, like that of security, comprises two notions: dynamic efficiency, which relates to the rate of economic growth, and static allocative efficiency, or the best possible allocation of the available resources among all possible alternative uses in a given time span. The subject is so large and wide-ranging that, given the limited space available here, it would seem to be the better part of wisdom to defer it to a thorough consideration on another occasion. All that need be said is that Taiwan's record of dynamic efficiency has been superior to its record of static efficiency. The situation (well recognized in developmental literature) is not atypical of the experience of rapidly developing economies. Inefficiencies in Taiwan seem to be especially noticeable in many areas of the bloated governmental bureaucracy's economic planning and management procedures, quality control, and in the overstaffed services sector. The problems are publicly acknowledged and repeated steps have been taken to correct them, which in itself is witness to the problems' obduracy.[16]

If static efficiency is imperfectly realized in market-oriented economies such as Taiwan, its attainment is much more problematical in administratively run economies, like the PRC. In the latter, static allocative inefficiency appears to be an inbuilt systemic problem traceable in large part to the absence of automatic price indicators that measure the opportunity cost of various competing allocative courses of action. This deficiency becomes increasingly troublesome as the administratively commanded economy grows and becomes more complex and, therefore, more susceptible to static resource misallocations. Visual impressions of the mainland economy as well as frequent official denunciations of "waste," lack of "economic accountability," and "managerial incompetence" are witness to the persistence of this problem in the developmental experience of the PRC. By and large it is reasonable to conclude that under both headings (static and dynamic efficiency) the performance of mainland China has been inferior to that of Taiwan.

Among the figures often cited by the authorities to illustrate progress of Taiwan's material welfare is the number of motorcycles per 1,000 persons, which was 55.7 in 1971 and 142.7 in 1977. The number of automobiles per 1,000 persons was 18 in 1976 and is expected to reach 34 in 1981. Legitimate doubts may be raised about the desirability of a projected 15 percent annual increase in automobile and motorcycle ownership in a city such as Taipei—already choked by over a quarter million cars—where the annual increase in road building is barely half that rate. Air, water, and noise pollution in Taiwan are among the world's worst. Of the dozen or so major rivers and streams on Taiwan, two-thirds are badly polluted, containing a high dose of zinc and hardly any oxygen. Damage to rivers and streams by industrial users, mainly, it would seem, large state-owned enterprises, has brought about the pollution of some 60,000 hecatres of irrigated farmland. Industrial waste dumped into rivers caused the deterioration of an additional 7,000 hectares of agricultural land in the last several years. There is evidence that the growing use of chemical fertilizers and pesticides carries with it land and plant pollution hazards. Pollution of coastal waters is also a problem. Concern has been expressed about the effect on marine life of the new nuclear power plant at Chinshan on the East China Sea. Sea water used for cooling is returned from the plant to the sea after use. In the rush to industrialize, environment-related doubts do not get much hearing in Taiwan, despite official protestations to the contrary. The Statute for the Encouragement of Investment, as amended in 1977, relaxed a number of regulations governing the use of industrial land. Most urban residential buildings in Taiwan are designed and built privately with little heed to overall urban planning concepts, with the result that buildings sprawl all over the place and open spaces are few and far between. There seems to be little doubt that until now the objective of conservation has been low on the scale of social priorities.

Despite the assurances by PRC authorities that environmental protection and resource conservation are actively pursued, air pollution in a number of mainland cities is quite advanced and water pollution is becoming a problem. Despite some evidence of ingenious recycling, natural resources tend to be used rather wastefully, especially in the rural industry sector.

Scientific and technical progress as a subgoal of the broader objective of growth has risen rapidly in recent years on the scale of Taiwan's social objectives. Scientific and technical progress tends to reduce the cost of carrying out other objectives. It is also counted on to help Taiwan retain its competitive edge in world markets against the onslaught of goods produced in countries with plentiful and lower-cost labor. Until now Taiwan has been an importer of increasingly advanced technology, including managerial know-how. This trend is likely to continue for some years to come as Taiwan switches its strategy of development to a technologically higher plateau dominated by capital-intensive large-scale steel, machine building, metalworking, precision, and petrochemical industries. However, already in some areas (for example, harbor construction) Taiwan is emerging as a pioneer and exporter of technologically superior processes. But by and large it is still at the copying and adapting stage through the use of licensing agreements, joint ventures, and direct investments. Comparatively little research and development work is done by Taiwan's industrial enterprises. The effort is mostly concentrated in universities and specialized research institutes.

The intellectual prerequisites for scientific and technical innovation have been laid in the years since 1945. When the Japanese left the island there were five institutions of higher learning and one teachers college. In 1976 higher educational institutions numbered 101 plus 11 teachers colleges. Nineteen universities and colleges offer graduate programs (one in 1950). By 1981 graduate enrollment is planned to reach 15,000. Of 1,000 persons in the 18–23 age bracket, 155 attend a college or university. In fact, given the still modest domestic employment opportunities for people with higher training, the expansion of higher education is perhaps running ahead of what the economy needs and can absorb in the foreseeable future. Much the greater part of Taiwan students sent for university study abroad do not return to Taiwan. Enormous progress has been made at the primary and secondary/vocational school levels. More than a quarter of the population attends school: 4.5 million people in 1976. There is thirst and respect for knowledge; learning is sought both for its own sake and as a means of social and economic mobility.

ECONOMIC INDEPENDENCE

National political sovereignty is thought to be fairly meaningless without a measure of economic independence. Taiwan has avoided excesses in this regard. Because of its small size and natural resource deficiency it cannot possibly aim at economic self-sufficiency. Because of its comparatively small domestic market and relatively low income level it cannot—like Japan—prevent foreigners from participating as owners (majority stockholders) in the product assets of the nation. On the contrary, Taiwan has actively courted foreign investment, granting it special privileges, incentives, and facilities.[17] A recent publication of the Ministry of Economic Affairs' Industrial Development and Investment Center urges foreign investors to "get in on the Taiwan bonanza!" Between 1952 and 1976 total private foreign investment in Taiwan amounted to U.S.$1.5 billion plus an additional U.S.$500 million from overseas Chinese sources. Yearly investments from abroad, which in 1952–59 averaged U.S.$20 million a year, rose to U.S.$115 million a year during 1960–65. In 1973, just before the oil crisis, the amount was U.S.$249 million, and U.S.$142 million in 1976. Of total private foreign investment, American investment represents roughly one-half, followed by the overseas Chinese, Japan, and the European Economic Community. The greater part of foreign investment has gone into manufacturing industries, especially electronics and electrical products, chemicals, petrochemicals, and basic metals, with a gradual shift toward capital- and technology-intensive heavy industries in recent years. Overseas Chinese investment has been concentrated in service industries. The evolution of private foreign and overseas Chinese investment approvals by ROC authorities may be seen from Figure 4.8. Symptomatic of the dangers inherent in heavy reliance on foreign sources of capital is the sharp reduction in the inflow of such capital between 1971 and 1972 (a period of the Republic of China's diplomatic reverses) and, much more so, in 1973–75 (world recession). It is not unreasonable to speculate that any significant shift in U.S.-Taiwan political and mutual security relations could have an adverse effect on foreign investors' confidence in Taiwan's future. A significant reduction in capital inflows from abroad would, in turn, seriously affect Taiwan's export trade and domestic economic development; ultimately, perhaps, the country's political stability. It should be recalled that foreign investments are concentrated in strategic sectors of Taiwan's economy (electronics, chemicals, machinery, equipment), increasingly so in those sectors intended to spur future

FIGURE 4.8

Amount of Investment Approved for Overseas Chinese and Foreign Investors, 1952–76

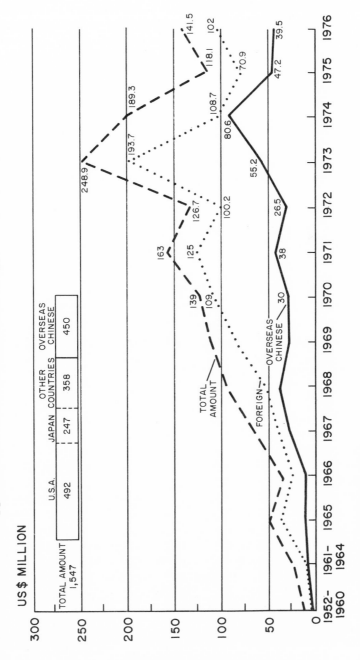

Source: ROC Ministry of Economic Affairs.

development and determine the future structure of the economy (metalworking, petrochemicals, and other heavy branches).

A different problem connected with large foreign equity participation in Taiwan's economy concerns the domestic political and cultural price that, some say, has to be paid to keep foreign investors happy.

Taiwan, too, is still rather heavily indebted to foreign lenders on government account (see Table 4.26). It would be interesting—space does not permit it here—to calculate the current debt service ratio, that is, the ratio of payments on foreign loans to GNP, which is likely to be quite high. The foreign trade ratio (the ratio of foreign commodity trade to gross national product plus imports) was .31 in 1976.

Thus while Taiwan's overt economic independency (solvency) has been amply demonstrated by the country's ability to meet its debt obligations and honor the commitments made to foreign investors regarding the repatriation of earnings on their capital, there is heavy reliance on the outside world (especially the United States, Japan, and two or three Arab oil supplying countries) for continued goods purchases, investment, technology transfers, and primary energy-raw materials supplies. Taiwan's record of successful navigation in such treacherous international waters witnesses the uncommon diplomatic skills of the country's leaders. Asked by a visiting American in 1978 which aspect of Taiwan's economy caused him the most worry, Minister of Economic Affairs K. S. Chang replied: "the United States."

PRC leaders have repeatedly insisted that the PRC has no foreign debts and that no foreign interests own any part of the domestic economy. The latter claim is correct. However, the "no foreign debts" assertion needs qualification. In 1976, according to estimates by the National Council for United States-China Trade, the PRC's repayment obligations for foreign trading partners amounted to $1.3 billion. The sum included long-term deferred payment obligations dating back to 1973 and 1974 (purchase of complete plants) and short-term credits. The debt of U.S.$1.3 billion represented about 23 percent of the PRC's total hard currency earnings in 1976, that is, just under what bankers regard as the warning debt service ratio of 25 percent.[18] The 1977 PRC indebtedness on foreign account was also of the order of U.S.$1.3 billion. More significantly, the PRC's post-1976 drive to modernize its economy implies heavy reliance and expenditure on advanced foreign technology.

In sum, Taiwan may be regarded as among the more successful examples of basically market-oriented developing economies, with the public sector acting as a major entrepreneurial leader of the developmental process. The creditable record must be seen in the context of Taiwan's initial poverty, absolute natural resource deficiency, formal political isolation, and heavy burden of defense expenditure.

TABLE 4.26

Principal Foreign Loans, as of December 31, 1974

	Agreement Amount	Disbursement	Principal Repaid	Outstanding Balance
Total Loan: U.S.$1,000	1,526,122	910,574	158,256	752,318
N.T.$1,000	1,331,918	1,331,918	263,461	1,068,457
Yen 1,000	53,910,180	49,499,074	21,227,992	28,271,082
U.S. AID*				
U.S.$	137,570	137,570	39,419	98,151
N.T.$	1,331,918	1,331,918	263,461	1,068,457
International Bank for Reconstruction and Development (U.S.$)	310,520	281,680	45,910	235,770
International Development Association (U.S.$)	15,756	15,756	411	15,345
Japan (Yen)	53,910,180	49,499,074	21,227,992	28,271,082
Export-Import Bank (U.S.$)	969,916	395,228	65,636	329,592
Asian Development Bank (U.S.$)	92,360	80,340	6,880	73,460

*Exclusive of Development Loan Fund and AID loans directly extended to local enterprises.
Source: TSDB, 1975, p. 221.

CONCLUSIONS

Our analysis of Taiwan's major societal objectives reveals

remarkable success as regards growth, stability, and equity of income distribution (with price stability being currently put to test by worrisome inflationary pressures);

a mixed, but overall creditable, performance as regards the objective of security (good with regard to security against physical risks; moderate to poor as regards risks—especially future ones—inherent in the operation of the economic system);

room for improvement in the areas of static efficiency, conservation, and innovation; and

an astute way of transforming heavy economic reliance on the outside world into respectable national economic independence.

It should be noted that—despite some official protestations to the contrary—the social security and conservation objectives have not been, thus far, high on the scale of Taiwan's social preferences, as these preferences emerged from the operation of the country's economic institutions. Nor has it been thought appropriate until now to enter the phase of autonomous scientific and technical innovation on a significant scale. In terms of the norms set by the system's effective decision makers, Taiwan has been highly successful in achieving what it had set out to do.

The PRC's interest in "liberating" Taiwan is not exclusively an expression of nationalism and ideology. It is also stimulated by economic considerations. Taiwan is a prosperous place, richly endowed with good-quality human resources and, increasingly, with capital equipment of a high order of modernity. Unification on PRC terms, that is, submergence of Taiwan by the PRC, is strongly resisted by Taiwan officials and the population alike on political, human, and other grounds. The analysis presented here reveals that Taiwan's living standards are superior to those on the mainland. Unification would inevitably lower the standard of living on Taiwan. Assuming that people are by and large economically rational, unification must surely be unacceptable to the people of Taiwan on economic grounds alone.

NOTES

Source Abbreviations for Taiwan

CF China Forum, Taipei.
DGBAS Directorate-General of Budget, Accounting, and Statistics (Executive Yuan, ROC).
ER Economic Review (Taipei: The International Bank of China), bimonthly.

EDROC Economic Development in the Republic of China (Taipei: Ministry of Economic Affairs, Republic of China), occasional.

EPT Economic Progress and Investment Climate in Taiwan, Republic of China (Taipei: Ministry of Economic Affairs, Industrial Development and Investment Center, 1977).

FCR Free China Review (Taipei: Chinese Information Service), Monthly.

MBSROC Monthly Bulletin of Statistics, The Republic of China (Taipei: Directorate-General of Budget, Accounting and Statistics, Executive Yuan, Republic of China).

MES Monthly Economic Survey (Taipei: The International Commercial Bank of China), monthly.

NC National Conditions (Taipei: Statistical Bureau, DGBAS, Executive Yuan, Republic of China), quarterly.

SDBI Statistical Data Book of the Interior (Taipei: Ministry of the Interior, Republic of China), annual.

SGANC Statistics on Government Administration and National Conditions, Republic of China (1972-1977) (Taipei: Research, Development, and Evaluation Commission, Executive Yuan, 1978).

SYROC Statistical Yearbook of the Republic of China (Taipei: Directorate-General of Budget, Accounting and Statistics, Executive Yuan, Republic of China), annual.

TSDB Taiwan Statistical Data Book (Taipei: Economic Planning Council, Executive Yuan, Republic of China), annual.

1. See Kung-chia Yeh, "Economic Growth: An Overview," in *Growth, Distribution, and Social Change: Essays on the Economy of the Republic of China*, ed. Yuan-li Wu and Kung-chia Yeh (Baltimore: School of Law, University of Maryland, Occasional Papers/Reprints Series in Contemporary Asian Studies, No. 3-1978 [15]), pp. 11–18. From 1969 to 1976 the non-OPEC average annual growth rate of real GNP for the developing countries was about 6 percent. For 22 "least developed countries" the rate was below 3.5 percent. Central Intelligence Agency (CIA), *Least Developed Countries: Economic Characteristics and Stake in North-South Issues*, Research Paper (May 1978), p. 7.

2. CIA, *China–Economic Indicators*, October 1977, p. 1.

3. Chi-ming Hou, "Institutional Innovations, Technological Change, and Agricultural Growth in Taiwan," in Wu and Yeh, *Growth, Distribution, and Social Change*, pp. 125–27. A broadly similar problem of factor productivity was observed in the PRC in the 1960s and 1970s. See Robert F. Dernberger, "The Program for Agricultural Transformation in the People's Republic of China," *Proceedings of the Seventh Sino-American Conference on Mainland China* (Taipei: Institute of International Relations, 1978).

4. In 1952 chemical fertilizer applied per hectare of planted rice area was 461 kilograms (100 kg nutrient weight). In 1974, 777 kg were applied per hectare (210 kg nutrient weight). In 1952–53 chemical fertilizer supplied per hectare of sugarcane planted area was 680 kg (157 kg nutrient weight). In 1974–75 the corresponding input was 1,270 kg (378 kg nutrient weight). *TSDB 1975*, pp. 61–62. On the comparative performance of intersectoral transformation of agriculture in the PRC, see Jan S. Prybyla, *The Chinese Economy: Problems and Policies* (Columbia: University of South Carolina Press, 1978), Chapter 3, pp. 38–40.

5. Yeh, "Economic Growth," p. 25.

6. *MBSROC*, April 1978, p. 5.

7. Yuan-li Wu and Kung-chia Yeh, "Taiwan's External Economic Relations," in Wu and Yeh, *Growth, Distribution, and Social Change*, pp. 173–75.

8. Ibid., p. 175. See also Kai-cheong Lee, "A Trade-Oriented Econometric Model of Taiwan, Republic of China," *ER*, January–February 1977, pp. 1–33.

9. Some useful studies of income distribution in Taiwan are: Yuan-li Wu, "Income Distribution in the Process of Economic Growth in Taiwan," in Wu and Yeh, *Growth, Distribution, and Social Change*, pp. 67–111; Ch'en T'ing-an, "Economic Growth, Income Distribution, and Fiscal Policy," *CF*, January 1978, 001-035; Wang-yong Kuo, "Income Distribution by Size in Taiwan Area–Changes and Causes," *ER*, July–August 1976, pp. 12–22; Han-yu Chang, "Income Disparity Under Economic Growth in Taiwan: Over Time Changes and Degree as Compared with Other Countries," *ER*, July–August 1977, pp. 7–20.

10. *EDROC*, pp. 35–36, based on a study by the Overseas Development Council; and *Investigation and Statistical Report on Individual Income Distribution in the Taiwan Area* (Taipei: Auditing Department, Executive Yuan, Republic of China, 1977). Also *SGANC*.

11. Y. L. Wu, "Income Distribution," pp. 78–79. The government claims that while farmers are worse off than industrial workers in terms of earnings, "they are catching up." Between 1971 and 1977 farmers' earnings reportedly rose 3.4 times faster than the salaries of government employees. In 1975 farm income was 65 percent of nonfarm income. By 1977 it was 76 percent. *FCR*, June 1978, p. 6, and July 1978, p. 7.

12. I am inclined to think that the Taiwan lowest:highest income differential of 1:4.2 is narrower than the comparable differential in the PRC. See J. S. Prybyla, "Work Incentives in The People's Republic of China," *Weltwirtschaftliches Archiv* (Kiel) 112, no. 4 (1976): 767–91.

13. Prybyla, *The Chinese Economy*, pp. 53–65; 107–32; and Chapters 3 and 5; and "A Note on Incomes and Prices in China," *Asian Survey* 15, no. 3 (March 1975): 262–78.

14. In 1976 Taiwan governmental expenditures on social security and welfare services represented 2.9 percent of total government expenditure, or U.S.$5 per head of population. *SYROC 1977*, p. 451.

15. Z. N. Lee, "An Evaluation of the Public Housing Policy of the Republic of China," *ER*, March–April 1977, pp. 7–14. A national housing fund has been established to help in the consltruction and rebuilding of 174,000 (mainly low-income) housing units during the Six-Year Economic Development Plan period (1976–81). In 1975 there were 154,000 dwelling units occupied by squatters.

16. In 1972 Taiwan had more than 7,000 laws and statutes. These were cut down to less than 4,000 by 1977. In earlier years people were required to supply the government with transcripts of their domicile records in 335 matters. Now such records are required in only 38 matters. *FCR*, June 1978, p. 16. In his oral report to the Legislative Yuan (June 13, 1978), premier Sun Yun-suan criticized the low efficiency and poor service of some government organizations and the poor discipline of government employees who have the most frequent direct contacts with people (presumably, what in the PRC is called addiction to "bureaucratic airs"). *FCR*, July 1978, pp. 56–60.

17. See, *Statute for Investment by Foreign Nationals* (Taipei: Ministry of Economic Affairs, Industrial Development and Investment Center, February 1977); and Hungdah Chiu and David Simon, eds., *Proceedings of Conference on Legal Aspect of United States-Republic of China Trade and Investment* (Baltimore: School of Law, University of Maryland, Occasional Papers/Reprints Series in Contemporary Asian Studies, No. 10, 1977).

18. New York *Times*, November 2, 1977, pp. 55, 57.

5

Taiwan in Peking's Strategy

King C. Chen

The United States recognized on January 1, 1979, the government of the People's Republic of China as "the sole legal government of China" and severed the diplomatic relations with the Republic of China on Taiwan. On the same day the U.S. government informed the ROC government of its decision to terminate the 1954 U.S.-ROC Mutual Defense Treaty at the end of 1979. Meanwhile, the remaining few hundreds of U.S. military personnel will soon be withdrawn from the island. In doing so, President Jimmy Carter has fully accepted Peking's three conditions for normalizing the U.S. relationship with the PRC.

The negotiations for normalization during the Carter administration have taken a winding road. At first, Secretary of State Cyrus Vance visited the PRC in late August 1977. Soon after Vance had left Peking, Vice-Premier Tend Hsiaoping made the Peking government's position known on September 6, 1977, that it had "rejected" Vance's reverse-liaison-and-embassy proposal for normalization and that Peking's patience with the question of normalization and Taiwan could not last forever.

In the spring of 1978 Peking's troubles with the Soviet-supported Vietnam softened its attitude toward Taiwan. Leonard Woodcock, U.S. chief liaison officer in Peking, felt the possibility of normalization at that time. In April–May of the same year the increasing favorable statements on U.S.-PRC normalization by President Carter, Secretary of State Vance, and National Security Advisor Zbigniew Brzezinski signaled the U.S. strong desire for a better relationship with Peking.* But the turning point was Brzezinski's visit in late May 1978 to China

---

*The following developments are favorable to the PRC. President Jimmy Carter stated at a news conference in April 1978 that he hoped that over a period of "a few

where he stated clearly that the United States had made up its mind to normalize its relations with the PRC.

In June 1978 Assistant Secretary of State Richard Holbrooke spoke in Hawaii, emphasizing "peaceful" settlement of the Taiwan issue.[2] In July U.S. Representative Lester L. Wolff (D., N.Y.) visited Peking and brought back Peking's message on Taiwan. He explained that Vice-Premier Teng Hsiao-ping and other officials in Peking had shown him a new conciliatory attitude toward Taiwan and had endorsed an approach to a peaceful settlement through negotiations with the government of the ROC on the island.

With a Middle East peace treaty in sight, President Carter set in October 1978. a deadline for normalization by January 1, 1979. His rationale for the deadline was that the unprecedented diplomatic success in concluding a Middle East peace treaty on the scheduled December 17, 1978, would be strong enough to head off Taiwan supporters' criticism of his full acceptance of Peking's three conditions for normalization.

Thus Taiwan had been "an obstacle" (in Jimmy Carter's words) to normalization for several years. But now, after the new U.S.-PRC relations were established, the United States still has commitments to Taiwan. The issue of Taiwan itself has not yet been settled (to be discussed later). In this context Taiwan is still strategically and politically important to Peking. The purpose of this chapter is to examine as closely as possible Peking's political and strategic positions on the island before and after the normalization.[3]

Undoubtedly there are several approaches to the study of Peking's perspectives. On the basis of a PRC-centered approach, four elements can be employed to serve as basic factors for analysis. Despite the vagueness of their meanings, these four elements are competing and complementing forces in formulating Peking's position.

FOUR ELEMENTS TO STUDY PEKING'S STAND

The first element is Chinese nationalism. After having suffered the humiliation of foreign encroachment for a century, China's desire to reunify and

---

months" the United States would "completely realize the hopes expressed in the Shanghai Communique." Secretary of State Vance said on April 30, 1978, at a CBS television interview that he hoped to normalize U.S.-Chinese relations in the first term of the Carter administration. National Security Advisor Zbigniew Brzezinski said on May 21 of the same year in Peking that the United States had "made up its mind" to normalize its relations with the PRC. In June and July the U.S. government agreed to the sales of airborne geological survey equipment (military-related technology) to China and sent a 14-member top scientist delegation, headed by President Carter's science adviser Frank Press, to China. In addition, six American oil companies (Pennzoil, Exxon, Union Oil of California, Phillips Petroleum, Standard Oil of Indiana, and Mobil), with U.S. Government support, have entered into negotiations with Peking for possible petroleum exploration and development of hydrocarbon resources in and off China. Subsequently, Energy Secretary James Schlesinger visited the PRC in the fall of 1978.[1]

rebuild itself to be a modern power is extremely strong. Such a sentiment has been expressed so abundantly by major political figures in the past that it does not need any elaboration here. However, the Sino-Indian conflicts in 1962 and the Sino-Soviet clashes in 1969 demonstrated the PRC's attitude toward unsettled territories. Peking's demand for the reunification of Taiwan with the mainland has stemmed from the same sentiment and motivation.

The second element is ideological perspective. Without exception, Peking clothes the problems of Taiwan in ideological terms. It accused the U.S. "imperialists" of "occupying Taiwan" for two decades until President Nixon's visit to the PRC in 1972, employed the theory of "class struggle" to judge Taiwan's society, and interpreted Taiwan's political, economic, and educational systems by using communist ideological jargon.

The third element is strategic value and energy interests. Knowing the strategic position of Taiwan and the naval facilities in the Pescadores, the Peking leaders stressed the definite necessity of keeping these islands out of the hands of unfriendly powers, especially the Soviet Union. Meanwhile, the vast, potentially energy-rich offshore areas surrounding Taiwan, including the Tiao Yu Tai (Senkaku) Islands, have attracted Peking's close attention, significantly enhancing the value of Taiwan.

The fourth element is factional politics. Despite nationalist sentiment, a similar ideological outlook, and common national interests, the PRC political factions have assumed different attitudes toward Taiwan in their power rivalry. The pragmatists have been generally moderate and tolerant; the radicals militant. Such differences are particularly apparent when the rivalry is in high gear. The struggle between the competing factions in 1976 prior to the arrest of the "Gang of Four" is a case in point.

The expression of Peking's views takes several forms: In inspiration it employs nationalist sentiment and communist ideology, while in operation it adopts united-front tactics and combines tolerance with militancy. It works with domestic and foreign channels, both at state-to-state and people-to-people levels.

PEKING'S TAIWAN UNIT

It should be first pointed out that after the "reopening" of China in 1971, Peking seems to have organized a special, informal, and unpublicized office (or "unit") to handle Taiwan affairs.[4] This office must have arranged numerous meetings and interviews in which the Peking leaders expressed their viewpoints. From the data I have collected, the structure can be tentatively drawn as follows:

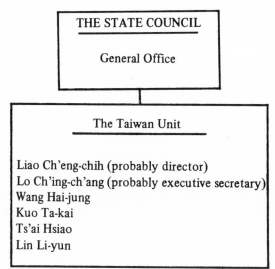

THE STATE COUNCIL

General Office

The Taiwan Unit

Liao Ch'eng-chih (probably director)
Lo Ch'ing-ch'ang (probably executive secretary)
Wang Hai-jung
Kuo Ta-kai
Ts'ai Hsiao
Lin Li-yun

Brief biographical notes may be helpful:

Liao Ch'eng-chih is a party Central Committee member and a veteran of Japanese and overseas Chinese affairs.

Lo Ch'ing-ch'ang is a party Central Committee member, deputy secretary-general of the State Council, and minister of intelligence of the PLA (People's Liberation Army).

Wang Hai-jung is deputy foreign minister.

Kuo Ta-kai is a member of the New China News Agency (NCNA) and formerly deputy director of the Information Department in the Foreign Ministry.

Ts'ai Hsiao is a party Central Committee member and is from Taiwan.

Lin Li-yun is a party Central Committee member, an interpreter, and a Taiwan Chinese from Japan.

In this group the important figure is Lo Ch'ing-ch'ang, who is probably in charge of this informal unit. This observation is made on the basis of his presence at almost all meetings with persons ralating to Taiwan. His double capacity as deputy secretary-general of the State Council and intelligence minister of the PLA indicates the necessity and significance of political and military coordination on Taiwan.

Where does the Taiwan unit rank among the government's agencies? How important is its role in the decision-making process? These questions cannot be answered in full at present, but preliminary findings suggest that the unit is probably located in the General Office of the State Council with roughly a cabinet ranking but without a cabinet status. Unlike the Commission of the Mongolian and Tibetan Affairs in Taipei, it is not a "window-dressing" agency, nor a decision-making unit. But it apparently has a function of collecting information, developing plans, and submitting recommendations for policy deliberation.

THE SHANGHAI COMMUNIQUE: CLARITY AND AMBIGUITY

The Joint Communique of December 15, 1978, on normalization reaffirms the principles agreed on by the United States and the PRC in the Shanghai Communique. A brief discussion of what position on Taiwan the Shanghai Communique has taken is necessary.

Undoubtedly, the Shanghai Communique brought the U.S.-PRC relationship to a new stage. On the Taiwan question, the communique is a document of both clarity and ambiguity; clarity, because both China and the United States hold the same position that all U.S. forces and military installations will be withdrawn from Taiwan; ambiguity, because both sides have not agreed on how the Taiwan question should be settled.

The clarity is evident in the U.S. troop withdrawal from Taiwan since 1972. The ambiguity is complicated by three nonagreements (not disagreements). First, while the United States has reaffirmed its interest in a "peaceful settlement" of Taiwan by the Chinese themselves, the Chinese insist that "the liberation of Taiwan is China's internal affair in which no other country has the right to interfere." Second, the United States does not "challenge"* China's unilaterally declared position of its opposition to "two Chinas," "one China, one Taiwan," "one China, two governments," and other devices, but this position is neither an agreement nor a disagreement. Third, there is no mention, let alone agreement, on the U.S.-Taiwan Mutual Defense Treaty. By keeping silent on this issue, the United States deliberately left it unsettled for future negotiations.

In an attempt to eliminate the ambiguity and to quicken the pace of the normalization process, Peking in 1974 set forth three conditions: withdrawal of U.S. troops from Taiwan, severance of U.S.-Taiwan diplomatic relations, and abrogation of the Mutual Defense Treaty. After a few years of delay and debate, the United States fully accepted them in December 1978.

TAIWAN IN PEKING'S STRATEGIC PERSPECTIVES

On numerous occasions Peking has invited a number of U.S. officials, legislators, foreign friends, journalists, and overseas Chinese to visit the PRC. Through meetings, interviews, and statements, Peking made known its attitude toward Taiwan. Apart from governmental communiques, Chou En-lai and his

---

*The English version differs significantly from the Chinese one. The Chinese text, "Pu T'i-ch'u I-i," literally means "not to raise different viewpoint (argument)."

associates elaborated their views on Taiwan in 23 statements to various visitors, especially the Taiwan Chinese.[5] For the sake of simplicity, I have summarized and reorganized their fundamental viewpoints on the following ten major issues and will discuss them in order of importance.

1. *"One China" (People's Republic of China) and "one legal government" (the Peking government).* This principle is unchangeable. Under this principle Peking firmly rules out the creation of "two Chinas," "one China, one Taiwan," "one China, two governments," an "independent Taiwan," or an "undetermined status of Taiwan." The settlement of Taiwan, accordingly, is China's domestic affair. The creation of the "liaison office" in Washington should not be interpreted as a compromise with Taiwan. Rather, it was established to facilitate a future settlement of the island.

2. *No "self-determination" or a "Far Eastern Switzerland" for Taiwan.* "Self-determination" is for those nations or areas whose political status is unsettled. Taiwan has already been returned to the motherland. Its status has been settled. There is, therefore, no need for "self-determination," let alone China's "protection" (an imperialist gimmick) of a "self-determined" Taiwan. The "Switzerland formula" is not possible because Taiwan cannot become an independent nation in the Far East. In this context Peking is not yet in a position to extend an invitation to Peng Ming-min, a leader of the Taiwan Independence Movement, to visit China.

3. *High autonomous status and long process of social transformation.* Whether Taiwan will be a province or an autonomous region after "liberation" (reunification) is a matter for future decision. Peking is flexible. But the island is very likely to have an autonomous status like that of Tibet prior to 1959. And it will require a long process of social transformation to integrate Taiwan into the Chinese political and social system. What is important, Chou En-lai emphasized, is that the Taiwan Chinese must be their own masters, managing their own affairs. All the people in the PRC are equal, it is claimed, and Han chauvinism will never be allowed to exist.

4. *Gradual transition of the economic system.* Taiwan has large investments of foreign capital from the United States and Japan; such foreign capital deforms Taiwan's socioeconomic structure. The economic system is a capitalist one under the exploiting and repressive Kuomintang government. After normalization (but not after reunification), the United States can keep its economic interests in Taiwan. If not, the withdrawal of foreign capital will be made up by government subsidies so as not to create an unemployment problem and economic difficulties. There will be no drastic economic measures, and there will be a long and gradual transition from private to public ownership.

5. *High living standard on Taiwan.* After "reunification" (liberation) the Chinese government will not lower Taiwan's living standard, which is now higher than the mainland's. Such a discrepancy is permissible because there are differences of living standards on the mainland, such as in Shanghai and other cities.

With the principle of self-reliance, every province, district, city, or commune pursues its own social and economic construction. They all seek to improve the quality of their lives by relying on their own economic and human resources.

6. *Peaceful and nonpeaceful liberation of Taiwan.* The question of whether "liberation" (reunification) will be peaceful or nonpeaceful depends on three conditions: the achievement of the socialist reconstruction in People's China; the favorable development of the international situation; and the readiness and collaboration of the people of Taiwan. The first two are now favorable, but the third is yet to develop. Peaceful liberation is Peking's first choice. If peaceful means will not work, however, Peking will employ nonpeaceful means, including armed blockade and attacks. To avoid bloodshed, Peking offers negotiations with delegates from Taiwan, governmental or private.

7. *Soviet interest in Taiwan.* The Soviet Union is competing for hegemony in Asia with the United States. To this end Moscow intends to gain access to Taiwan. The Soviets tried to explore the possibility of using the naval facilities in the Pescadores but were rejected by Chiang Kai-shek. This rejection will not end Moscow's interest in the island. Peking, nevertheless, will not allow the Soviet Union to gain what it wants from Taiwan.

8. *Recruitment of Taiwan Chinese.* Peking is enthusiastic about recruiting Taiwan Chinese as cadres to serve the people and government. Professionals in foreign countries are also welcome to return to China. But this plan requires a few more years of preparation: China has to prepare the professional and academic facilities, and the professional people have to become ideologically and psychologically ready in order to reduce the difficulties of adjustment after they return.

9. *Quemoy and Matsu.* Peking wants to possess these islands, but it may not seize them without Taiwan. This is a complex question, according to Chou En-lai. The bombardment of Quemoy and Matsu in 1958, for instance, was undertaken under a tacit and complex understanding: Peking understood that the U.S.-Taiwan Mutual Defense Treaty did not cover the islands, but the PRC had no plan to occupy them; Taiwan also understood that Peking would attack but not seize the islands. Peking wanted the bombardment to demonstrate the continuity of the civil war, while Taiwan needed it to support its claim to the mainland. The implication is that so long as the two island groups remain in Taiwan's hands, Taiwan is in a difficult position to declare independence.

10. *Tiao Yu Tai (Sekaku).* The Chinese government has repeatedly issued statements to the effect that Tiao Yu Tai is Chinese territory, and it will not change this position. When the Japanese surveyed that area, China made no protests; but if Japan should undertake oil or gas drilling, China will stop it. In terms of nationalism and energy interest, Tiao Yu Tai is as important as any other offshore island to China.

ANNIVERSARY MEETINGS FOR THE
FEBRUARY 28 INCIDENT

One of the several ways Peking seeks to "win over the hearts" (in Mao's words) of the Taiwan Chinese is the anniversary meeting for the February 28 Incident (1947), which was first held in 1973. The meeting, sponsored by the National Committee of the Chinese People's Political Consultative Conference, is based on united-front principles.* It has established a pattern: it is a sit-and-talk meeting (Tso-t'an hui), which indicates its ceremonial and study nature; there are 110–138 participants, of whom approximately 46 percent are Taiwan Chinese; and its components include party leaders, military personnel, administrators, nationality leaders, professors, writers, youths, women, and former Kuomintang generals, diplomats, and administrators. Liao Ch'eng-chih is the dominant figure, and Ts'ai Hsiao and Lin Li-yun are also quite active.[7]

Each year the participants reiterate the same themes: Taiwan must be liberated, the motherland must be united, and the Taiwan Independence Movement or "two-China" device is doomed to failure. They also discussed the three liberation conditions that always come out with an expected conclusion: the excellent situation in the socialist motherland, the favorable international situation, and the deteriorating condition on Taiwan.

Peking utilizes the meeting to convey two significant messages. First, Liao Ch'eng-chih has repeatedly claimed that the February 28 Incident was inspired by Mao's call in early 1947 for the creation of a "new high tide of the Chinese revolution."[8] By taking credit for the incident, the Chinese Communist party (CCP) contrives to establish the legitimacy and continuity of its leadership between the incident and any future political change on Taiwan. Second, Peking has offered peace talks with Taiwan. Such an offer was first made in 1973 by Fu Tso-yi, a former Kuomintang general. In subsequent meetings the offer has been reiterated with the emphasis that Taiwan cannot permanently rely on the United States and that the Taiwan Strait is no longer an obstacle to liberation—a hint of the use of cross-Strait missiles or other weapons. In applying coercion to back up persuasion, Peking displays its tactics of negotiation from strength.

THE UNIFICATION CAMPAIGN AND INVITATION TO CHINA

The campaign for the unification of Taiwan with the mainland is a nationalistic drive, designed to promote a peaceful settlement of the island. The

---

*By sponsoring the annual meeting, the Political Consultative Conference has resurrected its old function as a united-front organization. From its establishment in September 1949, the conference was designed and had functioned as a united-front organization. After the People's Congress was convened in September 1954, its power as a state organ was taken over by the Congress; but it remained a "united-front organization for uniting all nationalities, democratic classes, democratic parties and groups, people's bodies, overseas Chinese and other patriotic democrats . . . under the leadership of the Chinese Communist Party."[6]

drive started indirectly from the "Tiao Yu Tai protection" movement, which was originally a patriotic, nonpartisan protest. In January and April 1971, thousands of Chinese students participated in protest marches in New York, Washington, and San Francisco against Japan's claim to the Tiao Yu Tai islands. It was united and powerful for two reasons: the Chinese considered the islands historically Chinese territory, and the target was Japan—an aggressor in the recent past. Soon after, the drive split into pro-Peking and pro-Taiwan groups. Aided by Nixon's "opening" to China, the former group grew into a unit campaigning for unification.

Peking encouraged and invited the "Pao Tiao" (protection of Tiao Yu Tai) people to visit China and appealed to the overseas Chinese for support to the cause of unification. The drive gained momentum. Numerous Chinese and English papers and periodicals promoting the drive appeared in colleges in the United States. The movement called for U.S. troop withdrawal from Taiwan, the abrogation of the U.S.-ROC Mutual Defense Treaty, and U.S. recognition of the Peking government as the sole legal government of China; a Chinese settlement of the Taiwan question; abolishment of the ROC government in a year; and peaceful return of Taiwan to the PRC. To counteract this overseas campaign (mainly in the United States, Japan, and Hong Kong), the ROC firmly asserted that the real obstacle to unification is the CCP, which would have to be liquidated before unification could be achieved.[9] In a shift, both Peking and Taipei now courted the splintered Taiwan Independence Movement for support.[10]

There are approximately 60,000 Chinese in Japan, 50 percent of whom were born on Taiwan. Realizing the importance of the ethnic and cultural ties between the Chinese in Japan and Taiwan, Peking exchanged visits with Taiwan Chinese groups from Japan. Among all the visits, the Liao Ch'eng-chih mission in April 1973 truly reflected Peking's new efforts. The mission, which consisted of 55 members for a 33-day visit, was the largest political and goodwill group Peking has sent to Japan since 1971. Its components included deputies of the People's Congress, members of the Political Consultative Conference, party Central Committee members, youths, peasant and worker cadres, writers, educators, women, and Taiwan-born and Japan-educated people. The mission visited more than 17 cities and spent half of its time with the overseas Chinese. Liao and his group told the overseas Chinese that they should seek every opportunity to engage in propaganda activities toward Taiwan and that they were all welcome to visit the mainland.[11] It was an extremely impressive whirlwind-style mission.

Sports diplomacy was also employed. In addition to several Taiwan pingpong teams in 1972–74, the Athletic Delegation of Taiwan was invited to participate in the Third National Games in Peking in the fall of 1975. The "Taiwan" delegation came from six countries and consisted of 279 athletes and physical culture workers. It was the largest and most stimulating Taiwan sports team that ever visited China. The "one China" concept was "an important issue" at the games.[12]

To promote the unification drive further, Peking treated defectors from Taiwan with great publicity. All of the six known defectors since 1972 were received warmly.* Moreover, Peking launched psychological warfare by pardoning and releasing the remaining 293 Nationalist "prisoners of war" in March 1975† and the 144 captured secret agents from Taiwan in September of the same year. Although Peking interpreted such an act as a continuation of its POW policy, it was apparently designed to win some hearts in Taiwan.

DELAY-SETTLEMENT AND FACTIONAL POLITICS

If Peking's leaders had counted on President Nixon's "strong desire" to normalize relations with China and to "settle" the Taiwan issue during his second term, they must have been greatly disappointed. Up to early 1978, a Taiwan settlement had not only been delayed, but American ties with Taiwan had maintained about the same level as before in the military, economic, diplomatic, and cultural fields. U.S. arms sales to Taiwan had increased from $196 million in fiscal year 1974 to $293 million in 1976. Such sales increases included a highly advanced radar air defense system, Hawk ground-to-air missiles, and F-5E jet interceptors (from 120 to 180).[13] U.S. trade with Taiwan increased from $1.5 billion in 1971 to approximately $4.5 billion in 1976, while trade with Peking dropped from $934 million in 1974 to $336 million in 1976. Eight U.S. banks have opened branches in Taiwan, and several American oil companies—Amoco, Gulf, Clinton, Continental, and others—have obtained concessions from Taiwan for oil and gas exploration and have begun operations in waters surrounding Taiwan. These companies are planning the construction of five to ten production platforms in the Taiwan Strait at a cost of about $150 million each. In addition to Leonard Unger's ambassadorship to Taipei in 1974, five new Taiwan consulates were established in Atlanta, Portland, Kansas City, Guam, and American Samoa. Missions of "people's diplomacy" (cultural groups) have also actively increased their mutual visits between Taiwan and the United States. It was not until May–June 1978 that the U.S. government agreed to the sales of the military-related technology (airborne geological survey equipment)

---

*The defectors were Sung Wei-pin (diplomat, March 4, 1973); Chao Ming-che (air pilot, April 20, 1973); Wu Mou-huo (Lieutenant, April 2, 1974); K'uang Hui-sheng (Lieutenant, May 4, 1974); Yang Ming-yi (Lt. Colonel, November 15, 1975); and Li Yi (former Lt. General, December 12, 1975).

†Peking had previously pardoned and released 296 POWs: December 4, 1959, Tu Lu-ming and 32 others; November 28, 1960, Fan Han-chieh and 49 others; November 25, 1961, Liao Yao-hsiang and 67 others; April 9, 1963, Kang Tse and 34 others; December 12, 1964, Wang Ling-chi and 52 others; and April 16, 1966, Fang Chin and 56 others.

to Peking and held military sales of 60 F-4 fighter-bombers to Taiwan.

Another development was the Soviet Union's continuing interest in Taiwan. On May 12, 1973, a Soviet fleet from Vladivostok passed through the Taiwan Strait to the Indian Ocean. The Soviet ships signaled friendly greetings to the Chinese Nationalist vessels who, interestingly enough, after a moment of reluctance, replied in kind. Two weeks later another Soviet fleet sailed along the Taiwan east coast to the East China Sea. In the fall of that year Victor Louis, a well-known journalist from the Soviet Union, reportedly revisited Taiwan. In July 1976 rumors spread in Hong Kong that Moscow once again wanted to negotiate with Taiwan on the Pescadores.

Most of the above events were regarded by Peking as unfavorable developments caused by the delay of a settlement of the Taiwan issue. Some Chinese became impatient, and the delay became a factor in Chinese politics. It is no longer a secret that the pragmatists and radicals expressed different views toward Taiwan. The pragmatists, led by Chou En-lai, had long said that the PRC must be patient on the Taiwan question. China "can wait five years, ten years, or one hundred years" for the final return of Taiwan.[14] The pragmatists put first things first, and Taiwan is not to be "liberated" immediately.[15] Keng Piao, head of the Central Committee's International Liaison Department, stated in a secret speech in August 1976 that defense against the Soviet Union was Peking's most important problem and all other issues were secondary.[16]

The radicals, led by the group now known as the Gang of Four, were aggressive and impatient. Beginning with their opposition to the "reopening" of China, they criticized the pragmatists all the way.[17] They took every opportunity to express their impatient attitude on the military liberation of Taiwan, and they even utilized the criticize-Lin-Piao-and-Confucius movement to oppose Chou En-lai.[18]

A few examples will support this observation. On September 6, 1975, Chang Ch'un-ch'iao told the Athletic Delegation of Taiwan that military means should be used to back up a peaceful settlement of Taiwan.[19] In talking to Senator Hugh Scott's party in July 1976, three months before his arrest, Chang appeared to be extremely militant and aggressive. He insisted that peaceful unification was impossible and that Taiwan must be "liberated by force."[20] On that occasion Chang's audience included both U.S. visitors and Chinese political and military personnel. In arguing for his tough stand in front of both the Chinese and Americans, he acted as if he were the government's spokesman.

The radicals, moreover, allegedly tried to seize control of military and party affairs in Fukien, a key province facing Taiwan. Broadcasts from there in November 1976 charged that the Gang of Four had extended their sinister hands to Fukien, instructing a handful of people to practice revisionism and splitism and to engage in conspiracies, and that the Gang had also incited bourgeois factionalism and attempted to overthrow leading cadres in the party, government, and army and to seize leadership.[21] The provincial party leader, Liao Chih-kao, a close associate of Teng Hsiao-ping, had reportedly been physically attacked several times before Mao's death by the Gang of Four's followers. It was also reported that the radicals and their followers had staged military maneuvers in July 1976 along the Fukien coast, which involved naval, air, and ground forces and extended much farther into the Taiwan Strait than the PLA had previously gone. During the maneuvers the commander of the Fukien military region, General Pi Ting-chun, who had delayed his response to Chiang Ch'ing's request for support, was killed in a helicopter crash. But wall posters in Fukien have charged that the helicopter accident was engineered by the radicals' followers one day after the death in Peking of General Pi's father-in-law, General Chu Teh, who was also the "father" of the PLA.[22] Fukien was one of the several provinces and regions that faced serious troubles after the arrest of the Gang of Four, prompting Hua Kuo-feng to make a special effort to reorganize the province. If these reports were reliable, then the radicals did try, albeit unsuccessfully, to build up party and military bases in Fukien that could have posed a serious threat to Taiwan.

THE RANKING OF TAIWAN AND THE SOVIET FACTOR

In spite of the fact that the radical faction has been defeated, Peking's fundamental position on Taiwan has not changed. Peking upholds its territorial rights and sovereignty over the island and maintains that the settlement of Taiwan is a domestic issue in which no other country has the right to interfere. And yet, how high (or low) does the Taiwan issue rank among Peking's issue-policy priorities? From the data I have collected, the following ranking would seem to apply:

Soviet pressure
Economic development/modernization
Japanese cooperation
Taiwan-normalization
Internal stability and unity
Relations with Second and Third World countries
Taiwan-liberation/reunification.[23]

This tentative list is self-explanatory and does not need any elaboration except, perhaps, a word on the Soviet Union containment policy against China. Peking is apprehensive that Soviet containment (encirclement) is closing in upon the PRC. The Soviet Union has tried hard to gain footholds in Outer Mongolia, Japan, Indochina, and India and is applying a growing pressure on China. Although Peking has calculated, as Chou En-lai reported in 1973, that the Soviet Union would not wage a major war with China at present,[24] Peking is very much concerned about the weakness of these nations in dealing with the Soviets. In the Chinese interest, Peking urged other Asian nations to resist Soviet overtures and endorsed the continued stationing of U.S. troops in certain areas. Meanwhile, the PRC is trying by every possible means to strengthen its national defense, including the four unprecedented conferences on national defense in early February 1977 and several conferences on modernization in the spring of 1978. In sum, Peking is making a strenuous effort to cope with the Soviet threat.

So far as Taiwan is concerned, Peking fully realizes that it is not possible to "liberate" (reunify) Taiwan at the present time and that the normalization of Sino-American relations as a counter to the Soviet Union is in the best interests of the PRC. But Soviet interest in Taiwan may not be of a totally one-way traffic; Taiwan, for its own survival, may also develop an interest in Soviet approach. In late March 1978, Taiwan and the Soviet Union were reported to have held secret talks in Vienna on political and economic matters.[25] On July 18, 1978, Hsinhua (New China News Agency) accused President Chiang Ching-kuo of the ROC of hoping to disrupt the normalization process, "selling out to foreign interests," and attempting to "unite" with Soviet "revisionism."[26] Two days later an editorial of *Chung-yang jih-pao* (Central Daily News, the Kuomintang organ) denied Hsinhua's account and counteraccused the Peking government for "selling out" national interests to the Soviet Union.[27]

Whether Peking seriously believes Taiwan would turn to the Soviets is unclear. Yet Peking must have fully realized the possibility that if Peking forced Taiwan to a desperate situation, Taiwan may well resort to any available option for survival, including the extremely risky Soviet one. Vietnam's and Cuba's associations with the Soviet Union against the PRC and the United States have demonstrated clearly such a possibility. The Peking leaders are, of course, completely aware of the fact that a Soviet access to Taiwan and the use of Cam Ranh Bay (Vietnam) mean not only the further implication of the Taiwan issue but also a solid strategic close-in of the Soviet encirclement. In addition, the yet-to-grow navy of the PRC will most likely be kept in the watching eyes of the Soviet Pacific Fleet.

THE TIAO YU TAI INCIDENT

On April 12, 1978, when Japanese Foreign Minister Sunao Sonoda was just about to go to Peking for intensive negotiations on a Sino-Japanese peace treaty, 140 fishing boats from mainland China entered the 12-mile area of Tiao Yu Tai (Senkaku). Fifty of them were armed with machine guns. The Japanese government regarded it a "violation" of Japan's territorial waters and dispatched military aircraft and patrol boats to circle the Chinese boats. As the Japanese urged the Chinese to leave, the Chinese pointed their machine guns at the Japanese boats and shouted back that "Tiao Yu Tai is Chinese territory." Sung Wen, spokesman for the PRC embassy in Tokyo, stated on April 14 that the islands are part of territory of the People's Republic of China "as outlined in a Chinese Foreign Ministry statement on October 31, 1971."[28] Meanwhile, the ROC's Foreign Ministry issued a statement (also on April 14) reasserting Tiao Yu Tai as Chinese territory.[29] Such a situation lasted for a week.

The delicate and intriguing diplomatic maneuvers between Peking and Tokyo, at a time when the negotiations for a Chinese-sought "antihegemonic" (that is, anti-Soviet) peace treaty was just about to resume, resulted in the withdrawal of the Chinese fishing boats. The Peking government's position at that time was seen through the statements by Vice-Premier Keng Piao (April 15) and Liao Ch'eng-chih (May 1), president of Chinese-Japanese Friendship Association. Both made it clear that the event was "accidental." Keng Piao even evasively remarked that the issue of a much bigger near-by island, Taiwan, had not yet been solved, let alone the small Tiao Yu Tai.

Yet the Japanese government as well as the general public emotionally made the incident a big issue. Suddenly, anti-Chinese sentiment ran high in Tokyo and other major cities even after the withdrawal of the Chinese fishing boats. Japan, apparently, was applying strong pressure on the PRC for concessions at the delicate treaty negotiation time. As a result, Japan signed the treaty in August 1978 after having obtained Teng Hsiao-ping's promise that such a Tiao Yu Tai event would never happen again.

Several observations and comments can be drawn from this incident. First, Peking's strategy was to make concession on Tiao Yu Tai in order to lure Japan into the conclusion of the peace treaty. The low-profile statements by Keng Piao, Liao Ch'eng-chih, and other Chinese officials, such as "accident" and delay-settlement like the "bigger issue of Taiwan," were a shrewd strategic retreat. For a successful conclusion of such a treaty with Japan at this juncture is much more urgent and important than a settlement of the issue of Tiao Yu Tai; and to compare Tiao Yu Tai to the difficult-to-settle issue of Taiwan is to attempt to cover up Peking's concession to Japan. Clearly, Peking's "treaty first" strategy was the order of the day under which the Tiao Yu Tai issue must be pushed aside.

Second, Peking has made a shift from its fundamental position on the island. In 1974 Teng Hsiao-ping stated that the PRC would make no protest against Japan's surveying of the island, but if Japan undertook oil or gas drilling, the PRC would stop it.[30] Japan, at this incident, had accused the Chinese of "violating" Japanese "territorial waters" to which Peking had made no new claims nor protest. If the present situation is to last for a period of time, Japan may become "entitled" to the island. In that circumstance Peking will find it extremely difficult to stop Japan's oil or gas drilling there in the future. Consequently, such a strategic retreat will lead to the loss of the island to Japan.

Third, Peking's concession to Japan has obviously disappointed many Chinese. Despite elaborate explanations and skillful defense by Peking-supported journals,[31] the Peking government's evasive stand remains unconvincing to the independent mind of numerous Chinese.[32] As the ROC reasserted repeatedly Chinese sovereignty over Tiao Yu Tai, it seems to have won over a countless number of Chinese intellectuals around the world who had supported Peking in this fight from 1971 to 1978.

CONCLUDING OBSERVATIONS

The four elements discussed at the outset of the chapter have led us to see the issue from different perspectives. First, nationalism has played a leading role in Peking's persistent claim that Taiwan is an integral part of China. Needless to say, the other three elements have also contributed to enforcing this official stand. Despite U.S. pressure for a peaceful settlement, the unification campaign goes on unabated. Owing to the PRC's limited capabilities and the international environment, Peking will continue to postpone the "liberation" (reunification) of Taiwan but will not tolerate the creation of a "two-China" situation.

Second, immediately before the normalization, Peking's public accusations of the U.S. "imperialists' occupation" of Taiwan have been dropped, but not its attacks on Taiwan's "rich-poor" society, "dictatorial" politics, "capitalist" economic system, "bourgeois" education, and "poisonous" culture. The PRC, in ideological jargon, identified Taiwan as a preliberation area, waiting for eventual Marxist-Leninist rule. After the normalization, nevertheless, Peking's attitude turned soft and realistic toward Taiwan.

Third, strategic and energy factors have given an added value to Taiwan and tend to reinforce Peking's attitude toward the island. Together with the sentiment of nationalism, these factors have generated a dynamic force in Chinese politics as demonstrated over the Paracel Island operation (Chinese military occupation of the island after wiping out a South Vietnamese force from there in 1974). As Soviet sea power in Asia increases as a result of the 1978 Soviet-Vietnamese treaty and the world effort to search for energy doubles, Taiwan's importance to Peking will be on the rise.

Fourth, the factional conflict between the pragmatists and radicals over Taiwan became acute in 1976. The surprising, unsuccessful attempt of the radicals to gain power in Fukien in that year escalated the issue from debate to military-political action. Looking back, we are able to learn that factional politics over Taiwan had run much deeper than the outsiders

Peking has never ruled out a military liberation of Taiwan either before or after the normalization was accomplished. Should the situation develop in such a way as to require Peking to take military action, the proposal of "liberating Taiwan by force" will not remain a slogan or an academic issue but will become a realistic problem. There are two essential questions to be raised if Peking is to take Taiwan by force. First, under what circumstances will the PRC employ armed force? And second, what is the Chinese capability for such a military operation?

To answer the first question, it seems that under the following three circumstances the PRC will resort to force: (1) Taiwan's declaration of independence. If this should happen, it is highly likely that Peking would resort to force in an attempt to settle the issue once and for all. (2) The normalization followed by Soviet access to Taiwan. If the Soviet Union, against all the odds to be sure, should succeed in gaining a naval base in the Taiwan-Pescadores area after normalization, it could either escalate the Peking-Moscow tension or bring about a limited Peking-Moscow rapprochement. The tense situation might further draw Peking's attention away from Taiwan; but the limited rapprochement, again extremely unlikely, might result in a Moscow-Peking deal to dump Taiwan—an act similar to the U.S. derecognition of Taiwan. The subsequent development is predictable: Taiwan would face military pressure and/or economic blockade by the PRC. (3) After normalization, Peking would adopt a "soft and hard" strategy. As of January 3, 1979, the PRC has already offered conciliatory attitudes, peace talks, postal service, and trade to Taiwan. If Taiwan rejects them repeatedly, Peking would eventually apply economic blockade and even military pressure against Taiwan for reunification. It would take a long period of time to accomplish this goal, but the military means will be employed to back up this drive.

Perhaps the only effective deterrent to Peking's future military action is the development of a nuclear capability by Taiwan. At present, however, such a deterrent runs contrary to Taiwan's nonnuclear development policy.

On the second question of Chinese military capability, there are two major considerations: strategic capability and military strength. The continuance of strong Soviet military pressure in the north and troubles with Vietnam in the south will undoubtedly strategically limit Peking's ability to launch a military operation against Taiwan. As long as Sino-Soviet tensions and Sino-Vietnamese troubles remain unchanged, a war between the Soviet Union and the PRC can never be ruled out. And a two-war strategy against both the Soviet Union and Taiwan is very unlikely to be followed by Peking.

China also has only limited military capability against Taiwan. Even if Taiwan lacks nuclear weapons or outside assistance, an invasion would not be a simple operation. While it is clear that the PLA could take Quemoy and Matsu islands without too much difficulty, Taiwan is a different matter. The PRC does not yet have the capability of taking the island in a short period of time and, according to one estimate, the PLA could not land more than three divisions of assault troops on Taiwan.[33] In any event, should such an unfortunate war break out, the PLA would face a fierce resistance from the well-equipped and well-trained Taiwan army; the casualties on both sides would be extremely high.

Thus it is clear that Peking's political and strategic position on Taiwan has serious implications. Contrary to the Chinese government's statement of December 16, 1978, that the question of Taiwan "has now been resolved" between the United States and the PRC,[34] the problem itself is far from being settled. Although the Chinese government may continue to entertain an attitude as Keng Piao said in August 1976 that Peking would, for the time being, "allow the United States to guard" Taiwan for the PRC,[35] the problem eventually will have to be settled. Whether it will be peaceful unification, armed liberation, independence, or other actions will depend not only on the policies of the PRC and the United States, but on those of Taiwan and other major powers as well.

So far as the United States is concerned, normalization does not mean the end of the Taiwan issue. For, in addition to the need for the revision of more than 50 treaties and agreements with the ROC, President Carter has repeated U.S. continuing interests in the peaceful resolution of the Taiwan issue and limited arms sales to the island. Peking, nevertheless, either holds a different viewpoint or disagrees on these two issues. On the first issue, although Teng Hsiao-ping has said on January 2, 1979, to U.S. Representative John J. LaFalce (N.Y.) that he expected "a peaceful reunification" of Taiwan[36] and the Standing Committee of the National People's Congress has officially asked for trade and the exchange of mail service with the island, Teng did not promise China would not use force.[37] Moreover, the Chinese government's statement of December 16, 1978, made it clear that the way of reunification "is entirely China's internal affairs."[38] This means that Peking has reserved the right to use force in the future. Even if a peaceful reunification could be worked out, it would most likely follow the Tibet example as the Peking leaders have previously stated.

On the second issue of limited arms sales to Taiwan, the problem is thornier. Chairman Hua Kuo-feng said at his unprecedented press conference of December 16, 1978, that China "absolutely would not agree to this."[39] Even if the United States disregards Peking's opposition and sells arms to Taiwan, how long will such a deal last? And if the new Washington-Peking relations develop well in the near future, could the United States effectively resist Peking's pressures to stop the sales? In this context one can simply envision a short duration of U.S. arms sales to the island.

To the Asians, the U.S. prestige is at stake. While normalization is aimed at peace and stability in Asia, the U.S. interest in a peaceful resolution of the Taiwan issue is equally important to the maintenance of peace in the area. Presidents Nixon, Ford, and Carter have repeatedly committed themselves to this interest. It must be upheld without any reservation.

Yet, on January 9, 1979, Deputy Premier Teng Hsiao-ping said in Peking to a group of U.S. senators (led by Senator Sam Numm) that Taiwan could retain both its government and its armed forces and remain fully autonomous after its reunification with the mainland, but the Nationalists on Taiwan "must give up their *sovereignty*." More important is that the PRC, Teng continued, would use force against Taiwan for Taiwan's "indefinite *refusal*" to negotiate for reunification, and "an *attempt* by the Soviet Union to interfere in Taiwanese affairs."[40]

These circumstances (as stated by Teng) of the PRC's using force against Taiwan coincide accurately with what I have previously concluded: Taiwan's independence (sovereignty), Soviet access to Taiwan, and Taiwan's repeated rejection of reunification negotiations.

As Teng began to talk about the possibility of using force against Taiwan only nine days after the United States had recognized China, one would ask seriously: What would the United States do to its repeatedly pledged interest in "a peaceful resolution of the Taiwan issue"?

NOTES

1. See reports in the New York *Times* (hereafter *NYT*), April 12, May 21, June 28, July 15, 1978; and the *Wall Street Journal* (hereafter *WSJ*), July 26, September 6, 7, 1978.

2. Richard Holbrooke, "U.S. Policy in Asia: Changing Perspectives," *Current Policy*, No. 24 (Bureau of Public Affairs, U.S. Department of State, June 1978).

3. This is a political study rather than a legal judgment of the status of Taiwan. For legal considerations of Taiwan's status, see, among others, Hungdah Chiu, "China, the United States, and the Question of Taiwan," in *China and the Question of Taiwan, Documents and Analysis*, ed. Hungdah Chiu (New York: Praeger, 1973), pp. 112-91; Lung-chu Chen and M. W. Reisman, "Who Owns Taiwan: A Search for International Title," in *Taiwan's Future*, ed. Yung-Hwan Jo (Tempe: Center for Asian Studies, Arizona State University, 1974), pp. 170-239; and Frank P. Morello, *The International Legal Status of Formosa* (The Hague: Martinus Nijhoff, 1966).

4. This "unit" has been drawn up by the author, based on the sources in note 5 and interviews with State Department officials on November 5 and 19, 1976. On December 24, 1977, the director of the Investigation Bureau of the Justice Ministry in Taiwan (Taiwan's FBI) reported that in the past year the Chinese Communist Party and the State Council in Peking had respectively established "The Taiwan Office" and "The Taiwan Unit," and that branch offices had also been formed in Fukien and Kwangtung Provinces as well as in Hong Kong and at the PRC's Embassy in Japan. *Central Daily News*, December 25, 1977, p. 2. This report, albeit highly significant, remains to be confirmed.

5. Chou's associates included Teng Hsiao-ping, Chiao Kuan-hua, Lo Ch'ing-ch'ang, Chang Ch'un-ch'iao, Li Hsien-nien, Yü Chan, Keng Piao, Huang Hua, and Liao Ch'eng-chih. In the 25 published sources on their talks that I have collected, I found that, due to similar accounts written by different persons from one single group, they have actually made 23 statements relating to Taiwan. These sources are: (1) Seymour Topping in the New York *Times*, June 3, 1971, pp. 1-2; (2) The Committee of Concerned Asian Scholars, *China: Inside the People's Republic* (New York: Bantam Books, 1972), pp. 347-52 (an excerpt is in *NYT*, July 29, 1971, p. 6); (3) James Reston in *NYT*, August 10, 1971, p. 14; (4) William Hinton, "Chou En-lai," *New China*, January 1976, pp. 39-43; (5) Joseph J. Lee, "Peking's View of Taiwan: An Interview with Chou En-lai," in Jo, *Taiwan's Future*, pp. 65-70; (6) Sanford Lee, "China Offers to Talk with Taiwan," Toronto *Star*, October 19, 1972, p. 32; (7) Ts'ai K'an, "Chou En-lai Meets with Taiwan Chinese," *Ch'i-shih Nien-tai* (The Seventies) monthly, December 1972, pp. 38-39; (8) Parris Chang in *Hearings* before the Subcommittee on Future Foreign Policy Research and Development, 94th Cong., Parts I and II (Washington, D.C.: U.S. Government Printing Office, 1976), p. 278; (9) Yü Yu, "Chou En-lai's Conversations on Taiwan," *Ch'i-shih Nien-tai*, April 1973, pp. 30-31; (10) Ch'u Yen, "Conversations of Ch'iao Kuan-hua and Lo Ch'ing-ch'ang," *Ch'i-shih Nien-tai*, October 1973, pp. 63-65; (11) Fan Lan et al., "Teng Hsiao-ping on the Chinese Situation and the Taiwan Question," *Ch'i-shih Nien-tai*, December 1974, pp. 15-17 (a similar account appeared again in the additional section of the August 1977 issue of *Ch'i-shih Nien-tai*); (12) Mike Mansfield, *China: A Quarter Century After the Founding of the People's Republic* (Washington, D.C.: U.S. Government Printing Office, 1975), pp. 21-24; (13) Murrey Marder in the Washington *Post*, August 3, 1976, p. A3; (14) Daniel Southerland in the *Christian Science Monitor*, November 16, 1976, p. 3; (15) *Po-ch'eng Ch'ing-miao* (Berkeley Newsletter), November 1975, pp. 14-15; (16) Teng Hsiang-ping's talks with Cyrus R. Vance, October 11, 1975, in *Working Papers* (published by The Rockefeller Foundation, New York, October 1976), pp. 76-82; (17) Keng Piao's speech at the Institute of Diplomacy in Peking on August 24, 1976, in *Mei-chou Fei-ch'ing T'ung-hsin* (The Chinese Communist Affairs Weekly, Taipei), No. 503 (November 27, 1976), pp. 15-17; (18) Li Hsien-nien's interview, *Sunday Times* (Longon), March 27, 1977; (19) Li Hsien-nien's interview, *NYT*, August 30, 1977; (20) Teng Hsiao-ping's interview, *NYT*, September 7, 1977;

(21) Yü Chan's interview, *WSJ*, October 3, 1977; (22) Li Hsien-nien's interview, *WSJ*, October 4, 1977; (23) Huang Hua's Analytical Report on the World Situation of July 1977, *Fei-ch'ing Yüeh-pao* (Chinese Communist Affairs Monthly), November 1977, pp. 66–88; (24) Liao Ch'eng-chih on Foreign Relations, *Mei-chou Fei-ch'ing T'ung-hsin*, No. 587 (July 21, 1978), pp. 9–11; and (25) Teng Hsiao-ping's interview, *NYT*, December 3, 1978. All quotations and viewpoints in this section are based on these 25 published materials.

6. Editorial of *Jen-min Jih-pao* (hereafter *JMJP*), December 22, 1954.

7. *JMJP*, March 1, 1973; March 1, 1974; March 1 and 2, 1975; February 29, 1976; March 1 and 2, 1977; and March 1 and 2, 1978. Other participants from Taiwan were Chen Yi-sung (member of the People's Congress Standing Committee), Chiang Chung-kuang (professor), Chen Ting-mao (engineer), Tien Fu-ta (Kaoshan nationality, Democratic Self-Government League), Li Chun-ching (Democratic Self-Government League), Yeh Chi-tung, Tsai Tzu-min, Wu Ke-tai, and Chen Ping-chi (all participants in the February 28 uprising); Huang Chi-chun and Chen Lien-sheng (students); and Ko Lien-ying (Kaoshan nationality).

8. Mao Tse-tung, "Greet the New High Tide of the Chinese Revolution," in *Selected Works*, Vol. IV (Peking, 1961), pp. 119–27. This was an innerparty directive of February 1, 1947, from Mao to the Central Committee of the party.

9. *Chung-yang Jih-pao* (hereafter *CYJP*) (Taipei), January 4, February 1, 8, November 25, and December 10, 1972.

10. *NYT*, January 31, 1973, p. 13. For the splintered Taiwan Independence movement, consult Hung-mao Tien, "Taiwan in Transition: Prospects for Socio-Political Change," *China Quarterly*, No. 64 (December 1975), pp. 615–44.

11. *Ta Kung Pao* (Hong Kong), April 21; May 3, 14, 1973 (the world-renowned mathematician, Hua Lo-keng, was also with the mission).

12. *New China News Agency* (in English), October 22, 1975; *New China*, September 1976, pp. 36–37.

13. *CYJP*, June 29 and 30, 1976; *NYT*, August 4, 1976, pp. 1 and 3.

14. Teng Hsiao-ping's talks with Cyrus R. Vance, in *Working Papers*, pp. 81–82.

15. Charles H. Percy et al., *The United States and China: A Report to the Senate Foreign Relations Committee and the House International Relations Committee* (Washington, D.C.: U.S. Government Printing Office, 1975), pp. 10–11; quoted in "Schlesinger on China," editorial in *NYT*, October 18, 1976, p. 28; Daniel Southerland, "Mansfield: Sino-Soviet Rift to Stay," *Christian Science Monitor*, November 16, 1976, p. 3.

16. Keng Piao's speech of August 24, 1976.

17. For instance, Chou En-lai apparently was compelled by the radicals to explain why a compromise with the United States was necessary and different from that with the Soviet Union. See Chou's report to the Tenth Party Congress, *Peking Review*, Nos. 35 and 36 (September 7, 1973), p. 23. Also in August 1974 the radicals bitterly criticized those national betrayers who advocate "total Westernization" and ignore antiimperialism and antirevisionism. See Chen Chin, "Respect Confucianism, Study Classics, Worship the West, and Betray the Country," *Hung Ch'i*, No. 8 (1974), pp. 33–39. See similar criticisms in "Persist in the Philosophy of Struggle, Oppose the Way of the Golden Mean," *Xuexi Yu Pipan* (Study and Criticism), No. 5 (May 20, 1974); and Tsuan Feng, "On Capitalist Readers," *Xuexi Yu Pipan*, No. 5 (May 14, 1976).

18. "Gang of Four's Plots in the Movement to Criticize Lin Piao and Confucius," *Peking Review*, No. 16 (April 15, 1977), p. 29. Some of the China watchers who had previously misinterpreted this particular point must have been surprised by Peking's new charge under Hua Kuo-feng's leadership.

19. *Po-ch'eng Ch'ing-miao*, pp. 14–15.

20. Interview and conversations with members of the Scott party. A similar account was reported in the Washington *Post* and *NYT*, both dated August 3, 1976. Also Hugh

Scott's report, *The United States and China* (Washington, D.C.: U.S. Government Printing Office, September 1976), p. 3.

21. Fukien Provincial Service in Mandarin, 0900 GMT, November 14, 1976. *JMJP*, December 4, 1976, p. 4, also carried a similar report from Fuchow.

22. *NYT*, November 26, 1976, p. A3; *CYJP*, November 22, 1976; February 16, March 10 and 19, 1977.

23. After this ranking order was first drawn in late November 1976, the author saw on December 1976, the text of Keng Piao's speech of August 24, 1976, which substantiated, surprisingly, the order of priority. Some other available information after mid-December 1976 has also supported this ranking. See *NYT*, November 30, 1976, and February 21, 1977; Hsinhua (Peking), February 6, 1977; *Sunday Times* (London), March 27, 1977; and *NYT*, September 7, 1977.

24. Chou En-lai's secret speech of March 1973, and Huang Hua's speech of July 1977.

25. *NYT*, April 1, 1978, p. 4.

26. Hsinhua (Peking), July 18, 1978.

27. *CYJP*, July 20, 1978.

28. *NYT*, April 15, 1978, p. 1.

29. *CYJP*, April 15, 1978.

30. See earlier discussions on Tiao Yu Tai.

31. For instance, articles in *Ch'i-shih Nien-tai*, June 1978, pp. 10–21.

32. See, among others, articles in *Hsintu* (New Land) 1, no. 1 (July 1978): 8–29.

33. Brian Crozier, "The Art of Survival," *National Review*, December 6, 1974, p. 1402. Also see *NYT*, December 1, 1976, for the PLA's general strength.

34. "Statement of the Chinese Government," *Peking Review*, No. 51 (December 22, 1978), p. 8.

35. Keng Piao's speech, pp. 16–17.

36. *NYT*, January 3, 1979, p. 2.

37. Ibid.

38. *Peking Review*, No. 51 (December 22, 1978), p. 9.

39. Ibid., p. 10.

40. *NYT*, January 10, 1979, pp. 1, 8. (Emphasis added.)

6

The Question of Taiwan in Sino-American Relations

Hungdah Chiu

Since 1950 the question of Taiwan (Formosa) has been the most difficult issue in Sino-American relations. The two Taiwan Strait crises in 1954 and 1958 almost brought the United States into a major armed conflict with the People's Republic of China. In recent years the question of Taiwan has continued to be one of the major obstacles in the U.S. attempt to normalize relations with the PRC. On the other hand, the developments in the last three decades have also changed the nature of U.S. relations with the Republic of China in Taiwan from one based essentially on purely strategic considerations to one based on a mixture of strategic, economic, and moral considerations.

The ROC was the first of the developing countries to cease receiving U.S. aid; it has now become a major trading partner of the United States, with an annual volume of $7.5 billion. While the great majority of the American people would like to normalize relations with the PRC, they also want to maintain existing relations with the ROC. Therefore, there is little doubt that the question of Taiwan is one of the most important, complex, and difficult problems in U.S. foreign relations. This chapter seeks to provide a systematic analysis of the Taiwan question in the context of U.S.-PRC and U.S.-ROC relations.

THE ORIGIN OF THE TAIWAN QUESTION

In 1661 a Chinese general, Cheng Ch'eng-kung (Koxinga), drove the Dutch from Taiwan and formally established a Chinese administration there (see Document 1). In 1683, Cheng's grandson surrendered to the Ch'ing Empire (1644-1911), which administered the island as a prefecture of the mainland Fukien Province until 1885. In 1886 Taiwan was made a separate province of China. In

1895, after China was defeated in the First Sino-Japanese War (1894-95), Taiwan was ceded to Japan by the Treaty of Shimonoseki (see Document 2). On December 9, 1941, the ROC government made a formal declaration of war against Japan and declared "that all treaties, conventions, agreements, and contracts regarding relations between China and Japan are and remain null and void."[1] On November 26, 1943, at the Cairo Conference, President Chiang Kai-shek of the ROC, President Franklin D. Roosevelt of the United States, and Prime Minister Winston Churchill of Great Britain issued a joint communique, later known as the Cairo Declaration, declaring, among other things, that "all the territories Japan has stolen from the Chinese, such as Manchuria, Formosa, and the Pescadores, shall be returned to the Republic of China" (see Document 3).[2] On November 30, 1943, Marshall Stalin of the Soviet Union approved "the communique and all its contents" at the Teheran Conference.[3]

On July 26, 1945, the heads of government of the United States, ROC, and the United Kingdom further declared in the Potsdam Proclamation that "the terms of the Cairo Declaration shall be carried out."[4] This proclamation was adhered to by the Soviet Union on August 8, and by France on August 11.[5] On September 2, 1945, Japan signed the Instrument of Surrender[6] and accepted the provisions of the Potsdam Proclamation.

Pursuant to the provisions of the Instrument of Surrender, the Office of the Supreme Commander for the Allied Powers issued General Order No. 1, directing, inter alia, Japanese forces in China and Formosa to "surrender to Generalissimo Chiang Kai-shek."[7] On October 25, 1945, the ROC government took over Taiwan and the P'eng-hu Islands from the Japanese and on the next day announced that Taiwan had become a province of China. In 1946 the Province of Taiwan elected delegates to participate in the Constitutional National Assembly that enacted the present Constitution of the ROC. In 1947, in accordance with this Constitution, the Province of Taiwan elected 19 delegates to the National Assembly, 8 delegates to the Legislative Yuan (Congress), and 5 delegates to the Control Yuan.

Before 1949 there was virtually no discussion of the so-called question of Taiwan on the international level, and it was widely expected that the peace treaty with Japan would explicitly provide for the return of Taiwan to China.[8] It was not until mid-1949, when the Chinese Communists were about to take over the Chinese mainland, that the question of Taiwan gradually emerged.

On October 1, 1949, the Chinese Communists inaugurated the People's Republic of China in Peking. Between October 6 and 8, 1949, the U.S. Department of State convened a conference on Far Eastern problems attended by experts and officials. During the discussion the majority of the participants expressed the view that the ROC government was "finished" and that they were no longer interested in its fate. One participant, John K. Fairbank, said that the United States should not prevent the fall of Taiwan into the hands of the Chinese Communists.[9]

By December 1949 the Chinese Communists had virtually conquered the mainland of China, and the ROC government removed its seat to Taipei. At that time many American political and military leaders—such as ex-President Herbert Hoover, Secretary of Defense Louis Johnson, General Douglas MacArthur, Senators Robert A. Taft, William F. Knowland, and H. Alexander Smith, and Congressman Walter Judd—advocated the protection of Taiwan against a Communist invasion.[10] In late December 1949, the U.S. Joint Chiefs of Staff, under the chairmanship of General Omar Bradley, recommended helping the ROC government defend Taiwan and the dispatch of a military mission there.[11] A week later, at a meeting of the National Security Council, President Truman rejected the recommendation of the Joint Chiefs of Staff.[12]

On December 23, 1949, the U.S. Department of State sent a secret memorandum on Taiwan to its diplomatic and consular officers in the Far East, informing them of the hands-off policy of the United States toward Taiwan. The memorandum pointed out that the fall of Taiwan to the Chinese Communist forces was widely expected, the island had no special military significance and it was politically, geographically, and strategically a part of China, "though technical status of the island remains to be determined by the Japanese peace settlement," and "Formosa is exclusively the responsibility of the Chinese [ROC] government" (see Document 4).

President Truman made a statement on Taiwan at a press conference on January 5, 1950. He pointed out that, in keeping with the terms of the Cairo Declaration, the Potsdam Proclamation, and the terms of Japanese surrender, "Formosa was surrendered to Generalissimo Chiang Kai-shek, and for the past four years, the United States and the other Allied Powers have accepted the exercise of Chinese authority over the Island." The United States, Truman said, "has no predatory design on Formosa, . . . nor does it have any intention of utilizing its armed forces to interfere in the present situation." Specifically, "the United States Government will not provide military aid or advice to Chinese forces on Formosa."[13]

On the same day Secretary of State Acheson elaborated on the president's statement by saying that "when Formosa was made a province of China nobody raised any lawyers' doubts about that."[14] Furthermore, in Acheson's address before the National Press Club on January 12, 1950, he pointed out that the American defense perimeter in the western Pacific ran along the Aleutians through Japan and the Ryukyus to the Philippines. Taiwan was left out of this defense line.[15]

On February 9, 1950, in a reply to a series of questions on American policy toward China contained in a House resolution, the Department of State said that it would be unwise for the United States to establish a non-Chinese administration on Taiwan because the United States "do[es] not wish to create a Formosa *irredenta* issue about which the Chinese Communists could rally support within China" (see Document 5).

In Taiwan, President Chiang Kai-shek resumed his office on March 1, 1950. The Chinese government was preparing for the final showdown with the Chinese Communists in the last battle of the Chinese civil war, presumably to be fought sometime in the summer of 1950. Across the Taiwan Strait, the Chinese Communists were actively preparing for the invasion of Taiwan. Early in October 1949, after capturing Amoy, the victorious Comminist forces immediately launched an amphibious landing on Quemoy (Kinmen); but all three Communist divisions that landed were killed or captured by the Nationalist forces.[16]

In May 1950, crossing the 20-mile-wide Chiungchow Strait, Communist forces successfully landed on Hainan and rapidly captured the whole island. At that time it was widely expected that the Communist forces would soon invade Taiwan. Then a month later came the Korean War and the United States suddenly changed its position on the question of Taiwan. On June 27, 1950, President Truman declared that he had "ordered the Seventh Fleet to prevent any attack on Formosa"; and in the meantime he requested the ROC government on Taiwan to cease military operations against the mainland.

Concerning the status of Taiwan, Truman also drastically changed his January 5 position, saying that "the determination of the future status of Formosa must await the restoration of security in the Pacific, a peace settlement with Japan, or consideration by the United Nations."[17]

An aide-memoire of the United States to this effect was presented to the Chinese government on the same day by the U.S. chargé d'affaires at Taipei. At an Executive Yuan meeting of the Chinese government on June 28, it was decided to accept in principle the proposal of the U.S. government, and an order was immediately issued to Chinese military authorities to suspend operations against the mainland. In the meantime the ROC foreign minister, George K. C. Yeh, made a statement clarifying the Chinese response to the U.S. change of position on the status of Taiwan. Yeh said that the U.S. proposal "should in no way alter the status of Formosa as envisaged in the Cairo Declaration, nor should it in any way affect China's authority over Formosa." Moreover, the statement said that in accepting the American proposals, the Chinese government "does not intend to depart from its dual policy of resistance against the aggression of International Communism and the maintenance of the territorial integrity of China."[18]

Needless to say, the U.S. decision to intervene in the Taiwan situation compelled the PRC to delay its military campaign to "liberate" Taiwan, and therefore the PRC's response to the U.S. action was most unfavorable. On June 28 Mao Tse-tung, referring to Truman's January 5 statement, denounced the U.S. action as an "open exposure" of its "imperialist face."[19]

Chou En-lai, premier and foreign minister of the PRC, also declared on behalf of the PRC that Truman's statement and the American action "constitute armed aggression against the territory of China and are a gross violation of the United Nations Charter." Moreover, Chou stated that "no matter what obstructive action U.S. imperialists may take, the fact that Taiwan is part of

China will remain unchanged forever" and that "all the people of our country will certainly fight as one man and to the end to liberate Taiwan."[20]

Since June 27, 1950, when President Truman changed the American position on Taiwan, the question of Taiwan has become a major issue in U.S. relations with the PRC, ROC, and Japan.

THE QUESTION OF TAIWAN AT THE UNITED NATIONS

Soon after the establishment of the PRC on October 1, 1949, the PRC government demanded to be seated immediately in the United Nations, especially in the Security Council and the General Assembly. However, at that time the majority of the members of the United Nations still recognized the government of the ROC as representing China in this world body. As a result, when the Korean War broke out, the PRC was not in the United Nations. Although outside the United Nations, the PRC clearly recognized the importance of that organization in international relations. Therefore, on July 6, 1950, ten days after Truman's dispatch of the Seventh Fleet to the Taiwan Strait, PRC Premier and Foreign Minister Chou En-lai sent a cablegram to UN Secretary-General Trygve Lie saying that the U.S. action constituted "an act of open aggression which thoroughly violates the principle of the United Nations Charter forbidding any member to use force against the territorial integrity or political independence of any other state."[21]

On August 24, 1950, Chou sent another cablegram to the president of the Security Council and secretary-general of the United Nations, formally accusing the United States of armed aggression and requesting the Council to take action against the United States.[22] On August 29, 1950, the Security Council, at its 592nd meeting, decided to include the PRC's accusation in its agenda under the title "Complaint of armed invasion of Taiwan (Formosa)."

On September 17, 1950, Chou En-lai again cabled the Security Council, stating that, as "the sole legal government representing the Chinese people, and being the accuser in the case," his government had the right and necessity to send its delegation to attend and participate in the proceedings of the Security Council.[23] The Security Council adopted a resolution on September 29 to invite the representative of the PRC to attend its meetings held after November 15 concerning the discussion of the agenda item "Complaint of armed invasion of Taiwan (Formosa)."[24]

On October 23, 1950, the PRC accepted the invitation of the Council.[25] On November 27 the Council decided to consider the agenda item "Complaint of armed invasion of Taiwan (Formosa)," and on the same day a representative of the PRC took his seat at the Council table.[26]

The next day PRC representative Wu Hsiu-chuan made a lengthy speech denouncing the U.S. aggression against Taiwan.[27] He categorically rejected the U.S. view that the status of Taiwan "is undetermined." The status of Taiwan as an integral part of China, he stated, was clearly reflected in the Cairo Declaration, the Potsdam Proclamation, and the Japanese instrument of surrender. Therefore, when in 1945 the Chinese government accepted the Japanese surrender of Taiwan and exercised sovereignty over the island, Taiwan had become, not only de jure but also de facto, an inalienable part of China.

Since Taiwan is an inalienable part of Chinese territory, Wu said, the dispatch of the U.S. Seventh Fleet to the Taiwan Strait to prevent the Chinese people's "liberation" of the island constituted "armed aggression" against China. At the end of his long speech, Wu submitted a draft resolution calling upon the Security Council to condemn the United States for committing "open and direct aggression against Chinese territory" and "to demand the complete withdrawal by the Government of the United States of its forces of armed aggression from Taiwan."[28] This draft resolution, sponsored by the Soviet Union, was rejected by the Council by nine votes to one (Soviet Union), with one member not participating.[29]

During the same period, at the fifth session of the General Assembly, the Soviet Union and the United States each sponsored an agenda item concerning Taiwan. On September 20, 1950, the Soviet Union proposed that the question of U.S. aggression against China should be included in the Assembly's agenda. On September 26 the General Assembly included the item in its agenda under the title "Complaint by the USSR regarding aggression against China by the United States" and referred it to the First Committee.[30] On October 17 the PRC sent a cablegram to the United Nations, claiming its right to participate in the proceedings of the General Assembly, with particular reference to this agenda item. On November 15 the First Committee decided to invite the PRC to participate in the discussion of this item.[31]

On November 26 the PRC replied that it had appointed Wu Hsiu-chuan to participate in the discussion of the Soviets' proposed item in the First Committee, and the next day Wu took part in the committee's 407th meeting.[32] The next meeting of the committee was not held until December 7, and at that meeting it was decided to give priority to the French proposal on the "Intervention of the Central People's Government of the People's Republic of China in Korea"; discussion of the Soviet complaint against the United States was postponed.[33]

On December 16 Wu Hsiu-chuan issued a statement at Lake Success, New York, saying that the PRC firmly opposed and protested the Security Council's rejection of the PRC's proposal calling on the United States to withdraw from Taiwan.[34] He then distributed a speech that he had prepared but was kept from delivering to the First Committee.[35] On December 19, 1950, Wu's group left New York and returned to the PRC.

On February 2, 1951, the First Committee resumed consideration of the agenda item proposed by the Soviet Union, and its chairman notified the PRC of the date of the committee's next meeting, February 6. Chou En-lai replied on February 4 that the lengthy speech distributed by Wu on December 16, 1950, should be read and circulated before the committee's meeting.[36] On February 7 the committee rejected a Soviet draft resolution "to request the Security Council to take the necessary steps to ensure the immediate cessation of aggression against China by the United States."[37]

On September 20, 1950, when the Soviet Union requested the General Assembly to consider the question of U.S. aggression against China, the United States requested that the question of Formosa be included in the agenda of the fifth session of the General Assembly. On November 15 the First Committee decided to postpone its consideration of the U.S.-sponsored item until after the Soviet complaints regarding U.S. aggression against China and the ROC's complaints regarding Soviet aggression against China had been handled.[38] In early 1951, when the item was recalled, the United Stated supported a British move to adjourn consideration of the item "in view of the unsettled state of the situation in the Far East"; and on February 7 the First Committee decided to adjourn debate on the item.[39] Since then there has been no further consideration of this item in the United Nations.

Although UN consideration of the Taiwan question has not produced any substantive result, the positions taken by the ROC and the PRC toward the Taiwan question at the United Nations need special attention. Both the ROC and the PRC consider that the status of Taiwan as an integral part of Chinese territory has long been settled in accordance with several wartime agreements among the allies and is therefore outside the competence of the United Nations. Moreover, the PRC believes that the United Nations should deal only with the question of the "United States armed aggression against the Chinese territory of Taiwan." It categorically rejected any UN consideration of, or interference in, its effort to "liberate" Taiwan, whether by force or by peaceful means. In the past 30-odd years the PRC has consistently maintained this attitude.

The second time the question of Taiwan was raised at the United Nations was during the First Taiwan Strait Crisis in 1954–55. This episode will be discussed later in connection with the U.S.-ROC Treaty of Mutual Defense. In this section I shall cover only the UN side of the story.

After it suddenly opened fire on Quemoy on September 3, 1954, starting the First Taiwan Strait Crisis, the PRC, on October 10, 1954, sent a telegram to the United Nations requesting the ninth session of the General Assembly "to give its most serious attention" to no less than seven "facts relevant to the armed aggression against China's territory of Taiwan by the United States government." The cablegram specifically pointed out that "to liberate Taiwan is a matter of China's internal affairs" and "no foreign intervention will be tolerated."[40] It does not appear that the United Nations took any action on the cablegram, and this document appears to have been the PRC's last resort to the United Nations to protest the U.S. "armed aggression against Taiwan."

During the crisis, on January 19, 1955, President Eisenhower said in a press conference that he would like to see the United Nations try to arrange a cease-fire between the Nationalists and Communists.[41] On January 24, 1955, President Eisenhower, in his message to Congress asking for authorization to use

American forces to defend Taiwan and the Pescadores, said that the United States "would welcome any action by the United Nations which might, in fact, bring an end to the active hostilities in the area."[42] On the same day Chou En-lai issued a statement that rejected any cease-fire proposal, saying that this "is in fact an intervention in China's internal affairs for the alienation of China's territory."[43]

Despite the PRC's objection, New Zealand proposed to the UN Security Council, on January 28, 1955, that it consider the situation arising out of the occurrence of armed hostilities between the PRC and the ROC in the area of certain islands off the coast of mainland China.[44] On January 31 the Council decided to invite the PRC to participate in the discussion of this question.[45] On February 3, 1955, Chou En-lai sent a cablegram to the United Nations rejecting the invitation. The cablegram said that, inasmuch as the liberation of Taiwan was a sovereign right to the Chinese people and was an entirely internal affair of China, it was a violation of the UN Charter to suggest, as the New Zealand proposal did, that the Security Council should consider the question of hostilities between his government and the "Chiang Kai-shek regime." It further stated that so long as the PRC's place in the United Nations was usurped by the "Chiang Kai-shek group," the PRC would be unable to take part in the discussion of questions concerning China in the United Nations.[46]

The last time the question of Taiwan was raised at the United Nations was in connection with the discussion of the Chinese representation question at the 26th session of the UN General Assembly held in the fall of 1971. On October 25, 1971, when the debates on the Chinese representation question were about to conclude and the question was to be put to vote, Saudi Arabia made a last-minute proposal in order to save a seat for the ROC at the United Nations. The draft resolution proposed by Saudi Arabia provided, inter alia, the following:

> *The General Assembly* . . .
> Decides . . . that the People's Republic of China should assume its rightful place in the United Nations . . . and that at the same time, the Republic of China, i.e., the people of the island of Taiwan, should retain its seat in the United Nations, and in all the organizations related to it, until the people of the Republic of China, i.e., the people of the island of Taiwan, once enabled by a referendum or a plebiscite under the auspices of the United Nations to declare themselves on the following options:
> (a) Continued independence as a sovereign state . . .
> (b) Confederation with the People's Republic of China . . .
> (c) Federation with the People's Republic of China . . .[47]

Similarly, Tunisia also submitted a draft resolution, inviting the delegation of the ROC "to continue to sit under the name of Formosa in the General Assembly and the different organs of the United Nations in which it sits at present, with the exception of the Security Council. . . ."[48]

The UN General Assembly, however, adopted Resolution 2758 (XXVI) in the late evening of October 25, 1971, expelling the ROC. The Saudi draft resolution was not put to vote and the Tunisian draft resolution was withdrawn. Since the PRC took over the Chinese seat from the ROC at the United Nations, there has been no discussion of the Taiwan question there, since the PRC consider that question to be an internal Chinese matter.

THE QUESTION OF TAIWAN AND THE
JAPANESE PEACE SETTLEMENT

Before the outbreak of the Korean War in mid-1950, it was widely expected that the future peace treaty with Japan would explicitly provide for the return of the island to China, in accordance with several wartime agreements among the allies. The Korean War caused the United States to decide that this strategic island should not be controlled by a hostile regime. Therefore the United States had to devise a legal basis to justify its intervention to prevent the Chinese Communists' "liberation" of Taiwan. From the U.S. point of view, if Taiwan's status could be rendered "undetermined," then legally the United States would be in a better position to justify its dispatch of naval forces to the Taiwan Straits.[49] On the basis of this consideration the United States drafted the provisions concerning the status of Taiwan in the Japanese Peace Treaty.

The ROC government was in a dilemma. On the one hand, at that time it badly needed the U.S. naval force in the Taiwan Strait to prevent the Communist attack; and, if Taiwan was openly conceded in the proposed Japanese peace treaty to be an integral part of China, there would be no sound legal basis for the United States to intervene, since the "Taiwan questions" would be a purely Chinese affair. On the other hand, if the leaders of the ROC accepted an arrangement in the peace treaty that would detach Taiwan from China, they not only would lose their legal basis to govern Taiwan but also would forever be denounced as traitors by all Chinese. After protracted negotiation with the United States, the ROC agreed that in the proposed peace treaty with Japan, it would be sufficient for Japan to renounce its sovereignty over Taiwan and the Pescadores.

The United Stated initially planned to invite the ROC to the peace conference but subsequently changed its mind because of the strong objections raised by the United Kingdom and other countries that recognized the PRC as the legitimate government of China.[50] In June 1951, Secretary of State Dulles finally reached a compromise with the United Kingdom on the question of Chinese participation in the peace conference. According to this compromise, neither the ROC nor the PRC would be invited to the peace conference; after the conclusion of the multilateral peace treaty, Japan would conclude a bilateral peace treaty of similar content with the ROC or the PRC.[51]

Needless to say, the ROC was dissatisfied with such an arrangement. However, the political situation at that time was not favorable to the ROC's participation in the peace conference.[52] Therefore, the ROC had to accept this compromise, and the United States promised to persuade Japan to conclude a bilateral peace treaty with it.[53] On July 11, 1951, the United States published its draft peace treaty with Japan.

While the ROC was pressing its right to participate in the peace conference, the PRC asserted its right to participate in the same conference. On August 15, 1951, Chou En-lai issued a lengthy statement denouncing the American draft peace treaty with Japan.[54] It charged that the U.S. draft peace treaty violated the 1943 Cairo Declaration and the 1945 Potsdam Proclamation by failing to provide for the return of Taiwan and the Pescadores to the People's Republic of China.

Chou concluded his statement by strongly denouncing the exclusion of the PRC from the peace conference and said that such an action "completely violates a stipulation in the UN Declaration of January 1, 1942, to the effect that each of the signatory Powers pledged itself not to make a separate peace." In conclusion, Chou declared that without the participation of the PRC, the Central People's Government considered the peace treaty "illegal, and therefore null and void."

Despite the objections of the ROC and the PRC, the Japanese Peace Treaty was signed on September 8, 1951, at San Francisco.[55] With respect to the question of Taiwan, Article 2 of the treaty provides: "Japan renounces all right, title and claim to Formosa and the Pescadores." Article 26 provides that Japan will prepare to conclude a bilateral treaty with any state which "signed or adhered to the United Nations Declaration of January 1, 1942, and which is at war with Japan."

At the same time the United States continued to try to persuade Japan to conclude a bilateral peace treaty with the ROC. The most difficult problem in U.S.-Japan and U.S.-ROC preliminary negotiations on the ROC-Japanese Peace Treaty was whether the peace treaty should be applicable to all China, including those areas under the de facto control of the PRC. According to the understanding of the United States, in the future bilateral peace negotiations between the ROC and Japan, the latter would insist upon the inclusion of a territorial application clause saying that the peace treaty is applicable only to those areas under the control of the ROC. The degree to which the United States could influence Japan to conclude a peace treaty with the ROC depended largely upon whether the ROC would work out an acceptable formula to solve this problem.[56] In the meantime, U.S. Minister Ranking at Taipei also informed ROC Foreign Minister George Yeh that in any territorial formula for the bilateral ROC-Japanese peace treaty, it should avoid the possible implication of the wording that after the conclusion of the treaty, Taiwan had legally become a part of Chinese territory.[57]

The ROC could not accept any proposal in the peace treaty that would impair its claim to the Chinese mainland and its position in the United Nations as the only legal government of China.[58] Nevertheless, taking into consideration the political reality at that time, the ROC government accepted the U.S.

proposal to have a territorial clause in the peace treaty (though the form was still subject to future negotiation between the ROC and Japan); then the United States finally persuaded Japan to conclude a peace treaty with the ROC. On December 24, 1951, Japanese Prime Minister Yoshida sent a letter to Secretary of State Dulles saying that Japan was willing to conclude a peace treaty with the ROC based on the principles contained in the San Francisco Peace Treaty and with a territorial application clause for the ROC.[59] The letter was communicated to the ROC by the United States on January 16, 1952, and published in Tokyo on the same day.[60] On January 18, 1952, ROC Foreign Minister Yeh issued a statement saying that the ROC was preparing to enter into negotiations with Japan on the peace treaty.[61]

In February 1952 the ROC and Japan started negotiation on the bilateral peace treaty, which, with accompanying notes and other documents, was signed on April 28, 1952 (see Document 9). On the question of Taiwan, Article 2 of the treaty provides that "Japan has renounced all right, title and claim to Taiwan and P'eng-hu" in accordance with Article 2 of the San Francisco Peace Treaty. Article 4 of the treaty provides that "all treaties, conventions and agreements concluded before December 9, 1941, between China and Japan have become null and void as a consequence of the war." It is clear that under Article 4 the 1895 Sino-Japanese Treaty of Shimoneseki, ceding Taiwan to Japan, was abolished.

As for the territorial application clause, an exchange of notes accompanying the treaty provides that "the terms of the present Treaty shall, in respect of the Republic of China, be applicable to all territories which are now, or which may hereafter be, under the control of its Government."

On the same day that the ROC and Japan signed the bilateral peace treaty, the San Francisco Peace Treaty entered into force. On May 5, 1952, Chou En-lai again issued a statement declaring that the San Francisco Peace Treaty was in violation of preceding treaties agreed upon between the allies and was therefore "completely illegal and unreasonable."[62] On August 5, 1952, the ROC-Japan Peace Treaty entered into force.

THE FIRST TAIWAN STRAIT CRISIS AND THE 1954 U.S.-ROC TREATY OF MUTUAL DEFENSE

After the U.S.-imposed "neutralization" of Taiwan in mid-1950, the PRC temporarily had to delay its attack on Taiwan. Then, in the winter of 1950, the PRC participated in the Korean War through the dispatch of the so-called Chinese People's Volunteers to Korea. The PRC also actively supported the Vietnamese Communists in their fight against the French. The PRC forces entered Tibet in late 1950, and the PRC also engaged in the ruthless suppression of "counterrevolutionaries" or "bad elements" in mainland China.[63] Being preoccupied with these activities, it could not engage in an invasion of Taiwan.

The "neutralization" of Taiwan by the United States gave the ROC a breathing period. On July 31, 1950, General MacArthur paid a visit to Taipei to confer with President Chiang Kai-shek concerning the defense of Taiwan, and a week later the U.S. 13th Air Force set up liaison offices in Taipei.[64] On February 9, 1951, an agreement between the United States and the ROC came into force by which the United States agreed "to make available to the Republic of China . . . certain military materials for the defense of Taiwan against possible attack."[65] In May 1951 the U.S. Military Assistance Advisory group was established in Taiwan to aid in training the ROC armed forces. The United States also increased its economic aid to the ROC after the outbreak of the Korean War.[66] As a result the ROC government was able to maintain a comparatively stable currency and improve production in both agriculture and industry. In the military sphere the 600,000-member ROC force was reorganized, retrained, and modernized.

The PRC's entry into the Korean War did not change the U.S. policy of neutralizing Taiwan, and ROC forces were not permitted to attack the mainland. However, on February 2, 1953, President Eisenhower, in his first State of the Union message to the Congress, rescinded this restriction on the ROC forces:

> There is no longer any logic or sense in a condition that required the United States Navy to assume defensive responsibilities on behalf of the Chinese Communists. This permitted those Communists, with greater impunity, to kill our soldiers and those of our United Nations allies in Korea. I am, therefore, issuing instructions that the Seventh Fleet no longer be employed to shield Communist China. Permit me to make crystal clear—this order implies no aggressive intent on our part.[67]

The decision was hailed in the ROC. However, the ROC did not take any significant action against the mainland after Eisenhower's statement, though President Chiang Kai-shek reaffirmed the ROC's determination to restore the freedom of the Chinese people on the mainland.[68]

During the Korean War period, the United States entered into several mutual defense treaties with East Asian and Pacific countries, namely: Philippines, August 30, 1951;[69] Japan, September 8, 1951;[70] and Australia and New Zealand (ANZUS), September 1, 1951.[71]

On July 27, 1953, the Korean Military Armistice Agreement was signed,[72] and the United States concluded a mutual defense treaty with the Republic of Korea on October 1, 1953.[73] Under the circumstances, the ROC became the only country allied with the United States that lacked a mutual defense treaty. Also, after the cessation of hostilities in Korea, the reason for U.S. intervention in the Taiwan area was no longer valid.[74] Therefore, when Vice-President Richard Nixon visited the ROC in November 1953, the ROC proposed to him to conclude a mutual defense treaty. Later in the same year the ROC handed a draft treaty to U.S. Ambassador Rankin (December 1953).[75]

The United States at first was reluctant to enter into a mutual defense treaty, primarily because of a concern about being dragged into a conflict with the PRC by the future ROC "counterattack the mainland campaign." In 1954 the PRC began to put military pressure in the Taiwan Strait and the United States then began to give serious consideration to concluding a mutual defense treaty with the ROC.

On August 11, 1954, PRC Premier Chou En-lai said in his report on foreign affairs that "the people of China and the People's Liberation Army must redouble their efforts in every field, heighten their vigilance, avoid the pitfall of conceit, overcome all difficulties, and struggle to the end to fulfill the glorious task of liberating Taiwan and defending world peace!"[76] A few days later a joint declaration was issued by 19 parties and mass organizations of the PRC, including the Taiwan Democratic Self-Government League, which declared, inter alia, that "the Chinese People are determined to liberate Taiwan."[77] Militarily, the PRC deployed a force of more than 100,000 to the southern part of Fukien and assembed a great number of vessels in the vicinity of Amoy, Foochow, and Swatow. Then, on September 3, 1954, Communist guns suddenly opened fire on Quemoy, pouring 6,000 rounds onto the island.[78] This shelling contined for a number of days. The ROC forces of Quemoy immediately fought back. The ROC air force and navy also undertook operations against PRC batteries along the coast opposite Quemoy and PRC gunboats and motor junks near the coast of Fukien. Occasionally there were air and sea battles between the PRC and ROC forces.

In addition to Quemoy and the Matsu islands off the Fukien coast, the ROC also controlled the Tachen Islands (250 miles northwest of Taiwan) and Nanchi Island (140 miles northwest of Taiwan) off the Chekiang coast. In the middle of October 1954, the PRC began to fire on the Tachens; later, sea and air battles were fought between the PRC and the ROC forces near them. Amid this Communist military pressure against Quemoy and the Tachen Islands, the ROC and the United States began the serious negotiation of the mutual defense treaty in late October and the negotiation was concluded in late November 1954.

In the course of the negotiation, there were several controversial problems. The first one concerned the territorial scope for application of the treaty. The U.S. draft provided that the treaty would be applicable to "Taiwan and the Pescadores" only, and there was no mention of U.S. territory protected by the treaty. The ROC side considered that the omission of U.S. territory in the treaty would make it appear as if the ROC had accepted the ulilateral protection offered by the United States. Such a treaty could hardly be called a "mutual defense" treaty. For national prestige and dignity, the ROC refused to accept a treaty in the form of a guarantee of unilateral protection. Later the United States agreed to place part of its territy under the treaty, namely, "the island territories in the West Pacific under its jurisdiction" (Ryukyu islands and others).

Another ROC criticism of the U.S. draft was the lack of reference in the treaty to the offshore islands held by the ROC. The United States, however, was reluctant to commit itself to defending those islands since they were so close to the Communist-held mainland. After prolonged negotiation, a compromise formula was worked out. The treaty would provide that it may be "applicable to such other territories as may be determined by mutual agreement."[79]

The second problem concerned the ROC's freedom to take military action against the mainland. The U.S. side wanted to include a provision in the treaty to subject such action to "joint agreement." The ROC considered this to be a restriction on its sovereign rights and rejected the U.S. demand. Finally, a compromise formula was worked out to include the U.S. proposal in a separate exchange of notes, wherein the ROC agreed not to use force, without "joint agreement," except in a clear case of self-defense."[80]

The third problem concerned the duration of the treaty and the method of termination. The U.S. side proposed that the duration of the treaty should be ten years,[81] but this was rejected by the ROC, and later both sides agreed that treaty's duration should be "indefinite," but subject to one-year notice for termination.[82]

On December 2, 1954, the U.S.-ROC Mutual Defense Treaty[83] was signed at Washington (see Document 10). On December 8, 1954, PRC Premier and Foreign Minister Chou En-lai issued a lengthy statement denouncing the treaty and reaffirming the PRC's determination to "liberate" Taiwan.[84]

Meanwhile the PRC continued to exert military pressure on the Tachens; and on January 18, 1955, PRC forces, with air support, launched an amphibious attack against Yikiangshan, an islet of less than half a square mile, only eight miles from the Tachens. On January 20 the Communist forces captured the island, having suffered heavy casualties in the process; all 720 Nationalist defenders fought to the last man and none of them either surrendered to or was captured by the enemy.

It was clear at that time that the next target of the communist forces would be the Tachen Islands. In view of the gravity of the situation, President Eisenhower sent a message to Congress on January 24 saying that "Formosa and the Pescadores should not fall into the control of aggressive Communist forces" and asked for a congressional resolution authorizing the president to employ U.S. armed forces promptly and effectively for this purpose. The message also spoke of "taking into account closely related localities and actions" that might determine the failure or success of an attack on Formosa and the Pescadores.[85] On January 29, 1955, a congressional resolution to that effect (see Document 11) was adopted and promptly signed by President Eisenhower.

In order to avoid a major PRC-ROC armed conflict that might involve American forces in the defense of the Tachen Islands, the United States advised the ROC government to evacuate their forces, utilizing American assistance and convoy protection. the ROC government reluctantly accepted the advice, and all 15,000 troops and 17,132 civilians were evacuated to Taiwan in early February. Shortly after this evacuation the ROC government also evacuated its troops and civilians from Nanchi Island.[86] The redeployment left Quemoy and Matsu as the only two island groups off the mainland of China in the hands of the ROC.

The Mutual Defense Treaty was sent to the U.S. Senate for advice and consent on January 6, 1955. The Senate Foreign Relations Committee submitted its report on the treaty on February 8. Three understandings were made part of the committee report but not the resolution of consent. One of them concerns the status of Taiwan, which reads as follows: "It is the understanding of the Senate that nothing in the treaty shall be construed as affecting or modifying the legal status or sovereignty of the territories to which it applies." The committee's report urged the Senate to give its advice and consent to the ratification of this treaty (see Document 12). On February 9 the Senate, by a vote of 64 to 6, approved the treaty. On March 3, 1955, instruments of ratification were exchanged at Taipei between ROC Foreign Minister George K. C. Yeh and U.S. Secretary of State Dulles. On March 15, 1955, after his visit to Taiwan in early March, Dulles said in a press conference that the president of the United States presumably would order U.S. air and sea forces into action if there were an attack on the offshore islands that was a part of the larger assault on Taiwan, and that his recent discussions with President Chiang Kai-shek had taken account of the possibility that the United States might have to help defend these islands.[87] Faced with the strong stand of the United States, the PRC quietly dropped its desultory shelling of Matsu and Quemoy in late March.

THE INTERNATIONAL LEGAL STATUS OF TAIWAN

Because neither the San Francisco Japanese Peace Treaty nor the Sino-Japanese Peace Treaty explicitly provides for the return of Taiwan to China, the question of the legal status of Taiwan has become a complex and controversial issue among some scholars and several countries. This section attempts to make a concise analysis of this question.

The U.S. position on the status of Taiwan is, as stated by the late Secretary of State Dulles in a press conference held on December 1, 1954, "that technical sovereignty over Formosa and the Pescadores has never been settled" and that "the future title is not determined by the Japanese peace treaty, nor is it determined by the peace treaty which was concluded between the Republic of China and Japan."[88] On the other hand, the United States also recognizes that the ROC "effectively controls" Taiwan and the Pescadores.[89] In the 1954 U.S.-ROC Mutual Defense Treaty, Article 4 provides: "For the purposes of Articles 2 and 4, the terms 'territorial' and 'territories' shall mean in respect of the Republic of China, Taiwan and the Pescadores. . . ." Despite the inclusion of this provision in the treaty, the U.S. side denied that Article 4 constituted a recognition of the ROC's sovereignty over Taiwan. In his testimony before the Senate Foreign Relations Committee in connection with this treaty, Secretary of State Dulles said:

The question of the title [over Taiwan] is dependent upon developing facts. I do not deny the fact that this treaty is another of the successive events which may tend somewhat to strengthen the position of the Republic of China in relation to this area. *But certainly the United States has not the power alone by this treaty to convey title, because title is not in the United States. Nor does it purport to do so.*

Therefore, in my opinion the status of the Republic of China in relation to Formosa [Taiwan] is for all practical purposes unchanged and unaltered by this treaty.[90] (Emphasis added.)

The British government has taken a similar view. Thus, on February 4, 1955, British Secretary of State for Foreign Affairs Eden said in the House of Commons:

Under the Peace Treaty of April 1952, Japan formally renounced all right, title and claim to Formosa and the Pescadores; but again this did not operate as a transfer to Chinese sovereignty, whether to the People's Republic of China or to the Chinese Nationalist authorities. Formosa and the Pescadores are therefore, in the view of Her Majesty's Government, territory, the de jure sovereignty over which is uncertain or undetermined.[91]

The Anglo-American position appears to suggest that China could acquire de jure sovereignty over Taiwan only through provision on cession in a peace treaty. From the viewpoint of international law, such an assertion is questionable. For instance, in Lauterpacht's edition of Oppenheim it is stated:

Unless the parties stipulate otherwise, the effect of a treaty of peace is that conditions remain as at the conclusion of peace. . . . Thus . . . if nothing is stipulated regarding conquered territory, it remains in the hands of the possessor, who may annex it. But it is nowadays usual, *although not at all legally necessary*, for a conqueror desirous of retaining conquered territory to secure its cession in the treaty of peace.[92] (Emphasis added.)

The above rule is generally referred to as the principle of *uti possidetis* (as you possess, you shall continue to possess).

In 1912 Italy acquired Tripoli and Cyrenaica from Turkey without going through a formal treaty of cession. On October 15, 1912, three days before the signing of the formal peacy treaty, Turkey and Italy signed a protocol in which Turkey agreed to grant complete autonomy to these territories and thereby renounced sovereignty over them. The peace treaty, signed on October 18, did not provide for the transfer of these territories to Italy; but after the conclusion of the peace treaty, Italy announced their annexation.[93] No one raised any question about the legality of the Italian title to these territories.[94]

Consequently, the lack of explicit provisions on the transfer of Taiwan to China in the two peace treaties does not necessarily mean that China could not acquire de jure sovereignty over Taiwan. Some Western scholars of international law have expressed a similar view. For instance, D. P. O'Connell of Australia has said that after the Japanese renunciation of the island, it is "doubtful . . . whether there is any international doctrine opposed to the conclusion that [the Republic of] China appropriated the *terra derelicta* of Formosa by converting belligerent occupation into definite sovereignty."[95]

Similarly, F. P. Morello of the United States has argued that the ROC could acquire de jure sovereignty over Taiwan through prescription:

> Except for the claims of Red China, it can be said that the occupation of Formosa by the Nationalist [ROC] government has been undisturbed. In addition, this de facto exercise of governmental authority has been continuous for nineteen years [up to 1966]. The possession of Formosa by the Nationalist Government has been steadily maintained by an assertion of right. It follows that if the principle of prescription, as interpreted and applied within the framework of international law, is to be accepted in the case of China, then there can be no lawyer's doubts as to the legitimacy of Nationalist China's title to Formosa.[96]

An American authority on international law, Arthur Dean, has also commented on the question of the legal status of Taiwan:

> If Japan in its Treaty of Peace had formally ceded Formosa and the Pescadores to the Republic of China, the legal situation would have been clear. Since this was not done and since Japan renounced all right, title and claim to Formosa and the Pescadores, it is not clear just what would constitute a formal cession of title to the Republic of China. Perhaps an agreement with Japan would still be required. . . . It may well be, however, that from the standpoint of customary international law, at least, no cession is required. Nationalist China may have already acquired legal title to Formosa and the Pescadores by occupation or possibly by subjugation.
>
> As pointed out in 1933 by the Permanent Court of International Justice in the *Legal Status of Eastern Greenland Case*, acquisition of title by occupation involves "the intention and will to act as sovereign and some actual exercise or display of such authority." The occupation in order to vest title must be an effective occupation. . . . On the facts as I know them, Nationalist China has certainly satisfied the requirement of effective control, and such of its governmental acts as are known to me, as, for example, making

Formosa a Province of China, clearly indicate an intention and will to act as a sovereign.

Until the coming into force of the Japanese Peace Treaty on April 28, 1952, there was a formal obstacle to Nationalist China's acquiring legal title to Formosa by occupation in that technical sovereignty over Formosa and the Pescadores remained in Japan. They were, accordingly, not *terrae nullius* capable of being acquired by occupation. However, when Japan renounced all right, title and claim to Formosa and the Pescadores this obstacle was removed, unless the Peace Treaty is regarded as not merely divesting Japan's title but, in addition, also vesting in the signatories, or possibly [although I have not seen an adequate legal justification for this theory . . .] in the United Nations, the title, or at least the right to cede the title, to Formosa and the Pescadores. I suppose a case could also be made for Nationalist China's acquisition of title to Formosa through subjugation. Certainly there has been a conquest, but whether or not Nationalist China has turned the conquest into subjugation through formal annexation is not clear. Moreover, possibly on this theory Nationalist China did not have a legal right to annex Formosa without the acquiescence of the other states which participated in the conquest.[97]

It must be pointed out that to say the San Francisco Peace Treaty has vested the sovereignty of Taiwan and the Pescadores in its signatories is at least unreal, because the treaty itself does not say so; furthermore, none of the signatories has ever claimed to exercise a condominium over Taiwan. Similarly, the theory that sovereignty over Taiwan was vested in the United Nations as a result of the San Francisco Peace Treaty is equally unreal. So far no member of the United Nations has formally made such a claim, nor does the United Nations actually exercise any sovereignty over Taiwan. Therefore, so far as the ROC is concerned, it may reasonably be argued that Taiwan has been incorporated into its territory in accordance with the principle of occupation in international law.

The question raised by Dean—whether the ROC could conquer Taiwan without the acquiescence of the other World War II allies—might be problematical if there were no past international agreements and if Taiwan had never been a part of China, but it is universally known that Taiwan was a part of China before it was ceded to Japan in 1895. Moreover, the Cairo Declaration of 1943 explicitly stated that Taiwan "shall be restored to the Republic of China." The terms of this declaration were incorporated in the 1945 Potsdam Proclamation and accepted by Japan in its instrument of surrender. There is no doubt that the Japanese instrument of surrender is an international agreement binding upon all signatories.[98] Therefore, all the allies who signed the instrument of surrender are legally bound to accept the ROC claim to Taiwan and are not legally entitled to challenge the ROC conquest of Taiwan.

In any case, there appears to be strong legal ground to support the view that since the entry into force of the 1952 ROC-Japan bilateral peace treaty, Taiwan has become the de jure territory of the ROC. This interpretation of the legal status of Taiwan is confirmed by several Japanese court decisions. For instance, in the case of *Japan v. Lai Chin Jung*, decided by the Tokyo High Court on December 24, 1956, it was stated that "Formosa and the Pescadores came to belong to the Republic of China, at any rate on August 5, 1952, when the [Peace] Treaty between Japan and the Republic of China came into force. . . ."[99]

While the principles of international law stated above support the ROC's claim to Taiwan, the same reasoning would not support the PRC's claim to Taiwan for several reasons.

The PRC cannot invoke the 1952 ROC-Japanese Peace Treaty to support its claim that Taiwan is a part of China because the PRC denies the right of the ROC government to conclude any treaty in the name of China after October 1, 1949, the date of the establishment of the Central People's Government of the People's Republic of China. Similarly, as stated before, the PRC has categorically rejected the validity of the San Francisco Peace Treaty and therefore cannot invoke this treaty to its advantage.[100] Moreover, the principles of prescription and occupation that may justify the ROC's claim to Taiwan certainly are not applicable to the PRC because the application of these two principles to the Taiwan situation presupposes the validity of the two peace treaties by which Japan renounced its claim to Taiwan and thus makes the island *terra nullius*.[101]

Moreover, even assuming the Japanese renunciation of its claim to Taiwan in the two peace treaties was in the nature of an unilateral act, which does not need the recognition of the PRC, the PRC still could not acquire title over Taiwan through the international law principle of occupation or prescription because it had no physical control over the island. Nor could the PRC act through the ROC occupation to claim title over Taiwan because the PRC considers the ROC an "illegal group" or even "bandits." Clearly, the PRC can no more claim benefits through a group it does not recognize as legal than it can through a document it has declared illegal and void.

In view of the above-stated arguments, the PRC government and its writers have made various other arguments to support the PRC claim to Taiwan. Their main line of argument is that because Taiwan was originally Chinese territory, therefore a peace treaty to transfer the title back to China was not necessary. For instance, Shao Chin-fu wrote:

> After the Sino-Japanese War of 1894 the government of the Ching dynasty by signing the Treaty of Shimonoseki ceded Taiwan and P'eng-hu to Japan. With the outbreak of China's War of Resistance Against Japan in 1937, in accordance with international law, the treaties between the two countries became null and void. The Treaty of Shimonoseki was no exception. In 1945 after China's victory in the Anti-Japanese War, China recovered these two places from Japan.

No question has ever been raised about the legal status of Taiwan. Since Taiwan has always been Chinese territory, it is a matter of course for China to take it back like a thing restored to its original owner. It is not a case of China taking a new territory from Japan which must be affirmed by a peace treaty. Particularly since the United States and Britain signed the Cairo Declaration which clearly recognized that Taiwan and the P'eng-hu Islands are "territories Japan has stolen from the Chinese," and "shall be restored" to China, they are still less in a position to raise the so-called question of the legal status of Taiwan.[102]

International practice, however, does not support Shao's view. For instance, the provinces of Alsace and Lorraine were originally French territory but were ceded to Germany in 1871. Subsequently they were returned to France only through the Treaty of Versailles signed between the Allied and Associate Powers (including France) and Germany on June 28, 1919.[103] In other words, although France occupied the two provinces soon after the signing of the Armistice Agreement on November 11, 1918,[104] French sovereignty over its former territory did not automatically revert, but required the formal treaty mechanism. There does not appear to be any precedent or principle of international law supporting the PRC's position, as expressed by Shao Chin-fu, that on October 25, 1945, Taiwan's sovereignty was restored to China de jure and de facto.

Another PRC writer, Mei Ju-ao, argued that China had recovered its sovereign rights over Taiwan as a result of its abrogation of the Sino-Japanese treaties in its declaration of war against Japan issued on December 9, 1941. He wrote:

Simultaneously with its formal proclamation of war on Japan on December 9, 1941, China solemnly declared the abrogation of all treaties between China and Japan. Since the Shimonoseki Treaty, on the basis of which Japan occupied Taiwan, was among the treaties abrogated, Japan's rule over Taiwan naturally became groundless from that day. It is true that Taiwan was in fact under Japan's occupation during the war against Japan. But legally speaking, China has every right to consider that it had recovered its sovereign rights over Taiwan as from that day. . . . Taiwan has always been China's territory. It had been stolen by Japan for 50 years. Following the termination of the Second World War, China exercised the right conferred on it by international law as a nation victorious over Japan. On the basis of the proclamation it issued on December 9, 1941, China recovered Taiwan on October 25, 1945. This action by China is perfectly lawful. It is consistent with the terms of the Cairo Declatation and Potsdam Proclamation and Japan's instrument of surrender.[105]

Again, this argument can hardly find any support in the theory and practice of international law. For instance, in the renowned Lauterpacht-Oppenheim it is said: "Political and other treaties concluded for the purpose of setting up a permanent condition of things . . . are not *ipso facto* annulled by the outbreak of war; but nothing prevents the victorious party from imposing by the treaty of peace alteration in, or even the dissolution of such treaties."[106]

Based on the above analysis, it appears that the PRC's claim to Taiwan is primarily based on the theory of historical irredentism. PRC writers and officials have frequently argued that Taiwan was historically Chinese and that during the Japanese occupation (1895-1945) the people of Taiwan longed for a reunification with China. While this historical fact is true, it can hardly support the PRC's claim to Taiwan today for several reasons.

In the first place, during the period of Japanese occupation, China was run by the ROC government, which permitted free enterprise and a relatively free society. If the people of Taiwan knew at that time that China would become the totalitarian and highly regimented society it is today, it is unlikely that they would have longed for a unification. The fact that very few people from Taiwan participated in the Communist movement in China during the Japanese occupation period seems to support this point. And today it is self-evident that the people of Taiwan do not want to be united with the PRC.

Second, according to Edgar Snow, a close friend of Mao Tse-tung, in an interview with Mao at Yenan on July 16, 1936, Mao did not include Taiwan in China's "lost territories" to be regained from Japan. Mao said: "If the Koreans wish to break away from the chains of Japanese imperialism, we will extend them our enthusiastic help in their struggle for independence. The same thing applies for Formosa. . . ."[107] Therefore, the PRC's historical claim to Taiwan is not well-founded even in accordance with its leader's view.

Third, the principle of self-determination is now an accepted principle of international law and one that has not been opposed by the PRC. This principle would certainly overrule any historical claim of the PRC toward Taiwan, since the great majority of the people of Taiwan now oppose unification withs the PRC.

THE U.S.-PRC GENEVA TALKS AND THE SECOND TAIWAN STRAIT CRISIS OF 1958

In April 1955, Premier Chou En-lai led the PRC delegation to attend the Bandung Conference. His first speech, delivered on April 19, referred to "the tension created solely by the United States in the area of Taiwan" and showed little sign of a desire to compromise. However, after extensive discussions, he dramatically expressed a more conciliatory attitude at a luncheon given by the prime minister of Ceylon on April 23. He announced:

> The Chinese people are friendly to the American people. The Chinese people do not want to have a war with the United States of America. The Chinese Government is willing to sit down and enter into negotiations with the United States Government to discuss the

question of relaxing tension in the Far East and especially the question of relaxing tension in the Taiwan area.[108]

This offer was reiterated in Chou En-lai's final speech at the concluding session of the Bandung Conference, held the following day.[109]

The initial U.S. response was negative, but the PRC continued to keep its offer open and to advocate the "peaceful liberation" of Taiwan.[110] In a report to the Standing Committee of the PRC's National People's Congress on May 17, Chou En-lai renewed his offer and went on to state that the PRC was "willing to strive for the liberation of Taiwan by peaceful means so far as it is possible."[111] But he reiterated the PRC's claim to Taiwan by saying that "no negotiations should in the slightest degree affect the Chinese people's exercise of their own sovereign rights, their just demand and action, to liberate Taiwan."[112]

Subsequently, through the efforts of the United Kingdom and India, the United States and the PRC issued a communique on July 25, 1955, indicating their agreement to hold ambassadorial talks beginning on August 1, at Geneva.[113] The PRC-U.S. communique did not say that the talks would cover the Taiwan question, but this item may have been included in the "other practical matters now at issue" that were referred to in the comminique.[114] At a press conference held on July 26, 1955, Secretary of State Dulles said that the United States hoped "to find out in the forthcoming talks whether the Chinese Communists accept the concept of a cease-fire in accordance with the United Nations principle of avoiding any use or threat of force which could disturb the peace of nations."

The PRC also explained its position on Taiwan before the opening of the ambassadorial talks. In a long report entitled "The Present International Situation and China's Policy," Premier Chou En-lai told the National People's Congress on July 30, 1955, that the tension in the Taiwan area was "caused by the United States occupation of China's territory of Taiwan and its interference with the liberation of China's coastal island" and that "this is an international issue between China and the United States." The "liberation of Taiwan, however, "is a matter of China's internal affairs." Therefore, "these two questions cannot be mixed up" and only the first question could be subject to Sino-American negotiation.

Chou went on to say that there were two possible ways for the Chinese people to "liberate" Taiwan—by war or by peaceful means—and that the Chinese people were ready to use the latter. He also offered to negotiate "with the responsible local authorities of Taiwan to map out concrete steps for Taiwan's peaceful liberation." But he pointed out that "these would be negotiations between the central government and local authorities" and that "the Chinese people are firmly opposed to any ideas or plots of the so-called two Chinas."[115]

After making an "agreed announcement" on the return of civilians on September 10, 1955,[116] the United States and the PRC entered into negotiations on the Taiwan question in October. The United States proposed that both parties agree to renounce the use of force in the pursuit of their objectives in general and, more specifically, in the Taiwan area. The PRC did not object to the pledge as far as relations between the two countries were concerned. However, it emphasized that this pledge should not be confused with domestic tensions; the status of Taiwan was a domestic matter that the PRC would strive to settle by peaceful means if possible. It made clear that "this internal affair of China's cannot possibly be a subject of the Sino-American talks" and refused to include the nonuse of force in the Taiwan area in any declaration on nonuse of force.[117] Therefore, after prolonged negotiations on the different drafts proposed by each party, it was clear by mid-1956 that no agreement could be reached on this question.[118]

Meanwhile, the PRC had launched a peace offensive to "liberate" Taiwan. Soon after Chou En-lai's July 30, 1955, speech, a letter-writing campaign was launched. Many letters calling for the "peaceful liberation of Taiwan" were sent to the ROC leaders on Taiwan by their relatives, friends, former subordinates, teachers, and students on the mainland through radio broadcasts, newspapers, and other means.[119] On June 28, 1956, Chou En-lai issued a formal appeal to the ROC leaders for "peaceful liberation" in his report to the National People's Congress.[120]

The ROC immediately rejected Chou En-lai's offer. A government spokesman called it "an insulting gesture" because of "what needs liberation" is not Taiwan but the mainland. He regarded the "peace offensive" an an attempt to "bewitch the people of the Free World, wreck the unity among the free countries and isolate the United States."[121] On October 4, 1957, President Chiang Kai-shek told Sven Steenberg of West Germany that the ROC governmet "has already had too many painful experience in negotiating with Communists"; and he reaffirmed the ROC's rejection of the Communist "peace proposal" and the ROC's determination to restore the freedom of the Chinese on the mainland.[122]

In early 1958 the PRC had accused the United States of promoting "two Chinas" or other international solutions (such as a plebiscite or UN trusteeship) to the Taiwan question.[123] In April and June of the same year, the PRC criticized the U.S. attitude toward the ambassadorial talks in Geneva. In its June 30 statement on the talks, the PRC announced that unles they were resumed within 15 days, it could not "but consider that the United States" had "decided to break up the talks." The statement carried a threat to the effect that "the Chinese people are perfectly strong enough to liberate their territory Taiwan." It also denounced the U.S. effort to promote the situation of "two Chinas."[124]

After the period of the PRC's "utlimatum" had expired (it was extended for a few days on July 15), the United States on July 28 informed the PRC of its willingness to continue the talks at Warsaw instead of Geneva. There was no PRC response until September 6. Khrushchev and Mao Tse-tung held a secret meeting in Peking from July 31 to August 3, but they said nothing in their communique about Taiwan.[125] Around this time the PRC began a radio and press campaign for "liberating Taiwan." The PRC military movements and other preparations that were evident along the Chinese coast alarmed the ROC government, and a state of emergency was proclaimed in the offshore islands and the Taiwan Strait. On August 11 the United States released a memorandum on nonrecognition of the PRC that had been sent to all U.S. missions abroad. The memorandum, explaining several reasons for nonrecognition of the PRC, said "communism's rule in China is not permanent and that it one day will pass," and rejected the "two Chinas" solution. The PRC immediately denounced the memorandum as "shopworn" and the "occupation" of Taiwan as daydreaming on the part of those who were unaware of their own "impotence," for China had the "determination and strength" to liberate Taiwan.[126] At the same time, a Soviet broadcast in Chinese assured the PRC that it was not isolated in the world but had the support of the Soviet Union and other Communist countries.[127]

During this period it was clear that the PRC was attempting to resort to force to solve the Taiwan question; therefore President Eisenhower and his advisers were considering issuing a strong statement on U.S. intention before any actual attack could be made by the PRC. However, the warning was not issued until August 23, when the PRC started the second Taiwan Strait crisis.[128]

On August 23, 1958, the PRC suddenly began a massive artillery bombardment of Quemoy in which, from 6:30 to 8:30 P.M., Communist batteries rained 42,000 rounds of high explosives on the island. The PRC air and navy forces soon joined the action. PRC radios beamed broadcasts directly to the people on Quemoy, warning them of imminent landings of the "Liberation Army," demanding surrender of the defenders, and appealing for defectors. The PRC continued to bombard the island for several weeks and hoped to lay a successful siege so as to force its surrender. However, the ROC defenders stood firm and fought back. The United States gave the ROC force some limited logistic support by escorting the ROC supply ships to the three-mile limit off Quemoy. But the more significant U.S. reaction was President Eisenhower's statement on August 27, saying that the offshore islands were more important to the defense of Taiwan than they had been in the Taiwan Strait crisis of 1955, because there was now a "closer interlocking" between the defense system of the islands and Taiwan.[129]

On September 4 the PRC declared it was extending its territorial waters to 12 miles, thus including all offshore islands within its territorial waters.[130] The United States refused to recognize this extension, saying it was an "attempt to cloak aggressive purposes." On September 7 the U.S. navy continued to escort ROC supply ships to three miles from Quemoy.[131]

On the same day that the PRC extended its territorial waters, U.S. Secretary of State Dulles called on the PRC to negotiate and implied that the United States would not avoid resort to force in the Taiwan Strait if compelled to use force (see Document 13). Two days later Chou En-lai replied, reaffirming the PRC's claim to Taiwan but expressing willingness to resume the ambassadorial talks with the United States. The next day Soviet Premier Khrushchev sent a letter to President Eisenhower supporting the PRC's claim to Taiwan[132] On September 15 the ambassadorial talks were resumed at Warsaw.

During the crisis the tone of the ROC leaders was very conciliatory. On September 15, 1958, President Chiang emphasized in his answer to questions submitted by the New York *Journal-American* that the Communists' shelling and encircling was "in actuality a prelude to an invasion of Taiwan." On September 29 President Chiang told a group of reporters that Quemoy and Matsu "do not constitute an obstacle to peace" and that every time it was the Communists who started the hostilities in the offshore islands. He said that the bases of the ROC's counterattack "are not on Quemoy and Matsu" but "are on the mainland itself." He also warned that if the Communists "should continue to bomb these islands in an attempt to re-blockade them," the ROC "shall . . . take retaliatory actions against Communist bases on the mainland."[133]

The PRC continued to bomb Quemoy. From August 23 to October 4 the PRC fired a total of 444,433 rounds on Quemoy. The United States supplied some new weapons to the ROC, including eight-inch howitzers capable of firing tactical atomic shells and air-to-air "Sidewinder" missiles. The ROC air force also won several battles and shot down 31 Communist planes. On October 5 the PRC unilaterally announced a cease-fire and offered to conduct direct peace talks with the ROC government. On October 20, on the eve of U.S. Secretary of State Dulles' visit to Taipei, the PRC fired on Quemoy again. On October 23, the United States and the ROC issued a joint communique in which the ROC, while affirming that "the restoration of freedom to its people on the mainland is its sacred mission," nevertheless recognized that "the principal means of successfully achieving its mission is the implementation of Dr. Sun Yat-sen's three people's principles and not the use of force" (see Document 15). The communique reaffirmed U.S. support of the ROC to resist PRC aggression.

Facing the determined effort of the United States and the ROC to resist the PRC's military action, the PRC apparently had to drop its attempt to "liberate Taiwan" by force and began to indicate that this goal was a long-term one. Earlier, in mid-September 1958, after the United States determined to intervene in the Taiwan Strait crisis, Peking Radio said that the PRC would be ready to wait "five to ten years" to settle the problem of Taiwan.[134] Then, on October 13 PRC Defense Minister P'eng Teh-huai said that he would not be surprised if the civil war, which started in 1928, between the Nationalists and the Communists continued for another "thirty years"; and he rejected any American interference in that civil war.[135] Finally, on October 25 Defense Minister P'eng announced an "even-day" cease-fire, that is, the PRC refrained from shelling Quemoy on even-numbered days (see Document 16). This has been the military situation in the Taiwan Strait up to the present.

At Warsaw the United States and the PRC representatives held ten talks on Taiwan. But before the tenth meeting on November 7, PRC Vice-Premier and Foreign Minister Ch'en Yi told Gordon Clark of the Montreal *Star* that the PRC would not guarantee anyone the renunciation of force regarding Taiwan. Certainly realizing the United States intended to separate the question of the off-shore islands and the question of Taiwan, Ch'en Yi pointed out: "Quemoy, Matsu, Taiwan and the Pescadores must be liberated as a whole. We will not allow the handing over of Quemoy in exchange for placing Taiwan under trusteeship. . . . Nor can we accept demilitarization or referring the matter to the UN or the International Court of Justice."[136] Thus, in November 1958, while the military crisis subsided, the question of Taiwan remained unsolved in PRC-U.S. relations.[137] The PRC apparently, however, dropped its attempt to seize Taiwan by force for an indefinite period. It was reported that Mao Tse-tung said in an interview held in 1959 that "[the Chinese territory] is spacious, and for the time being we can get along without these islands [Taiwan and the offshore islands] " (see Document 18).

THE THIRD TAIWAN STRAIT CRISIS AND THE PERIOD OF STALEMATE IN U.S.-PRC RELATIONS, 1962-71

After the Second Taiwan Strait Crisis was over, the United States tried to change its strategy at the Warsaw Talks with the PRC, attempting to bypass the Taiwan issue and to discuss other matters of mutual interest. However, the PRC responded by tying every subject under discussion to the question of Taiwan. For instance, when the United States proposed the exchange of correspondents between the two countries, the PRC insisted on including a clause on "the question of withdrawal of all U.S. armed forces from China's territory Taiwan" in the proposed agreement, that was unacceptable to the United States.[138] On September 5, 1960, Premier Chou En-lai told British correspondent Felix Greene that "so long as the United States continues to occupy Taiwan, there can be no basic improvement in the relations between the United States and China."[139] Three days later a *People's Daily* editorial entitled "100 Meetings of Sino-U.S. Talks" blamed the United States for failure to reach an agreement with the PRC on the question of Taiwan at the talks.[140] The editorial reiterated the PRC position on Taiwan and denounced the alleged American attempt to create "two Chinas."

On many occasions the PRC manifested its determination to "liberate" Taiwan and reasserted its claim to the island. For instance, on July 17 and 19, 1960, the PRC conducted an "armed demonstration" by bombing Quemoy to protest President Eisenhower's visit to the ROC.[141] On February 1, 1962, an enlarged celebration of the 300th anniversary of the recovery of Taiwan by Cheng Ch'en-kung (the Chinese general who drove the Dutch from Taiwan in 1662) was held in Peking.[142]

In late 1958 the PRC began to launch the Great Leap Forward Movement for "Socialist Reconstruction" and to establish the People's Commune that later proved to be an economic disaster. In 1961-62 food shortages and unrest were acute in many parts of the mainland. Moreover, in the first half of 1962 there were numerous natural calamities, such as drought, flood, and pestilence, in many provinces of the mainland. In May 1962 some 100,000 refugees from southern China flooded into Hong Kong, although a substantial number of them were soon rounded up and turned back to the mainland.[143] Internationally, the PRC was preoccupied with tensions along its border with the Soviet Union and India and increased American military involvement in Vietnam.[144]

During this period the ROC obviously saw an opportunity to "recover" the mainland. In President Chiang Kai-shek's New Year's Day message to the Chinese people for 1962, he declared:

> Our armed forces have made adequate preparations for the counter-offensive, and, therefore, are capable of moving into action at any time. Have no fear of being alone in rising against the Communists. Have no fear of lack or shortage of supplies or help. Both will be forthcoming once you take action.[145]

Then additional manpower was conscripted into the ROC armed forces, and a provisional national defense special assessment was imposed for the period May 1, 1962, to June 30, 1963.[146] In the early months of 1962, several high American officials, including Averell Harriman and Allen Dulles, visited Taiwan. Their purpose was presumably to discourage the Nationalist eagerness for an invasion of the mainland, but the PRC might have believed just the opposite. The same applies to the appointment in May of a new American ambassador to the ROC, Admiral Alan G. Kirk, who had had extensive experience with amphibious operations during World War II.[147]

As a result, during June 1962 the PRC heavily reinforced its forces opposite Taiwan.[148] On June 23 the PRC official news agency maintained that "the Chiang Kai-shek [clique] . . . with the support and encouragement of U.S. imperialism, is prepared for . . . an invasion of the coastal areas of the mainland."[149] It said the Americans wanted "to kill two birds with one stone." If Chiang's invasion succeeded, it would "deal a blow to the prestige" of the PRC. On the other hand, if it failed, then his strength would be greatly weakened, thus facilitating the American imperialists' "kicking him out" and using a new puppet to take over Taiwan. On the same day, at a special meeting in Warsaw, American Ambassador to Poland John Moors Cabot reportedly informed PRC Ambassador Wang that the United States would not support the Nationalists' attempt to invade the mainland.[150] This American position was reaffirmed by President Kennedy in his press conference held on June 27. He stressed the defensive character of the American commitment to the ROC, but he also strongly reaffirmed his predecessor's statements that the United States would defend Taiwan and the offshore islands if necessary.[151] After the United States made known its position for not supporting the ROC invasion of the mainland, the Soviet Union announced its support of the PRC. On July 2 Soviet Premier Khrushchev said that "any one who dares to attack the People's Republic of China will meet a crushing rebuff from the great Chinese people and the people of the Soviet Union and the whole socialist camp."[152] A few days later PRC Vice-Premier and Foreign

Minister Ch'en Yi expressed the PRC's gratitude for Soviet support but again held the United States responsible for any possible invasion of the mainland "on a big scale or a small scale."[153]

After the American reaffirmation of the defensive character of its commitment to the ROC, the possibility of a military confrontation in the Taiwan Strait gradually abated, though the ROC did launch several commando raids against the mainland coast in late 1962 and early 1963.[154] The Third Taiwan Strait Crisis was over.

Since 1963 the Taiwan Strait has been relatively quiet, and the so-called even-day cease-fire in the Quemoy islands, which was initiated by the PRC in late October 1958, has been tacitly observed by both sides. The United States, while affirming and reaffirming its commitment to the defense of Taiwan, has, since the 1958 ROC-U.S. Joint Communique (see Document 15), shifted to a de facto "two Chinas" policy. Thus when Secretary of State Rusk told a BBC representative on March 3, 1961, that the Chinese Nationalist leaders "were to us and are a much more genuine representation of the China that we have known," he made it clear that he was "talking in this context about the great cultural heritage of China," thus dissipating the possible implication of the U.S. recognition of the ROC government as the only legal government of China.[155] Similarly, the joint communique issued on August 2, 1961, at the conclusion of ROC Vice-President Ch'en Cheng's visit to the United States, while reiterating U.S. support of the ROC government, failed to support the ROC's claim to be the only legal government of China.[156]

To the PRC, the failure to take Taiwan by force compelled it to take a long-range political approach to the Taiwan question; this approach necessitates keeping the issue of sovereignty over Taiwan alive. Otherwise, a de facto status quo could gradually crystallize into a de jure situation, undermining the PRC's ultimate goal of "liberating" Taiwan. Therefore, despite the impasse on the question of Taiwan at the Warsaw talks, the PRC continued the talks as a channel of communication with the United States.[157] At times Peking makes overtures to the ROC leaders, and rumors of Peking-Taipei peace negotiations occasionally appear in the press.[158] The PRC loses no opportunity to announce its determination to "liberate" Taiwan. In international affairs the PRC refuses to participate in any international organization or conference, governmental or nongovernmental, when a delegation from the ROC or Taiwan is also present.[159]

On January 27, 1964, the PRC announced the establishment of diplomatic relations with France and agreed to exchange ambassadors within three months.[160] This time the ROC, perhaps at the suggestion of the United States, did not follow its usual practice of breaking diplomatic relations with any state recognizing the PRC, though it did make a strong protest to the French government.[161] As France also made no move to initiate such a break, the PRC's Foreign Ministry issued a statement on January 28 reminding France that the "government of the People's Republic of China" was the "sole legal government representing all the Chinese people," that "recognition of the new government of a country naturally implies ceasing to recognize the old ruling group over-thrown by the people of that country," and that "the Chinese Government deems it necessary to reaffirm that Taiwan is part of China's territory and that any attempt to detach Taiwan from China or otherwise to create 'two Chinas' is absolutely unacceptable to the Chinese Government and people."[162] This state-ment put France in a difficult position, since, prior to its recognition of the PRC, it had hoped to make an arrangement whereby it could recognize "two Chinas."[163] Perhaps under the pressure of the PRC, French President de Gaulle said in a statement on February 10 that France recognized only one China.[164] On the same day the ROC severed relations with France.[165]

On October 16, 1964, the PRC announced its first successful test of a nuclear device.[166] But no pronouncement on the "liberation of Taiwan" was made in connection with this event. This attitude was understandable, since the use of nuclear weapons to attack Taiwan would certainly contradict the alleged purpose of the PRC's "liberation" of Taiwan: to "save" the inhabitants of Taiwan from the "yoke" of "the Chiang Kai-shek clique" and "American imperialism."

After the end of the Third Taiwan Strait Crisis in 1962, the United States gradually began to reconsider its China policy and made efforts to test the PRC's willingness to accept a "two Chinas" solution of the Taiwan problem. On December 13, 1963, U.S. Assistant Secretary of State for Far Eastern Affairs Roger W. Hilsman delivered a lengthy speech on China policy. In this speech he clearly pointed out that the United States would "fully honor our close and friendly ties with the people of the Republic of China on Taiwan and with their Government" and that "so long as Peiping insists on the destruction of this rela-tionship as the *sine qua non* for any basic improvement in relations between our-selves and Communist China, there can be no prospect for such an improve-ment."[167] But he concluded his speech by sayin that "we pursue today toward Communist China a policy of the open door: We are determined to keep the door open to the possibility of change, not to slam it shut against any develop-ments which might advance our national good, serve the free world, and benefit the people of China."[168] This overture for improving relations with the PRC, together with other similar speeches made by Averell Harriman and Dean Rusk, was rejected by a *People's Daily* article on February 19, 1964, which insisted on American withdrawal from Taiwan and the Taiwan Strait as a precondition for improving relations.[169]

Similarly, after the PRC became a nuclear power in 1964 and following the 47 to 47 vote on the Chinese representation question in the 1965 UN General Assembly, there were growing pressures for the United States to change its China policy. Therefore, in March 1966 hearings on China policy were held by the Committee on Foreign Relations of the U.S. Senate. Many participants in the hearings favored shifting China policy to "containment without isolation." In this connection Professor A. Doak Barnett's statement is representative:

A shift of American policy on the United Nations issue—and, in fact, any significant change in our posture toward Peking—will inevitably require some modification of our policy toward the Nationalist regime on Taiwan. For many reasons—political, strategic, and moral—we should continue defending Taiwan against attack and should firmly support the principle of self-determination in regard to the 13 million inhabitants of the island. But we will not be able to continue sustaining the fiction that the Nationalist regime is the government of mainland China.

Our view of the Nationalist regime should be one in which we recognize it as the legal government of the territories it now occupies, essentially Taiwan and the Pescadores, rather than as the government of all China; this, one might note, is essentially the position which the Japanese Government already maintains in regard to the Nationalists. We should do all we can to obtain representation for the Taipei regime in the United Nations and to urge the international community to accept and support it as the government of its present population and territory. But we cannot indefinitely sustain the fiction that it is the government of all China.[170]

Officially Secretary of State Dean Rusk told the Subcommittee on the Far East and the Pacific of the House Committee on Foreign Affairs on March 16, 1966, that the United States "do[es] not seek to overthrow by force the Peiping regime" and announced ten main elements in American policy toward Communist China that repeated the U.S. treaty commitment to the ROC on Taiwan and the continued support of the ROC's representation in the United Nations, yet indicated a desire to improve relations with the PRC.[171]

While the Americans were engaged in a controversial debate on China policy, the PRC started the "Great Proletarian Cultural Revolution in the late spring of 1966 and did not show any interest in various suggestions made, in the course of the American debate, to improve PRC-U.S. relations. Thus on March 29, 1966, the PRC responded with an article in the *People's Daily* that again denounced the "American occupation of Taiwan" and rejected the American overture.[172] Furthermore, a *People's Daily* editorial of June 27, 1966, did not compromise on the Taiwan question.[173] Even at the height of the Cultural Revolution, the question of Taiwan was still being mentioned, though in very short but adamant terms. On October 1, 1968, the PRC's national day, Lin Piao, then Mao's heir-designate, said: "We definitely will liberate Taiwan and are ready at all times to wipe out all enemies who dare to invade us!" Chou En-lai said more simply: "We definitely will liberate Taiwan!"[174] The PRC also maintained its uncompromising position on the "two Chinas" situation. For instance, when the national emblem of the ROC appeared in a Soviet publication, the PRC protested strongly to the Soviet government.[175] On November 26, 1968, the PRC issued a statement on the Warsaw talks saying that "the Chinese Government will never barter away principles [that is, America must withdraw from Taiwan] ."[176]

Moreover, all available materials concerning the Cultural Revolution have indicated that the question of Taiwan, "two Chinas," or "one China, one Taiwan" has never been an issue among contending Communist leaders. As a matter of fact, the attitude of deposed leaders such as Liu Shao-ch'i and P'eng Chen toward this question was in no way different from that of other Communist leaders.

The Cultural Revolution created great turmoil on the mainland and seemingly presented another opportunity for the ROC to "recover" the mainland. But the ROC seemed to take a very cautious attitude. In his 1967 New Year's message President Chiang emphasized that the "counterattack" against the mainland must be political rather than military.[177] Perhaps to test the American response to the possibility of ROC action against the mainland, ROC Ambassador Chow Shu-kai told reporters on January 10, 1967, that because of the turmoil on the mainland, 1967 might be the decisive year for ROC recovery of the mainland.[178] But the U.S. response was immediate and negative. Department of State spokesman Robert J. MacCloskey, referring to the exchange of notes accompanying the 1954 Sino-American Defense Treaty (see Document 10), said that the ROC should not resort to offensive action against the mainland without prior consultation and agreement with the United States.[179] In May Vice-President Yen Chia-kan of the ROC was invited by President Johnson to visit the United States, but the joint statement issued by them on May 10 merely said: "They agreed that the struggle for power is far from over and that developments on the Chinese mainland are closely related to the peace and security of Asia. They further agreed to consult on future developments on the Chinese mainland."[180] Probably as a result of the unfavorable response from the American side, President Chiang specified in his 1967 National Day (October 10) message that the "counterattack" should be considered 70 percent political and 30 percent military.[181] Throughout the Cultural Revolution (1966–69) the ROC's attitude was cautious, and no military action was undertaken against the mainland. However, it did improve its international status significantly. In January 1966, 57 states maintained diplomatic relations with the ROC; by June 1968 it has increased to 64, while the PRC then had diplomatic relations with only 45 states. In the United Nations the resolution to expel the ROC and to seat the PRC was defeated in 1968 by a decisive vote of 58–44, with 23 abstentions.

In 1969 the Cultural Revolution began to subside, but the tension in PRC-Soviet relations increased, culminating in armed conflict in Chengpao (Damansky) Island in March 1969. The PRC also began to show concern over the alleged Soviet "counterrevolutionary collusion with the Chiang Kai-shek bandit gang."[182] It is amid that background that the PRC began to take active measures to end its international isolation. While the PRC still maintained its uncompromising attitude toward the question of Taiwan, it was willing to make a tactical retreat by not tying that question to the establishment of diplomatic relations with other countries. Thus, after negotiations with Canada on establishing diplomatic relations were deadlocked for more than a year because the

PRC insisted that Canada recognize PRC sovereignty over Taiwan,[183] the PRC finally agreed to drop the issue by agreeing to a formula under which Canada was required "to take note" of the PRC's position on Taiwan in the joint communique issued on October 13, 1970.[184] With respect to some countries, the PRC even showed flexibility by not including the Taiwan question in the communique announcing the establishment of diplomatic relations.

On the part of the United States, the Nixon administration, inaugurated in January 1969, undertook cautious steps to improve relations with the PRC. First, it withdrew the Seventh Fleet from periodic patrol in the Taiwan Strait.[185] Then certain trade and travel restrictions applied to those areas of China under the PRC control since the early 1950s were removed.[186] Furthermore, in 1970 the United States announced that it would not oppose the admission of the PRC to the United Nations if that admission were not at the expense of the ROC.[187]

In the meantime, President Nixon and other high administration officials made a series of statements beginning in early 1969 on the American desire to improve relations with the PRC.[188] The most significant was President Nixon's foreign policy message to Congress on February 25, 1971, in which he said:

> We are prepared to establish a dialogue with Peking. We cannot accept its ideological precepts, or the notion that Communist China must exercise hegemony over Asia. But neither do we wish to impose on China an international position that denies its legitimate national interests.

> The evolution of our dialogue with Peking cannot be at the expense of international order or our own commitments. Our attitude is public and clear. We will continue to honor our treaty commitments to the security of our Asian allies. An honorable relationship with Peking cannot be constructed at their expense. . . .

> In that connection, I wish to make it clear that the United States is prepared to see the People's Republic of China play a constructive role in the family of nations. The question of its place in the United Nations is not, however, merely a question of whether it should participate. It is also a question of whether Peking should be permitted to dictate to the world the terms of its participation. For a number of years attempts have been made to deprive the Republic of China of its place as a member of the United Nations and its Specialized Agencies. We have opposed these attempts. We will continue to oppose them.[189]

The PRC's official response for this Nixon overture was negative; an article in the authoritative *Peking Review* denounced Nixon for "still . . . engaging in his criminal 'two Chinas' plot."[190] Unexpectedly, in April the PRC's team agreed to participate in the 31st World Table Tennis Championships held at Nagoya, Japan. While there, the Chinese invited the American team to visit mainland

China and, as a result, started "Ping Pong Diplomacy."[191] The PRC also admitted several American reporters to mainland China. These gestures produced a widely favorable reaction in the United States and elsewhere. Nevertheless, there has not been the slightest hint that the PRC might make concessions to the United States on the question of Taiwan.[192] Thus, when the U.S. State Department said on April 28, 1971, that the legal status of Taiwan is undetermined (see Document 19), the PRC issued a categorical rejection.[193] The PRC also made it clear that no seat for the ROC or Taiwan in the United Nations would be tolerated.[194]

On July 15, 1971, after a secret visit by Secretary of State Kissinger to Peking, President Nixon suddenly announced that he had reached agreement with Premier Chou En-lai to visit the PRC at an appropriate date before May 1972 for the purpose of seeking "the normalization of relations between the two countries and also to exchange views on questions of concern to the two sides."[195] Many countries interpreted Nixon's move as one that would ultimately lead to the abandonment of the ROC by the United States; as a consequence, many countries shifted their recognition to the PRC. Then, in October 1971, amid the UN debates on the Chinese representation question, Secretary of State Kissinger again visited the PRC, presumably on a mission to arrange a forthcoming Nixon visit. However, many countries who apparently interpreted Kissinger's trip as an indication that the United States lacked interest in preserving a seat for the ROC at the United Nations shifted their attitude toward the Chinese representation question. On October 25, 1971, the ROC was compelled to announce its withdrawal from the United Nations a few minutes before the 26th session of the General Assembly passed the Albania-sponsored resolution to seat the PRC and to oust the ROC by a decisive vote of 76–35, with 17 abstentions.[196] On November 15, 1971, the PRC delegation took its place in the United Nations,[197] and the U.S. delegation joined other delegations in welcoming the PRC's participation at the United Nations. Thus the 21 years' stalemate in U.S.-PRC relations since the Korean War began to thaw.

FROM THE SHANGHAI COMMUNIQUE OF 1972 TO THE ESTABLISHMENT OF DIPLOMATIC RELATIONS IN 1979

On February 27, 1972, when President Nixon concluded his visit to the PRC, a joint communique was issued at Shanghai; this historical document has been usually referred to as the Shanghai Communique (see Document 21).[198] This document is peculiar in diplomatic history because it states, in the words of Nixon, "frankly the significant differences between the two sides on major issues rather than smoothing them over."[199]

With respect to the question of Taiwan, the PRC stated its claim of being the sole legal government of China and its conviction that Taiwan is a province of China. It asserted that the liberation of Taiwan was China's internal affair in which no country had a right to interfere and demanded that all American forces and military installations be withdrawn from Taiwan. The communique concluded by stating that "the Chinese government firmly opposes any activities which aim at the creation of 'one China, one Taiwan,' 'one China, two governments,' 'two Chinas,' an 'independent Taiwan' or advocate that 'the status of Taiwan remains to be determined.'"

The wording of the U.S. section on Taiwan avoided a clash by stating simply: "The United States acknowledge that all Chinese on either side of the Taiwan Strait maintain there is but one China and that Taiwan is a part of China. The United States government does not challenge that position. It affirms its interest in a peaceful settlement of the Taiwan question by the Chinese themselves." The United States also stated its ultimate objective of withdrawing American troops from Taiwan but did not put any final date on that withdrawal, and it agreed in the meantime to reduce its forces and installations on Taiwan progressively "as the tension in the area diminishes."

Despite the disagreement on the Taiwan problem, both the PRC and the United States agreed on improving their trade, cultural exchange, and other relations and they also agreed to move toward the normalization of relations. The communique was silent on the subject of U.S.-ROC diplomatic relations and the Mutual Defense Treaty. Subsequently, the PRC announced the so-called three conditions for normalization of relations that include, in addition to the withdrawal of U.S. troops mentioned in the Shanghai Communique, the termination of U.S. diplomatic relations and of the Mutual Defense Treaty with the ROC. President Nixon in his *Memoirs* and other public statements has never indicated that he ever agreed to or intended to accept the latter two conditions. On the contrary, he and U.S. high officials, before and after his visit, repeatedly assured the ROC that the treaty would remain unaffected.[200] On March 3, 1972, U.S. Assistant Secretary of State Marshall Green brought President Nixon's message of reassurance to the ROC leaders, pledging that "faithfully honoring all our commitment remain[s] a cornerstone of U.S. policy."[201] It was reported that since the Nixon trip and before he resigned in the summer of 1974, he and high officials under his administration had assured the ROC on 52 occasions that the United Stated intended to honor its commitments.[202] In any case, President Nixon was in no position to accept the PRC's conditions for normalization before his resignation because he was facing impeachment and he badly needed the support of the conservative senators in the Congress.

Whether the Shanghai Communique represents a change in the U.S. position on the legal status of Taiwan is an interesting question. Soon after the issuance of the Shanghai Communique, Assistant Secretary of State for East Asian Affairs Marshall Green denied that the communique represented any change in the position held by the U.S. since 1950—the status of Taiwan is as yet undetermined.[203] The PRC remained silent for a year, then on February 28, 1973, Fu Tso-yi, a former ROC general who defected to the Communist side and who was then vice-chairman of the Chinese People's Political Consultative Conference, claimed that "in the Shanghai Communique, the United States recognizes Taiwan as part of China's territory."[204] A similar view was also expressed in an internal document of the PRC.[205]

Recently it was disclosed that at the time of negotiating the Shanghai Communique, Secretary of State Henry Kissinger wanted to accept the PRC's position on Taiwan by stating in the communique that the United States "accepts" rather than "does not challenge" the belief of "all Chinese" in one China. But Kissinger was rebuffed in that attempt, possibly by President Nixon.[206] In any case, the phrase "does not challenge" in the communique is not equivalent to a recognition of the PRC's claim to Taiwan but would virtually rule out U.S. support for an independent Taiwan,[207] as was advocated by some dissident elements indigenous to the province. While the question of Taiwan remains an obstacle to the relations between the two countries, they apparently agreed to shelve, at least in the foreseeable future, this question for the sake of improving relations on other fronts.

Despite U.S. assurance of its support of the ROC after the issuance of the Shanghai Communique, many countries considered that the American abandonment of the ROC would be merely a matter of time. Therefore, many countries that had formerly recognized the ROC shifted their recognition to the PRC one after the other. Among these countries, the most important one was Japan, which recognized the PRC on September 29, 1972, and severed diplomatic relations and terminated all treaties with the ROC. Cultural, economic, and trade relations between Japan and the ROC, however, have been maintained through ostensibly "unofficial organs." This means of maintaining Japan-ROC relations has come to be known as the Japan formula."[208]

After his third visit to Peking, Secretary of State Henry Kissinger announced on February 23, 1973, that the United States and the PRC agreed to establish a "liaison office" in each other's capital. Each "liaison office," Kissinger said, "would handle trade as well as all other matters except the strict formal diplomatic aspects of the relationships." Although "not a formal diplomatic office," it "would cover the whole gamut of relationships," he emphasized; and its personnel would have diplomatic privileges and immunities and facilities for communicating with their home country in code.[209]

In May the United States and the PRC opened their respective liaison offices. The United States appointed David Bruce, one of the most distinguished American ambassadors, as chief of the liaison office in Peking. The PRC appointed Huang Chen, former PRC ambassador to France and then the only Chinese diplomat with membership in the Central Committee of the Chinese Communist party, as chief of liaison office in Washington. Before his arrival, on April 20, President Nixon approved S.1315 (Public Law 93-22), an act to extend diplomatic privileges and immunities to the liaison office of the PRC and to the members thereof.[210] The United States and the PRC for all practical purposes established semidiplomatic relations.

In August 1974 President Nixon was compelled to resign as a result of the Watergate scandal, and Vice-President Gerald Ford succeeded to the presidency.

President Ford's attitude toward the U.S. commitment to the ROC was rather ambivalent. When Vice-President Rockefeller went to Taiwan in April 1975 to attend the burial ceremony of late President Chiang Kai-Shek, he did not say a word on the U.S. commitment to the ROC. It was not until after the collapse of South Vietnam on April 30, 1975, that the president reaffirmed U.S. "commitments to Taiwan" at his press conference held on May 7, 1978.[211]

In December 1975 President Ford visited the PRC. Although nothing concrete regarding normalization was mentioned after the visit, it was disclosed later by Teng Hsiao-ping, vice-premier of the State Council of the PRC, in an interview with directors of the Associated Press in Peking on September 6, 1977, that President Ford did "promise" in that visit that if he were reelected he would resolve the Taiwan problem and establish full relations with Peking in the same way as the Japanese.[212] Ford, however, had a different version of the story and said that he did suggest the so-called Japanese formula as "a possibility" for normalization, but he added that "any change toward normalization must be predicated on the peaceful solution of the Taiwan-People's Republic of China Situation."[213]

During the 1976 presidential campaign, Jimmy Carter stated, in the second televised debate with President Ford on October 6, this position on the Taiwan Question:

> In the Far East I think we need to continue to be strong, and I would certainly pursue the normalization of relations with the People's Republic of China . . . but I would never let that friendship [with the PRC] stand in the way of the preservation of the independence and freedom of the people of Taiwan.[214]

He was, however, silent on the U.S.-ROC treaty and diplomatic relations. His attitude remained the same after he became president on January 20, 1977. On May 12, 1977, President Carter held a press conference on his China policy. While affirming his "commitment to the . . . Shanghai Communique," and to the normalization of the U.S. relationship with the PRC, he also said that the United States "do[es]n't want to see the Taiwanese people punished or attacked."[215]

On June 29, 1977, seven weeks before his scheduled visit to the PRC, Secretary of State Cyrus Vance gave a speech before the Asian Society on "United States and Asia," in which he summarized the position of the Carter administration's China policy as follows:

> Our policy toward China will continue to be guided by the principles of the Shanghai Communique, and on that basis we shall seek to move toward full normalization of relations. We acknowledge the view expressed in the Shanghai Communique that there is but one China. We also place importance on the peaceful settlement of the Taiwan question by the Chinese themselves.[216]

The next day President Carter said at a press conference that he hoped that the United States "can work out an agreement with the People's Republic of China, having full diplomatic relations with them, and still make sure that the peaceful life of the Taiwanese, the Republic of China, is maintained."[217]

Since both Vance and Carter were silent on treaty and diplomatic relations with the ROC, there was widespread belief that the Carter administration was going to normalize relations with the PRC by accepting the PRC's three conditions. ROC Foreign Minister Shen Chang-huan issued a statement on July 1, voicing strong exception to Vance's China policy part of his speech. Shen's statement reminded the United States, among others, that "the Republic of China and the United States have been friends of long standing. The two countries have diplomatic relations and are allies by virtue of the Mutual Defense Treaty."[218]

Carter's intention to accept the PRC's three conditions drew sharp criticism and opposition from many senators, congressmen, public opinion leaders, and the general public.[219] It was later disclosed by the Washington *Post* that at a meeting held on July 30, presided over by the president himself, Carter decided to postpone, but definitely not to reject, the recommendation to abandon Taiwan formulated in President Review Memorandum No. 24 because the time was not propitious for so dramatic a shift in China policy. Therefore, Vance's mission to the PRC became an exploratory one and he would have authority to talk and listen but not to accept the three conditions demanded by the PRC.[220]

Vance visited the PRC on August 20-27, 1977, and the official report of the U.S. government indicated only that he had made clear to the PRC leaders that the United States would continue to be guided by the Shanghai Communique in dealing with China.[221] However, ten days after the Vance visit, on September 6, Vice-Premier Teng Hsiao-ping said that Vance did suggest a formula to swap between U.S. missions in Peking and Taipei—setting up a liaison office in Taipei and an embassy in Peking—but this was rejected by the PRC.[222] PRC high officials also indicated that they would not renounce the use of force to liberate Taiwan, nor could they tolerate any U.S. unilateral statement expressing U.S. vital interests in the peace and stability in the Taiwan region or arm sales to Taiwan after normalization.[223]

Since the PRC has refused to make any pledge, and has even ruled out a unilateral declaration by the United States on the peaceful settlement of the Taiwan question, and faced with strong congressional and public opposition to the abandonment of Taiwan, the Carter administration has had to postpone its attempt to normalize relations with the PRC.

In May 1978 President Carter's National Security Adviser Zbigniew Brzezinski visited the PRC. He told the Chinese side that the United States was determined to seek normalization of relations with the PRC, but he apparently made no progress on the Taiwan impasse.[224] Then, on July 13, 1978, it was reported by United Press International that President Carter told the private Trilateral Commission that he intended to normalize relations with the PRC if the latter accept the following conditions:

U.S. trade and aid to the ROC government on Taiwan, including military assistance, must continue after full diplomatic relations are established with the PRC.
A U.S. trade office would be established in Taiwan after the embassy is closed.
The PRC must make clear, through a formula to be agreed upon, that it would not use force in seeking to unite Taiwan to the Chinese Mainland.

On December 15, 1978, President Carter dramatically announced to the world that the United States and the PRC would establish diplomatic relations on January 1, 1979 (see Document 26). He also declared that he would sever diplomatic relations with the ROC on that date, terminate the Mutual Defense Treaty with the ROC a year from that date, and withdraw all U.S. forces from Taiwan within four months (see Document 27). There was neither a PRC commitment to refrain from using force against Taiwan nor a unilateral U.S. commitment to the security of Taiwan. The president's statement accompanying the Joint Communique on establishing diplomatic relations did state that "the United States continues to have an interest in the peaceful resolution of the Taiwan issue and expects that the Taiwan issue will be settled peacefully by the Chinese themselves" (see Document 27). The PRC immediately issued a response to this statement, insisting that the decision as to the method by which Taiwan would be brought back to PRC control was part of China's "internal affairs" for "unifying the country" (see Document 28). It is elementary that a country may use force in its internal affairs, so the Carter statement on the peaceful resolution of the Taiwan issue was in fact and in law rejected by the Chinese. As a matter of fact, at a press conference held in Peking on January 5, 1979, Vice-Premier Teng Hsiao-ping publicly acknowledged that the Chinese cannot restrict themselves by renouncing the possibility of using force for the unification of Taiwan and the mainland. He also said the future of Taiwan "is entirely an internal Chinese affair" but that Peking would "take note" of President Carter's wish that the dispute be settled peacefully.[225]

Peking flatly refused to agree to U.S. arms sales to Taiwan in the post-normalization period, though it decided to establish diplomatic relation with the United States despite this disagreement. The United States, however, made a further concession to the PRC by pledging "to sell a limited amount of arms to Taiwan for defensive purpose" (see Document 29) only. The United States also committed itself to a one-year moratorium on new U.S. weapons sales to Taiwan in 1979, except those already in the pipeline due to previous agreements.[226]

With respect to the legal status of Taiwan, the United States said in the Joint Communique that it "acknowledges the Chinese position that there is but one China and Taiwan is part of China." And it is within that context that "the people of the United States will maintain cultural, commercial, and other unofficial relations with the people of Taiwan." Deputy Assistant Secretary of State for East Asian and Pacific Affairs Roger Sullivan told the Taiwan press on December 27, 1978, that the United States did not recognize the PRC's sovereign claim to Taiwan in the Joint Communique.[227] Be that as it may, the PRC has purposely mistranslated the word "acknowledges" into *Cheng-jen* in the Chinese version of the communique, which means, if retranslated into English, "recognizes." The United States, however, did not challenge the Chinese use of the word *cheng-jen* in the Chinese version of the Joint Communique. It is possible, therefore, that at a later date the PRC may seek to rely on its version of the Communique to claim that the United States had effectively "recognized" its sovereign claim to Taiwan.

Furthermore, in the Joint Communique, the United States stated that it would maintain only "unofficial relations with the people of Taiwan." Such an arrangement would, at least in the eyes of the PRC, constitute a tacit recognition of the PRC's sovereign claim to Taiwan. In view of the above analysis, if the PRC chose in the future to interfere with U.S. economic, trade, and financial relations with the ROC, or with arms sales to the ROC government, the United States would be in a poor legal position to resist.

President Carter's sudden recognition of the PRC and his acceptance of virtually all the latter's demands, needless to say, were a shock to the ROC. While leaders of the ROC had expected President Carter's move sometime in the near future, they could not understand why the president had acted abruptly at that time, giving them only seven hours' notice.[228] They were particularly upset by the lack of U.S. assurance on the security of Taiwan. Thus, when President Carter sent a delegation headed by Deputy Secretary of State Warren Christopher to Taiwan on December 28–29, 1978, to discuss postnormalization U.S.-ROC relations, the ROC made several basic demands, namely, that future U.S.-ROC relations be maintained on a government-to-government basis, that the United States take concrete and effective measures to assure the security of Taiwan, that the United States continue to supply adequate arms to the ROC, and others (see Documents 31 and 32).

The Christopher mission did not succeed in reaching an overall agreement with the ROC on the future of U.S.-ROC relations, though both sides agreed to hold further negotiations in the United States on the subject. They also agreed that pending the final agreement on principles and concrete arrangements concerning their future relations, existing cultural, commercial, and other relations should be continued without interruption until March 1, 1979. Thus, on December 30, 1978, President Carter issued a memorandum to all U.S. departments and agencies instructing them that all existing treaties and agreements between the United States and the ROC "shall continue in force" and "whenever any law, regulation, or order of the United States refers to a foreign country, nation, state, government, or similar entity, departments and agencies shall construe those terms and apply those laws, regulations, or orders to include Taiwan" (see Document 32).

U.S.-ROC RELATIONS IN THE POSTNORMALIZATION PERIOD

US-ROC negotiations on maintaining trade, cultural, and other relations in the postnormalization period were resumed in Washington in early January 1979, but no substantive progress was made for several weeks because the ROC insisted on having official, that is, government-to-government, relations with the United States while the latter insisted, at least formally, on unofficial relations. According to the U.S. proposal, a new American Institute in Taiwan would be created to take over all functions of former U.S. embassy and consular services in Taiwan. The Institute would be a nonprofit private corporation, incorporated under District of Columbia law, but would be staffed by veteran diplomats or other civil servants "temporarily" on leave of absence from the U.S. government.[229] Despite the ROC's objection, the U.S. State Department incorporated the Institute on January 10, 1979,[230] and urged the ROC to create a similar unofficial organ to replace its embassy and consular services in the United States.

After several weeks of deadlock over this issue, the United States sent an ultimatum to Taipei, calling for an agreement to nongovernmental relationships by February 10 or a complete rupture in U.S.-ROC ties.[231] A few days later, however, the United States made a minor concession by agreeing to let the ROC issue an executive order to create a Cordination Council for North American Affairs to serve as a counterpart of the American Institute in Taiwan. The Council will have an office in Washington and branch offices in New York, Chicago, Atlanta, Houston, Seattle, San Francisco, Los Angeles, and Honolulu. The United States would call the Council an "unofficial" organ, while the ROC could maintain that it is of an "official nature."[232]

The United States also agreed to grant the following privileges and immunities to the Council and its personnel on the condition that similar privileges and immunities be extended to the American Institute in Taiwan and its personnel by the ROC: the privilege of a secure pouch; the right to send and receive coded messages; customs courtesies, involving such matters as freedom from customs inspections and duties; tax exemption of the Council and its personnel; inviolability of the premises of the Council; and immunity of appropriate members of the Council from criminal and civil liability for any acts commited in the performance of their duties.[233]

With respect to the ROC demand for a security guarantee for Taiwan, which was supported by many members of the Congress, the Carter administration asserts such a guarantee is unnecessary, whether in the form of a presidential declaration or a congressional resolution.[234] At the Senate Foreign Relations Committee's hearings on the Taiwan Enabling Act held on February 5, 1979, Secretary of Defense Harold Brown told the committee that any PRC military attack against Taiwan is extremely unlikely for the foreseeable future, for the following reasons: the PRC has limited amphibious capabilities; the island of Taiwan is heavily fortified and would be costly to take; the action could make the PRC more vulnerable to a Soviet attack; the PRC will be faced with a hostile Vietnam for many years to come, which will require the PRC to maintain substantial military forces near the Sino-Vietnamese border; and an attack on Taiwan would reverse the political gains made in the West by the PRC and jeopardize continued U.S. help for PRC's modernization.[235]

The great majority of the senators in the committee, however, were less optimistic on the future security of Taiwan. Their view, as summarized in the Senate Foreign Relations Committee's Report on the Taiwan Enabling Act, is as follows:

> . . . Committee members indicated their belief that it is prudent to consider the possibility that current circumstances could change. This is especially true in light of the recent PRC attack on Vietnam. Vice-Premier Teng is 74 years old and has twice been purged from office. Chinese foreign policy could again dramatically change. A Sino-Soviet detente would free large numbers of Chinese troops currently near the Soviet border. The Chinese might miscalculate U.S. resolve to continue providing security to Taiwan. Or Taiwan could take action such as declaring its independence, acquiring nuclear weapons, or cooperating closely with the Soviet Union, any of which might trigger a PRC reaction.
>
> There are several possible "nonpeaceful" alternatives open to Peking with regard to reunification. They include an economic boycott, a military blockade, seizure of the offshore islands, invasion of Taiwan, and nuclear blackmail. . .
>
> A more effective way for the PRC to strangle Taiwan economically would be a military blockade, which some argue might have sanction in international law for those countries which regard Taiwan as part of China. The blockade probably would not require air superiority if Peking were to call on its 73 fleet class submarines. Without the U.S. Seventh Fleet, Taiwan has a very limited anti-submarine warfare capability. . . .[236]

Moreover, in evaluating the security problem of Taiwan, one should also take into account the peculiar features of the Taiwan economy. Taiwan's economy is highly exported-oriented: at present, it is perhaps more dependent than any other country upon its exports. In 1978 Taiwan's worldwide exports comprised 48 percent of its GNP (about 11 billion out of 22 billion GNP). Direct foreign investment and technological inflow are indispensable elements of the economic viability of Taiwan. Foreign investment in Taiwan now amounts to only U.S. $2 billion and *in theory* could be replaced by domestic investment. In practice, however, the importance of foreign investment lies, not in its amount, but in its psychological impact on domestic investors. Without foreign investment, domestic investors would lose confidence in their own investments there;

and if foreign investment slowed down or fled, then domestic investment would do likewise.

Past experience indicates that foreign direct investment in Taiwan has apparently been very sensitive to political events. As a recent study indicates,

> the rate of U.S. investment in Taiwan dropped in 1971 and 1972, probably as a result of the ROC's international setbacks during those years and doubt its future. . . .
>
> The flow of direct investment from Japan, including investments by "overseas Chinese" resident in Japan, rose steadily during 1965–1970, immediately after the establishment of the export processing zones. The rate of flow fell in 1972, reflecting the same concern felt by U.S. investors.[237]

In view of these economic realities, both the Senate and the House considered that some form of security guarantee for Taiwan was necessary. It was thought that such a guarantee should be in the form of assurances to Taiwan that the United States remains seriously concerned for Taiwan's future. At the same time, any guarantee should avoid offending the PRC. After extensive discussions in the Congress and between the congressional leaders and the Carter administration, it was agreed that the legislation on Taiwan should provide that "any effort to determine the future of Taiwan by other than peaceful means, including by boycotts or embargoes, a threat to the peace and security of the Western Pacific area and of grave concern to the United States."[238] The Taiwan legislation was finally passed by the House (March 26, 1979) and the Senate (March 29, 1979) under the title Taiwan Relations Act (see Document 35) and, in addition to the provision mentioned above, also included the following security measures for Taiwan:

The United States will assist the people on Taiwan to maintain a sufficient self-defense capacity through the provision of arms of a defensive character.

The United States shall maintain the capacity to resist any resort to force or other forms of coercion that would jeopardize the security, or the social or economic system, of the people on Taiwan.

Taiwan shall be exempted from the $1,000 per capita income restriction on the availability of the Overseas Private Investment Corporation (OPIC) insurance to developing countries for three years.

The House Committee on Foreign Affairs, the Senate Foreign Relations Committee, and other appropriate committees of the Congress shall monitor the implementation of the Taiwan Relations Act.

SECONDARY OPTIONS OF THE ROC IN TAIWAN
IN RESPONSE TO NORMALIZATION

U.S.-ROC relations in political, economic, cultural, and other fields have been very close. So far as possible, the ROC would like to maintain these relations, in spite of its disappointment over the U.S. recognition of the PRC. The ROC government would consider secondary options only if it felt the United States was going to withdraw its support for the ROC, either immediately or in the long term. Before analyzing these secondary options, however, it is necessary to dispose of the possibility of a negotiated settlement between the ROC and the PRC.

When a PRC official talks about "negotiations" with the ROC, he invariably refers to what Peking calls the "peaceful liberation or unification," that is, the eventual reintegration, of Taiwan into the Communist-controlled mainland. This differs from the historic West German offer to enter into relations with East Germany, for example, since the office was preconditioned on West German recognition of the legitimacy of the German Democratic Republic within the territory under its control. Unless the PRC were willing to offer the ROC a solution to the Taiwan issue along the lines of the German model, whereby the PRC would recognize the legitimacy of the ROC, there would be no reason for the ROC to enter into negotiations with the PRC if Taiwan does not, in fact, want to surrender.

Some U.S. scholars and PRC officials have suggested that Taiwan could be made an autonomous region within the PRC. This offer is equally unacceptable to the ROC for the simple reason that Peking's credibility in this connection has long been undermined by its dealings with Tibet. Tibet signed an agreement with the PRC in 1951, by the terms of which the PRC promised autonomous status to Tibet. But the Communists later sent a large occupation force to Tibet, settled many Han Chinese there, and finally massacred thousands of Tibetans in the name of suppressing a "rebellion" in 1959. The atrocities committed by the PRC in Tibet were condemned by the International Commission of Jurists as constituting "genocide."[239]

Another important consideration in evaluating the PRC's offer of autonomy for Taiwan is the complex and unpredictable nature of power politics and policy struggles in the PRC. Experiences in the last three decades clearly demonstrate that power and policy struggles in the PRC have swung periodically like a pendulum between two opposing extremes. One has witnessed, for example, the rise and fall of powerful figures such as Liu Shao-ch'i (chairman of the PRC, 1958-66), Lin Piao (Mao's heir-designate in 1969), and the Gang of Four headed by Mao's wife Chiang Ching. The present leader, Teng Hsiao-ping, was twice humiliated and purged out of power in the last decade. If the ROC became an autonomous region of the PRC, it would lose its international personality and its ability to acquire necessary defensive weapons abroad; and, as the PRC politics are anything but stable and are, above all, mysterious to the outsiders, there would be no credible assurance that Taiwan's autonomy would be respected by future PRC leaders.

Moreover, the internal situation in the ROC would also preclude its leaders from entering into negotiations with the PRC, unless the negotiations were based on the German model. The great majority of people on the island are Taiwanese-Chinese or Taiwan-born mainlanders. If the ROC leadership were to negotiate with the PRC for a so-called peaceful liberation or unification, virtually the entire population would interpret the government's action as a sellout. This could well provoke a widespread rebellion against the government. In view of this, any U.S. attempt to pressure the ROC to negotiate with the PRC would probably be rejected, because any negotiation, in the ROC's view, would be seen as the equivalent of surrender or suicide. This is all the more so because U.S.-arranged negotiations with the Communists in comparable situations in the past, such as in Vietnam and Laos, have rarely if ever been successful; each ended in the surrender of the non-Communist side. The only partial exception has been Korea, but this resulted from the United States maintenance of substantial combat forces there after the signing of the armistice agreement. Moreover, the United States had also concluded a security treaty with the Republic of Korea.

Now let us turn to the secondary options available to the ROC in response to normalization. It is generally agreed that there are three such options: to declare independence, to go nuclear, or to seek a relationship with the Soviet Union. The reason that the word "secondary" is used here is that none of these options would be a happy one for the ROC to choose, although it could nevertheless resort to one or more of them if it eventually concluded that the United States was going to "abandon" it.

The first option would be to declare Taiwan an independent state. It is unlikely that the present ROC leaders would adopt such a policy, since they would thereby label themselves as "traitors" to Chinese history; this alternative should not be ruled out, as an increasing number of Taiwanese-Chinese are continuing to move into the decision-making levels of the ROC government. Independence would be more favorably looked upon if the PRC increased its military, political, or economic pressure on Taiwan. In that event, the United States would be placed in an embarrassing position if it seemed to disregard the validly expressed aspirations of the people of Taiwan for self-determination. On the other hand, if the United States supported the independence of Taiwan, that support would disrupt all its relations with the PRC.

Another possible course of action within this option would have the ROC adopt a "two-Chinas" policy by *formally* declaring the suspension of its claim to sovereignty over the mainland and asserting the limitation of its jurisdiction to the territory now under its effective control. Since all U.S. treaties with the Republic of China since 1949 have been modified to apply only to the territory actually under ROC control, the proposed declaration would have no effect on the validity of existing treaty relations. On the other hand, the ROC would probably strengthen its position with the American public and thereby make it more difficult for the Washington government to abandon the ROC.

A second option for the ROC is to develop and deploy nuclear weapons. While there is no doubt that the ROC has the technological know-how and industrial base for manufacturing nuclear weapons, the United States could retaliate by cutting off supplies of nuclear fuels for Taiwan's nuclear power plants. However, there are alternative sources of nuclear fuel supplies. Moreover, what political, moral, and economic benefits would the United States gain by exerting pressure on Taiwan to prevent it from manufacturing nuclear weapons for self-defense—after throwing Taiwan out of the U.S. mutual defense system and leaving the 17 million people there with very little choice but to defend themselves against a country of 900 million people, armed with nuclear weapons? As a knowledgeable commentator has observed,

> there are potential alternative sources of [nuclear] fuel and it is quite possible that, having facilitated Taiwan's extraordinary success and then having, in effect, thrown Taiwan completely back on its own resources, the United States would prove unwilling to take military or severe economic action against a Taiwanese government which refused to allow continued inspection [of its nuclear reactors and development]. Such action would be morally questionable and politically dangerous, and would shock other U.S. allies. The legality of such actions would be dubious and the pressure from Taiwan's political supporters and foreign investors would be intense.[240]

The last option open to the ROC would be to enter into some kind of relationship with the Soviet Union. The strategic importance of the island of Taiwan does not require much elaboration. In this connection it is perhaps sufficient to quote from a speech by former PRC Foreign Minister Ch'iao Kuan-hua, delivered at Tientsin on May 20, 1975:

> From the geographic point of view, Taiwan is very important. Hence, the Soviet Union is watching this area and attempts to avail itself of an opportunity to set its foot on it. On the other hand, Taiwan is taking advantage of its important position to play political maneuvers between the United States, Soviet Union and Japan.[241]

Taiwan would be especially useful for the operation of the Soviet navy in the western Pacific. A Soviet base on Taiwan would threaten the sea lanes to the south of Japan and the security of the Philippines. Similarly, PRC control over Taiwan would shift the strategic balance to the disadvantage of the Soviet

Union. It is true that the Soviet leadership would have to consider the political costs involved in developing a closer relationship with the ROC, but a limited rapprochement or unpublicized coordination in limited areas of parallel interest, without the formality of diplomatic relations, should not be ruled out.[242] At present the ROC government officially excludes any such possibility of relations with the Soviet Union,[243] but this policy could change if the ROC were facing strong economic, political, and military pressure from the PRC, combined with a lack of support, especially in regard to military assistance and arms sales, from the United States. In any case, the government and the people of the ROC would like to maintain their close relations with the United States and do not want to develop an uncertain relationship with the Soviet Union. However, if faced with the PRC threat and desertion by the United States, they could resort to whatever means available to them to prevent a PRC takeover of Taiwan.

CONCLUDING OBSERVATIONS

Despite the PRC's statement in the 1972 Shanghai Communique that "the Taiwan question is the crucial question obstructing the normalization of relations between China and the United States" and the U.S. refusal, up to December 15, 1978, to give up its support to Taiwan, since 1972 the United States and the PRC have in fact normalized their relations in almost all areas, with the major exception of raising the status of representation in each other's capital to the "ambassadorial" level. This is because the raison d'etre of the U.S.-PRC rapprochement in 1972 was based on their common interest in coping with the "Soviet threat and expansion." As long as the Soviet "threat" exists, the United States and the PRC would maintain their present cordial relations, despite the existence of the Taiwan question and the lack of the diplomatic formality of "embassy" representation between them.

It is unlikely that any faction in power in the PRC would be in a position to give up the PRC's claim to Taiwan because of China's historic claim to the island. However, this does not mean that the PRC may not have any flexibility on the Taiwan question. For instance, the PRC could maintain its claim to the island but agree to shelve the question for a number of years. If the PRC leaders intended to do that, they could again find ample support in Mao's teachings. In 1959 Mao said that "it is unimportant if they [the United States] do not return Taiwan to us for another 100 years" (see Document 18). At present the PRC's policy toward Taiwan appears to attempt to legally reduce the Taiwan question to one of domestic Chinese affairs. At the appropriate time the PRC would use political, economic, and military pressure to unite Taiwan with the mainland. However, if the United States stands firm and is patient, there is good reason to believe that the PRC would become flexible on the Taiwan question. Past experience in dealing with the PRC supports this analysis. Since 1955 the PRC had insisted that unless the Taiwan question were solved, it would not deal with the

United States. In the early 1970s the PRC was willing to drop the Taiwan question's priority in its foreign policy agenda and to talk to the United States on
other matters of common concern.

There is, however, a limit on the PRC's flexibility regarding the question
of Taiwan. To the PRC, as long as Taiwan is controlled by the present ROC government, which considers itself as the genuine representative of the Chinese culture and history, there is always the possibility of "peaceful unification" and the
PRC can wait. However, if Taiwan declared itself an independent "Republic of
Taiwan," the entire situation would change. If that should happen and the PRC
did not take swift action to crush the new republic, then an independent Taiwan
might be gradually accepted by the international community as an independent
state vis-a-vis China. This in turn would make it legally and politically more difficult for the PRC to reunite Taiwan with the mainland. Therefore, the emergence
of an independent "Republic of Taiwan" would be a great inducement to the
PRC to take military action against Taiwan and would thus lead to tension in
East Asia,[244] possibly to an armed conflict involving the United States and
Japan.

Public opinion in the United States before President Carter's recognition
of the PRC clearly demonstrated that the latter's three conditions for accepting
the U.S. recognition were unacceptable. A poll conducted by Harris-ABC News
Survey between June 27 and July 1, 1978, indicated that by a 66 to 19 percent
margin Americans were opposed to a U.S. withdrawal of recognition of the ROC
government in Taiwan, and by 64 to 19 percent an almost identical majority
wanted the United States to maintain its Mutual Defense Treaty with the ROC.[245]

On the congressional side, a poll conducted by the American Conservative
Union (ACU) released on October 12, 1978, indicated that 56 senators were
opposed to the severance of diplomatic relations and the termination of the
treaty with the ROC as conditions for normalizing relations with the PRC. Eight
other senators were leaning toward such a move. Only 3 senators favored accepting the PRC's conditions, while 23 were undecided and 9 refused to answer the
poll.[246] An earlier poll by the ACU showed that 264 members of the House
opposed any change in U.S.-ROC relations, while only six favored accepting the
PRC's conditions; the remaining members were undecided or refused to answer
the poll.[247]

Externally, before President Carter's recognition of the PRC, it appeared
that Japan opposed an American normalization of relations with the PRC if
there were no credible guarantee on the security of Taiwan.[248] The Soviet Union
also reacted strongly to the Carter administration's attempt to play the "China
card" against it.[249] Moreover, needless to say, termination of the Mutual Defense Treaty with the ROC must impair American credibility as an ally.

Some China specialists had argued that the United States must normalize
relations, that is, establish full diplomatic relations, with the PRC, even on the
latter's terms, in order to consolidate cordial U.S.-PRC relations. Some even
argued that failure to complete the process of normalization would enhance the

possibility of a Sino-Soviet rapprochement. However, recent diplomatic history does not support such a view. The Soviet Union has maintained diplomatic relations with the PRC since 1949, concluded an alliance treaty with it in 1950, and provided large amounts of military and economic aid, including atomic reactors, to the PRC. However, this has not prevented the subsequent deterioration of Sino-Soviet relations. Therefore, there is no reason to believe that the establishment of diplomatic relations between Washington and Peking will ensure a future U.S.-PRC friendship. Moreover, at present, the PRC has not changed its ultimate national goal of eliminating "American imperialism," together with the "Soviet social imperialism." By entering into full diplomatic relations with the United States, the PRC could only be changing its priority of enemies, moving the United States from the status of No. 1 enemy to No. 2. In a secret speech delivered in August 1976, Chinese Politburo member Keng Piao analyzed U.S.-PRC relations within the context of the PRC's strategic confrontation with the Soviet Union and the PRC's ultimate goal of driving the United States out of East Asia as follows:

> Just let the United States defend us against the influence of Soviet revisionism and guard the coast of the East China sea so that we can have more strength to deal with the power in the north and engage in state construction. When the time is right, we will be candid and say: "please, Uncle Sam, pack up your things and go."[250]

The argument for the "China card," that is, normalization to create pressure on Moscow to be more conciliatory regarding U.S.-Soviet relations, is equally unconvincing. As some commentators pointed out, playing the China card, instead of pressuring the Soviet to become more conciliatory, could produce just the opposite result, provoking the Soviets to take drastic action. As Hans J. Morgenthau said:

> While the China Card does not frighten the Russians at present, it may provoke them to pre-emptive action [against China]. . . . In terms of American interests, playing the Chinese Card, prematurely at present, would achieve the exact opposite of what it is intended to do. It would provoke, rather than frighten, the Russians. . . .[251]

Similarly, Edward N. Luttwak has observed:

> [By playing the China card] we may lose more than we gain. For example, the Russians might react by sponsoring a North Korean attack against the South. This would not only punish us directly but it might also out maneuver our own move, if Peking found itself compelled to compete with Moscow in supporting the North against the South, and ourselves [just like the Vietnam War situation].

Whatever the war's outcome, United States cooperation with Peking would be unlikely to survive the strain.[252]

Moreover, developments after President Carter's recognition of the PRC appear to indicate that, instead of America's playing the China card, the Chinese are playing the America card. As a commentator observed:

> The U.S. did find that its longtime policy assumption that the West could only benefit from the Sino-Soviet dispute is false. Not only may the new Soviet-American agreement on strategic arms limitation have been jeopardized by Washington's rapprochement with Peking, but the Chinese attact on Vietnam and the serious possibility for a time of a Soviet reprisal affected world peace.
>
> The Carter administration sought, it seems, to play its "China card" against the Kremlin but found that Peking was actually using Washington for leverage against Moscow.[253]

The domestic attitude toward playing the China card should not be ignored. In the Harris-ABC poll mentioned above, it was revealed that, by a ratio of 71 to 20 percent, a majority opposed the notion that "the United States [should] work together with Communist China as a force against Russia." Also an overwhelming majority of 81 to 11 percent of Americans were opposed to "the sale of U.S. electronic military defense systems" to the PRC. The results indicate that the idea of playing the China card is viewed by the general public as a high-risk course that could lead to involvements that the American people are not now prepared to make.

Under the above-stated analysis, the most sensible policy for the United States toward the question of normalization would have been to maintain the status quo and wait until the PRC became more reasonable and flexible with respect to Taiwan.[254] This policy would have received the support of the great majority of the American people, congressional members, and U.S. allies and would also have been consistent with the principles of justice, international law, and respect for human rights.

The Carter administration, however, in total disregard of the above-stated rational approach toward the question of normalization, in disregard of public opinion, and without prior consultation of the Congress (see Document 25), suddenly decided to recognize the PRC and to virtually dump Taiwan on December 15, 1978. There have been many criticisms on Carter's dramatic move and his lack of concern for U.S. credibility in the world and for the security of the 17 million people in Taiwan in making the deal with the PRC.[255] As the *Wall Street Journal* commented:

> U.S. acceptance of Peking's claim to rule over Taiwan is no mere confirmation of a "simple reality," as President Carter described it. . . . In trying to minimize the importance of what the U.S. has

surrendered for a remarkably low price, the President has aggravated the damage the agreement itself has done to the political credibility of this administration. . . .

[The President] has paid a high price in conceding the People's Republic's claims to Taiwan with so little assurance of Taiwan's security. Taiwan has developed, under U.S. protection, into an Eastern showcase for Western principles of economic development. Its divergent path from that of the mainland has been one of the world's best examples of the superiority of those principles over those employed in the People's Republic and other Communist nations. . . .

In return for this recognition and the withdrawal of the U.S. military alliance with Taiwan, the U.S. has received . . . a statement that Peking has not contradicted U.S. insistence that reunification not be attempted by force.

It will be argued by the administration that Peking could go no further without losing face. . . . Perhaps so, but the concern for Chinese face betrays a certain lack of concern for U.S. or Taiwanese face. To whatever degree the charges of a U.S. "sell-out" have meaning in Asia and the world, it will be another in a series of signals that the U.S. has become an unreliable ally in facing up to pressures from politically determined Communist nations. Face is indeed important in politics. It is the task of U.S. administrations to worry about U.S. face.[256]

Among the general public, more than 80 percent of letters, cables, or phone calls to the White House expressed their disapproval of president's act, especially his failure to assure the security of Taiwan. A New York *Times*-CBS survey conducted the weekend after President Carter's December 15 announcement found that Americans opposed closer ties with China at the expense of Taiwan by a 45 percent to 27 percent margin. The same poll found the public believing that the PRC will get a greater benefit from increased trade than the United States.[257] Even after more than a month of publicity and explanation by the Carter administration, a substantial plurality of the American people still disapproves recognizing Peking at the expense of relations with Taiwan by a 46 percent to 32 percent margin, according to a New York *Times*-CBS survey conducted from January 23 to 26, 1979.[258] Many members of the Congress also criticized the secret diplomacy of President Carter, his unilateral decision to terminate the security treaty with Taiwan, and his failure to provide assurance for Taiwan's security.[259]

Internationally, while President Carter's move did receive verbal approval from three principal European allies—the United Kingdom, France, and West Germany—the latter, however, did show their concern over the reaction from the Soviet Union.[260] While Japan, because it had recognized the PRC in 1972, publicly did not disapprove Carter's move, some Japanese leaders and commentators did show their concern over the wisdom of the U.S. dumping of Taiwan. As the Japan *Times* commented,

According to the State Department, explicit assurances from Peking were not necessary because Communist China's chief concern is with the Soviet troops massed along its northern border. Moreover, China "understands" the U.S. expectation of continued peace in the Taiwan area.

But that is tenuous reasoning, indeed. Even without questioning the stability of the present Peking regime, there is the Chinese "record" of changing courses with bewildering speed. Only a few years ago, China was accusing Japan of "militarism" and the U.S. of "imperialism." It could switch directions again. This does raise the question of trustworthiness. . . .

[The United States] chose to abrogate its security treaty commitment with Taiwan. Although it is the first of the more than 40 postwar pacts of a similar nature the U.S. has abandoned in peacetime, it does raise serious questions on American credibility, especially with its allies in this part of the world. . . .

The American break with Taiwan has other ramifications in raising doubts among other U.S. allies whether they too might become expendable in the future. Despite strong and repeated denials by American officials, the impression remains that the U.S. is gradually retreating from the East Asian region. . . .[261]

The Philippines' reaction is more direct and articulate. Foreign Minister Carlos P. Romulo warned on January 2, 1979, that U.S. abrogation of the U.S.-ROC Mutual Defense Treaty would further cast doubt on the credibility of U.S. commitment to its allies.[262] The Israelis also saw the U.S. dumping of Taiwan as a dangerous precedent. As one correspondent observed:

The establishment of diplomatic relations between Washington and Peking has shaken [Israeli] officials here. If the United States can so abruptly switch friends in the Far East, embracing China while abandoning Taiwan and abrogating the defense treaty with it, then Israelis fear it can also do so in the Middle East.[263]

The Soviet Union also showed its displeasure with President Carter's move on China, especially the inclusion of a passage in the Joint Communique opposing "hegemony," which is a Chinese codeword for Soviet "expansionism" and has been used in Chinese-Soviet polemics.[264] The Soviet Union quietly suspended the second Strategic Arms Control Talks with the United States, increased its press attacks on China, and apparently urged Vietnam to launch a large-scale invasion of Cambodia to eliminate Chinese influence there,[265] which again appeared to cause the PRC to invade Vietnam.[266]

The ROC's reactions to President Carter's move have been stated before, but it is necessary to emphasize here Taiwan's view of Carter's so-called peaceful resolution of the Taiwan question. To the ROC leaders, as expressed by Premier Sun Yun-suan at a December 21, 1978, press conference, the U.S. emphasis on some unspecified "peaceful resolution" can only mean an implicit understanding with Peking to press the government of the ROC, perhaps by withholding arms deliveries, perhaps by curbing trade or cultural ties, perhaps by further downgrading the unofficial relations, to open such negotiations with the Communists—a move that to the ROC leaders would certainly mean the end of the ROC government and the abandonment of 17 million people to totalitarian Communist rule.[267]

In view of the foregoing analysis of President Carter's ill-considered move, it is understandable that the Congress has insisted that it should take certain credible measures to assure the security of Taiwan and the continuation of the close economic, cultural, and other relations between the two countries so as to restore U.S. credibility as an ally. Such measures are absolutely necessary, as former President Nixon—the architect of U.S.-PRC rapprochement—said in his letter dated February 14, 1979, to Representative Lester L. Wolff, chairman of the House Subcommittee on Asian and Pacific Affairs:

> Normalization of U.S. relations with the PRC is indispensable in furthering our goal of building a structure of peace in Asia and the world. But at a time when U.S. credibility as a dependable ally and friend is being questioned in a number of countries, it is also vitally important that the Taiwan issue be handled in a way which will reassure other nations—whether old friends, new friends, potential friends or wavering friends—that it is safe to rely on America's word and to be America's friend.[268]

NOTES

1. *Contemporary China, A Reference Digest* 1, no. 15 (December 15, 1941): 1. Japan began an undeclared war on China on July 7, 1937, and China resisted that undeclared war without technically announcing the existence of a state of war until December 9, 1941.

2. At the time of drafting the Joint Communique, the Chinese insisted upon the inclusion of the wording ". . . Formosa . . . shall be restored to the Republic of China." See Chinese record of November 26, 1943, meeting at Cairo, in *China and the Question of Taiwan: Documents and Analysis*, ed. Hungdah Chiu (New York: Praeger, 1973), pp. 205–07.

3. *Foreign Relations of the United States, Diplomatic Papers: The Conferences at Cairo and Teheran 1943* (Washington, D.C.: U.S. Government Printing Office, 1961), pp. 565–66.

4. *Foreign Relations of the United States, Diplomatic Papers: The Conference of Berlin (The Potsdam Conference) 1945*, Vol. 2 (Washington, D.C.: U.S. Government Printing Office, 1960), p. 1474–76.

5. Ibid., pp. 1474 (Soviet Union) and 1555–56 (France).

6. In complete text of document, see *United States Statutes At Large*, Vol. 59, Part II (Washington, D.C.: U.S. Government Printing Office, 1946).

7. Marjorie M. Whiteman, *Digest of International Law*, Vol. 3 (Washington, D.C.: U.S. Government Printing Office, 1964) pp. 487–88.

8. For instance, D. Barry Kirkham wrote that "had the Communists not come to power on the mainland, Formosa undoubtedly would have been ceded to China by express

terms of the [San Francisco Peace] Treaty." See his "The International Legal Status of Formosa," in *Canadian Yearbook of International Law*, Vol. 4 (Vancouver: The Publication Center, University of British Columbia, 1968), p. 147.

9. See U.S. Department of State, *Transcript of Proceedings: Conference on Problems of United States Policy in China* (Washington, D.C.: Division of Central Services, 1949). For Fairbank's statement, see pp. 138–39.

10. See Tang Tsou, *American Failure in China, 1941-50* (Chicago: University of Chicago Press, 1963), pp. 528–31.

11. See *Time* 60, no. 1 (January 2, 1950): 11–12.

12. *Time* 60, no. 2 (January 9, 1950): pp. 9–10.

13. See *American Foreign Policy, 1950-1955, Basic Documents*, Vol. 2 (Washington, D.C.: U.S. Government Printing Office, 1951), pp. 1667–69.

14. See ibid., pp. 2449–51.

15. *Department of State Bulletin* 22, no. 551 (January 23, 1950): 116.

16. A. Doak Barnett, *China on the Eve of Communist Takeover* (New York: Praeger, 1963), p. 310.

17. *American Foreign Policy, 1950-1955*, p. 2468.

18. *China Handbook 1951* (Taipei: China Publishing Co., 1951), p. 115.

19. Chinese People's Institute of Foreign Affairs, ed., *Oppose U.S. Occupation of Taiwan and "Two Chinas" Plot* (Peking: Foreign Languages Press, 1958), p. 3.

20. Ibid., pp. 5–6.

21. Hsinhua News Agency, *Daily News Release*, No. 427 (Peking: China Information Bureau, Press Administration, July 7, 1950), p. 51.

22. UN Doc. S/1715, August 24, 1950.

23. *Yearbook of the United Nations 1950* (New York: Columbia University in cooperation with the United Nations, 1950), p. 289.

24. Ibid., p. 291.

25. Ibid., p. 292.

26. Ibid.

27. The complete text of Wu's speech can be found in UN Security Council, *Official Records*, 5th Year, 527th Meeting, No. 69, August 29, 1950, pp. 5–10 (S/P.V. 527).

28. Ibid., p. 293.

29. Ibid., p. 294.

30. Ibid.

31. Ibid.

32. Ibid., p. 295.

33. Ibid., pp. 296–97.

34. See *Daily News Release*, No. 576 (December 19, 1950), pp. 133–34.

35. *Daily News Release*, No. 577 (December 20, 1950), pp. 143–52.

36. See "Foreign Minister Chou En-lai Replies Arbelaez's Cable," NCNA-Peking, February 5, 1951, in *Daily News Release*, No. 617 (February 9, 1951), p. 21.

37. *Yearbook of the United Nations 1951* (New York: Columbia University Press, 1952), pp. 259, 261.

38. *Yearbook of the United Nations 1950*, p. 298.

39. *Yearbook of the United Nations 1951*, p. 262.

40. *Daily News Release*, No. 1758 (October 11, 1954), pp. 117–19.

41. *Keesing's Contemporary Archives*, Vol. 10 (1955–56) (London: Keesing's Publications), p. 14017.

42. Ibid., p. 14018.

43. *Oppose U.S. Occupation of Taiwan*, p. 29.

44. *Yearbook of the United Nations 1955* (New York: Columbia University Press, 1956), p. 55. The Soviet Union also proposed on January 30, 1955, that the Security Council consider the question of acts of aggression committed by the United States against Communist China in the area of Taiwan and other Chinese islands.

45. Ibid., p. 57.

46. Ibid., p. 58.

47. UN Doc. A/L. 638, October 25, 1971, in *UN General Assembly Official Records*, 26th Session, Annexes, Agenda item 93, p. 5.

48. UN Doc. A/L. 640, October 25, 1971, in ibid., p. 6.

49. For instance, on October 20, 1950, Dulles told ROC Ambassador Koo that "if the United States already regarded Taiwan as purely Chinese territory . . . the United States would lose her grounds for dispatching the Seventh Fleet to protect Taiwan. . . ." See *Chin-shan ho-yüeh yu chung-jih ho-yüeh ti kuan-hsi* (The relationship between the San Francisco peace treaty and the Sino-Japanese peace treaty) (Edited and published by Taipei: Chung-hua min-kuo wai-chiao wen-t'i yen-chiu hui, 1966), p. 6.

50. See ibid., pp. 76–82, for Anglo-American negotiations on the question of Chinese participation in the peace conference. The Chinese records show that the United Kingdom insisted that the PRC be invited to the peace conference and that the peace treaty should provide for "ceding Taiwan to China," pp. 76–77.

51. Information conveyed by Dulles to Ambassador Koo on June 15, 1951, at U.S. Department of State, in ibid., p. 78.

52. See record of conversation between Foreign Minister George Yeh and Minister Rankin, dated August 23, 1951, in ibid., pp. 155–58.

53. See the statement read by American Minister Rankin to ROC Foreign Minister George Yeh on August 23, 1951, in ibid., p. 155. See also the Chinese note to U.S. Minister Rankin, dated September 26, 1951, in ibid., pp. 166–67.

54. For text of Chou's statement, see *Daily News Release*, No. 777 (August 16, 1951), pp. 75–78.

55. *3 United States Treaties and Other International Agreements* (hereafter UST) 3169; *Treaties and Other International Agreements Series* (hereafter TIAS) 2490; *United Nations Treaty Series* (hereafter UNTS) 45.

56. Statement read by American Minister Rankin to ROC Foreign Minister Yeh on August 23, 1951, in *Chin-shan ho-yüeh yu Chung-jih ho-yüeh ti kuan-hsi*, p. 156.

57. See record of conversation between Foreign Minister Yeh and Minister Rankin, September 17, 1951, in ibid., p. 165.

58. See record of conversation between Foreign Minister Yeh and Minister Rankin, August 30, 1951, in ibid., p. 160.

59. Chinese translation of the letter in ibid., pp. 185–87.

60. Ibid., pp. 185, 187.

61. Ibid., p. 187.

62. *Chung-hua jen-min kung-ho kuo tui-wai kuan-hsi wen-chien chi* (Compilation of documents relative to the foreign relations of the People's Republic of China), Vol. II, 1951–53 (Peking: Shih-chieh chih-shih ch'u-pan she, 1958), p. 66.

63. See Richard L. Walker, *China Under Communism: The First Five Years* (New Haven, Conn.: Yale University Press, 1955), pp. 11–17, 214–32.

64. *China Handbook 1951*, p. 494.

65. Agreement Relating to the Furnishing of Certain Military Material to China for the Defense of Taiwan, exchange of notes at Taipei, January 30 and February 9, 1951. 2 UST 1499; TIAS, No. 2293; 132 UNTS 273.

66. See *China Handbook 1952–53* (Taipei: China Publishing Co., 1952), pp. 142–43.

67. *American Foreign Policy, 1950–1955, Basic Documents*, p. 2475.

68. For example, see President Chiang's statement issued on March 1, 1953, as summarized in *China Handbook 1953–54* (Taipei: China Publishing Co., 1953), p. 483.

69. 3 UST 160; TIAS No. 5289; 473 UNTS 133.

70. 3 UST 3329; TIAS No. 2491. Later replaced by Treaty of Mutual Cooperation and Security, Washington, January 19, 1960. 11 UST 1632; TIAS No. 4509; 373 UNTS 186.

71. 3 UST 3420; TIAS No. 2493; 131 UNTS 83.

72. 4 UST 234; TIAS No. 2782.

73. 5 UST 2368; TIAS 3097; 238 UNTS 199.

74. See Document 12.

75. See *Kuo-chia chien-she ts'ung-k'an* (National reconstruction series), Vol. 3, *Wai-chiao yu ch'iao-wu* (Diplomacy and overseas Chinese affairs) (Taipei: Cheng-chung shu-ch'u, 1971), p. 154.

76. *Important Documents Concerning the Question of Taiwan* (Peking: Foreign Languages Press, 1955), p. 126.

77. For the whole text, see *Daily News Release*, No. 1717 (August 23, 1954), pp. 243–45.

78. This is the beginning of the so-called First Taiwan Strait Crisis. For a detailed analysis of this crisis, see J. H. Kalicki, *The Pattern of Sino-American Crises, Political-Military Interactions in the 1950s* (London: Cambridge University Press, 1975), pp. 120–55.

79. See *Kuo-chia chien-she ts'ung-k'an*, p. 155.

80. See ibid., pp. 155–57.

81. See interview with George K. C. Yeh in *Chung-kuo Shih-pao* (China Times), Taipei, October 28, 1971, p. 2. Yeh was ROC foreign minister in charge of negotiating the treaty.

82. At the time of negotiation, the ROC side wanted the one-year termination notice changed to two years, but the proposal was rejected by the United States. Information supplied by a reliable source.

83. Accompanied by an exchange of notes dated December 10, 1954. See note 80 and accompanying text. The note was not made public until February 7, 1955.

84. Chou's statement was translated in *Oppose U.S. Occupation of Taiwan and "Two Chinas" Plot*, pp. 18–27.

85. See *Keesing's Contemporary Archives*, Vol. 10 (1955–56), pp. 14017–18.

86. See *China Handbook, 1955–56* (Taipei: China Publishing Co., 1955), pp. 7–11.

87. *American Foreign Policy, 1950–1955, Basic Documents*, pp. 2491–93.

88. Whiteman, *Digest of International Law*, p. 564.

89. For example, see exchange of notes accompanying the 1954 ROC-U.S. Mutual Defense Treaty in Document 10.

90. *Executive Sessions of the Senate Foreign Relations Committee (Historical Series)*, Vol. VII (84th Cong., 1st sess., 1955) (Washington, D.C.: U.S. Government Printing Office, 1978), p. 316. See also the Senate's understanding in approving the Treaty in Document 12.

91. Whiteman, *Digest of International Law*, p. 565.

92. L. Oppenheim, *International Law*, Vol. 2, 7th ed. H. Lauterpacht, ed. (London: Longmans, Green, 1952), p. 611.

93. Ibid.

94. International lawyer Diena regarded this as a dereliction of these territories by Turkey and Italy's occupation of them as the occupation of a no man's land. Ibid., p. 611.

95. D. P. O'Connell, "The Status of Formosa and the Chinese Recognition Problem," *American Journal of International Law* 50, no. 2 (April 1956): 415.

96. Frank P. Morello, *The International Legal Status of Formosa* (The Hague: Martinus Nijhoff, 1966), p. 92.

97. Arthur Dean, "International Law and Current Problems in the Far East," *Proceedings of the American Society of International Law*, 49th Annual Meeting (1955), pp. 86, 95, 96–97.

98. Document 6. The instrument's treaty character seemed beyond doubt in that, as in the case of other treaties concluded by the United States, it was printed in the *United States Statutes at Large*, Vol. 59, Part II, pp. 1734–39.

99. Materials on Succession of States, UN Doc. ST/LEG/SER. B/14 (New York: United Nations, 1967), p. 70. Similarly, in the case of *Chang Fukue v. Chang Chin Min*, decided by the Osaka District Court on June 7, 1960, the court said:

The determination as to whether the parties have lost the Japanese nationality they had once held should be made on the basis of the Formosan Register of Personal Status established for the Formosans as a special category, separately from the Family Register of Japan, ever since the establishment of Japanese sovereignty over Formosa. It is therefore proper to understand that those who held such personal status in the Register referred to above have lost Japanese nationality and acquired the nationality of the Republic of China with the establishment of permanent sovereignty of the Republic of China, i.e., with the entry into force of the Peace Treaty in 1952 when the *de jure* change of sovereignty over that territory. . . .

Ibid., p. 71.

100. See note 54.

101. Of course, if Japan in fact renounced the island of Taiwan on October 25, 1945, and the island became *terra nullius* at that time, then the ROC certainly could acquire sovereignty over the island by occupation. And the PRC, claiming to be the successor of the ROC government, could also invoke the principle of occupation to its advantage. However, it should be noted that there is no document to support the view that Japan had renounced the title to Taiwan on October 25, 1945.

102. Shao Chin-fu, "The Absurd Theory of 'Two Chinas' and Principles of International Law," *Kuo-chi wen-t'i yen-chiu* (Studies in international problems), No. 2 (Peking 1959), p. 14.

103. The relevant provisions of the Versailles Treaty are as follows:

Section V.
ALSACE-LORRAINE

The HIGH CONTRACTING PARTIES, recognising the moral obligation to redress the wrong done by Germany in 1871 *both to the rights of France and to the wishes of the population of Alsace and Lorraine*, which were separated from their country in spite of the solemn protest of their representatives at the Assembly of Bordeaux,

Agree upon the following Articles:

Article 51.

The territories which were ceded to Germany in accordance with the Preliminaries of Peace signed at Versailles on February 26, 1871, and the Treaty of Frankfort of May 10, 1871, are restored to French sovereignty as from the date of the Armistice of November 11, 1918.

The provisions of the Treaties establishing the delimitation of the frontiers before 1871 shall be restored. (Emphasis added.)

Fred L. Isreal and Emanuel Chill, *Major Peace Treaties of Modern History, 1648-1967*, Vol. II (New York: McGraw-Hill, 1967), p. 1311. It should be noted that the treaty paid equal importance to French historical right and to the wishes of the inhabitants in returning the Alsace-Lorraine to France.

104. The Conditions of An Armistice with Germany signed on November 11, 1918, provided that Germany should immediately evacuate from "invaded countries . . . as well as Alsace-Lorraine. . . ." *American Journal of International Law*, Vol. 13 (1919), Supplement, p. 97.

105. See his "Strip the Aggressor of Its Legal Cloak," *Jen-min jih-pao* (People's Daily), January 31, 1955, p. 3; English translation under the title "The Aggressor and the Law, *People's China*, No. 5 (March 1, 1955), p. 10.

106. Oppenheim, *International Law*, p. 304.

107. See his *Red Star Over China* (New York: Grove Press), 1961, p. 96.

108. Kenneth T. Young, *Negotiating with the Chinese Communists* (New York: McGraw-Hill, 1968), p. 44.

109. Ibid., p. 45.

110. See ibid.

111. Ibid., pp. 46-67.

112. Ibid., p. 47.

113. See ibid., pp. 47-50, 52.

114. See ibid., pp. 52-53.

115. *Oppose U.S. Occupation of Taiwan and "Two Chinas" Plot*, pp. 35-36.

116. For the text of the agreement, see *Department of State Bulletin* 33, no. 847 (September 19, 1955): 456-57. Reproduced in Young, *Negotiating with the Chinese Communists*, pp. 412-13.

117. See Young, *Negotiating with the Chinese Communists*, pp. 94-95.

118. See ibid., pp. 95-110.

119. See Lewis Gilbert, "Peking and Taipei," in *Formosa Today*, ed. Mark Mancall (New York: Praeger, 1964), pp. 112-20.

120. See Chou En-lai's Report to the Third Session of the First National People's Congress, June 28, 1956, in *Oppose the U.S. Occupation of Taiwan and "Two China" Plot*, pp. 41-51.

121. See The New York *Times*, June 30, 1956, p. 2.

122. See *President Chiang Kai-Shek: Selected Speeches and Messages in 1957* (Taipei: Government Information Office) pp. 45-46.

123. See Chou En-lai's Report to the Fifth Session of the First National People's Congress, February 10, 1958, in *Oppose U.S. Occupation of Taiwan and "Two Chinas" Plot*, pp. 55-56, 57-58.

124. "Chinese Government's Statement on Sino-American Ambassadorial Talks," *Peking Review* 1, No. 19 (July 8, 1958): 21-22.

125. See Young, *Negotiating with the Chinese Communists*, pp. 139-41.

126. *American Foreign Policy, Current Documents, 1958* (Washington, D.C.: U.S. Government Printing Office, 1962), pp. 1138-43, 142; and Young, *Negotiating with the Chinese Communists*, p. 142.

127. Donald S. Zagoria, *The Sino-Soviet Conflict, 1956-61* (Princeton, N.J.: Princeton Univeristy Press, 1962), p. 210.

128. Young, *Negotiating with the Chinese Communists*, p. 143.

129. Ibid., p. 144.

130. For the text of the PRC's declaration, see *Peking Review* 1, no. 28 (September 8, 1958): p. 21.

131. See G. Barraclough, *Survey of International Affairs, 1956-1958* (London: Oxford University Press, 1962), pp. 568-69.

132. See *Peking Review* 1, no. 28 (September 9, 1958): pp. 15-16; and *Soviet News*, No. 3911 (London: Press Department of the Soviet Embassy, September 9, 1958), pp. 193-95. For President Eisenhower's reply, see *Department of State Bulletin* 39, no. 1005 (September 29, 1958): 498. Khrushchev again sent a letter to Eisenhower on September 19, 1958. See *Soviet News*, No. 3917 (September 22, 1958), pp. 221-23.

133. Both interviews reprinted in Hungdah Chiu, ed., *China and the Question of Taiwan: Documents and Analysis* (New York: Praeger, 1973), pp. 283-85.

134. Young, *Negotiating with the Chinese Communists*, p. 161.

135. See P'eng's message to compatriots on Taiwan, October 13, 1958. *Chung-hua jen-min kung-ho kuo tui-wai kuan-hsi wen-chien chi* (Compilation of documents relating to the foreign relations of the People's Republic of China), Vol. 5 (1958) (Peking: Shih-chieh chih-shih ch'u-pan she, 1959), p. 176.

136. *China and U.S. Far East Policy, 1945-1967* (Washington, D.C.: Congressional Quarterly Service, 1967), p. 90.

137. For a thorough analysis of the Second Taiwan Strait Crisis, see Kalicki, *The Pattern of Sino-American Crisis*, pp. 168–208.

138. See the statement issued by the spokesman for the information department of the PRC Foreign Ministry on the question of exchanging correspondents between China and the United States, September 13, 1960. *Peking Review* 3, no. 37 (September 14, 1960: pp. 29–31.

139. Premier Chou En-lai's Replies to Questions Submitted by Felix Greene, September 5, 1960, in *Oppose the New U.S. Plots to Create "Two Chinas"* (Peking: Foreign Languages Press, 1962), pp. 22–24.

140. English translation of the editorial in *Peking Review* 3, no. 37 (September 14, 1960): 26–29.

141. See "Message of the Fukien Front Command of the Chinese People's Liberation Army to Compatriots in Taiwan, Penghu, Quemoy and Matsu, June 17, 1960," *Peking Review* 3, no. 25, (June 21, 1960): 3–4.

142. *Jen-min jih-pao* (People's Daily), February 2, 1962, p. 4.

143. Frank Robertson, "Refugees and Troop Moves—a Report from Hong-Kong," *China Quarterly*, No. 11 (July-September, 1962), pp. 111–15.

144. See Harold C. Hinton, *Communist China in World Politics* (Boston: Houghton Mifflin, 1966), pp. 296, 324, 350.

145. *China Yearbook 1962-63* (Taipei: China Publishing Co., 1963), p. 1012.

146. Ibid., p. 342.

147. See Hinton, *Communist China in World Politics*, p. 271.

148. Max Frankel, "Red China Building up Troops and Jet Units Opposite Quemoy," New York *Times*, June 21, 1962, pp. 1, 5.

149. NCNA Correspondent, "Chiang Kai-shek Gang Prepares for Military Adventure," June 29, 1962, *Peking Review* 5, no. 26 (June 29, 1962): 5–6.

150. Young, *Negotiating with the Chinese Communists*, p. 250.

151. Ibid., p. 251.

152. Hinton, *Communist China in World Politics*, p. 272.

153. "Ch'en Yi Condemns U.S. Imperialism," *Peking Review* 5, no. 29 (July 20, 1962): 21.

154. *China Yearbook, 1963-64* (Taipei: China Publishing Co., 1964), pp. 2–4; "Guerrilla War Hits Red China," *U.S. News and World Report*, March 4, 1963, pp. 40–44.

155. *American Foreign Policy, 1961, Current Documents* (Washington, D.C.: U.S. Government Printing Office, 1965), p. 946.

156. Ibid., pp. 949–51.

157. Kenneth T. Young, *Diplomacy and Power in Washington-Peking Dealings: 1953-1967* (Chicago: University of Chicago Center for Policy Study, 1967), p. 18.

158. For example, see Edgar Snow, *The Other Side of the River: Red China Today* (New York: Random House, 1961), pp. 765–66.

159. For example, see "No 'Two Chinas' in Gymnastics," *Peking Review* 7, no. 32 (August 7, 1964): 5, 27.

160. Stephen Erasmus, "General de Gaulle's Recognition of Peking," *China Quarterly*, No. 18 (April-June 1964), p. 195.

161. Ibid., p. 197.

162. Hinton, *Communist China in World Politics*, pp. 150–51.

163. Drew Middleton, "De Gaulle Tries to Retain Tie with Nationalist China," New York *Times*, January 26, 1964, pp. 1, 4.

164. Hinton, *Communist China in World Politics*, p. 151.

165. On February 15 a PRC chargé d'affaires arrived in Paris; on February 23 a French chargé d'affaires took up residence in Peking. In April ambassadors were exchanged. Erasmus, "De Gaulle's Recognition of Peking," p. 197.

166. See Hungdah Chiu, "Communist China's Attitude Towards Nuclear Tests," *China Quarterly*, No. 21 (January-March 1965), p. 96.

167. *American Foreign Policy, Current Documents, 1963* (Washington, D.C.: U.S. Government Printing Office, 1967), p. 759.

168. Ibid., p. 761.

169. See excerpts of the article in *American Foreign Policy, Current Documents, 1964* (Washington, D.C.: U.S. Government Printing Office, 1967), pp. 876–77.

170. *U.S. Policy with Respect to Mainland China*, Hearings before the Committee on Foreign Relations, U.S. Senate, 89th Cong., 2d sess., March 8, 10, 16, 18, 21, 28, 30, 1966 (Washington, D.C.: U.S. Government Printing Office, 1966), pp. 14–15.

171. See *American Foreign Policy, Current Documents, 1966* (Washington, D.C.: U.S. Government Printing Office, 1969), pp. 650–59.

172. Observer, "Old Tune, New Plot," English translation in *Peking Review* 9, no. 14 (April 1, 1966): 13–15.

173. Editorial, "The Five-star Red Flag Must be Planted on Taiwan Province," *Jen-Min jih-pao* (People's Daily), June 27, 1966; English translation in *Peking Review* 14, no. 19 (May 7, 1971): 13–14.

174. *Peking Review* 9, no. 40 (October 4, 1968): 14, 15.

175. See PRC Foreign Ministry's Note to the Soviet Embassy in China, March 21, 1968, *Peking Review* 11, no. 13 (March 29, 1968): 9.

176. See *Peking Review* 11, no. 48 (November 29, 1968): 31.

177. *China Yearbook 1967-68* (Taipei: China Publishing Co., n.d.) p. 653. See also "General Chiang Termed Wary on Red China," New York *Times*, January 19, 1967, p. 2.

178. Associated Press, Washington, January 10, 1967, in *Chung-yang jih-pao* (Central daily news), international ed., January 11, 1967, p. 1.

179. United Press International, Washington, *Tsing-tao jih-pao* (Hong Kong), January 12, 1967, p. 2.

180. *Department of State Bulletin* 56, no. 1458 (June 5, 1967): 849.

181. *Free China Review* 17, no. 11 (November 1967): 88.

182. See *Peking Review* 12, no. 11 (March 14, 1969): 13.

183. See Jay Walz, "Canada's Talks on Ties to Peking Appear Stalled," New York *Times*, August 3, 1969, p. 15.

184. "Canada Establishes Diplomatic Relations with the Chinese People's Republic," *External Affairs* (Ottawa) 22, no. 11 (November 1970): 378.

185. "7th Fleet Cut Seen in the Taiwan Straits," United Press International, Tokyo, December 24, 1969, in New York *Times*, December 25, 1969, p. 8. See also New York *Times*, March 19, 1970, p. 14.

186. In April 1970 the United States authorized the selctive licensing of goods for export to the PRC. During 1970 the United States validated passports for 270 Americans to visit the PRC. See Nixon's message to the Congress on February 25, 1971, "U.S. Foreign Policy for the 1970's, Building for Peace," *Department of State Bulletin* 64, no. 1656 (December 14, 1970): 384.

187. See U.S. Representative Christopher H. Phillips' statement at 25th session of the General Assembly of the United Nations in late 1970. *Department of State Bulletin* 63, no. 1642 (December 14, 1970): 734.

188. For example, Marshall Green, assistant secretary of state for East Asian and Pacific affairs, told the Subcommittee on Asian and Pacific Affairs, Committee on Foreign Affairs of the House of Representatives, on October 6, 1970:

> For our part, we will continue to reiterate our willingness to remain responsive to any indications of reduced hostility from Peking, to cooperate in removing tensions and to enter into a constructive dialogue eventually leading to more relations. We will attempt to convince Peking that we are not seeking to "contain and isolate" China and that we favor China's emergence from isolation.
>
> . . .

Excerpt in *Current Scene* (Hong Kong) 9, no. 3 (March 7, 1971): 23. For excerpts of similar statements by Nixon, Secretary of State Rogers, and Green, see ibid., pp. 22–24.

189. Nixon, "U.S. Foreign Policy for the 1970's" p. 383.

190. "A Look at Nixon's Foreign Policy Report, Big Exposure of U.S. Imperialism's World Hegemony Ambition," *Peking Review* 14, no. 11 (March 12, 1971): p. 27.

191. See "Chinese Table Tennis Team in Nagoya," *Peking Review* 14, no. 16 (April 16, 1971): pp. 11–12.

192. See Tillman Durdin, "China's U.S. Policy, a Chasm Still Separates Two Governments," New York *Times* News Service; *Asahi Evening News*, Tokyo, May 8, 1971, p. 4.

193. See Commentator, "Fresh Evidence of the U.S. Government's Hostilities toward the Chinese People," *Jen-min jih-pao* (People's Daily), May 4, 1971. The ROC also took strong exception to the American view the status of Taiwan. See Document 20.

194. See Takashi Oka, "Chou Ties U.N. Seat to Taipei's Ouster," New York *Times*, July 1, 1971, pp. 1, 32.

195. "Transcript of the President's Statement," New York *Times*, July 17, 1971, p. 4.

196. Resolution 2758 (XXVI), *UN Monthly Chronicle* 8, no. 10 (November 1971): 61.

197. *UN Monthly Chronicle* 8, no. 11 (December 1971), p. 26.

198. English text in *Peking Review*, 15, no. 9 (March 3, 1972): 5; *Department of State Bulletin* 64, no. 1708 (March 20, 1972): 435–38. Text reproduced in Document 21.

199. *The Memoirs of Richard Nixon* (New York: Grosset and Dunlap, 1978), p. 576.

200. President Nixon explained the U.S. position before he went to the PRC as follows:

> In my address announcing my trip to Peking, and since then, I have emphasized that our new dialogue with the PRC would not be at the expense of friends . . . with the Republic of China, *we shall maintain our friendship, our diplomatic ties, and our defense Commitment.* . . . (Emphasis added.)

"U.S. Foreign Policy for the 1970's, The Emerging Structure of Peace, A Report to the Congress by Richard Nixon," February 9, 1972, in *Department of State Bulletin* 64, no. 1707 (March 13, 1972): 330.

This position was affirmed by Secretary of State Henry Kissinger at a press conference held on February 27, 1972, after the issuance of the Shanghai Communique. The pertinent colloquy is as follows:

> Q. Why did not the United States Government reaffirm its treaty commitment to Taiwan, as the President and you have done on numerous occasions?
>
> Dr. Kissinger: Let me . . . state in response to this and any related question—and let me do it once and not repeat it: We stated our basic position with respect to this issue in the President's world report (of February 9, 1972) in which we say that this treaty will be maintained. Nothing has changed in that position . . . the position of the world report stands and has been unaltered.

"President Nixon's Visit to the PRC—News Conference of Dr. Kissinger and Mr. Green," (Shanghai, February 27, 1972), in *Department of State Bulletin* 66, no. 1708 (March 20, 1972): 428.

201. Lee Lescaze, "U.S. Aide Reassures Taiwan with Pledge Backing Treaty," *International Herald Tribune*, Paris, March 4–5, 1972, p. 2.

202. Joseph Lelyveld, "A 1½-China Policy," New York *Times Magazine*, April 6, 1975, p. 71.

203. "Transcript of ['Meet the Press'] T.V. Interview with [Marshall] Green," *Mainchi Daily News*, March 29, 1972, p. 2.

204. "'February 28' Uprising in Taiwan Province Marked," *Peking Review* 16, no. 10 (March 9, 1973): 11.

205. In a military document distributed to the company level and above entitled "The Great Victory of Chairman Mao's Revolutionary Diplomatic Line," prepared by the Political Department of Kunming Military Region on April 4, 1973, it is stated: "The Shanghai Communique . . . has forced U.S. imperialism to recognize that Taiwan is a part of Chinese territory." Translated by the author from the Chinese text reprinted in *Chinese Communist Internal Politics and Foreign Policy*, (Taipei: Institute of International Relations, 1974), p. 180.

206. Stanely Karnow, "Our Next Move on China," New York *Times Magazine*, August 14, 1977, p. 34.

207. See "Harvard Expert's View, U.S. Stand on Taiwan Is Seen As Peril to Nixon-Chou Accord," *International Herald Tribune*, Paris, March 6, 1972, p. 2. See also Ralph N. Clough, *Island China* (Cambridge, Mass.: Harvard University Press, 1978), p. 3.

208. The "unofficial organs" are run by foreign service officials "on leave" from each other's foreign ministry, but their seniority in the service will not be interrupted during their "leave of absence" for service in the "unofficial organs." For a study of the so-called Japanese formula, see David N. Rowe, *Informal "Diplomatic Relations": The Case of Japan and the Republic of China, 1972-1974* (Hamden: Conn.: Shoe String Press, 1975); James William Morely, "The Japanese Formula for Normalization and Its Relevance for U.S. China Policy," in *Normalizing Relations with the People's Republic of China: Problems, Analysis and Documents*, ed. Hungdah Chiu (Baltimore: University of Maryland School of Law, 1978), pp. 121-36, and Clough, *Island China*, pp. 189-201.

209. New York *Times*, February 23, 1973, p. 14.

210. *United States Statute At Large*, Vol. 87, p. 24.

211. See New York *Times*, May 7, 1975, pp. 1, 6.

212. See Fox Butterfield, "U.S.-China Talks: Peking, While Rejecting Proposals, Still Appears Flexible on Taiwan," New York *Times*, September 8, 1977, p. A3.

213. "Ford Asserts He Called Severing of Taiwan Ties Only a Possibility," New York *Times*, September 8, 1977, p. A3.

214. Excerpt from Paul Chan and James Reardon-Anderson, "Documentation, Chronology and Bibliography," *Contemporary China* 2, no. 1 (Spring 1978): 63.

215. Excerpt in ibid., p. 64.

216. Excerpt in ibid., p. 65.

217. Excerpt in ibid.

218. See Document 24.

219. Numerous articles and editorials appeared during July-August 1977 opposing the severing of U.S. ties with and terminating the security treaty with the ROC. For example, see Joseph J. Sisco (former undersecretary of state and then president of the American University), "Secretary Vance's Trip to Peking," *Wall Street Journal*, July 8, 1977; Edward N. Luttwak," United States Policy: Between the Two Chinas," New York *Times*, August 1, 1977, p. 23; George W. Ball (former undersecretary of state), "Against 'Cravenly Yielding' to Peking," New York *Times*, August 24, 1977, p. 31, to mention just a few. See also an open letter to President Carter signed by 3,500 Americans, urging him "to continue diplomatic ties with the Republic of China on Taiwan." The signers include Robert Murphy (former undersecretary of state), Frederick Seitz (president of Rockefeller University), C. Martin Wilbur (former president of the Association for Asian Studies), New York *Times*, August 14 (Sunday), 1977, p. E18, and many other prominent Americans. Earlier a Potomac Associates poll conducted in April 1977 indicated that 47 percent of Americans oppose derecognizing the ROC as a quid pro quo for normalizing relations with the PRC, while only 28 percent approved that condition.

220. Rowland Evans and Robert Novak, "A Stall on the Taiwan Question," Washington *Post*, August 17, 1977.

221. "Vance Briefs Carter On His Discussion with Top Chinese," New York *Times*, August 29, 1977, p. 7.

222. Louis D. Boccardi, "Teng Says Vance Tip Set Back Normal Ties," New York *Times*, September 7, 1977, pp. A1, A2.

223. See PRC Vice Foreign Minister Yu Chan's interview in *Wall Street Journal*, October 3, 1977, and Vice Premier Li Hsien-nien's interview in *Wall Street Journal*, October 4, 1977. Excerpt in Chan and Anderson, "Documentation" pp. 66–67.

224. See *Department of State Bulletin* 78, no. 2016 (July 1978): 27–28.

225. See "Relations with U.S. will grow fast, opening 'Wide Vistas,' Teng says," and "Teng Says 'nothing new,' State Department finds," *The Sun* (Baltimore)' January 6, 1979, p. A2. The same position was reiterated on January 30, 1979, during Teng's visit in the United States. See Bernard Gwertzman, "Teng, on Capital Hill, Says Peking Must Keep Taiwan Options Open," New York *Times*, January 31, 1979, pp. A2, A6.

226. See Earnest B. Furgurson, "Taiwan will be safe, top spokesman assert, Some others wonder," *The Sun* (Baltimore)‚ December 18, 1978, pp. A1, A2; and Don Oberdorfer, "U.S. Sets '79 Moratorium on New Arms to Taiwan," Washington *Post*, January 12, 1979.

227. *Chung-juo shih-pao* (China Times), Taipei, December 28, 1978, p. 1.

228. The State Department instructed U.S. Ambassador Unger in Taipei to give the ROC only one-hour advance notice of the president's surprise move. Ambassador Unger, however, disregarded the instruction and informed the ROC leaders as soon as he received the message, so the ROC government received a seven-hour advance notice of the president's dramatic action.

229. S. 245, submitted to Senate on January 29, 1979. Text in *Taiwan*, Hearings before the Senate Committee on Foreign Relations, 96 Cong., 1st Sess. on S.245 (February 5, 6, 7, 8, 21, and 22, 1979) (Washington, D.C.: U.S. Government Printing Office, 1979), pp. 3–10.

230. Text of Articles of Incorporation of the American Institute in Taiwan can be found in *Taiwan Enabling Act*, Report of the Senate Foreign Relations Committee on S.245 (Washington, D.C.: U.S. Government Printing Office, 1979), pp. 69–71.

231. Bernard Gwertzman, "Senate Panel Balks at Letting U.S. Shift Funds to New Office in Taipei," New York *Times*, February 13, 1979, p. A6.

232. See "Taipei to Set Up New Organization to Continue Its Ties With the U.S.," New York *Times*, February 16, 1979, p. A3, and "Coordination Council for N. American Affairs to Start Operation March 1," *News From China*, February 27, 1979, p. 79–0260. See also Document 34.

233. See *Taiwan Enabling Act Report*, pp. 29–30.

234. See Deputy Secretary of State Warren Christopher's statement at Senate hearings on Taiwan, February 5, 1979, *Taiwan Hearings*, p. 24.

235. See *Taiwan Hearings*, pp. 32–35.

236. *Taiwan Enabling Act Report*, pp. 11–12.

237. Yuan-li Wu and K. C. Yeh, "Economic Impact of Alternative US-ROC Relations," *International Trade Law Journal* 3, no. 1 (Fall 1977): 152, 156.

238. See Bernard Gwertzman, "Compromise on Taiwan Security Reported Imminent in Congress," New York *Times*, February 21, 1979, pp. A1, A7, and Henry L. Trewhitt, "Compromise Reached on Taiwan issue," *The Sun* (Baltimore), February 22, 1979, p. A2.

239. See International Commission of Jurists, editor and publisher, *The Question of Tibet and the Rule of Law* (Geneva, 1959). For text of PRC-Tibetan Agreement of 1951, see *Taiwan Hearings*, pp. 98–99.

240. William E. Overholt, "Nuclear Proliferation in Eastern Asia," *Pacific Community, An Asian Quarterly Review* 8, no. 1 (October 1976): 50. See also Ernest Lefever,

"U.S. Security Ties and the Nuclear Option: South Korea and Taiwan," in *Forum on the U.S. and East Asia* (Taipei: Asia and the World Forum, 1977), pp. 133-235.

241. Warren Kuo, *Foreign-Policy Speeches by Chinese Communist Leaders 1963-1975* (Taipei: Institute of International Relations, 1976), p. 34. At the 1951 MacArthur hearings of the Senate Committees on Armed Services and Foreign Relations, General Bradley said that Formosa [Taiwan]"has great strategic value in the hands of an enemy . . . (because of Formosa's) naval and air bases which would extend the action of ships and planes a considerable distance along the lines of our [US]communication between the Philippines, Okinawa and Japan. . . ." *Military Situation in the Far East*, Hearings before Senate Committee on Armed Services and Committee on Foreign Relations, 82nd Cong., 1st sess., May-June 1951 (Washington, D.C.: U.S. Government Printing Office, 1951), p. 882. General MacArthur said at the hearings, "I believe that from our standpoint we would practically lose the Pacific Ocean if we give up or lose Formosa." Ibid., p. 53.

At the 1955 Senate Executive Session on the U.S.-ROC Mutual Defense Treaty, Admiral Radford said: "Formosa [Taiwan], in unfriendly hands, because of its size, would accommodate air forces that could force us to abandon our base at Okinawa; I mean, they would outflank us, and . . . with jet aircraft the threat to the Philippines, Okinawa, would be very, very great." *Executive Sessions of the Senate Foreign Relations Committee*, p. 143.

242. For example, see Edwin J. Feulner, Jr., "Asia, Taiwan and the Man," *Asia Mail* 2, no. 8 (May 1978): 17, and a more comprehensive analysis of the problem in John W. Garver, "Taiwan's Russian Option: Image and Reality," *Asian Survey* 18, no. 7 (July 1978): 751-66.

243. At present, the ROC government refuses to let Soviet commercial ships enter Taiwan ports even if they are delivering ROC crews rescued by the Soviet ship. The ROC port authorities have usually sent a motorboat to pick up a rescued ROC crew from the Soviet ship three miles off the ROC coast. See several interesting stories reported in Kao Yuan, "Soviet Russia's Cargo Ships and Chinese Crews," *Chung-ho yüeh-Kan* (Scooper Monthly), No. 114 (Taipei, May 1978), pp. 29-35.

244. See the following excerpts from two commentators: "There are those who argue that a declaration of independence [by Taiwan] is the one thing that could precipitate a Chinese attack. As long as everyone agrees that Taiwan is China, it is reasoned, China can afford to temporize; a claim to independence would make it now or never for Peking," Joseph Lelyveld, "A 1½-China Policy," New York *Times Magazine*, April 6, 1975, p. 78. "Support for independence for Taiwan would damage U.S. relations with both China and Japan. The Chinese would, justifiably, regard this course as violating the spirit if not the letter of the Shanghai communique, and they would be likely to renew military threats to Taiwan," Ralph N. Clough, *East Asia and U.S. Security* (Washington, D.C.: Brookings Institution, 1975), p. 139.

245. Released on September 11, 1978 (1SSN 0046-6875). For earlier polls done by various organizations, see Y. M. Kau, "Public Opinion and Our China Policy," *Asian Affairs, An American View* 5, no. 3 (January-February 1978): 133-47.

246. On July 25, 1978, the Senate by a vote of 94 to 0 adopted an amendment to the International Security Assistance Act of 1978 stating that "it is the sense of the Senate that there should be prior consultation between the Congress and the executive branch on any proposed policy changes affecting the continuation in force of the Mutual Defense Treaty of 1954 [with the Republic of China]." *Congressional Record*, 95th Cong., 2d sess., No. 113 (July 25, 1978), p. S11726. Later the amendment was revised by inserting the word "Congress" to replace "Senate." See *Congressional Record*, No. 138 (September 7, 1978), p. H9229. See Document 25.

247. Information supplied by American Conservative Union.

248. See Morley, "The Japanese Formula for Normalization," p. 136.

249. See "Brezhnev Attacks United States for Trying 'to Play Chinese Card,'" New York *Times*, June 26, 1978, pp. A1, A4. See also the following view expressed by Dr.

Georgi Arbatov, Director of the Institute for U.S. and Canadian Studies of the Soviet Academy of Sciences to an American correspondent:

> If normalization of your U.S. relations with China is part of a general move toward detente, it will be understood as such. Our relations with Peking may also change in time. But if you normalize with China in a way that has definite military and political undertones of anti-Soviet nature, it may be seen as a sign of something very sinister.

Time, November 6, 1978, p. 45.

In another interview, Arbatov observed:

> [If China becomes] some sort of military ally to the West, even an informal ally. Then the whole situation would look different to us. We would have to reanalyze our relationship with the West. If such an axis is built on an anti-Soviet basis, then there is no place for detente, even in a narrow sense. For instance, what sense would it make for us to agree to reduce armaments in Europe if armaments are simply to be channeled by the West to the eastern front?

"Soviet Cautions U.S. on Pact with China," New York *Times*, November 13, 1978, p. A7.

250. Cited from Richard Baum, "Jimmy Carter & China," *Asia Mail* 2, no. 7 (April 1978): 14.

251. "Gambling on China," New York *Times*, July 25, 1978, p. 415.

252. "United States Policy: Between the Two Chinas," New York *Times*, August 1, 1977, p. 23.

253. Michael Parks, "Sino-Soviet tensions near danger level," *The Sun* (Baltimore), March 11, 1979, p. A4.

254. See also James Reardon-Anderson, "Peking and Washington: The Politics of Abnormalization," *Contemporary China* 2, no. 1 (Spring 1978): 3-12.

255. To mention just a few, William Safire, "Reading Teng's Mind," New York *Times*, December 21, 1978; John B. Oakes, "America's Loss of Face," New York *Times*, December 29, 1978, p. A23; Joseph Kraft, "The Sino-American Normalization, Regent in Peking," *The Sun* (Baltimore), December 19, 1978, p. A19; S. Robert Chiappinelli, "Shunning of Taiwan a 'national shame,' scholar says," Providence *Bulletin*, December 18, 1978, p. B1; George Bush, "Our Deal with Peking: All Cost, No Benefit," Washington *Post*, December 24, 1978; William J. Porter, "What Carter Gets Us Into," *Christian Science Monitor*, January 10, 1979; and John Maclean, "Questions about Taiwan's Future," Chicago *Tribune*, December 24, 1978.

256. "China's Price," *Wall Street Journal*, December 18, 1978, p. 28.

257. AP (Washington), "Chinese concession reported," *The Sun* (Baltimore), January 5, 1979, p. A4.

258. "Poll Finds 46 Percent Still Oppose Ties With China at Taiwan's Expense," New York *Times*, January 29, 1979.

259. For example, see Adam Clymer, "Old China Debate Flares," New York *Times*, December 17, 1978, pp. 1, 18, and Warren Weaver, Jr., "Treaty Termination May Spur Senators," New York *Times*, December 18, 1978, p. A13.

260. See Terence Smith, "Carter and European Leaders Seek to Assure Soviet on Ties to China," New York *Times*, January 7, 1979, pp. 1, 13.

261. Masaru Ogawa, "Our Times—U.S.-China Normalization," Japan *Times*, December 24, 1978, pp. 1, 4. See also editorial of *Sankei Shimbun*, January 1, 1979, and comments in *Asahi Shimbun*, January 1, 1979, all calling for review of U.S.-Japanese relations in view of the abrogation of U.S.-ROC Mutual Defense Treaty.

262. UPI-Manila, January 2, 1979, cited from *Lien-ho pao* (United daily news), international air edition, January 3, 1979, p. 1.

263. Henry S. Bradsher, "Angry Israelis Now See U.S.-Taiwan Break as Dangerous Precedent," Washington *Star*, December 18, 1978.

264. David K. Shipler, "Soviet, Citing Its Note to Carter, Indicates Concern on China Ties," New York *Times*, December 22, 1978. See also "Soviet warns of danger in U.S.-China relations," *The Sun* (Baltimore), December 19, 1978, p. A2; "U.S. forging 'bloc,' Soviet says," *The Sun* (Baltimore), December 18, 1978; and David K. Shipler, "Two Soviet Officials See Danger in U.S.-China Relations," New York *Times*, December 17, 1978, p. 19; and Bernard Gwertzman, "Soviet Reluctance on Final Arms Pact Linked to China Ties," New York *Times*, December 25, 1978, pp. A1, A4.

265. See Edward K. Wu, "New regime installed in Cambodia, Vietnam reports rebels it backed have taken over," *The Sun* (Baltimore), January 9, 1979, pp. A1, A2.

266. See "A War of Angry Cousins, China's 'Punitive action' against Vietnam has global implications." *Time* 113, no. 10 (March 5, 1979): 35.

267. Michael Parks, "Taiwan doubts Carter's sincerity in promising safeguards," *The Sun* (Baltimore), December 22, 1978.

268. Text of letter released by Congressman Wolff on February 23, 1979.

Selected Documents

DOCUMENT 1

Koxinga-Dutch Treaty, February 1, 1662

Treaty made and agreed upon; from the one side, by His Highness the Lord Teibingh Tsiante Teysiancon Koxin, who has besieged Castle Zeelandia on Formosa since 1st May 1661 up till this first day of February 1662; and from the other side, as representing the Dutch Government, by the Governor of the said Castle, Frederick Coyett and his Council, consisting of the undernoted eighteen Articles:

I. All hostilities committed on either side to be forgotten.

II. Castle Zeelandia, with its outworks, artillery, remaining war-materials, merchandise, money, and other properties belonging to the Honourable Company, to be surrendered to Lord Koxinga.

III. Rice, bread, wine, arack, meat, pork, oil, vinegar, ropes, canvas, pitch, tar, anchors, gunpowder, bullets, and linen, with such other articles as may be required by the besieged during their voyage to Batavia, to be taken on board the Company's ships in keeping with instructions from the before-mentioned Governor and Council.

IV. All private movable property inside the Castle or elsewhere belonging to officers of the Dutch Government, shall first be inspected by Koxinga's delegates, and then placed on board the said ships.

V. In addition to these goods, each of the twenty-eight Councillors shall be permitted to take with him two hundred *rijksdaalders*, and twenty chosen civilians an aggregate sum of one thousand *rijksdaalders*.

VI. After inspection, the Dutch soldiers may come forth with flying banners, burning fusees, loaded rifles, and beating drums, marching thus for embarkation under command of the Governor.

VII. The names of all Chinese debtors or lease-holders in Formosa, with particulars of claims against them, shall be copied out from the Company's books, and handed to Lord Koxinga.

VIII. All the Government archives may be taken to Batavia.

IX. Every servant of the Company, now imprisoned by the Chinese in Formosa, shall be liberated within eight or ten days, and those who are in China, as soon as possible. Servants of the Company who are not imprisoned in Formosa shall be granted a free pass to reach the Company's ships in safety.

X. The said Lord Koxinga shall now return to the Company the four captured boats, with all their accessories.

XI. He shall also provide a sufficient number of vessels to take the Honourable Company's people and goods to their ships.

XII. Vegetables, flesh-meat, and whatever else may be necessary to sustain the Company's people during their stay, shall daily be provided by his Highness's subjects at a reasonable price.

XIII. So long as the Honourable Company's people remain on land before embarkation, no soldier or other subject of Lord Koxinga shall be permitted to enter the Castle (unless . . . on service for the Company). to approach the outworks nearer than the gabions, or to proceed further than the palisades erected by order of His Highness.

XIV. No other than a white flag shall float from the Castle until the Honourable Company's people have marched out.

XV. Those who guard the stores shall remain in the Castle two or three days after the other people and goods have been taken on board, and thereafter they shall proceed themselves to the vessels.

XVI. As soon as this Agreement is signed, sealed, and sworn to on both sides, each according to his own country's customs, Lord Koxinga shall deliver to one of the Dutch ships two hostages, viz. the Mandarin or Captain Moor Ongkun and Pimpan Jamoosje of the political Council. On the other side, and as representing the Company, Lord Koxinga shall receive custody of Mr. Jan Oetgens van Waveren, an official second in rank to the Governor, and Mr. David Harthouwer, also a member of the Formosa Council. Each of these hostages shall remain in a previously fixed place until everything has been carried out in accordance with the terms of this contract.

XVII. Chinese prisoners at present in the Castle or on the Company's ships shall be released in exchange for any of our people who have been seized by the subjects of Lord Koxinga.

XVIII. All misunderstandings, and every important matter overlooked in this Agreement, shall immediately be dealt with to the satisfaction of both parties, upon notice having been given from either side.

William Campbell, *Formosa Under the Dutch* (London: Kegan Paul, Trench, Trubner, 1903), pp. 455–56.

DOCUMENT 2

Treaty of Shimonoseki, April 17, 1895

His Majesty the Emperor of Japan, and His Majesty the Emperor of China, desiring to restore the blessings of peace* to their countries and subjects and to remove all cause for future complications, have named as their Plenipotentiaries for the purpose of concluding a Treaty of Peace. . . .

. . .

ARTICLE II

Territorial Cessions by China to Japan.

China cedes to Japan in perpetuity and full sovereignty the following territories, together with all fortifications, arsenals, and public property thereon:

. . .

Island of Formosa

(b) The island of Formosa, together with all islands appertaining or belonging to the said Island of Formosa.

Pescadores Group

(c) The Pescadores Group, that is to say, all islands lying between the 119th and 120th degrees of longitude east of Greenwich, and the 23rd and 24th degrees of north latitude.

. . .

ARTICLE V

Right of Inhabitants to Emigrate from
Territory Ceded to Japan

The inhabitants of the territories ceded to Japan who wish to take up their residence outside the ceded districts shall be at liberty to sell their real property and retire. For this purpose a period of two years from the date of the exchange of the ratifications of the present Act shall be granted. At the expiration of that period those of the inhabitants who shall not have left such territories shall, at the option of Japan, be deemed to be Japanese subjects.

---

*War was declared by Japan against China on August 3, 1894.

Excerpts from *Hertslet's China Treaties*, I (London: His Majesty's Stationery Office, 1908), 362, 363, 364. The treaty entered into force on May 8, 1895.

DOCUMENT 3

The Cairo Declaration, November 26, 1943

Press Communique

President Roosevelt, Generalissimo Chiang Kai-shek and Prime Minister Churchill, together with their respective military and diplomatic advisers, have completed a conference in North Africa. The following general statement was issued:

"The several military missions have agreed upon future military operations against Japan. The three great Allies expressed their resolve to bring unrelenting pressure against their brutal enemies by sea, land and air. This pressure is already rising.

"The three great Allies are fighting this war to restrain and punish the aggression of Japan. They covet no gain for themselves and have no thought of territorial expansion. It is their purpose that Japan shall be stripped of all the islands in the Pacific which she has seized or occupied since the beginning of the First World War in 1914, and that all the territories Japan has stolen from the Chinese, such as Manchuria, Formosa, and the Pescadores, shall be restored to the Republic of China. Japan will also be expelled from all other territories which she has taken by violence and greed. The aforesaid three great powers, mindful of the enslavement of the people of Korea, are determined that in due course Korea shall become free and independent.

"With these objects in view the three Allies, in harmony with those of the United Nations at war with Japan, will continue to persevere in the serious and prolonged operations necessary to procure the unconditional surrender of Japan."

Foreign Relations of the United States, Diplomatic Papers: The Conferences at Cairo and Tehran 1943 (Washington, D.C.: U.S. Government Printing Office, 1961), pp. 448-49. The communique was released to the press by the White House on December 1, 1943, and was printed, with slight editorial variations, in *Department of State Bulletin* 9, no. 232 (December 4, 1943): 393.

DOCUMENT 4

U.S. Department of State's Policy Memorandum on Formosa, December 23, 1949

Department of State
Policy Information Paper—Formosa. Special Guidance No. 28,
December 23, 1949.

I. Problem

To formulate information policy which will minimize damage to United States prestige and others' morale by the possible fall of Formosa to the Chinese Communist forces.

II. Background

A. Comment on Formosa is on the increase as the Communist advances on the Chinese mainland leave the island as the last substantial part of China under Nationalist control. Attention is focused by three principal elements:

1. Communists, world-wide, who charge the United States with conspiring to build the island into a fortress to be taken over by the United States (if it does not already control it), thereby trying to brand the United States with the mark of aggressive imperialism, and also hoping to get us involved in a risky and unpromising venture;

2. Pro-Nationalists (principally in the United States) who consider Formosa a redoubt in which the Government could survive, and who tend to create an impression the United States is delinquent if it fails to "save Formosa";

3. Groups in the United States who are inclined to be critical of the United States for failure to act to prevent loss of the island to the Communists, largely because of [the] mistaken popular conception of its strategic importance to United States Defense in the Pacific.

B. Loss of the island is widely anticipated, and the manner in which civil and military conditions there have deteriorated under the Nationalists adds weight to the expectation. Its fall would threaten:

1. Loss of United States prestige at home and abroad to the extent we have become committed in the public mind to hold it;

2. Damage to the morale of other nations, particularly in the Far East, which are disturbed by the Communist gains and fear its possible further advances.

C. Formosa, politically, geographically, and strategically, is part of China in no way especially distinguished or important. Although ruled by the Japanese (as "Taiwan") for 50 years, historically it has been Chinese. Politically and militarily it is a strictly Chinese responsibility.

It is true that the technical status of the island remains to be determined by the Japanese peace settlement, but the Cairo agreement and the Potsdam declaration and the surrender terms of September 2, 1945, looked to its return to China and the United States facilitated its take-over by Chinese troops shortly after V-J Day.

Even the small United States military advisory group sent there at Chinese Government request was completely withdrawn a year ago. Merely a handful of military attaché personnel with diplomatic status remains. The United States never has had military bases there, and never has sought any special concessions there.

ECA [Economic Cooperation Administration] work done on the island, particularly through the Joint Commission on Rural Reconstruction, has been of purely economic and technical nature for assistance in improvement of conditions, and no quid pro quo has been sought.

D. United States public opinion has concerned itself primarily with the question of the island's strategic importance; there has been insistent demand from a few sources for military action by the United States, but it has not assumed significant proportions. Rather, public opinion obviously is divided and uncertain, and there is no apparent consensus for a particular course of active intervention.

III. Treatment

A. If rising public interest warrants it, gradually increasing attention may be paid Formosa, to establish publicly the facts indicated below. Overseas use should be made of unofficial materials in public analysis and comment appearing both at home and abroad, as well as official statements as they may appear. Label conflicting public statements properly as "individual expressions of opinion," as "unofficial," etc.

B. All material should be used best to counter the false impressions that:

1. Formosa's retention would save the Chinese Government;

2. The United States has a special interest in or "designs on" the island or any military bases on Formosa;

3. Its loss would seriously damage the interests of either the United States or of other countries opposing communism;

4. The United States is responsible for or committed in any way to act to save Formosa.

C. Without evidencing undue preoccupation with the subject, emphasize as appropriate any of the following main points:

1. Formosa is exclusively the responsibility of the Chinese Government:

(a) Historically and geographically a part of China;

(b) The national government has run the island's affairs since the take-over and is responsible for present conditions there;

(c) The United States has assumed no responsibilities or obligations, actual or moral.

2. Formosa has no special military significance:

(a) It is only approximately 100 miles off the China coast;

(b) Other potential objects of Communist aggression are closer to points on the Chinese mainland than to Formosa;

(c) China has never been a sea power and the island is of no special strategic advantage to the Chinese Communist armed forces.

3. Economic assistance in Formosa has been for economic and social purposes, has been consistent with demonstrated United States concern for the welfare of the Chinese generally, and has involved no thought of special concessions for the United States.

4. In areas of insistent demand for United States action, particularly in the United States itself, we should occasionally make clear that seeking United States bases on Formosa, sending in troops, supplying arms, dispatching naval units, or taking any similar action would:

(a) Accomplish no material good for China or its Nationalist regime;

(b) Involve the United States in a long-term venture producing at best a new area of bristling stalemate, and at worst possible involvement in open warfare;

(c) Subject the United States to a violent propaganda barrage and to reaction against our "militarism, imperialism, and interference" even from friendly peoples, and particularly from Chinese, who would be turned against us anew;

(d) Eminently suit purposes of the U.S.S.R., which would like to see us "substantiate" its propaganda, dissipate our energies and weaken effectiveness of our policies generally by such action.

5. In reflecting United States unofficial demands for action of various kinds in Formosa, avoid giving them prominence unwarranted by their limited (usually individual) source, and make clear that the total of such demands evidences concern and frustration in some quarters but does not add up to a consensus on any particular position different from that officially taken.

D. Avoid:

1. Speculation which would show undue concern with whether Nationalists can hold the island or when Communists may take it;

2. References which would indicate important strategic significance, or that the island is a political entity;

3. In output to China, any emphasis on bad conditions in Formosa under the Nationalists, although to other areas reference can be made among reasons why Nationalists are vulnerable there as elsewhere;

4. Statement that Formosa's final status still is to be determined by the Japanese peace treaty;

5. Name "Taiwan"; use "Formosa."

Military Situation in the Far East, hearings before the Committee on Armed Services and the Committee on Foreign Relations, U.S. Senate, 82d Cong., 1st sess., Part III (Washington, D.C.: U.S. Government Printing Office, 1951), pp. 1667–69.

DOCUMENT 5

Review of U.S. Policy in Relation to China

The Committee on Foreign Affairs, to whom was referred the resolution (H. Res. 452) requesting the State Department to furnish full and complete answers to certain questions relating to the foreign policy of the United States in the Far East, having considered the same, report adversely thereon and recommend that the resolution . . . not pass.

The recommendation of the committee is based on the fact that answers to the questions contained in the resolution have been furnished the committee by the Department of State. With the exception of portions of two answers, the publication of which portions is felt by the Department of State would be incompatible with the public interest, the answers are included in this report for the information of the Members of the House, and are as follows:

Question 1

With respect to the President's° statement of January 5, 1950, on policy regarding Formosa—

. . .

Question 1 (d)

Have the following been considered by the Executive as alternatives to the policy enunciated in said statement?

(1) Insistence on the execution of the terms of the Cairo Declaration, which provided for the return of Formosa to the Republic of China.

Comment.—This cannot properly be considered an alternative to the policy enunciated by the President. The President's statement of January 5, 1950, contained a re-affirmation of the Cairo Declaration on the part of the United States in respect to the disposition of Formosa. Formosa has been administered since 1945 by China, the surrender of Japanese forces on Formosa having been made to the Generalissimo Chiang Kai-shek.

(2) Consideration of Formosa as a possession of Japan to be administered by the victor powers until eventual disposition under a peace settlement with Japan.

(3) A plebiscite in Formosa, under the auspices of the Far Eastern Commission or a special commission of the UN, to determine whether the inhabitants desire—

(a) to continue as a province of and the seat of government of the Republic of China; (b) to be placed under a United Nations trusteeship; or (c) to become an independent nation.

Comment.—These alternatives were considered. As has been noted under (1) above, Formosa has been administered by China since 1945, when Japanese forces on the island surrendered to Generalissimo Chiang Kai-shek. It was incorporated into China as a province. It is now the seat of the Chinese Government. The Allied Powers associated in the war against Japan have not questioned these steps. The United States Government has not questioned these steps because they were clearly in line with its commitments made at Cairo and reaffirmed at Potsdam. In other words, the Allied Powers including the United States have for the past 4 years treated Formosa as a part of China.

For the United States Government, at this date, to seek to establish a non-Chinese administration on Formosa, either through SCAP or a United Nations or FEC-sponsored plebiscite, would be almost universally interpreted in mainland China and widely interpreted throughout Asia as an attempt by this Government to separate Formosa from China in violation of its pledges and contrary to its long-standing policy of respecting the territorial integrity of China. The important point from the standpoint of our interests in Asia, including mainland China, is not the technical justifications which we might urge for taking such steps but rather the way such action on our part would be viewed by the people of Asia. In this connection we do not wish to create a Formosa *irredenta* issue about which the Chinese Communists could rally support within China and with which they could divert attention from Soviet actions in the North. We must not place ourselves in the unenviable position of the U.S.S.R. with regard to the integrity of China and must remain free to take the position that anyone who violates the integrity of China is the enemy of China and is acting contrary to our own interests.

These are compelling reasons for rejecting alternatives stated above. There are, of course, additional practical difficulties. The seat of the Chinese Government is now on Formosa and that island, with Hainan, is the only remaining substantial territory now under its control. There is no evidence that the Chinese Government would willingly accomplish its own demise by acquiescing in either of the proposed alternatives. There is likewise the question of military force to carry out the course of action proposed if the Chinese Government refuses its consent, and to defend the island if either proposal were effected. The United Nations, of course, has no forces and it seems clear that any defense of the island would finally rest upon the United States.

In any case the conduct of a plebiscite for the purpose of determining the wishes of the inhabitants on the future disposition of Formosa is beyond the competence of the Far Eastern Commission. The Far Eastern Commission by its terms of reference is "to formulate the policies, principles, and standards in conformity with which the fulfillment by Japan of its obligations under the terms of surrender may be accomplished." The terms of reference also provide that "the Commission shall not make recommendations with regard to the conduct of military operations nor with regard to territorial adjustments."

"Replies by the U.S. Department of State to a Series of Questions Contained in House Resolution 452, 81st Cong., 2d sess.; Report of the House Committee on Foreign Affairs, February 9, 1950." *American Foreign Policy, 1950–1955, Basic Documents*, Vol. 2 (Washington, D.C.: U.S. Government Printing Office, 1957), pp. 2456–58.

DOCUMENT 6

President Truman's Statement on the Mission of the U.S. Seventh Fleet in the Formosa Area, June 27, 1950

The attack upon Korea makes it plain beyond all doubt that communism has passed beyond the use of subversion to conquer independent nations and will now use armed invasion and war. It has defied the orders of the Security Council of the United Nations issued to preserve international peace and security. In these circumstances, the occupation of Formosa by Communist forces would be a direct threat to the security of the Pacific area and to United States forces performing their lawful and necessary functions in that area.

Accordingly, I have ordered the Seventh Fleet to prevent any attack on Formosa. As a corollary of this action, I am calling upon the Chinese Government on Formosa to cease all air and sea operations against the mainland. The Seventh Fleet will see that this is done. The determination of the future status of Formosa must await the restoration of security in the Pacific, a peace settlement with Japan, or consideration by the United Nations.

American Foreign Policy, 1950-1955, Basic Documents, Vol. 2 (Washington, D.C.: U.S. Government Printing Office, 1957), p. 2468.

DOCUMENT 7

PRC Foreign Minister Chou En-lai's Statement Refuting Truman's Statements of June 27, 1950, and June 28, 1950

After instigating the puppet government of Syngman Rhee in South Korea to provoke civil war in Korea, President Truman of the United States of America made a statement on June 27, declaring that the United States Government had decided to prevent by armed force our liberation of Taiwan.

On Truman's order, the U.S. Seventh Fleet has moved to the coast of Taiwan.

On behalf of the Central People's Government of the People's Republic of China, I declare that Truman's statement of June 27 and the action of the U.S. navy constitute armed agression against the territory of China and are a gross violation of the United Nations Charter. This violent, predatory action by the United States Government comes as no surprise to the Chinese people but only increases their wrath, because the Chinese people have, over a long period, consistently exposed all the conspiratorial schemes of U.S. imperialism to commit aggression against China and seize Asia by force. In his statement, Truman merely discloses his premediated plan and puts it into practice. In fact the attack by the puppet Korean troops of Syngman Rhee on the Korean Democratic People's Republic at the instigation of the United States Government was a premeditated move by the United States, designed to create a pretext for the United States to invade Taiwan, Korea, Vietnam and the Philippines. It is nothing but a further act of intervention by U.S. imperialism in the affairs of Asia.

On behalf of the Central People's Government of the People's Republic of China, I declare that, no matter what obstructive action U.S. imperialists may take, the fact that Taiwan is part of China will remain unchanged forever. This is not only a historical fact; it has also been confirmed by the Cairo and Potsdam Declarations and the situation since the surrender of Japan. All the people of our country will certainly fight as one man and to the end to liberate Taiwan from the grasp of the U.S. aggressors. The Chinese people, who have defeated Japanese imperialism and Chiang Kai-shek, the hireling of U.S. imperialism, will surely succeed in driving out the U.S. aggressors and in recovering Taiwan and all other territories belonging to China.

Chinese People's Institute of Foreign Affairs, ed., *Oppose U.S. Occupation of Taiwan and "Two Chinas" Plot* (Peking: Foreign Languages Press, 1958), pp. 5-6.

DOCUMENT 8

PRC Foreign Minister Chou En-lai's Statement on the U.S. Proposal of the Japanese Peace Treaty, August 15, 1951

The Central People's Government of the People's Republic of China considers that the Draft Peace Treaty with Japan as proposed by the United States and British Governments is a draft which violates international agreements and is therefore basically unacceptable and that the conference which has been scheduled to meet on September 4 at San Francisco, under the compulsion of the United States Government, and which audaciously excludes the People's Republic of China is a conference which repudiates international commitments and therefore basically cannot be recognized.

Whether considered from the procedure through which it was prepared or from its contents, the United States-British Draft Peace Treaty with Japan flagrantly violates these important international agreements to which the United

States and British Governments were signatories, viz., the United Nations Declaration of January 1, 1942, the Cairo Declaration, the Yalta Agreement, the Potsdam Declaration and Agreement, and the Basic Post-Surrender Policy for Japan which was adopted by the Far Eastern Commission on June 19, 1947. The United Nations Declaration provides that no separate peace should be made. The Potsdam Agreement states that the "preparatory work of the peace settlements" should be undertaken by those states which were signatories to the terms of surrender imposed upon the enemy state concerned. . . .

[T]he United States has monopolized the task of preparing the Draft Peace Treaty with Japan as now proposed, excluding most of the states that had fought against Japan and particularly the two principal Powers in the war, China and the Soviet Union, from the preparatory work for the peace treaty. . . .

[I]n violation of the agreement under the Cairo Declaration, the Yalta Agreement and the Potsdam Declaration, the Draft Treaty only provides that Japan should renounce all right to Taiwan and the Pescadores as well as to the Kurile Islands, the southern part of Sakhalin and all islands adjacent to it, without mentioning even one word about the agreement that Taiwan and the Pescadores be returned to the People's Republic of China and that the Kurile Islands be handed over to, and the southern part of Sakhalin and all islands adjacent to it be returned to, the Soviet Union.

With a view to expediting the concluding of a separate peace treaty with Japan, the United States Government, in its notification for the convocation of the San Francisco Conference, openly excludes the People's Republic of China—the principal Power which had fought against Japan—and thus completely violates a stipulation in the United Nations Declaration of January 1, 1942, to the effect that each of the signatory Powers pledged itself not to make a separate peace. . . .

Now, the Central People's Government of the People's Republic of China once again declares: If there is no participation of the People's Republic of China in the preparation, drafting and signing of a peace treaty with Japan, whatever the contents and results of such a treaty, the Central People's Government considers it all illegal, and therefore null and void.

Hsinhua News Agency, *Daily News Release*, No. 777 (Peking: China Information Bureau, Press Administration, August 16, 1951), pp. 75–78.

DOCUMENT 9

Treaty of Peace between the Republic of China and Japan, April 28, 1952

Article I

The state of war between the Republic of China and Japan is terminated as from the date on which the present Treaty enters into force.

Article II

It is recognized ·that under Article 2 of the Treaty of Peace with Japan signed at the city of San Francisco in the United States of America on September 8, 1951 (hereinafter referred to as the San Francisco Treaty), Japan has renounced all right, title and claim to Taiwan and the Paracel Islands.

Article III

The disposition of property of Japan and of its nationals in Taiwan (Formosa) and Penghu (the Pescadores), and their claims, including debts, against the authorities of the Republic of China in Taiwan (Formosa) and Penghu (the Pescadores) and the residents thereof, and the disposition in Japan of property of such authorities and residents and their claims, including debts, against Japan and its nationals, shall be the subject of special arrangements between the Government of the Republic of China and the Government of Japan. The terms nationals and residents whenever used in the present Treaty include juridical persons.

Article IV

It is recognized that all treaties, conventions and agreements concluded before December 9, 1941, between China and Japan have become null and void as a consequence of the war.

. . .

Article X

For the purposes of the present Treaty, nationals of the Republic of China shall be deemed to include all the inhabitants and former inhabitants of Taiwan (Formosa) and Penghu (the Pescadores) and their descendants who are of the Chinese nationality in accordance with the laws and regulations which have been or may hereafter be enforced by the Republic of China in Taiwan (Formosa) and Penghu (the Pescadores); and juridical persons of the Republic of China shall be deemed to include all those registered under the laws and regulations which have been or may hereafter be enforced by the Republic of China in Taiwan (Formosa) and Penghu (the Pescadores).

. . .

Protocol

At the moment of signing this day the Treaty of Peace between the Republic of China and Japan (hereinafter referred to as the present Treaty), the undersigned Plenipotentiaries have agreed upon the following terms which shall constitute an integral part of the present Treaty:

. . .

2. The commerce and navigation between the Republic of China and Japan shall be governed by the following Arrangements:

. . .

(d) In the application of the present Arrangements, it is understood:
(i) that vessels of the Republic of China shall be deemed to include all those registered under the laws and regulations which have been or may hereafter be enforced by the Republic of China in Taiwan (Formosa) and Penghu (the Pescadores); and products of the Republic of China shall be deemed to include all those originating in Taiwan (Formosa) and Penghu (the Pescadores); and

. . .

The Arrangements set forth in this paragraph shall remain in force for a period of one year as from the date on which the present Treaty enters into force.

. . .

Exchange of Notes

(I) Note from the Japanese Plenipotentiary to the Chinese Plenipotentiary
No. 1.

Taipei, April 28, 1952

Excellency,

In regard to the Treaty of Peace between Japan and the Republic of China signed this day, I have the honor to refer, on behalf of my Government, to the understanding reached between us that the terms of the present Treaty shall, in respect of the Republic of China, be applicable to all the territories which are now, or which may hereafter be, under the control of its Government.

I shall be appreciative, if you will confirm the understanding set forth above.

I avail myself of this opportunity to convey to Your Excellency the assurance of my highest consideration.

(signed) Isao Kawada

His Excellency
     Monsieur Yeh Kung Chao,
         Plenipotentiary of the Republic of China

(II) Note from the Chinese Plenipotentiary to the Japanese Plenipotentiary
No. 1.

Taipei, April 28, 1952

Excellency,

In connection with the Treaty of Peace between the Republic of China
and Japan signed this day, I have the honor to acknowledge receipt of Your
Excellency's Note of to-day's date reading as follows:
[Test of Japanese note]
I have the honor to confirm, on behalf of my Government, the under-
standing set forth in Your Excellency's Note under reply.
I avail myself of this opportunity to convey to Your Excellency the as-
surance of my highest consideration.

(signed) Yeh Kung Chao

His Excellency
     Mr. Isao Kawada,
         Plenipotentiary of Japan

. . .

Agreed   Minutes

I

Chinese Delegate:
It is my understanding that the expression "or which may hereafter be"
in the Notes No. 1 exchanged to-day can be taken to mean "and which may
hereafter be." Is it so?
Japanese Delegate:
Yes, it is so. I assure you that the Treaty is applicable to all the territories
under the control of the Government of the Republic of China.

. . .

(signed) Yeh Kung Chao
(signed) Isao Kawada

United Nations Treaty Series, Vol. 138, pp. 38, 40, 42, 44, 46, 48, 50, 52. The treaty
came into force on August 5, 1952.

DOCUMENT 10

Mutual Defense Treaty between the United States and the Republic of China, December 2, 1954

The Parties to this Treaty,

Reaffirming their faith in the purposes and principles of the Charter of the United Nations and their desire to live in peace with all peoples and all Governments, and desiring to strengthen the fabric of peace in the West Pacific Area,

Recalling with mutual pride the relationship which brought their two peoples together in a common bond of sympathy and mutual ideals to fight side by side against imperialist aggression during the last war,

Desiring to declare publicly and formally their sense of unity and their common determination to defend themselves against external armed attack, so that no potential aggressor could be under the illusion that either of them stands alone in the West Pacific Area, and

Desiring further to strengthen their present efforts for collective defense for the preservation of peace and security pending the development of a more comprehensive system of regional security in the West Pacific Area,

Have agreed as follows:

Article I

The Parties undertake, as set forth in the Charter of the United Nations, to settle any international dispute in which they may be involved by peaceful means in such a manner that international peace, security and justice are not endangered and to refrain in their international relations from the threat or use of force in any manner inconsistent with the purposes of the United Nations.

Article II

In order more effectively to achieve the objective of this Treaty, the Parties separately and jointly by self-help and mutual aid will maintain and develop their individual and collective capacity to resist armed attack and communist subversive activities directed from without against their territorial integrity and political stability.

Article III

The Parties undertake to strengthen their free institutions and to cooperate with each other in the development of economic progress and social well-being and to further their individual and collective efforts toward these ends.

Article IV

The Parties, through their Foreign Ministers or their deputies, will consult together from time to time regarding the implementation of this Treaty.

Article V

Each Party recognizes that an armed attack in the West Pacific Area directed against the territories of either of the Parties would be dangerous to its own peace and safety and declares that it would act to meet the common danger in accordance with its constitutional processes.

Any such armed attack and all measures taken as a result thereof shall be immediately reported to the Security Council of the United Nations. Such measures shall be terminated when the Security Council has taken the measures necessary to restore and maintain international peace and security.

Article VI

For the purposes of Articles II and V, the terms "territorial" and "territories" shall mean in respect of the Republic of China, Taiwan and the Pescadores; and in respect of the United States of America, the island territories in the West Pacific under its jurisdiction. The provisions of Articles II and V will be applicable to such other territories as may be determined by mutual agreement.

Article VII

The Government of the Republic of China grants, and the Government of the United States of America accepts, the right to dispose such United States land, air and sea forces in and about Taiwan and the Pescadores as may be required for their defense, as determined by mutual agreement.

Article VIII

This Treaty does not affect and shall not be interpreted as affecting in any way the rights and obligations of the Parties under the Charter of the United Nations or the responsibility of the United Nations for the maintenance of international peace and security.

Article IX

This Treaty shall be ratified by the Republic of China and the United States of America in accordance with their respective constitutional processes and will come into force when instruments of ratification thereof have been exchanged by them at Taipei.

Article X

This Treaty shall remain in force indefinitely. Either Party may terminate it one year after notice has been given to the other party.

IN WITNESS WHEREOF, The undersigned Plenipotentiaries have signed this Treaty.

DONE in duplicate, in the Chinese and English languages, at Washington on this Second day of the Twelfth month of the Forty-third Year of the Republic of China, corresponding to the Second day of December of the Year One Thousand Nine Hundred and Fifty-four.

For the Republic of China:
(signed) George K. C. Yeh
For the United States of America:
(signed) John Foster Dulles

Exchange of Notes

I
The Secretary of State to the Chinese Minister
of Foreign Affairs
Department of State
Washington

December 10, 1954

Excellency:

I have the honor to refer to recent conversations between representatives of our two Governments and to confirm the understandings reached as a result of those conversations, as follows:

The Republic of China effectively controls both the territory described in Article VI of the Treaty of Mutual Defense between the Republic of China and the United States of America signed on December 2, 1954, at Washington and other territory. It possesses with respect to all territory now and hereafter under its control the inherent right of self-defense. In view of the obligations of the two Parties under the said Treaty and of the fact that the use of force from either of these areas by either of the Parties affects the other, it is agreed that such use of force will be a matter of joint agreement, subject to action of an emergency character which is clearly an exercise of the inherent right of self-defense. Military elements which are a product of joint effort and contribution by the two Parties will not be removed from the territories described in Article VI to a degree which would substantially diminish the defensibility of such territories without mutual agreement.

Accept, Excellency, the assurances of my highest consideration.

John Foster Dulles
Secretary of State of the United States of America

His Excellency George K. C. Yeh
Minister of Foreign Affairs of the Republic of China

II

December 10, 1954

Excellency:

I have the honor to acknowledge the receipt of Your Excellency's Note of today's date, which reads as follows:

[See note I]

I have the honor to confirm, on behalf of my Government, the understanding set forth in Your Excellency's Note under reply.

I avail myself of this opportunity to convey to Your Excellency the assurances of my highest consideration.

George K. C. Yeh
Minister for Foreign Affairs
of the Republic of China

His Excellency John Foster Dulles
Secretary of State of the United States of America

United Nations Treaty Series, Vol. 248, pp. 214–16, 226, 228. The treaty came into force on March 3, 1955.

DOCUMENT 11

U.S. Congressional Authorization for the President to Employ the Armed Forces of the United States to Protect Formosa, the Pescadores, and Related Positions and Territories of That Area

Whereas the primary purpose of the United States, in its relations with all other nations, is to develop and sustain a just and enduring peace for all; and

Whereas certain territories in the West Pacific under the jurisdiction of the Republic of China are now under armed attack, and threats and declarations have been and are being made by the Chinese Communists that such armed attack is in aid of and in preparation for armed attack on Formosa and the Pescadores,

Whereas such armed attack if continued would gravely endanger the peace and security of the West Pacific Area and particularly of Formosa and the Pescadores; and

Whereas the secure possession by friendly governments of the Western Pacific Island chain, of which Formosa is a part, is essential to the vital interests of the United States and all friendly nations in or bordering upon the Pacific Ocean; and

Whereas the President of the United States on January 6, 1955, submitted to the Senate for its advice and consent to ratification a Mutual Defense Treaty between the United States of America and the Republic of China, which recognizes that an armed attack in the West Pacific Area directed against territories, therein described, in the region of Formosa and the Pescadores, would be dangerous to the peace and safety of the parties to the treaty: Therefore be it

Resolved by the Senate and House of Representatives of the United States of America in Congress assembled, That the President of the United States be and he hereby is authorized to employ the Armed Forces of the United States as he deems necessary for the specific purpose of securing and protecting Formosa and the Pescadores against armed attack, this authority to include the securing and protection of such related positions and territories of that area now in friendly hands and the taking of such other measures as he judges to be required or appropriate in assuring the defense of Formosa and the Pescadores.

This resolution shall expire when the President shall determine that the peace and security of the area is reasonably assured by international conditions created by action of the United Nations or otherwise, and shall so report to the Congress.

United States Statutes At Large, Vol. 69 (1955), p. 7. The resolution was repealed on October 26, 1974, see Vol. 88, Part 2 (1974), p. 1439.

DOCUMENT 12

U.S. Senate, Committee on Foreign Relations, Report on Mutual Defense Treaty with the Republic of China, February 8, 1955

The Committee on Foreign Relations, to whom was referred the Mutual Defense Treaty with the Republic of China (Ex. A, 84th Cong., 1st sess.), signed at Washington on December 2, 1954, reports the treaty to the Senate, and recommends that its advice and consent to ratification be given at an early date. . . .

5. SCOPE OF UNITED STATES COMMITMENT (ART. V)

Article V, which contains the heart of the treaty, is virtually identical with the provisions of article IV of the Philippines and ANZUS Defense Treaties. In the first paragraph, each party recognizes that—

an armed attack in the West Pacific Area directed against the territories of either of the parties would be dangerous to its won peace and safety and declares that it would act to meet the common danger in accordance with its constitutional processes.

The basic provision is one which has repeatedly received the committee's attention, and requires little comment. It embodies the now familiar "Monroe Doctrine formula," encountered in the previous defense pacts, and the concept that any action taken by the United States must be in accordance with our constitutional processes. Put somewhat differently, there is no question of any automatic commitment such as was discussed with respect to the "attack upon one is an attack upon all" concept of the North Atlantic Treaty. The power of the United States Government to act under this treaty remains precisely as it is defined in the Constitution, without impairing either the right of the Congress to declare war, or the authority of the President to act as Commander in Chief and as director of this Nation's foreign relations. The problem was examined in some detail by the committee in its reports on the Southeast Asia Collective Defense Treaty (Ex. Rept. No. 1, 84th Cong.) and the Mutual Defense Treaty with Korea (Ex. Rept. No. 1, 83d Cong.).

The committee considered carefully the wording of article V and the nature of our commitments under that article. In order to clear up any doubt on this point, it was agreed that its report should include the following statement:

> It is the understanding of the Senate that the obligations of the parties under article V apply only in the event of external armed attack; and that military operations by either party from the territories held by the Republic of China, shall not be undertaken except by joint agreement.

The understanding reflects an agreement manifested by the Government of the United States and the Government of the Republic of China in an exchange of notes dated December 10, 1954, under which the use of force from the areas specified must be pursuant to joint agreement, except for emergency actions by way of self-defense.

Finally, in the event of such armed attack as is envisaged by paragraph 1 of article V, the parties agree, in paragraph 2, that—

> all measures taken as a result thereof shall be immediately reported to the Security Council of the United Nations. Such measures shall be terminated when the Security Council has taken the measures necessary to restore and maintain international peace and security.

The paragraph reflects the position of both signatories as members of the United Nations.

6. THE TREATY AREA

Article VI defines the treaty area. It declares that, for the purposes of articles II and V, the terms "territorial" and "territories" shall mean—

in respect of the Republic of China, Taiwan and the Pescadores; and in respect of the United States of America, the island territories in the west Pacific under its jurisdiction.

The treaty area is thus defined in a limited way and as such does not extend the obligation of the United States to defend any territories other than Formosa and the Pescadores. Embraced within the prorection given our own "island territories in the west Pacific" are such groups as the Ryukus (including Okinawa), the trust territories (former Japanese mandated islands) and Guam.

However, article VI expressly contemplates that the obligations of articles II and V of the treaty may be made applicable—

to such other territories as may be determined by mutual agreement.

During the hearings, some members of the committee expressed concern lest the words "mutual agreement" be interpreted as permitting an important extension of our treaty commitments without the approval of the Senate. Secretary Dulles assured the committee, however, that as in the case of the Southeast Asia Collective Defense Treaty—

an agreement to extend the coverage of the China Defense Treaty to additional territories would in practical terms amount to an amendment of the treaty, and should be submitted to the Senate for its advice and consent.

Nevertheless, the committee, with the aim of avoiding any doubts as to the nature of the "mutual agreement" required, decided to include the following statement in this report:

It is the understanding of the Senate that the "mutual agreement" referred to in article VI, under which the provisions of articles II and V may be made applicable to other territories, shall be construed as requiring the advice and consent of the Senate of the United States.

8. STATUS OF FORMOSA AND THE PESCADORES

China ceded Formosa and the Pescadores to Japan by the 1895 Treaty of Shimonoseki after the Sino-Japanese War. At the Cairo Conference in 1943, President Roosevelt, Prime Minister Churchill, and Generalissimo Chiang Kaishek agreed that Formosa and the Pescadores "shall be restored to the Republic of China." At the Potsdam Conference this decision was confirmed in the proclamation defining the terms for Japanese surrender, July 26, 1945. Administrative control of the island was turned over to the Republic of China subsequent to the Japanese surrender in September 1945.

Formosa became the seat of the National Government of the Republic of China in December 1949. By the peace treaty of September 8, 1951, signed with the United States and other powers, Japan renounced "all right, title, and claim to Formosa and the Pescadores." The treaty did not specify the nation to which such right, title, and claim passed. Although the Republic of China was not a signatory to the treaty it and the parties at the conference expressly recognized that it did not dispose finally of Formosa and the Pescadores. The Republic of China concluded a separate peace treaty with Japan on April 27, 1952, "on the same or substantially the same terms" as specified in article 26 of the Japanese treaty.

At a press conference on December 1, 1954, Secretary of State Dulles was asked whether the treaty recognized the claim of the Republic of China to sovereignty over the mainland. He replied: "It does not deal specifically with that matter one way or another." Later, during a discussion of this question in executive session, he informed the committee that the reference in article V to "the territories of either of the parties" was language carefully chosen to avoid denoting anything one way or another as to their sovereignty.

It is the view of the committee that the coming into force of the present treaty will not modify or affect the existing legal status of Formosa and the Pescadores. The treaty appears to be wholly consistent with all actions taken by the United States in this matter since the end of World War II, and does not introduce any basically new element in our relations with the territories in question. Both by act and by implication we have accepted the Nationalist Government as the lawful authority on Formosa.

To avoid any possibility of misunderstanding on this aspect of the treaty, the committee decided it would be useful to include in this report the following statement:

> It is the understanding of the Senate that nothing in the treaty shall
> be construed as affecting or modifying the legal status or sovereignty
> of the territories to which it applies.

11. CONCLUSIONS

Our Government has determined that it is in the national interest that Formosa and the Pescadores be kept in friendly hands, as an important anchor in the defensive chain from the Aleutians to Australia. It is, therefore, of great importance that this policy, which until now has been voluntary and unilateral, be supported by a concrete undertaking to take appropriate action to help defend Formosa and the Pescadores against armed attack. By doing this in terms which cannot be misunderstood, it is hoped that the Communist military regime will be deterred from further attempts to aggrandize its position in the Far East at the expense of the free world. At the same time, the treaty will give further evidence of our intention not to abandon a wartime ally who fought valiantly in a long and exhausting struggle against a common foe. Finally, it is believed that the treaty, by putting the world on notice as to our intention, will contribute to the peace and security of a dangerous and sensitive zone.

For these reasons, the Committee on Foreign Relations urges the Senate to give its advice and consent to the ratification of this treaty.

Mutual Defense Treaty with the Republic of China, Senate, 84th Cong., 1st sess., Executive Report No. 2 (Washington, D.C.: U.S. Government Printing Office, 1955), pp. 1, 4, 5-6, 8.

DOCUMENT 13

U.S. Secretary of State Dulles' Statement, September 4, 1958

I have reviewed in detail with the President the serious situation which has resulted from aggressive Chinese Communist military actions in the Taiwan (Formosa) Straits area. The President has authorized me to make the following statement.

1. Neither Taiwan (Formosa) nor the islands of Quemoy and Matsu have ever been under the authority of the Chinese Communists. Since the end of the Second World War, a period of over 13 years, they have continuously been under the authority of Free China, that is, the Republic of China.

2. The United States is bound by treaty to help to defend Taiwan (Formosa) from armed attack and the President is authorized by Joint Resolution of the Congress to employ the armed forces of the United States for the securing and protecting of related positions such as Quemoy and Matsu.

3. Any attempt on the part of the Chinese Communists now to seize these positions or any of them would be a crude violation of the principles upon which world order is based, namely, that no country should use armed force to seize new territory.

4. The Chinese Communists have, for about 2 weeks, been subjecting Quemoy to heavy artillery bombardment and, by artillery fire and use of small naval craft, they have been harassing the regular supply of the civilian and military population of the Quemoys, which totals some 125 thousand persons. The official Peiping radio repeatedly announces the purpose of these military operations to be to take by armed force Taiwan (Formosa), as well as Quemoy and Matsu. In virtually every Peiping broadcast Taiwan (Formosa) and the offshore islands are linked as the objective of what is called the "Chinese People's Liberation Army."

5. Despite, however, what the Chinese Communists say, and so far have done, it is not yet certain that their purpose is in fact to make an all-out effort to conquer by force Taiwan (Formosa) and the offshore islands. Neither is it apparent that such efforts as are being made, or may be made, cannot be contained by the courageous, and purely defensive, efforts of the forces of the Republic of China, with such substantial logistical support as the United States is providing. . . .

7. The President and I earnestly hope that the Chinese Communist regime will not again, as in the case of Korea, defy the basic principle upon which world order depends, namely, that armed force should not be used to achieve territorial ambitions. Any such naked use of force would pose an issue far transcending the offshore islands and even the security of Taiwan (Formosa). It would forecast a widespread use of force in the Far East which would endanger vital free world positions and the security of the United States. Acquiescence therein would threaten peace everywhere. We believe that the civilized world community will never condone overt military conquest as a legitimate instrument of policy.

8. The United States has not, however, abandoned hope that Peiping will stop short of defying the will of mankind for peace. This would not require it to abandon its claims, however ill-founded we may deem them to be. I recall that in the extended negotiations which the representatives of the United States and Chinese Communist regime conducted at Geneva between 1955 and 1958, a sustained effort was made by the United States to secure, with particular reference to the Taiwan area, a declaration of mutual and reciprocal renunciation of force, except in self-defense, which, however, would be without prejudice to the pursuit of policies by peaceful means. The Chinese Communists rejected any such declaration. We believe, however, that such a course of conduct constitutes the only civilized and acceptable procedure. The United States intends to follow that course, so far as it is concerned, unless and until the Chinese Communists, by their acts, leave us no choice but to react in defense of the principles to which all peace-loving governments are dedicated.

Department of State Bulletin 39, no. 1004 (Spetember 22, 1958), pp. 445–46.

DOCUMENT 14

PRC's Declaration on the Territorial Sea, September 4, 1958

The Government of the People's Republic of China declares:

1. The breadth of the territorial sea of the People's Republic of China shall be twelve nautical miles. This provision applies to all territories of the People's Republic of China, including the Chinese mainland and its coastal islands, as well as Taiwan and its surrounding islands, the Penghu Islands, the Tungsha Islands, the Hsisha Islands, the Chungsha Islands, the Nanshal Islands and all other islands belonging to China which are separated from the mainland and its coastal islands by the high seas.

2. China's territorial sea along the mainland and its coastal islands takes as its baseline the line composed of the straight lines connecting base-points on the mainland coast and on the outermost of the coastal islands; the water area extending twelve nautical miles outward from this baseline is China's territorial sea. The water areas inside the baseline, including Pohai Bay and the Chiungchow Straits, are Chinese inland waters. The islands inside the baseline, including Tungyin Island, Kaoteng Island, the Matsu Islands, the Paichuan Islands, Wuchiu Island, the Greater and Lesser Quemoy Islands, Tatan Island, Erhtan Island and Tungting Island, are islands of the Chinese inland waters.

3. No foreign vessels for military use and no foreign aircraft may enter China's territorial sea and the air space above it without the permission of the Government of the People's Republic of China.

While navigating Chinese territorial sea, every foreign vessel must observe the relevant laws and regulations laid down by the Government of the People's Republic of China.

4. The principles provided in paragraphs 2 and 3 likewise apply to Taiwan and its surrounding islands, the Penghu Islands, the Tungsha Islands, the Hsisha Islands, the Chungsha Islands, the Nansha Islands, and all other islands belonging to China.

The Taiwan and Penghu areas are still occupied by the United States by armed force. This is an unlawful encroachment on the territorial integrity and sovereignty of the People's Republic of China. Taiwan, Penghu and such other areas are yet to be recovered, and the Government of the People's Republic of China has the right to recover these areas by all suitable means at a suitable time. This is China's internal affair, in which no foreign interference is tolerated.

––––––––––––––

Peking Review 1, no. 28 (September 9, 1958): 21.

DOCUMENT 15

ROC-U.S. Joint Communique, October 23, 1958

Consultations have been taking place over the past three days between the Government of the United States and the Government of the Republic of China pursuant to Article IV of the Mutual Defense Treaty. These consultations had been invited by President Chiang Kai-shek. The following are among those who took part in the consultations:

For the Republic of China:

President Chiang Kai-shek

Vice-President—Premier Chen Cheng

Secretary-General to the President Chang Chun

Minister of Foreign Affairs Huang Shao-ku

Ambassador to the United States George K. C. Yeh

For the United States of America:

Secretary of State John Foster Dulles

Assistant Secretary of State Walter S. Robertson

Ambassador to the Republic of China Everett F. Drumright.

The consultations had been arranged to be held during the two weeks when the Chinese Communists had declared they would cease fire upon Quemoy. It had been hoped that, under these circumstances, primary consideration could have been given to measures which would have contributed to stabilizing an actual situation of nonmilitancy. However, on the eve of the consultations, the Chinese Communists, in violation of their declaration, resumed artillery fire against the Quemoys. It was recognized that under the present conditions the defense of the Quemoys, together with the Matsus, is closely related to the defense of Taiwan and Penghu.

The two Governments recalled that their Mutual Defense Treaty had had the purpose of manifesting their unity "so that no potential aggressor could be under the illusion that either of them stands alone in the West Pacific Area." The consultations provided a fresh occasion for demonstrating that unity.

The two Governments reaffirmed their solidarity in the face of the new Chinese Communist aggression now manifesting itself in the bombardment of the Quemoys. This aggression and the accompanying Chinese Communist propaganda have not divided them, as the Communists have hoped. On the contrary, it has drawn them closer together. They believe that by unitedly opposing aggression they serve not only themselves but also the cause of peace. As President Eisenhower said on September 11, the position of opposing aggression by force is the only position consistent with the peace of the world.

The two Governments took note of the fact that the Chinese Communists, with the backing of the Soviet Union, avowedly seek to conquer Taiwan, to eliminate Free China and to expel the United States from the Western Pacific generally, compelling the United States to abandon its collective security arrangements with free countries of that area. This policy cannot possibly succeed. It is hoped and believed that the Communists, faced by the proven unity, resolution and strength of the Governments of the United States and the Republic of China, will not put their policy to the test of general war and that they will abandon the military steps which they have already taken to initiate their futile and dangerous policy.

In addition to dealing with the current military situation, the two Governments considered the broad and long-range aspects of their relationship.

The United States, its Government and its people, have an abiding faith in the Chinese people and profound respect for the great contribution which they have made and will continue to make to a civilization that respects and honors the individual and his family life. The United States recognizes that the Republic of China is the authentic spokesman for Free China and of the hopes and aspirations entertained by the great mass of the Chinese people.

The Government of the Republic of China declared its purpose to be a worthy representative of the Chinese people and to strive to preserve those qualities and characteristics which have enabled the Chinese to contribute so much of benefit to humanity.

The two Governments reaffirmed their dedication to the principles of the Charter of the United Nations. They recalled that the treaty under which they are acting is defensive in character. The Government of the Republic of China considers that the restoration of freedom to its people on the mainland is its sacred mission. It believes that the foundation of this mission resides in the minds and the hearts of the Chinese people and that the principal means of successfully achieving its mission is the implementation of Dr. Sun Yat-sen's three people's principles (nationalism, democracy and social well-being) and not the use of force.

The consultations which took place permitted a thorough study and re-examination of the pressing problems of mutual concern. As such, they have proved to be of great value to both Governments. It is believed that such consultations should continue to be held at appropriate intervals.

American Foreign Policy, Current Documents, 1958 (Washington, D.C.: U.S. Government Printing Office, 1962), pp. 1184–85.

DOCUMENT 16

PRC Defense Minister P'eng Teh-huai's Second Message to Compatriots in Taiwan, October 25, 1958

Compatriots, military and civilian, in Taiwan, Penghu, Quemoy and Matsu:

We are fully aware that the overwhelming majority of you are patriots, and only extremely few among you are willing slaves of the Americans. Compatriots! Chinese problems can only be settled by us Chinese. If they are difficult to settle for the time being, things can be talked over at length. The American political broker Dulles likes to poke his nose into other people's business. He wants to take a hand in the matter of the long-standing dispute between the Kuomintang and the Communist Party, and order Chinese to do this or that, to harm the interests of the Chinese and serve the interests of the Americans. That is to say: step one, to isolate Taiwan; step two, to place Taiwan under trusteeship. If things do not turn out to their liking, they can resort to the most sinister measures. Do you know how General Chang Tso-lin met his death? There is a place called Huangkutun in northeast China, and it was there that he was done to death. No imperialist in the world has any conscience. And the American imperialists are especially vicious, at least no better than the Japanese who did Chang Tso-lin to death. Compatriots! I advise you to be a little more careful. I advise you not to depend too much on other people, lest all your rights and authority be taken away. To arrange things between our two Parties is very easy. I have already ordered our troops at the Fukien front not to shell the airfield in Quemoy and the wharf, beach and ships at Liaolo Bay on even days of the calendar, so that the compatriots, both military and civilian, on the big and small islands of Greater Quemoy, Lesser Quemoy, Tatan, Erhtan and others may all get sufficient supplies, including food, vegetables, edible oils, fuels and military equipment, to facilitate your entrenchment for a long time to come. If you are short of anything, just say so and we will give it to you. It is time now to turn from foe into friend. Your ships and aircraft should not come on odd days. We will not necessarily conduct shelling on odd days. But you should refrain from coming, to avoid possible losses. In this way, half of each month will be free for transportation, and supplies would not be lacking. Some of you suspect that we want to undermine the unity between your troops and civilians and between your officers and men. No, compatriots! We hope you will strengthen your unity, so as to act in unison in facing up to the foreigners. Fight-fight-stop-stop, half-fight, half-stop: this is no trick but a normal thing in the present specific circumstances. Our refraining from shelling the airfield, the wharf, the beach and the ships is still conditional on not introducing American escorts. Exception will be taken if there should be escorts. In the Chiang-Dulles talks, you have suffered a little loss. Now you have only the right of speaking for "Free China"; in addition, you are still permitted to represent a small part of the overseas Chinese. The Americans have conferred upon you the title of a small China. On October 23, the U.S. Department of State published an interview Dulles had given to a correspondent of a British broadcasting company which was recorded in advance on October 16. The interview was made public as soon as Dulles took off from Taiwan. Dulles said that he saw a China of the Communists, that, since this country actually exists, he was willing to deal with it, and so on. Thank heaven, our country is seen by an American lord. This is a big China. Under the force of circumstances, the Americans have changed their policy and treated you as a "de facto political unit," that is to say, in fact, not as a country. Such a "de facto political unit" is still needed by the Americans at the initial stage starting from the present time. That means isolating Taiwan. In the second stage, Taiwan is to be placed under trusteeship. Friends of the Kuomintang! Do you not yet sense this danger? Where is the way out? Please think it over. The document issued after the Chiang-Dulles talks this time was only a communique devoid of legal force. It is easy to shake yourselves free, depending on whether you have the determination or not. There is only one China, not two, in the world. On this we agree. All Chinese people, including you and compatriots abroad, absolutely will not allow the American plot forcibly to create two Chinas to come true. The present age is an age full of hope. All patriots have a future and should not be afraid of the imperialists. Of course, we are not advising you to break with the Americans right away. That would be an unrealistic idea. We only hope that you will not yield to American pressure, submit to their every whim and will, lose your sovereign rights, and so finally be deprived of shelter in the world and thrown into the sea. These words of ours are well-intentioned and bear no ill-will. You will come to understand them by and by.

Peng Teh-huai
Minister of National Defense

Peking Review 1, no. 35 (October 28, 1959): 5.

DOCUMENT 17

Ely Maurer, "Legal Problems Regarding Formosa and the Offshore Islands"

International Legal Problems

On the international front it is best to examine the problem of Formosa separately from the problem of the offshore islands [Quemoy and Matsu in the vicinity of the coast of Fukien Province].

In giving the historical background of Formosa it has been pointed out that at Cairo the Allies stated it was their purpose to restore Formosa to Chinese sovereignty and that at the end of the war the Republic of China receive the surrender of Japanese forces on Formosa. It has also been pointed out that under the Japanese Peace Treaty Japan renounced all right, title, and claim to Formosa. However, neither in that treaty nor in any other treaty has there been any definitive cession to China of Formosa. The situation is, then, one where the Allied Powers still have to come to some agreement or treaty with respect to the status of Formosa. Any action, therefore, of the Chinese Communist regime to seize Formosa constitutes an attempt to sieze by force territory which does not belong to it. Such a siezure is prohibited by law and the United Nations Charter as an attempt to settle claim to territory by force. It would thus appear that the United States is within its legal rights in taking action to defend Formosa.

With respect to the offshore islands the situation is admittedly somewhat different. There is no question that these islands are a part of the state of China. It may be admitted further that these islands are close to the mainland of China. However, the offshore islands have been in the possession and effective control of the Government of the Republic of China since its inception, except for the period of the Japanese war. Since 1949 a status quo has come into existence vis-a-vis the Peiping regime. It is this status quo which the Chinese Communists have threatened with the menace of armed force. It is our view that we have here in fact a situation comparable to that which obtained in Korea preceding the invasion of south Korea by north Korea. In other words, the action of the Chinese Communists in taking warlike measures is an effort to change the status quo and to gain additional territory by force in violation of the prohibitions of the United Nations Charter.

It has been urged that this is essentially a civil war and therefore it is improper for the United States to participate with the Government of the Republic of China in defense of the offshore islands. It should first be pointed out that it is too narrow to look upon the conflict merely as a civil war. Even as early as the end of the war with Japan the Soviet Union, in violation of its treaty with the Chinese Nationalists, turned over large stores of equipment and in other ways furnished material aid to the Chinese Communists. Since that time the Soviet Union has continued giving large assistance to the Chinese Communist regime. Thus much of the ammunition, artillery, and planes that are at present being used by that regime derive from Russian sources. And the Soviet Union is allied by military treaty with the Chinese regime. On the other hand the United States has vital interests in the Formosa area and is allied with the Republic of China in a Mutual Defense Treaty and has agreements to supply arms for defensive purposes. In the circumstances it seems fair to say that we are here involved in what is realistically an international dispute which the Communist regime is attempting to settle by force.

Further, with respect to the argument that this is a civil war, it will be recalled that this was the same argument that was made by Vishinsky regarding the north Korean invasion of south Korea. It was an argument however which the United Nations paid no heed to but, instead, viewed the action of the north Koreans as one of aggression which came under the ban of the United Nations Charter.

. . .

On this phase of the matter it is our view, then, that the United States would be justified from an international standpoint in cooperating with the Republic of China in the defense of the offshore islands and Formosa.

Department of State Bulletin 39, no. 1017 (December 22, 1958): 1009–10. Maurer was assistant legal adviser for Far Eastern affairs at the time of presenting this address before the Washington chapter of the Federal Bar Association on November 20, 1958.

DOCUMENT 18

From a 1959 Mao Interview

The Words and Deeds of the Leaders of the Communist Party of China.— Concerning an Interview With Mao Tse-tung. (By Eduardo Mora Valverde, member of the leadership of the People's Vanguard Party of Costa Rica. *Izvestia*, June 19, p. 2. 2,000 words. Condensed text:) . . . [At a meeting of leaders of a number of Latin American Communist and Workers' Parties with Comrade Mao Tse-tung on March 3, 1959, he declared:]

"We have thrown out the North American imperialists from the continent, but they are holding out on Taiwan. We have warned them to get out of there, but they refuse. Perhaps you can suggest some means to us. You know about the events of last year. The island of Quemoy has a population of only 80,000, but it is now known to the entire world. The U.S.A. does not object to the islands of Quemoy and Matsu being given back to us, but in return it wishes to retain Taiwan for itself. This would be an unprofitable deal. We had better wait; let Chiang Kai-shek stay on Quemoy and Matsu, and we shall get them back later, together with the Pescadores and Taiwan. Our territory is spacious, and for the time being we can get along without these islands."

But Mao Tse-tung continued developing his idea, and in the course of the interview another Mao Tse-tung, quite unlike the one we had known before, gradually began to appear before us. His words astonished us. He said: "We do not want conciliation with the U.S.A. The United States must submit to us. Otherwise we do not wish to enter into negotiations with them. It is unimportant if they do not return Taiwan to us for another 100 years. If they do not recognize us, then we have no desire to recognize them either. . . ."

Current Digest of the Soviet Press 16, no. 25 (July 15, 1964): 5–6. The article is reprinted from the magazine *Problemy mira i sotsializma* [Problems of peace and socialism], No. 6, in somewhat condensed form.

DOCUMENT 19

U.S. Department of State's Statement on the Status of Taiwan, April 28, 1971

. . . Press Officer Charles Bray . . . gave the following description of the U.S. attitude toward mainland China.

"We must deal with the practical situation as we find it. We recognize the Republic of China and have diplomatic relations with it. We have a treaty commitment to the defense of Taiwan and the Pescadores Islands on one hand. On the other hand, mainland China has been controlled and administered by the People's Republic of China for 21 years and for some time we have been dealing with that government on matters affecting our mutual interest."

. . .

Bray, in a prepared statement on the question about who exercises sovereignty over Taiwan, said:

"In our view sovereignty over Taiwan and the Pescadores is an unsettled question subject to future international resolution. Both the Republic of China and the People's Republic of China disagree with this conclusion. Both consider Taiwan and the Pescadores Islands are part of the sovereign state of China."

"Obviously we cannot hope to resolve the dispute between these two rival governments," Bray added.

"Our position has been and remains very firmly that whatever the ultimate resolution of the dispute between the Republic of China on Taiwan and the PRC on the mainland, it should be accomplished by peaceful means."

[He] said there were two ways this could be worked out—internationally, or directly by the two governments.

. . .

He said that the statement on Taiwan was a considered statement. He explained that the U.S. regards the status of the island as unsettled, because in the Cairo and Potsdam declarations of World War II, the allied powers "stated as their purpose that Taiwan should be part of China."

"This statement of purpose was never formally implemented or executed," he said.

There was an opportunity at the time of the San Francisco 1951 treaty of peace with Japan to settle the question of Taiwan, but the subject was not dealt with.

"We regard the Republic of China as exercising legitimate authority over Taiwan and the Pescadores by virtue of the fact that Japanese forces occupying Taiwan were directed to surrender to the force of the Republic of China," he said.

Bray also recalled President Truman's June 27, 1950, statement, when he announced that the U.S. Seventh Fleet was being interposed between Taiwan and the mainland of China, that the determination of the future status of Taiwan "must await the restoration of security in the Pacific, a peace settlement with Japan or consideration of the United Nations."

The Nixon administration also follows this policy, Bray said.

Excerpt from Associated Press, Washington, D.C., April 29, 1971, in *China Post* (Taipei), April 30, 1971, p. 1.

DOCUMENT 20

ROC Foreign Ministry Statement, April 30, 1971

The government of the Republic of China is astounded by Mr. Bray's remarks on the so-called status of Taiwan and the Pescadores and by his proposal for a direct negotiation between the government of the Republic of China and the Peiping regime. Soon after the Chinese government learned of the aforementioned statements, a ranking official of the Ministry of Foreign Affairs made enquiry at the embassy of the United States on April 29th.

Subsequently, Foreign Minister Chow Shu-kai asked American Ambassador Walter P. McConaughy for a conference at 11 a.m. on April 30. The Minister expressed the Chinese Government's extreme concern with and took strong exception to the contents of the State Department press officer's remarks.

Mr. Chow pointed out that both the Cairo Declaration and the Postdam Declaration clearly provided that Taiwan and the Pescadores should be returned to the Republic of China. Moreover, the Sino-Japanese Peace Treaty signed in 1952 and the Sino-American Mutual Defense Treaty signed in 1954 have definitely recognized Taiwan and the Pescadores as part of the territories of the Republic of China. It is, therefore, beyond comprehension that the State Department press officer should have made at this time a statement touching upon the legal status of Taiwan and the Pescadores.

Minister Chow stressed the necessity for the U.S. government to make a clarification of this matter as soon as possible.

In reply, the American Ambassador told the Foreign Minister that he had made a telegraphic enquiry about this incident to the State Department and was instructed to assure the Chinese government that Mr. Bray's statement does not represent any change in the U.S. policy concerning the status of Taiwan and the Pescadores and the Republic of China's legitimate jurisdiction over Taiwan and the Pescadores.

The Ambassador added that it is the consistent policy of the United States that issues relating to this area should be settled by peaceful means, but this should not be construed as the United States advocating a direct negotiation between the Chinese Government and the Peiping regime.

Minister Chow made particular mention to the American Ambassador of the statement made by President Richard M. Nixon on the evening of April 29th (Washington time) at a press conference that any such suggestion for a direct negotiation is completely unrealistic. As far as the Chinese government is concerned, it is simply inconceivable.

Minister Chow emphatically asked the American Ambassador to convey the Chinese Government's firm and just stand to the State Department, to which the American ambassador agreed.

The Ministry of Foreign Affairs has also instructed today the Chinese embassy in Washington to make a strong representation to the State Department to the same effect.

News from China (New York: Chinese Information Service, May 1, 1971), No. P71–352.

DOCUMENT 21

The Shanghai Communique, February 28, 1972

President Richard Nixon of the United States of America visited the People's Republic of China at the invitation of Premier Chou En-lai of the People's Republic of China from February 21 to February 28, 1972. Accompanying the President was Mrs. Nixon, U.S. Secretary of State William Rogers, Assistant to the President Dr. Henry Kissinger, and other American officials.

President Nixon met with Chairman Mao Tse-tung of the Communist Party of China on February 21. The two leaders had a serious and frank exchange of views on Sino-US relations and world affairs.

During the visit, extensive, earnest and frank discussions were held between President Nixon and Premier Chou En-lai on the normalization of relations between the United States of America and the People's Republic of China, as well as on other matters of interest to both sides. In addition, Secretary of State William Rogers and Foreign Minister Chi Peng-fei held talks in the same spirit.

President Nixon and his party visited Peking and viewed cultural, industrial and agricultural sites, and they also toured Hangchow and Shanghai where, continuing discussions with Chinese leaders, they viewed similar places of interest.

The leaders of the People's Republic of China and the United States of America found it beneficial to have this opportunity, after so many years without contact, to present candidly to one another their views on a variety of issues. They reviewed the international situation in which important changes and great upheavals are taking place and expounded their respective positions and attitudes.

The U.S. side stated: Peace in Asia and peace in the world requires efforts both to reduce immediate tensions and to eliminate the basic causes of conflict. The United States will work for a just and secure peace: just, because it fulfills the aspirations of peoples and nations for freedom and progress; secure, because it removes the danger of foreign aggression. The United States supports individual freedom and social progress for all the peoples of the world, free of outside pressure or intervention. The United States believes that the effort to reduce tensions is served by improving communication between countries that have different ideologies so as to lessen the risks of confrontation through accident, miscalculation or misunderstanding. Countries should treat each other with mutual respect and be willing to compete peacefully, letting performance be the ultimate judge. No country should claim infallibility and each country should be prepared to re-examine its own attitudes for the common good. The United States stressed that the peoples of Indochina should be allowed to determine their destiny without outside intervention; its constant primary objective has been a negotiated solution; the eight-point proposal put forward by the Republic of Vietnam and the United States on Jaunary 27, 1972 represents a basis for the attainment of that objective; in the absence of a negotiated settlement the United States envisages the ultimate withdrawal of all U.S. forces from the region consistent with the aim of self-determination for each country of Indochina. The United States will maintain its close ties with and support for the Republic of Korea to seek a relaxation of tension and increased communication in the Korean peninsula. The United States places the highest value on its friendly relations with Japan; it will continue to develop the existing close bonds. Consistent with the United Nations Security Council Resolution of December 21, 1971, the United States favors the continuation of the ceasefire between India and Pakistan and the withdrawal of all military forces to within their own territories and to their own sides of the ceasefire line in Jammu and Kashmir; the United States supports the right of the peoples of South Asia to shape their own future in peace, free of military threat, and without having the area become the subject of great power rivalry.

The Chinese side stated: Wherever there is oppression, there is resistance. Countries want independence, nations want liberation and the people want revolution—this has become the irresistible trend of history. All nations, big or small, should be equal; big nations should not bully the small and strong nations should not bully the weak. China will never be a superpower and it opposes hegemony and power politics of any kind. The Chinese side stated that it firmly supports the struggles of all the oppressed people and nations for freedom and liberation and that the people of all countries have the right to choose their social systems according to their own wishes and the right to safeguard the independence, sovereignty and territorial integrity of their own countries and oppose foreign aggression, interference, control and subversion. All foreign troops should be withdrawn to their own countries.

The Chinese side expressed its firm support to the peoples of Vietnam, Laos and Cambodia in their efforts for the attainment of their goal and its firm support to the seven-point proposal of the Provisional Revolutionary Government of the Republic of South Vietnam and the elaboration of February this year on the two key problems in the proposal, and to the Joint Declaration of the Summit Conference of the Indochinese Peoples. It firmly supports the eight-point program for the peaceful unification of Korea put forward by the Government of the Democratic People's Republic of Korea on April 12, 1971, and the stand for the abolition of the "U.N. Commission for the Unification and Rehabilitation of Korea." It firmly opposes the revival and outward expansion of Japanese militarism and firmly supports the Japanese people's desire to build an independent, democratic, peaceful and neutral Japan. It firmly maintains that India and Pakistan should, in accordance with the United Nations resolutions on the India-Pakistan question, immediately withdraw all their forces to their respective territories and to their own sides of the ceasefire line in Jammu and Kashmir and firmly supports the Pakistan Government and people in their struggle to preserve their independence and sovereignty and the people of Jammu and Kashmir in their struggle for the right of self-determination.

There are essential differences between China and the United States in their social systems and foreign policies. However, the two sides agreed that countries, regardless of their social systems, should conduct their relations on the principles of respect for the sovereignty and territorial integrity of all states, non-aggression against other states, non-interference in the internal affairs of other states, equality and mutual benefit, and peaceful coexistence. International disputes should be settled on this basis, without resorting to the use or threat of force. The United States and the People's Republic of China are prepared to apply these principles to their mutual relations.

With these principles of international relations in mind the two sides stated that:

—progress toward the normalization of relations between China and the United States is in the interests of all countries;

—both wish to reduce the danger of international military conflict;

—neither should seek hegemony in the Asia-Pacific region and each is opposed to efforts by any other country or group of countries to establish such hegemony; and

—neither is prepared to negotiate on behalf of any third party or to enter into agreements or understandings with the other directed at other states.

Both sides are of the view that it would be against the interests of the peoples of the world for any major country to collude with another against other countries, or for major countries to divide up the world into spheres of interest.

The two sides reviewed the long-standing serious disputes between China and the United States. The Chinese side reaffirmed its position: The Taiwan question is the crucial question obstructing the normalization of relations between China and the United States; the Government of the People's Republic of China is the sole legal government of China; Taiwan is a province of China which has long been returned to the motherland; the liberation of Taiwan is China's internal affair in which no other country has the right to interfere; and all U.S. forces and military installations must be withdrawn from Taiwan. The Chinese Government firmly opposes any activities which aim at the creation of "one China, one Taiwan," "one China, two governments," "two Chinas," and "independent Taiwan" or advocate that "the status of Taiwan remains to be determined."

The U.S. side declared: The United States acknowledges that all Chinese on either side of the Taiwan Strait maintain there is but one China and that Taiwan is a part of China. The United States Government does not challenge that position. It reaffirms its interest in a peaceful settlement of the Taiwan question by the Chinese themselves. With this prospect in mind, it affirms the ultimate objective of the withdrawal of all U.S. forces and military installations from Taiwan. In the meantime, it will progressively reduce its forces and military installations on Taiwan as the tension in the area diminishes.

The two sides agreed that it is desirable to broaden the understanding between the two peoples. To this end, they discussed specific areas in such fields as science, technology, culture, sports and journalism, in which people-to-people contacts and exchanges would be mutually beneficial. Each side undertakes to facilitate the further development of such contacts and exchanges.

Both sides view bilateral trade as another area from which mutual benefit can be derived, and agreed that economic relations based on equality and mutual benefit are in the interest of the peoples of the two countries. They agree to facilitate the progressive development of trade between their two countries.

The two sides agreed that they will stay in contact through various channels, including the sending of a senior U.S. representative to Peking from time to time for concrete consultations to further the normalization of relations between the two countries and continue to exchange views on issues of common interest.

The two sides expressed the hope that the gains achieved during this visit would open up new prospects for the relations between the two countries. They believe that the normalization of relations between the two countries is not only in the interest of the Chinese and American peoples but also contributes to the relaxation of tension in Asia and the world.

President Nixon, Mrs. Nixon and the American party expressed their appreciation for the gracious hospitality shown them by the Government and people of the People's Republic of China.

Department of State Bulletin 66, no. 1708 (March 20, 1972): 435–38.

DOCUMENT 22

Deputy Secretary Warren Christopher's Address at Occidental College, June 11, 1977

I want to talk to you today about one of the foreign policy issues presently at the center of my desk: the normalization of U.S. relations with other governments.

It is an issue that arises in a variety of current and important situations but, before getting down to cases, I think it is important to understand why it is generally in the interest of the United States to exchange diplomats with other governments and, where possible, to exchange ideas, goods, and people as well....

We live, in sum, in an interdependent world. And in one way or another, we find our fate and our futures tied increasingly to those of other peoples. If we cannot communicate easily with them, we cannot effectively promote our own interests or build new bonds of common interest.

This brings me to my central point: We believe that diplomatic relations help us to discharge our basic duty to protect the interests of our government and our citizens. By keeping open a channel of communication with other countries, we best serve our long-range objective of encouraging the growth of democratic institutions.

We do not look at the normalization of relations as an end in itself. Rather, diplomatic relations, once established and maintained, enable us to communicate with other governments directly, to state our views and listen to theirs, to avoid misunderstandings and to exert influence. In short, they help us to accomplish more than we can without them....

We maintain diplomatic relations with many governments of which we do not necessarily approve. The reality is that, in this day and age, coups and other unscheduled changes of government are not exceptional developments. Withholding diplomatic relations from these regimes, after they have obtained effective control, penalizes us. It means that we forsake much of the chance to influence the attitudes and conduct of a new regime. Without relations, we forfeit opportunities to transmit our values and communicate our policies. Isolation may well bring out the worst in the new government.

For the same reasons, we eschew withdrawal of diplomatic relations except in rare instances, for example, the outbreak of war or events which make it physically impossible to maintain a diplomatic presence in another capital.

If we continue to withhold diplomatic relations, this hesitancy invites confusion and can become the center of a touchy political issue. Eventual establishment of diplomatic relations then comes, wrongly, to be considered as a form of approval. In short, it means that someday, when we seek to normalize relations, we will be painting on a dirty canvas.

Indeed, efforts to restore relations once broken often encounter special difficulties. Inevitably, constituencies in both countries develop an emotional investment in the absence of relations. Financial claims and counterclaims pile up, and there is a backlog of issues which might have been resolved if normal relations had existed. Faced with this legacy of problems, the process of restoring relations must be approached with great care and deliberation. . . .

Fully aware of the difficulties involved, we are bent on shortening the list. Let me give a few examples of the kinds of steps being taken, under President Carter's leadership, to establish normal diplomatic relations with other countries. . . .

The People's Republic of China, of course, presents a unique situation. For over two decades we stared across the Pacific at this giant with fear, hostility, and little communication.

Then, six years ago, began the dramatic process of establishing relations with the People's Republic of China. This process was complicated by the fact that we maintained relations with another government as the Government of China.

In 1972, under the carefully crafted framework of the Shanghai Communique, we agreed to move forward toward normalization of relations. The Chinese stated in that communique that there was but one China, and we did not challenge that view. We have since exchanged liaison offices—not embassies—in Peking and Washington.

When Secretary Vance goes to Peking later this year, we hope to discuss with the leaders of the People's Republic of China ways to move forward in our relationship. The main obstacle to full normalization is the question of Taiwan, an issue of genuine concern to the American people. It is a question we believe should be settled peacefully—and by the Chinese themselves. . . .

In sum, we believe normal diplomatic relations are an asset to promote other objectives, an asset we cannot deny ourselves, without incurring substantial cost. As Churchill put it: "When relations are most difficult, that is the time diplomacy is most needed."

There is no certainty that two nations will be able to resolve their disputes by talking about them. But without effective communications, without some form of dialogue, the odds are high that there will be no progress at all. This is true, as each of you knows, among individuals. So it is among nations, as well.

Department of State Press Release, No. 269 (June 10, 1977).

DOCUMENT 23

Secretary of State Vance's Address before the Asia Society, June 29, 1977

Turning to China, after 25 years of confrontation we are carrying on a constructive dialogue with the People's Republic of China.

Vast differences in culture, social systems, ideology, and foreign policy still separate our two countries. But the Chinese and American people no longer face each other with the hostility, misunderstanding, and virtually complete separation that existed for two decades.

We consider friendly relations with China to be a central part of our foreign policy. China's role in maintaining world peace is vital. A constructive relationship with China is important, not only regionally, but also for global equilibrium. Such a relationship will threaten no one. It will serve only peace.

The involvement of a fourth of mankind in the search for the solution of global issues is important.

In structuring our relationship with the Chinese, we will not enter into any agreements with others that are directed against the People's Republic of China. We recognize and respect China's strong commitments to independence, unity, and self-reliance.

Our policy toward China will continue to be guided by the principles of the Shanghai Communique, and on that basis we shall seek to move toward full normalization of relations. We acknowledge the view expressed in the Shanghai Communique that there is but one China. We also place importance on the peaceful settlement of the Taiwan question by the Chinese themselves.

Department of State Bulletin 77, no. 1988 (August 1, 1977): 141–42.

DOCUMENT 24

ROC Foreign Minister Shen Chang-huan's Statement, July 1, 1977

Having read the speech made by Secretary of State Cyrus Vance on June 29, 1977 at the Asia Society, I am constrained to take strong exception to the statement of China policy as reflected in that speech.

It may be recalled that following the announcement of the "Shanghai Communique" in February 1972, my government registered a strong protest with the United States government and has since repeatedly pointed out that the illusions the U.S. entertains towards the Chinese Communists not only seriously affect the rights and interests of the Republic of China, but will also bring immeasurable damage to the entire free world.

I must now frankly point out that it is extremely dangerous for the United States to consider friendly relations with the Chinese Communists to be a central part of its foreign policy and for the United States to believe that the Chinese Communists can play a vital role in maintaining world peace.

We should not have forgotten that the Chinese Communists have massacred as many as sixty million people after their occupation of the Chinese mainland, and that more than 150,000 American youths lost their lives or were wounded during the Korean War with the direct intervention of the Chinese Communists. It is a well known fact that the Chinese Communists actively supported the North Vietnamese in the Vietnam War. Presently, the Chinese Communists are continuing their support of Communist elements in Southeast Asia, Latin America and Africa, with a view to subverting the free and independent governments and to advance their cause of world communization. It would be a total disregard of the historical lessons as well as the reality if the United States were to believe that the Chinese Communists are capable of playing any role in maintaining international peace. Such a policy would not only be unhelpful to the cause of world peace, but may lead to new threats of war.

The Republic of China and the United States have been friends of long standing. The two countries have diplomatic relations and are allies by virtue of the mutual defense treaty. The government of the Republic of China, as a loyal ally of the United States, has always respected moral principles and faithfully adhered to its treaty obligations. Deep and sincere friendship have been existing between the peoples of the two countries.

My government and people are dedicated to peace and freedom. We have devoted ourselves to the promotion of democracy, the development of economy and the betterment of the standard of living of our people. Internationally, we have done our utmost to promote mutual assistance and cooperation with free countries in many parts of the world, with a view to contributing to world peace.

On the other hand, the Chinese Communists took power with sheer violence. Internally, Communist tyranny has deprived the people of all fundamental human rights. To the outside world, they export revolution, engaging in infiltration and subversive activities in many free countries. With such sharp contrasts, should the United States choose to recognize the Chinese Communists by abandoning the long standing friendly relations with the Republic of China, it would not only seriously damage the rights and interests of the Republic of China and jeopardize the security of the 16 million Chinese on Taiwan, but would also violate the lofty ideals upon which the American nation was built and the moral principles emphasized by the Carter administration and thus erode the credibility of the United States among the free peoples the world over.

It has been the consistent position of the government of the Republic of China to carry out its responsibility of delivering our 800 million compatriots from Communist tyranny by political means, while the Chinese Communists have never given up their design to "librate" Taiwan by force. The "peaceful settlement" theme being harped by the Chinese Communists is but an attempt on their part to forcibly impose their tyrannic rule on the 16 million Chinese on Taiwan.

The Chinese people in Taiwan, who enjoy freedoms and fundamental human rights, can never accept Communist enslavement and persecution. For these reasons, I must reiterate that the government and the people of the Republic of China will in no circumstances enter into any negotiation with the Chinese Communists.

I earnestly hope that the United States of America, being the leader of the free world, will abandon forthright all illusions, perceive her own real interests and carefully weigh her moral and historic responsibility towards the future of the free world as a whole.

Finally, I wish to state most emphatically that the government and the people of the Republic of China will continue to strive unceasingly towards the established goal in the spirit of self-respect and self-reliance.

News from China, No. P.77–624 (July 1, 1977).

DOCUMENT 25

An Amendment to the International Security Assistance Act of 1978 Concerning the Mutual Defense Treaty with the ROC

United States Republic of China Mutual Defense Treaty

Sec. 26. (a) The Congress finds that—

(1) the continued security and stability of East Asia is a matter of major strategic interest to the United States;

(2) the United States and the Republic of China have for a period of twenty-four years been linked together by the Mutual Defense Treaty of 1954;

(3) the Republic of China has during that twenty-four-year period faithfully and continually carried out its duties and obligations under that treaty; and

(4) it is the responsibility of the Senate to give its advice and consent to treaties entered into by the United States.

(b) It is the sense of the Congress that there should be prior consultation between the Congress and the executive branch on any proposed policy changes affecting the continuation in force of the Mutual Defense Treaty of 1954.

Congressional Record, 95th Cong., 2d sess., No. 138 (September 7, 1978), p. H9229. The amendment was adopted by the Congress on September 12, 1978.

DOCUMENT 26

Joint Communique on the Establishment of Diplomatic Relations between the United States of America and the People's Republic of China, January 1, 1979

(The communique was released on December 15, 1978, in Washington and Peking)

The United States of America and the People's Republic of China have agreed to recognize each other and to establish diplomatic relations as of January 1, 1979.

The United States of America recognizes the Government of the People's Republic of China as the sole legal Government of China. Within this context, the people of the United States will maintain cultural, commercial, and other unofficial relations with the people of Taiwan.

The United States of America and the People's Republic of China reaffirm the principles agreed on by the two sides in the Shanghai Communique and emphasize once again that:

●Both wish to reduce the danger of international military conflict.

●Neither should seek hegemony in the Asia-Pacific region or in any other region of the world and each is opposed to efforts by any other country or group of countries to establish such hegemony.

●Neither is prepared to negotiate on behalf of any third party or to enter into agreements or understandings with the other directed at other states.

●The Government of the United States of America acknowledges* the Chinese position that there is but one China and Taiwan is part of China.

●Both believe that normalization of Sino-American relations is not only in the interest of the Chinese and American peoples but also contributes to the cause of peace in Asia and the world.

The United States of America and the People's Republic of China will exchange Ambassadors and establish Embassies on March 1, 1979.

---

*The Chinese text translated the word "acknowledges" into *Cheng-jen*, which, if retranslated into English, would mean "recognize."
Department of State Bulletin 79, no. 2022 (January 1979): 25.

DOCUMENT 27

United States Statement Accompanying the Joint Communique on the Establishment of Diplomatic Relations between the United States and the People's Republic of China, December 15, 1978

As of January 1, 1979, the United States of America recognizes the People's Republic of China as the sole legal government of China. On the same date, the People's Republic of China accords similar recognition to the United States of America. The United States thereby establishes diplomatic relations with the People's Republic of China.

On that same date, January 1, 1979, the United States of America will notify Taiwan that it is terminating diplomatic relations and that the Mutual Defense Treaty between the United States and the Republic of China is being terminated in accordance with the provisions of the Treaty. The United States also states that it will be withdrawing its remaining military personnel from Taiwan within four months.

In the future, the American people and the people of Taiwan will maintain commercial, cultural, and other relations without official government representation and without diplomatic relations.

The Administration will seek adjustments to our laws and regulations to permit the maintenance of commercial, cultural, and other nongovernmental relationships in the new circumstances that will exist after normalization.

The United States is confident that the people of Taiwan face a peaceful and prosperous future. The United States continues to have an interest in the peaceful resolution of the Taiwan issue and expects that the Taiwan issue will be settled peacefully by the Chinese themselves.

The United States believes that the establishment of diplomatic relations with the People's Republic will contribute to the welfare of the American people, to the stability of Asia where the United States has major security and economic interest, and to the peace of the entire world.

Department of State Bulletin 79, no. 2022 (January 1979): 26.

DOCUMENT 28

People's Republic of China Statement Accompanying the Joint Communique on the Establishment of Diplomatic Relations between the United States and the PRC, December 15, 1978

As of January 1, 1979, the People's Republic of China and the United States of America recognize each other and establish diplomatic relations, thereby ending the prolonged abnormal relationship between them. This is a historic event in Sino-U.S. relations.

As is known to all, the Government of the People's Republic of China is the sole legal Government of China and Taiwan is a part of China. The question of Taiwan was the crucial issue obstructing the normalization of relations between China and the United States. It has now been resolved between the two countries in the spirit of the Shanghai Communique and through their joint efforts, thus enabling the normalization of relations so ardently desired by the people of the two countries. As for the way of bringing Taiwan back to the embrace of the motherland and reunifying the country, it is entirely China's internal affair.

At the invitation of the U.S. Government, Teng Hsiao-ping, Vice-Premier of the State Council of the People's Republic of China, will pay an official visit to the United States in January 1979, with a view to further promoting the friendship between the two peoples and good relations between the two countries.

Peking Review 21, no. 51 (December 22, 1978): 8–9.

DOCUMENT 29

Chairman Hua's Press Conference on Establishing Diplomatic Relations with the United States, Peking, December 16, 1978

Hua Kuo-feng, Chairman of the Central Committee of the Communist Party of China and Premier of the State Council, gave a press conference in Peking's Great Hall of the People on the morning of December 16 in connection with the establishment of diplomatic relations between the People's Republic of China and the United States of America.

Chairman Hua started the press conference by reading out the joint communique on the establishment of diplomatic relations between China and the

United States and the statement of the Government of the People's Republic of China. He then answered questions from newsmen.

Question: Chairman Hua, will you please speak about the significance of the normalization of Sino-U.S. relations?

Answer: The normalization of Sino-U.S. relations has long been a wish of the Chinese and American peoples. Our great leader the late Chairman Mao Tse-tung and our esteemed Premier Chou En-lai paved the way for opening Sino-U.S. relations. During the visit of President Nixon and Dr. Kissinger to China in 1972, the Chinese and U.S. sides issued the Shanghai Communique, which started the process of normalizing Sino-U.S. relations. Thanks to the joint efforts of the leaders, governments and peoples of the two countries in the past few years, Sino-U.S. relations have now been normalized. Former U.S. President Ford, many of the senators and congressmen and other friends from all walks of life have all played their part towards this end. Now, President Carter, Dr. Brzezinski and Secretary of State Vance have all made valuable contributions to the eventual normalization of our relations.

The establishment of diplomatic relations between China and the United States is a historic event. It opens up broad vistas for enhancing understanding and friendship between the two peoples and promoting bilateral exchanges in all fields. It will also contribute to peace and stability in Asia and the world as a whole. The Chinese and American peoples are happy about it and I believe the people all over the world will be happy at the news too.

Q: Chairman Hua, my question is: What policy will the Chinese Government adopt towards Taiwan in the new circumstances when relations between China and the United States have been normalized?

A: Taiwan is part of China's sacred territory and the people in Taiwan are our kith and kin. It is the common aspiration of all the Chinese people including our compatriots in Taiwan to accomplish the great cause of reunifying the country with Taiwan returning to the embrace of the motherland. It has been our consistent policy that all patriots belong to one big family whether they come forward early or late. We hope that our compatriots in Taiwan will join all the other Chinese people including our compatriots in Hongkong and Macao and overseas Chinese in making further contributions to the cause of reunifying China.

Q: Can you say that after normalization China will object to a visit to Taiwan by an American official?

A: The relations between China and the United States have been normalized after the joint efforts of both sides which have reached an agreement and have now issued the joint communique. And the answer to your question is clearly stated in the joint communique which I quote: "The United States of America recognizes the Government of the People's Republic of China as the sole legal Government of China. Within this context, the people of the United States will maintain cultural, commercial, and other unofficial relations with the people of Taiwan." So the answer is very clear in this paragraph. There will only be unofficial relations.

Q: Will the United States be permitted to continue providing Taiwan with access to military equipment for defensive purposes?

A: Paragraph two of the joint communique which I announced just now says: "The United States of America recognizes the Government of the People's Republic of China as the sole legal Government of China. Within this context, the people of the United States will maintain cultural, commercial, and other unofficial relations with the people of Taiwan." In our discussions on the question of the commercial relations, the two sides had differing views. During the negotiations the U.S. side mentioned that after normalization it would continue to sell limited amount of arms to Taiwan for defensive purposes. We made it clear that we absolutely would not agree to this. In all discussions the Chinese side repeatedly made clear its position on this question. We held that after the normalization continued sales of arms to Taiwan by the United States would not conform to the principles of the normalization, would be detrimental to the peaceful liberation of Taiwan and would exercise an unfavourable influence on the peace and stability of the Asia-Pacific region. So our two sides had differences on this point. Nevertheless, we reached an agreement on the joint communique.

Q: Mr. Chairman, may I ask you please about the possibility of a worsening of relations with Russia as a result of what you have announced today, since the Russians may be very suspicious of your joining more closely with the Americans. Do you feel that it may lead to a worsening of relations with Moscow?

A: We think that the normalization of relations between China and the United States and the signing of the Treaty of Peace and Friendship Between China and Japan are conducive to peace and stability in the Asia-Pacific region and the world as a whole. Does this mean the formation of an axis or alliance of China, Japan and the United States? We say that it is neither an alliance nor an axis. China and the United States have now normalized their relations and the relations between the United States and the Soviet Union have also been normalized. Therefore it is out of the question that the normalization of relations is directed at any country.

Here I would like to make an additional explanation. China has now normalized relations with the United States and Japan and signed a treaty of peace and friendship with Japan. This is beneficial to the development of relations between countries in the Asia-Pacific region and to the peace and stability of the Asia-Pacific region and the world as a whole. Undoubtedly, of course, it is also favourable to the struggle of all peoples against hegemonism. We have mentioned our opposition to hegemonism in our joint communique. We oppose both big hegemony and small hegemony, both global hegemony and regional hegemony. This will be conducive to the peace of the whole world.

Q: I would like to ask you if there were any Chinese compatriots from Taiwan involved at any stage in the discussions towards normalization?

A: No.

Huang Hua, Chinese Foreign Minister, and Chang Wen-chin, Vice-Foreign Minister, attended the press conference. More than 100 Chinese and foreign correspondents were present.

———————

Peking Review 21, no. 51 (December 22, 1978): 9–11.

DOCUMENT 30

ROC Foreign Minister Y. S. Tsiang's Statement at the ROC-U.S. Talks on Postnormalization Relations, December 28, 1978

The Republic of China has been a long-standing ally of the United States of America. The government and people of the Republic of China have persistently cooperated with the United States in maintaining world peace and upholding the principles of justice. On December 16 [Taipei time], however, President Carter abruptly announced his decision to sever diplomatic relations with our country, to serve notice of his intention to recognize the Chinese Communist regime as of January 1, 1979, and to terminate the Sino-American Mutual Defense Treaty.

I do not consider that the U.S. government has any justifiable cause at all to unilaterally announce its intention to terminate the defense treaty which, as you know, is a treaty of alliance. In addition, so long as the defense treaty between our countries continues to remain in full force and effect, I cannot understand how President Carter can take the position that the diplomatic relations between our two countries can be terminated before that treaty of alliance comes to an end.

We strongly oppose this decision which we believe is wrong, and which has most seriously impaired the rights and interests of this country. We are convinced that it will also impair the long-term interests of the United States and endanger the peace and stability of the Asian-Pacific region. Although President Carter's decision is so far-reaching, we were advised of it only seven hours before it was made public. This is not the way for a leading world power to treat a long-standing ally and it has aroused indignation among the Chinese people both at home and abroad. President Chiang Ching-kuo has made a solemn statement on our position on this unfortunate event. I will not repeat it, but I do hereby lodge a further protest on behalf of my government against the decision of President Carter.

I will now state the fundamental position of my government as the basis of the talks between our two governments.

First, since the founding of the Republic of China in 1911, she has maintained close and friendly relations with the United States. The people of the United States fought shoulder to shoulder with our people during the Second World War.

The close cooperation with the United States continued after the seat of our government moved to Taipei, with the United States government providing us with military and economic aid to help us build our armed forces and expedite our economic development. We have now become your country's eighth trading partner and our total volume of trade with your country has outstripped that of the Chinese Communist regime by nearly ten times. Today we have economic and cultural relations with more than 140 countries and territories. We also maintain diplomatic ties with more than twenty countries.

The Republic of China continues to be an independent sovereign state with an efficient government supported by her people. She has consistently made positive contributions to security, stability and peace in the West Pacific. The U.S. government must recognize these realities.

Second, President Carter has repeatedly expressed his concern for the security and well-being of the people of the Republic of China. This concern must be backed with assurance of security for this region. To build such an assurance merely on the judgment and expectation that the Chinese Communists would not invade Taiwan by the use of force is unrealistic, dangerous, and would have serious consequences. Therefore, the United States must provide concrete and specific measures, through appropriate legislation, to ensure the security of the Republic of China, including the uninterrupted supply of weapons which we need now and in the future.

Finally, I must point out that there are now some 59 treaties and agreements, as well as other arrangements between our two countries. Furthermore, additional agreements and other government-to-government arrangements will be required from time to time to meet future needs. Appropriate legislative measures, therefore, must be taken by your government to ensure that existing treaties, agreements and arrangements continue to remain in full force and effect; and new ones be entered into between our two countries. All these, I emphasize, are essential to the maintenance of future ties between our two countries.

News from China, P. 78–1344 (December 28, 1978).

DOCUMENT 31

President Chiang Ching-kuo's Five Principles on U.S.-ROC Relations in the Postnormalization Period, December 29, 1978

[President Chiang Ching-kuo informed Deputy Secretary of State Christopher that future ties between the Republic of China and the United States must rest on five underlying principles—reality, continuity, security, legality, and governmentality. The President's statement is summarized by Dr. James Chu-yul Soong, Deputy-Director of the Government Information Office, as follows:]

The Republic of China is an independent sovereign state with a legitimately established government based on the Constitution of the Republic of China. It is an effective government, which has the wholehearted support of her people. The international status and personality of the Republic of China cannot be changed merely because of the recognition of the Chinese Communist regime by any country of the world. The legal status and international personality of the Republic of China is a simple reality which the United States must recognize and respect.

The United States has expressed its intention that it will continue to maintain cultural, economic, trade, scientific, technological, and travel relations with the Republic of China. The ties that bound our two countries and people together in the past, however, include much more than these. The Republic of China is ready and willing to continue these traditional ties. The United States, on the other hand, must also realize the importance of the continuity of these ties, not only in their present scope, but also on an expanded scale to meet future needs.

The security of the Asian-Pacific region is also of utmost importance to the well-being and livelihood of the 17 million people on Taiwan, as well as American interests in the area.

The Sino-U.S. Mutual Defense Treaty signed in 1954 was designed to be a vital link in the chain of collective defense system of free countries in the West Pacific. The situation in this region has not changed. It is still unstable and insecure. The threat of invasion and subversion by Communist forces to the free nations of Asia, particularly after the fall of Vietnam, is even more serious than before.

Hence, the U.S. unilateral action to terminate the Sino-U.S. Mutual Defense Treaty will further destabilize this region and might create a new crisis of war. Thus, in order to ensure the peace and security of the West Pacific, which includes that of the Republic of China, it is imperative that the United States take concrete and effective measures to renew its assurances to countries in this region.

We are ready and determined to continue to do our share in securing stability and peace in the West Pacific. But in order to do this, we must have sufficient capabilities to defend ourselves, and thereby protect our neighbors. President Carter has indicated that he is still concerned about the peace, security, and prosperity of this region after the termination of the Sino-U.S. Mutual Defense Treaty, and will continue to supply the Republic of China with defense weapons. The U.S. must give us assurances of a legal nature which would ensure the fulfillment of this commitment.

We are at present faced with the pragmatic problems involved in continuing and maintaining 59 treaties and agreements, as well as other arrangements, between our two countries. Since both the Republic of China and the United States are governed by law, the private interests of both Chinese and American citizens require the protection of definite legal provisions. Appropriate legislative measures in both countries must therefore be taken to provide legal basis on which these security, commercial, and cultural treaties and agreements can continue to remain in full force and effect.

The complex nature of the activities of mutual interest to our two countries makes it impossible for them to be carried out by any private organization or individual. To facilitate the continuation and expansion of all relations between our two countries, it is necessary that government-to-government level mechanisms be set up in Taipei and Washington. This model alone can serve as the framework on which the future relationship of our two countries can be constructed.

News from China, P. 78–1348 (December 29, 1978).

DOCUMENT 32

President Carter's Memorandum for All Departments and Agencies on Future Relations with the People of Taiwan, December 30, 1978

As President of the United States, I have constitutional responsibility for the conduct of the foreign relations of the nation. The United States has announced that on January 1, 1979, it is recognizing the government of the People's Republic of China as the sole legal government of China and is terminating diplomatic relations with the Republic of China. The United States has also stated that, in the future, the American people will maintain commercial, cultural and other relations with the people of Taiwan without official government representation and without diplomatic relations. I am issuing this memorandum to facilitate maintaining those relations pending the enactment of legislation on the subject.

I therefore declare and direct that:

(A) Departments and agencies currently having authority to conduct or carry out programs, transactions, or other relations with or relating to Taiwan are directed to conduct and carry out those programs, transactions, and relations beginning January 1, 1979, in accordance with such authority and, as appropriate, through the instrumentality referred to in paragraph D below.

(B) Existing international agreements and arrangements in force between the United States and Taiwan shall continue in force and shall be performed and enforced by departments and agencies beginning January 1, 1979, in accordance with their terms and, as appropriate, through that instrumentality.

(C) In order to effectuate all of the provisions of this memorandum, whenever any law, regulation, or order of the United States refers to a foreign country, nation, state, government, or similar entity, departments and agencies shall construe those terms and apply those laws, regulations, or orders to include Taiwan.

(D) In conducting and carrying out programs, transactions, and other relations with the people on Taiwan, interests of the people of the United States will be represented as appropriate by an unofficial instrumentality in corporate form, to be identified shortly.

(E) The above directives shall apply to and be carried out by all departments and agencies, except as I may otherwise determine.

I shall submit to the Congress a request for legislation relative to non-governmental relationships between the American people and the people on Taiwan.

This memorandum shall be published in the FEDERAL REGISTER.

(signed) Jimmy Carter

Federal Register 44, no. 3 (January 4, 1979): 1075.

DOCUMENT 33

ROC Statement on U.S. Termination of Mutual Defense Treaty, January 2, 1979

(On January 1, 1979, the U.S. government notified the ROC government of its decision to terminate the Mutual Defense Treaty as of December 31, 1979.

In response to that notice, the ROC Government issued the following statement.)

The government of the Republic of China has scrupulously observed its obligations under the Mutual Defense Treaty, and has never violated any provisions of that treaty. For the U.S. government to unilaterally give notice of termination for no justifiable ground is wholly unthinkable.

In accordance with the principles of international law, the cause and spirit constitute the basis of the provisions of a treaty. To terminate the Mutual Defense Treaty unilaterally without prior consultations violates the basic spirit of the provisions of that treaty.

There has been no vital change of circumstances since the signing of the Mutual Defense Treaty and the termination of the treaty can never be justified on the ground of *rebus sic stantibus* (the principle of changed circumstances).

The government of the Republic of China deplores the unilateral termination of the Mutual Defense Treaty and has lodged its strong protest with the government of the United States. . . .

News from China, P. 79–0002 (January 2, 1979).

DOCUMENT 34

ROC President Chiang Ching-kuo's Statement on Establishing a New Organization to Administer New Relations with the United States, February 15, 1979

The unilateral announcement of the U.S. government last December 15 terminating diplomatic relations with us and recognizing the tyrannical Chinese Communists was a historic tragedy affecting the whole world. In the last two months, we have endured the heavy pain in our hearts in order to negotiate and talk with the United States amidst danger and concern. We wanted to do all we could to mitigate damage from the tragedy and protect the interest of the country and people. In this period, we have done everything we could to carry out our country's fundamental policy. We especially appreciate the support of our compatriots at home and abroad. From beginning to end, they have trusted and encouraged the government and have contributed their wisdom and assistance to the country. We also have been deeply moved by the voice of justice persistently heard in the U.S. Congress and among the multitudes of the American people. This voice has given us warm sympathy and support. It has expressed the profound friendship between the peoples of the Republic of China and the United States and at the same time has indicated that justice still prevails.

In order to restructure and seek the continued development of relations between our two countries, we have decided to set up a new organization.* Reality requires that this time-honored and extremely close relationship be perpetuated, so we must swallow the bitter and handle the situation with all the fortitude at our command. We are also showing the Chinese people's ability to overcome extreme hardship with maximum courage and perserverance. As the negotiations between the two countries proceed, I must emphasize to all the people of the nation that the Republic of China's fundamental policy of anti-Communism and national recovery will never be changed. Current difficulties can in no way shake our confidence and determination. To the contrary, we shall execute our national policy more vigorously, courageously and determinedly. Politically, we shall remain in the democratic camp and safeguard human rights. Economically, we shall strengthen our construction program to sustain steady growth. Militarily, we shall fortify national defense to ensure national security. As long as we remain unafraid, do what we should, maintain our optimism and self-confidence and uphold our position with self-reliance, we can turn adversity to our advantage, open up a fresh vista and create a new horizon.

With the weighty mandate of the people and in the face of national danger and difficulty, I have steadfastly urged myself to proceed with caution and courage and have never allowed myself the illusion that I can afford a single moment of negligence or laxity. I appreciate wholeheartedly the people's total and unreserved support of the government. I want to pledge anew that I shall contribute all that I have and join with my compatriots in partaking of both joy and sorrow. I shall unite with them indestructibly to carry out our common ideal and reach our common goal. We must march forward together courageously until we have won the final victory.

----

*Coordination Council for North American Affairs.
Free China Weekly 20, no. 6 (February 18, 1979): 1.

DOCUMENT 35

Taiwan Relations Act, 1979

SHORT TITLE

Section 1. This Act may be cited as the "Taiwan Relations Act".

FINDINGS AND DECLARATION OF POLICY

SEC. 2. (a) The President having terminated governmental relations between the United States and the governing authorities on Taiwan recognized by the United States as the Republic of China prior to January 1, 1979, the Congress finds that the enactment of this Act is necessary—

(1) to help maintain peace, security, and stability in the Western Pacific; and

(2) to promote the foreign policy of the United States by authorizing the continuation of commercial, cultural, and other relations between the people of the United States and the people on Taiwan.

(b) It is the policy of the United States—

(1) to preserve and promote extensive, close, and friendly commercial, cultural, and other relations between the people of the United States and the people on Taiwan, as well as the people on the China mainland and all other peoples of the Western Pacific area;

(2) to declare that peace and stability in the area are in the political, security, and economic interests of the United States, and are matters of international concern;

(3) to make clear that the United States decision to establish diplomatic relations with the People's Republic of China rests upon the expectation that the future of Taiwan will be determined by peaceful means;

(4) to consider any effort to determine the future of Taiwan by other than peaceful means, including by boycotts or embargoes, a threat to the peace and security of the Western Pacific area and of grave concern to the United States;

(5) to provide Taiwan with arms of a defensive character; and

(6) to maintain the capacity of the United States to resist any resort to force or other forms of coercion that would jeopardize the security, or the social or economic system, of the people on Taiwan.

(c) Nothing contained in this Act shall contravene the interest of the United States in human rights especially with respect to the human rights of all the approximately 18 million inhabitants of Taiwan. The preservation and enhancement of the human rights of all the people on Taiwan are hereby reaffirmed as objectives of the United States.

IMPLEMENTATION OF UNITED STATES POLICY WITH REGARD TO TAIWAN

SEC. 3. (a) In furtherance of the policy set forth in section 2 of this Act, the United States will make available to Taiwan such defense articles and defense services in such quantity as may be necessary to enable Taiwan to maintain a sufficient self-defense capability.

(b) The President and the Congress shall determine the nature and quantity of such defense articles and services based solely upon their judgment of the needs of Taiwan, in accordance with procedures established by law. Such determination of Taiwan's defense needs shall include review by United States military authorities in connection with recommendations to the President and the Congress.

(c) The President is directed to inform the Congress promptly of any threat to the security or the social or economic system of the people on Taiwan and any danger to the interests of the United States arising therefrom. The President and the Congress shall determine, in accordance with constitutional processes, appropriate action by the United States in response to any such danger.

APPLICATION OF LAWS; INTERNATIONAL AGREEMENTS

SEC. 4. (a) The absence of diplomatic relations or recognition shall not affect the application of the laws of the United States with respect to Taiwan, and the laws of the United States shall apply with respect to Taiwan in the manner that the laws of the United States applied with respect to Taiwan prior to January 1, 1979.

(b) The application of subsection (a) of this section shall include, but shall not be limited to, the following:

(1) Whenever the laws of the United States refer or relate to foreign countries, nations, states, governments, or similar entities, such terms shall include and such laws shall apply with respect to Taiwan.

(2) Whenever authorized by or pursuant to the laws of the United States to conduct or carry out programs, transactions, or other relations with respect to foreign countries, nations, states, governments, or similiar entities, the President or any agency of the United States Government is authorized to conduct and carry out, in accordance with section 6 of this Act, such programs, transactions, and other relations with respect to Taiwan (including, but not limited to, the performance of services for the United States through contracts with commercial entities on Taiwan), in accordance with the applicable laws of the United States.

(3) (A) The absence of diplomatic relations and recognition with respect to Taiwan shall not abrogate, infringe, modify, deny, or otherwise affect in any way any rights or obligations (including but not limited to those involving contracts, debts, or property interests of any kind) under the laws of the United States heretofore or hereafter acquired by or with respect to Taiwan.

(B) For all purposes under the laws of the United States, including actions in any court in the United States, recognition of the People's Republic of China shall not affect in any way the ownership of or other rights or interests in properties, tangible and intangible, and other things of value, owned or held on or prior to December 31, 1978, or thereafter acquired or earned by the governing authorities on Taiwan.

(4) Whenever the application of the laws of the United States depends upon the law that is or was applicable on Taiwan or compliance therewith, the

law applied by the people on Taiwan shall be considered the applicable law for that purpose.

(5) Nothing in this Act, nor the facts of the President's action in extending diplomatic recognition to the People's Republic of China, the absence of diplomatic relations between the people on Taiwan and the United States, or the lack of recognition by the United States, and attendant circumstances thereto, shall be construed in any administrative or judicial proceeding as a basis for any United States Government agency, commission, or department to make a finding of fact or determination of law, under the Atomic Energy Act of 1954 and the Nuclear Non-Proliferation Act of 1978, to deny an export license application or to revoke an existing export license for nuclear exports to Taiwan.

(6) For purposes of the Immigration and Nationality Act, Taiwan may be treated in the manner specified in the first sentence of section 202(b) of that Act.

(7) The capacity of Taiwan to sue and be sued in courts in the United States, in accordance with the laws of the United States, shall not be abrogated, infringed, modified, denied, or otherwise affected in any way by the absence of diplomatic relations or recognition.

(8) No requirement, whether expressed or implied, under the laws of the United States with respect to maintenance of diplomatic relations or recognition shall be applicable with respect to Taiwan.

(c) For all purposes, including actions in any court in the United States, the Congress approve the continuation in force of all treaties and other international agreements, including multilateral conventions, entered into by the United States and the governing authorities on Taiwan recognized by the United States as the Republic of China prior to January 1, 1979, and in force between them on December 31, 1978, unless and until terminated in accordance with law.

(d) Nothing in this Act may be construed as a basis for supporting the exclusion or explusion of Taiwan from continued membership in any international financial institution or any other international organization.

OVERSEAS PRIVATE INVESTMENT CORPORATION

SEC. 5. (a) During the three-year period beginning on the date of enactment of this Act, the $1,000 per capita income restriction in clause (2) of the second undesignated paragraph of section 231 of the Foreign Assistance Act of 1961 shall not restrict the activities of the Overseas Private Investment Corporation in determining whether to provide any insurance, reinsurance, loans, or guaranties with respect to investment projects on Taiwan.

(b) Except as provided in subsection (a) of this section, in issuing insurance, reinsurance, loans, or guaranties with respect to investment projects on Taiwan, the Overseas Private Insurance Corporation shall apply the same criteria as those applicable in other parts of the world.

THE AMERICAN INSTITUTE IN TAIWAN

SEC. 6. (a) Programs, transactions, and other relations conducted or carried out by the President or any agency of the United States Government with respect to Taiwan shall, in the manner and to the extent directed by the President, be conducted and carried out by or through—

(1) The American Institute in Taiwan, a nonprofit corporation incorporated under the laws of the District of Columbia, or

(2) such comparable successor nongovernmental entity as the President may designate, (hereafter in this Act referred to as the "Institute").

(b) Whenever the President or any agency of the United States Government is authorized or required by or pursuant to the laws of the United States to enter into, perform, enforce, or have in force an agreement or transaction relative to Taiwan, such agreement or transaction shall be entered into, performed, and enforced, in the manner and to the extent directed by the President, by or through the Institute.

(c) To the extent that any law, rule, regulation, or ordinance of the District of Columbia, or of any State or political subdivision thereof in which the Institute is incorporated or doing business, impedes or otherwise interferes with the performance of the functions of the Institute pursuant to this Act, such law, rule, regulation, or ordinance shall be deemed to be preempted by this Act.

SERVICES BY THE INSTITUTE TO UNITED STATES CITIZENS ON TAIWAN

SEC. 7. (a) The Institute may authorize any of its employees on Taiwan—

(1) to administer to or take from any person an oath, affirmation, affidavit, or deposition, and to perform any notarial act which any notary public is required or authorized by law to perform within the United States;

(2) to act as provisional conservator of the personal estates of deceased United States citizens; and

(3) to assist and protect the interests of United States persons by performing other acts such as are authorized to be performed outside the United States for consular purposes by such laws of the United States as the President may specify.

(b) Acts performed by authorized employees of the Institute under this section shall be valid, and of like force and effect within the United States, as if performed by any other person authorized under the laws of the United States to perform such acts.

TAX EXEMPT STATUS OF THE INSTITUTE

SEC. 8 (a) The Institute, its property, and its income are exempt from all taxation now or hereafter imposed by the United States (except to the extent that section 11 (a) (3) of this Act requires the imposition of taxes imposed under chapter 21 of the Internal Revenue Code of 1954, relating to the Federal Insurance Contributions Act) or by any State or local taxing authority of the United States.

(b) For purposes of the Internal Revenue Code of 1954, the Institute shall be treated as an organization described in sections 170(b)(1)(A), 179(c), 2055(a), 2106(a)(2)(A), 2522, and 2522b).

FURNISHING PROPERTY AND SERVICES TO AND OBTAINING SERVICES FROM THE INSTITUTE

SEC. 9. (a) Any agency of the United States Government is authorized to sell, loan, or lease property (including interests therein) to, and to perform administrative and technical support functions and services for the operations of, the Institute upon such terms and conditions as the President may direct. Reimbursements to agencies under this subsection shall be credited to the current applicable appropriation of the agency concerned.

(b) Any agency of the United States Government is authorized to acquire and accept services from the Institute upon such terms and conditions as the President may direct. Whenever the President determines it to be in furtherance of the purposes of this Act, the procurements of services by such agencies from the Institute may be effected without regard to such laws of the United States normally applicable to the acquisition of services by such agencies as the President may specify by Executive order.

(c) Any agency of the United States Government making funds available to the Institute in accordance with this Act shall make arrangements with the Institute for the Comptroller General of the United States to have access to the books and records of the Institute and the opportunity to audit the operations of the Institute.

TAIWAN INSTRUMENTALITY

SEC. 10. (a) Whenever the President or any agency of the United States Government is authorized or required by or pursuant to the laws of the United States to render or provide to or to receive or accept from Taiwan, any performance, communication, assurance, undertaking, or other action, such action shall, in the manner and to the extent directed by the President, be rendered or provided to, or received or accepted from, an instrumentality established by Taiwan which the President determines has the necessary authority under the laws applied by the people on Taiwan to provide assurances and take other actions on behalf of Taiwan in accordance with the Act.

(b) The President is requested to extend to the instrumentality established by Taiwan the same number of offices and complement of personnel as were previously operated in the United States by the governing authorities on Taiwan recognized as the Republic of China prior to January 1, 1979.

(c) Upon the granting by Taiwan of comparable privileges and immunities with respect to the Institute and its appropriate personnel, the President is authorized to extend with respect to the Taiwan instrumentality and its appropriate personnel, such privileges and immunities (subject to appropriate conditions and obligations) as may be necessary for the effective performance of their functions.

SEPARATION OF GOVERNMENT PERSONNEL FOR
EMPLOYMENT WITH THE INSTITUTE

SEC. 11. (a) (1) Under such terms and conditions as the President may direct, any agency of the United States Government may separate from Government service for a specified period any officer or employee of that agency who accepts employment with the Institute.

(2) An officer or employee separated by an agency under paragraph (1) of this subsection for employment with the Institute shall be entitled upon termination of such employment to reemployment or reinstatement with such agency (or a successor agency) in an appropriate position with the attendant rights, privileges, and benefits which the officer or employee would have had or acquired had he or she not been so separated, subject to such time period and other conditions as the President may prescribe.

(3) An officer or employee entitled to reemployment or reinstatement rights under paragraph (2) of this subsection shall, while continuously employed by the Institute with no break in continuity of service, continue to participate in any benefit program in which such officer or employee was participating prior to employment by the Institute, including programs for compensation for job-related death, injury, or illness; programs for health and life insurance; programs for annual, sick, and other statutory leave; and programs for retirement under any system established by the laws of the United States; except that employment with the Institute shall be the basis for participation in such programs only to the extent that employee deductions and employer contributions, as required, in payment for such participation for the period of employment with the Institute, are currently deposited in the program's or system's fund or depository. Death or retirement of any such officer or employee during approved service with the Institute and prior to reemployment or reinstatement shall be considered a death in or retirement from Government service for purposes of any employee or survivor benefits acquired by reason of service with an agency of the United States Government.

(4) Any officer or employee of an agency of the United States Government who entered into service with the Institute on approved leave of absence without pay prior to the enactment of this Act shall receive the benefits of this section for the period of such services.

(b) Any agency of the United States Government employing alien personnel on Taiwan may transfer such personnel, with accrued allowances, benefits, and rights, to the Institute without a break in service for purposes of retirement and other benefits, including continued participation in any system established by the laws of the United States for the retirement of employees in which the alien was participating prior to the transfer to the Institute, except that employment with the Institute shall be creditable for retirement purposes only to the extent that employee deductions and employer contributions, as required, in payment for such participation for the period of employment with the Institute, are currently deposited in the system's fund or depository.

(c) Employees of the Institute shall not be employees of the United States and, in representing the Institute, shall be exempt from section 207 of title 18, United States Code.

(d)(1) For purposes of sections 911 and 913 of the Internal Revenue Code of 1954, amounts paid by the Institute to its employees shall not be treated as earned income. Amounts received by employees of the Institute shall not be included in gross income, and shall be exempt from taxation, to the extent that they are equivalent to amounts received by civilian officers and employees of the Government of the United States as allowances and benefits which are exempt from taxation under section 912 of such Code.

(2) Except to the extent required by subsection (a)(3) of this section, service performed in the employ of the Institute shall not constitute employment for purposes of chapter 21 of such Code and title II of the Social Security Act.

REPORTING REQUIREMENTS

SEC. 12. (a) The Secretary of State shall transmit to the Congress the text of any agreement to which the Institute is a party. However, any such agreement the immediate public disclosure of which would, in the opinion of the President, be prejudicial to the national security of the United States shall not be so transmitted to the Congress but shall be transmitted to the Committee on Foreign Relations of the Senate and the Committee on Foreign Affairs of the House of Representatives under an appropriate injunction of secrecy to be removed only upon due notice from the President.

(b) For purposes of subsection (a), the term "agreement" includes—

(1) any agreement entered into between the Institute and the governing authorities on Taiwan or the instrumentality established by Taiwan; and

(2) any agreement entered into between the Institute and an agency of the United States Government.

(c) Agreements and transactions made or to be made by or through the Institute shall be subject to the same congressional notification, review, and approval requirements and procedures as if such agreements and transactions were made by or through the agency of the United States Government on behalf of which the Institute is acting.

(d) During the two-year period beginning on the effective date of this Act, the Secretary of State shall transmit to the Speaker of the House of Representatives and the Committee on Foreign Relations of the Senate, every six months, a report describing and reviewing economic relations between the United States and Taiwan, noting any interference with normal commercial relations.

RULES AND REGULATIONS

SEC. 13. The President is authorized to prescribe such rules and regulations as he may deem appropriate to carry out the purposes of this Act. During the three-year period beginning on the effective date of this Act, such rules and regulations shall be transmitted promptly to the Speaker of the House of Representatives and to the Committee on Foreign Relations of the Senate. Such action shall not, however, relieve the Institute of the responsibilities placed upon it by this Act.

CONGRESSIONAL OVERSIGHT

SEC. 14. (a) The Committee on Foreign Affairs of the House of Representatives, the Committee on Foreign Relations of the Senate, and other appropriate committees of the Congress shall monitor—

(1) the implementation of the provisions of this Act;

(2) the operation and procedures of the Institute;

(3) the legal and technical aspects of the continuing relationship between the United States and Taiwan; and

(4) the implementation of the policies of the United States concerning security and cooperation in East Asia.

(b) Such committees shall report, as appropriate, to their respective Houses on the results of their monitoring.

DEFINITIONS

SEC. 15. For purposes of this Act—

(1) the term "laws of the United States" includes any statute, rule, regulation, ordinance, order, or judicial rule of decision of the United States or any political subdivision thereof; and

(2) the term "Taiwan" includes, as the context may require, the islands of Taiwan and the Pescadores, the people on those islands, corporations and other entities and associations created or organized under the laws applied on those islands, and the governing authorities on Taiwan recognized by the United States as the Republic of China prior to January 1, 1979, and any successor governing authorities (including political subdivisions, agencies, and instrumentalities thereof).

AUTHORIZATION OF APPROPRIATIONS

SEC. 16. In addition to funds otherwise available to carry out the provisions of this Act, there are authorized to be appropriated to the Secretary of State for the fiscal year 1980 such funds as may be necessary to carry out such provisions. Such funds are authorized to remain available until expended.

SEVERABILITY OF PROVISIONS

SEC. 17. If any provisions of this Act or the application thereof to any person or circumstance is held invalid, the remainder of the Act and the application of such provision to any other person or circumstance shall not be affected thereby.

EFFECTIVE DATE

SEC. 18. This Act shall be effective as of January 1, 1979.

Congressional Record–House 125, No. 38 (March 16, 1979): H1668-70.

Selected Bibliography

BOOKS

Asian American Assembly for Policy Research. *Position Paper I. A Review of U.S.-China Relations*. Baltimore: Occasional Papers/Reprints in Contemporary Asian Studies, No. 11-1977, University of Maryland School of Law, 1978.

Barclay, George W. *Colonial Development and Population in Taiwan*. Princeton, N.J.: Princeton University Press, 1954.

Barnds, William J., ed. *China and America: The Search for a New Relationship*. New York: New York University Press (Council on Foreign Relations), 1977.

Barnett, A. Doak. *China and the Major Powers in East Asia*. Washington, D.C.: Brookings Institution, 1977.

——. *China Policy, Old Problems and New Challenges*. Washington, D.C.: Brookings Institution, 1977.

Bellows, Thomas J. *Taiwan's Foreign Policy in the 1970s: A Case Study of Adaptation and Viability*. Baltimore: Occasional Papers/Reprints in Contempory Asian Studies, No. 4-1977, University of Maryland School of Law, 1977.

Bueler, William M. *U.S. China Policy and the Problem of Taiwan*. Boulder: Colorado Associated University Press, 1971.

Campbell, William. *Formosa Under the Dutch*. London: Kegan Paul, Trench, Trubner, 1903.

Chaffee, Frederick H. et al. *Area Handbook for the Republic of China*. Foreign Area Studies. Washington, D.C.: U.S. Government Printing Office, 1968.

Chen, Lung-chu and Harold D. Lasswell. *Formosa, China, and the United Nations*. New York: St. Martin's Press, 1967.

Chien, Fredrick F. *More Views of a Friend*. Taipei: Government Information Office, 1975.

China Yearbook. Taipei: China Publishing Co., annual publication since 1950.

Chinese People's Institute of Foreign Affairs. *Oppose U.S. Occupation of Taiwan and "Two China" Plot*. Peking: Foreign Languages Press, 1958.

Chin-shan ho-yueh yu chung-jih ho-yueh ti kuan-hsi (The relationship between the San Francisco Peace Treaty and the Sino-Japanese Peace Treaty). Edited and published by Chung-hua min-kuo wai-chiao wen-t'i yen-chiu hui, 1966.

Chiu, Hungdah, ed. *China and The Question of Taiwan: Documents and Analysis*. New York: Praeger, 1973.

——. *Normalizing Relations with the People's Republic of China: Problems, Analysis and Documents*. Baltimore: Occasional Papers/Reprints Series in Contemporary Asian Studies, No. 2-1978(14), University of Maryland School of Law, 1978.

Chiu, Hungdah and David Simon, eds. *Proceedings of Conference on legal Aspect of United States–Republic of China Trade and Investment* (A Regional Conference of the American Society of International Law). Baltimore: Occasional Papers/Reprints Series in Contemporary Asian Studies, No. 10-1977, University of Maryland School of Law, 1977.

Clough, Ralph N. *East Asian and U.S. Security*. Washington, D.C.: Brookings Institution, 1975.

——. *Island China*. Cambridge, Mass.: Harvard University Press, 1968.

Clough, Ralph N., Robert B. Oxnam, and William Watts. *The United States and China: American Perceptions and Future Alternatives*. Washington, D.C.: Potomac Associates, 1977.

Cohen, Jerome Alan, and Hungdah Chiu. *People's China and International Law: A Documentary Study*. 2 vols. Princeton, N.J.: Princeton University Press, 1974.

Cohen, Jerome Alan, Edward Friedman, Harold C. Hindon, and Allen S. Whiting. *Taiwan and American Policy, The Dilemma in U.S.-China Relations*. New York: Praeger, 1971.

Croizier, Ralph C. *Koxinga and Chinese Nationalism: History, Myth, and the Hero*. Cambridge, Mass.: Harvard University Press, 1977.

Davidson, James W. *The Island of Formosa*. N.p., 1903; reprinted Taipei: Wen hsing shu chu, 1964.

Fairbank, John K. *Chinese American Interactions, A Historical Summary*. New Brunswick, N.J.: Rutgers University Press, 1975.

Feulner, Edwin J., Jr., ed. *China–The Turning Point*. Washington, D.C.: Council on American Affairs, 1976.

Goddard, W. G. *Formosa: A Study in Chinese History.* London: Macmillan, 1966.

Goldwater, Barry M. *China and the Abrogation of Treaties.* Washington, D.C.: Heritage Foundation, 1978.

Gordon, Leonard H. D. *Taiwan: Studies in Chinese Local History.* New York: Columbia University Press, 1970.

Ho, Samuel P. S. *Economic Development of Taiwan, 1860–1970.* New Haven, Conn.: Yale University Press, 1978.

Hsiao, Gene T., ed. *Sino-American Detente and Its Policy Implications.* New York: Praeger, 1974.

Hsieh, Chiao-min. *Taiwan-ilha Formosa: A Geography in Perspective.* Washington, D.C.: Butterworths, 1964.

Hsieh, S. C., and T. H. Lee. *Agricultural Development and Its Contributions to Economic Growth in Taiwan-Input-Output and Productivity Analysis of Taiwan Agricultural Development.* Taipei: Joint Commission on Rural Reconstruction, 1966.

Hsu, Wen-hsiung. "Chinese Colonization of Taiwan." Ph.D. dissertation, University of Chicago, 1975.

Huang Ching-chia. *Jih-chü shih-ch'i chih T'ai-wan chih-min-ti fa-chih yü chih-min t'ung-chih* (Taiwan Colonial legal system and colonial rule under the Japanese occupation). Taipei: privately published, 1960.

Huang, Mab. *Intellectual Ferment for Political Reforms in Taiwan, 1971–73.* Ann Arbor: University of Michigan Press, 1976.

Important Documents Concerning the Question of Taiwan. Peking: Foreign Languages Press, 1955.

Jacoby, Neil H. *U.S. Aid to Taiwan: A Study of Foreign Aid, Self-Help and Development.* New York: Praeger, 1966.

Jo, Yung-Hwan, ed. *Taiwan's Future.* Tempe: Union Research Institute for Center for Asian Studies, Arizona State University, May 1974.

Kalicki, J. H. *The Pattern of Sino-American Crisis.* London: Cambridge University Press, 1975.

Kerr, George H. *Formosa: Licensed Revolution and the Home Rule Movement 1895–1945.* Honolulu: University Press of Hawaii, 1974.

Koo, Anthony Y. C. *The Role of Land Reform in Economic Development: A Case Study of Taiwan.* New York: Praeger, 1968.

Kuo Ting-yee. *T'ai-wan shih-shih kai-shu* (General history of Taiwan). Third printing. Taipei: Cheng chung shu chu, 1964.

Li, Victor H. *De-recognizing Taiwan: The Legal Problems.* Washington, D.C.: Carnegie Endowment for International Peace, 1977.

Lien Chen-tung. *Chiang tsung-t'ung yü T'ai-wan sheng ti kuang-fu ch'ung-chien* (President Chiang and the Restoration and reconstruction of the Taiwan Province). Two volumes. Taipei: Chung-yang wen-wu kung-ying she, 1967.

Lien Heng. *T'ai-wan t'ung shih* (A comprehensive history of Taiwan). Two volumes. Edited from 1921 Taiwan edition. Taipei: Chung hua ts'ung shu wei yuan hui, 1954.

Lin Hsiung-hsiang and Huang Wang-cheng, eds. *Tai-wan sheng t'ung-chih kao* (Draft history of Taiwan Province), Vol. 9, *Ke-min chih-k'ang jih pien* (History of revolution-resistance against Japan). Taipei: T'ai-wan sheng wen hsien wei yuan hui, 1954.

Lumbey, F. A. *The Republic of China Under Chiang Kai-shek: Taiwan Today.* London: Barrie and Jenkins, 1976.

MacFarquhar, Roderick. *Sino-American Relations, 1949–71.* New York: Praeger, 1972.

Mancall, Mark. ed. *Formosa Today.* New York: Praeger, 1968.

Mendel, Douglas. *The Politics of Formosan Nationalism.* Berkeley: University of California Press, 1970.

Moorsteen, Richard, and Morton Abramowitz. *Remaking China Policy.* Cambridge, Mass.: Harvard University Press, 1971.

Morello, Frank P. *The International Legal Status of Formosa.* The Hague: Martinus Nijhoff, 1966.

Myers, Ramon H., ed. *Two Chinese States: U.S. Foreign Policy and Interests.* Stanford, Calif.: Hoover Institution Press, 1978.

National Conditions. Taipei: Statistical Bureau, DGBAS, Executive Yuan, Republic of China, Quarterly.

Normalization of Relations with the People's Republic of China: Practical Implications. Hearings before the Subcommittee on Asian and Pacific Affairs of the House Committee on International Relations, 95th Cong., 1st Sess.

(September 20, 21, 28, 29; October 11, and 13, 1977). Washington, D.C.: U.S. Government Printing Office, 1977.

Oksenberg, Michel and Robert B. Oxnam. *China and America: Past and Future.* (Headline Series, No. 235.) New York: Foreign Policy Association, 1977.

Prybyla, Jan S. *The Societal Objective of Wealth, Growth, Stability, and Equity in Taiwan.* Baltimore: Occasional Papers/Reprints in Contemporary Asian Studies, No. 4–1978 (16), University of Maryland School of Law, 1978.

Rankin, Karl L. *China Assignment.* Seattle: University of Washington Press, 1964.

Rowe, David Nelson. *Informal "Diplomatic Relations": The Case of Japan and the Republic of China, 1972–1974.* Hamden, Conn.: Shoe String Press, 1975.

Shen, R. H., ed. *Agriculture's Place in the Strategy of Development: The Taiwan Experience.* Taipei: Joint Commission on Rural Reconstruction, 1974.

Sheng, Ching-i and others. *T'ai-wan Shih* (The history of Taiwan). Taipei: Taiwan Historical Commission, 1977.

Sigur, Gaston J. *The Asian Alliance: Japan and United States Policy.* New York: National Strategy Information Center, 1972.

Sih, Paul K. T. *Taiwan in Modern Times.* Jamaica, N.Y.: St. John's University Press, 1973.

Sino-American Relations: A New Turn. A Trip Report [by Senator John Glenn and others] to the Senate Committee on Foreign Relations, January 1979. Washington, D.C.: U.S. Government Printing Office, 1979.

Statistical Data Book of the Interior. Taipei: Ministry of Interior, Republic of China, annual publication.

Statistical Yearbook of the Republic of China. Taipei: Directorate-General of Budget, Accounting and Statistics, Executive Yuan, Republic of China, Annual.

Taiwan. Hearings before the Senate Committee on Foreign Relations, 96th Cong., 1st sess. (February 5, 6, 7, 8, 21, and 22, 1979). Washington, D.C.: U.S. Government Printing Office, 1979.

Taiwan Enabling Act. Report of the Senate Foreign Relations Committee on S. 245. Washington, D.C.: U.S. Government Printing Office, 1979.

Tsou, Tang. *Embroilment over Quemoy: Mao, Chiang, and Dulles.* Salt Lake City: University of Utah Press, 1959.

Tsurumi, E. Patricia. *Japanese Colonial Education in Taiwan, 1895–1945*. Cambridge, Mass.: Harvard University Press, 1977.

United States-China Relations: The Process of Normalization of Relations. Hearings before a House Special Subcommittee on Investigations of the Committee on International Relations, 94th Cong. (November 18, December 8 and 17, 1975; February 2, 1976). Washington, D.C.: U.S. Government Printing Office.

United States Security Agreement and Commitments Abroad, Republic of China. Hearings before the Subcommittee on United States Security Agreements and Commitments Abroad of Committee on Foreign Relations, U.S. Senate, 91st Cong., 2d sess., Part 4 (November 24, 25 and 26, 1969, and May 8, 1970). Washington, D.C.: U.S. Government Printing Office, 1970.

Whiting, Allen S. *China and the United States: What Next?* (Headline Series, No. 230.) New York: Foreign Policy Association, 1976.

Williams, Jack F., ed. *The Taiwan Issue*. East Lansing, Mich.: East Asian Series/ Occasional Paper No. 5, May 1976.

Wilson, Richard W. *Learning to Be Chinese: The Political Socialization of Children in Taiwan*. Cambridge: M.I.T. Press, 1970.

Wu, Yuan-li. *U.S. Policy and Strategic Interests in the Western Pacific*. New York: Crane, Russak and Co.,; St. Lucia: University of Queensland Press, 1975.

Wu, Yuan-li and Kung-chia Yeh, eds. *Growth, Distribution, and Social Change: Essays on the Economy of the Republic of China*. Baltimore: Occasional Papers/Reprints in Contemporary Asian Studies, No. 3–1978 (15), University of Maryland School of Law, 1978.

Yang, Martin M. C. *Socio-Economic Results of Land Reform in Taiwan*. Honolulu: University Press of Hawaii, for East-West Center, 1970.

Yen, Sophia Su-fei. *Taiwan in China's Foreign Relations, 1836–1874*. Hamden, Conn.: Shoe String Press, 1965.

Young, Kenneth T. *Negotiating with the Chinese Communists: The United States Experience, 1953–1963*. New York: McGraw-Hill, 1968.

ARTICLES

American Chamber of Commerce in the Republic of China. "US-Republic of China Economic Relationship: A Businessman's View." *International Trade Law Journal* 3, no. 1 (Fall 1977): 130–38.

Appleton, Sheldon. "Taiwanese and Mainlanders on Taiwan: A Survey of Student Attitudes." *China Quarterly*, No. 44 (October-December 1970), pp. 38-65.

Baum, Richard. "Jimmy Carter & China." *Asia Mail* 2, no. 7 (April 1978): 1, 10, 14.

Chang Han-yu and Ramon H. Meyers. "Japanese Colonial Development Policy in Taiwan, 1895-1906: A Case of Bureaucratic Entrepreneurship." *Journal of Asian Studies* 22, no. 4 (August 1963): 433-49.

Chen, Lung-chu, and W. M. Reisman. "Who Owns Taiwan: A Search for International Title." *Yale Law Journal* 81, no. 4 (March 1972): 599-671.

Chiu, Hungdah. "Certain Legal Aspects of Recognizing the People's Republic of China." *Case Western Reserve Journal of International Law*, to be published in 1979.

———. "Normalizing Relations with China: Some Practical and Legal Problems." *Asian Affairs, An American View* 5, no. 2 (November-December 1977): 67-87.

Chen, King C. "Peking's Attitude Toward Taiwan." *Asian Survey* 17, no. 10 (October 1977): 903-18.

Copper, John F. "Taiwan's Energy Situation." In *National Energy Profiles*, edited by Kenneth R. Stunkel. New York: Praeger, 1979.

———. "Taiwan's Strategy and America's China Policy." *ORBIS* 21, no 2 (Summer 1977): 261-76.

Durdin, Tillman. "Chiang Ching-kuo and Taiwan: A Profile." *ORBIS* 18, no. 4 (Winter 1975): 1023-42.

———. "Chiang Ching-kuo's Taiwan." *Pacific Community* 7, no. 1 (October 1975): 92-117.

Feulner, Edwin J. "Chiang Ching-kuo: Asia, Taiwan & the Man." *Asia Mail* 2, no. 8 (May 1978): 1, 8, 17.

Findley, Paul. "U.S. Congress & China." *Asia Mail* 2, no. 4 (January 1978): 1, 8.

Garver, John W. "Taiwan's Russian Option: Image and Reality." *Asian Survey* 18, no. 7 (July 1978): 751-66.

Heuser, Robert. "Legal Aspects of Trade with and Investment in the Republic of China: The German Experience." *International Trade Law Journal*. 3, no. 1 (Fall 1977): 172-88.

Hsiung, James C. "U.S. Relations with China in the Post-Kissingerian Era: A Sensible Policy for the 1980s." *Asian Survey* 17, no. 8 (August 1977): 691–710.

Jain, J. P. "The Legal Status of Formosa." *American Journal of International Law* 57, no. 1 (January 1963): 25–45.

Javits, Jacob R. "Washington's Connections: Tokyo, Seoul & Taipei." *Asia Mail* 2, no. 6 (March 1978): 1, 8, 19.

Karnow, Stanley. "Our Next Move on China." New York *Times Magazine*, August 14, 1977.

Kau, Michael Y. M. et al. "Public Opinion and our China Policy." *Asian Affairs, An American View* 5, no. 3 (January-February 1978): 133–47.

Kennedy, Edward M. "China Ties Urged." *Asia Mail* 2, no. 11 (August 1978): 1, 9.

Kim, H. N. "The Tanaka Government and the Politics of the Sino-Japanese Civil Aviations Pact, 1972–1974." *World Affairs* (Washington), 137 (1975): 386–402.

Lamley, Harry J. "The 1895 Taiwan Republic." *Journal of Asian Studies* 27, no. 4 (August 1968): 739–62.

Lelyveld, Joseph. "A 1½ China Policy." New York *Times Magazine*, April 6, 1975.

Lerman, Arthur J. "National Elite and Local Politicians in Taiwan." *American Political Science Review* 71, no. 4 (December 1977): 1406–22.

Myers, Ramon H. "Taiwan under Ch'ing Imperial Rule, 1684–1895: The Traditional Economy." *Journal of the Institute of Chinese Studies of the Chinese University of Hong Kong* 5, no. 2 (1972): 373–411.

——. "Taiwan under Ch'ing Imperial Rule, 1684–1895: The Traditional Order." *Journal of the Institute of Chinese Studies of the Chinese University of Hong Kong* 4, no. 2 (1971): 495–522.

——. "Taiwan under Ch'ing Imperial Rule, 1684–1895: The Traditional Society." *Journal of the Institute of Chinese Studies of the Chinese University of Hong Kong* 5, no. 2 (1972): 413–53.

Myers, Ramon H., and Adrienne Ching. "Agricultural Development in Taiwan Under Japanese Colonial Rule." *Journal of Asian Studies* 23, no. 4 (August 1964): 555–70.

O'Connell, D. P. "The Status of Formosa and the Chinese Recognition Problem." *American Journal of International Law* 52, no. 2 (April 1956): 405–16.

Perrolle, Pierre M. "Does the PRC Consider Taiwan Analogous to Tibet." *Contempory China* 2, no. 1 (Spring 1978): 58–61.

Reardon-Anderson, James. "Peking and Washington: The Politics of Abnormalization." *Contemporary China* 2, no. 1 (Spring 1978): 3–12.

Scalapino, Robert A. "Approaches to Peace and Security in Asia: The Uncertainty Surrounding American Strategic Principles." *Current Scene* 16, nos. 8 and 9 (August-September 1978): 1–18.

——. "China and the Balance of Power." *Foreign Affairs* 52, no. 1 (January 1974): 349–85.

——. "The Question of 'Two Chinas.'" In *China in Crisis*, Vol. 2; *China's Policies in Asia and America's Alternatives*, edited by Tang Tsou. Chicago: University of Chicago Press, 1968.

Schiebel, Joseph. "The Soviet Union and the Sino-American Relationship." *ORBIS* 21, no. 1 (Spring 1977): 77–94.

Schroder, Norma. "America's Economic Stake in Taiwan." *International Trade Law Journal* 3, no. 1 (Fall 1977): 40–48.

Solomon, Richard H. "Thinking Through the China Problem." *Foreign Affairs* 56, no. 2 (1977): 324–56.

Tai, Hung-chao. "The Kuomintang and Modernization in Taiwan." In *Authoritarian Politics in Modern Society*, edited by Samuel P. Huntington and Clement H. Moore. New York: Basic Books, 1970.

Tien, Hung-mao. "Taiwan in Transition: Prospects for Socio-Political Change." *China Quarterly*, No. 64 (October-December 1975), pp. 615–44.

Wei, Yung. "Modernization Process in Taiwan: An Allocative Analysis." *Asian Survey* 16, no. 3 (March 1976): 249–69.

——. "The Republic of China in the 1970s: Striving for a Future of Growth, Equity and Security." *International Trade Law Journal* 3, no. 1 (Fall 1977): 2–11.

——. "Unification or Confrontation: An Assessment of Future Relations between Mainland China and Taiwan." In *The Politics of Division, Partition, and Unification*, edited by Ray E. Johnston. New York: Praeger, 1976.

Weiss, Thomas. "Taiwan and U.S. Policy." *ORBIS* 12, no. 4 (Winter 1969): 1165–87.

Whiting, Allen S. "Taiwan's Future." *Asia Mail* 2, no. 8 (May 1978): 1, 8.

Wilson, Richard W. "A Comparison of Political Attitudes of Taiwanese Children and Mainlander Children on Taiwan." *Asian Survey* 8, no. 12 (December 1968): 980–1000.

Wu, Yuan-li, and Kung-chia Yeh. "Economic Impact of Alternative US-Republic of China Relations." *International Trade Law Journal* 3, no. 1 (Fall 1977): 139–71.

Index

Italy, 162

Japan, 8, 11, 50, 51, 53, 55, 58, 64,
    66, 72, 79, 82, 84, 91, 107, 119,
    120, 122, 130, 132, 133, 135,
    138, 148, 149, 150, 158, 163–
    64, 164, 165, 166, 167, 176,
    181, 191, 193, 196, 197, 201–
    02, 219; conflict with China on
    Taiwan, 16, 16–17; control of
    Taiwan, 7, 17, 20–24, 216;
    dispute over Senkaku Islands,
    61, 139–40 (see also Sino-
    Japanese War; Sino-Japanese
    Peace Treaty)
Japan formula, 2, 181, 182, 207
Japan v. Lai Chin Jung (Tokyo High
    Court, 1956), 165
Japanese Communist party, 27
Japanese Instrument of Surrender
    (1945), 148, 152, 164, 166, 216
Johnson, Louis, 149
Johnson, Lyndon B., 177
Joint Chiefs of Staff (U.S.), 149
Judd, Walter, 149
Judicial Yuan, 45

K'ang Yu-wei, 18
Kansas City, establishment of the ROC
    consulate in, 136
Kaohsiung, 16, 46, 95
Kau, Y. M., 209
Keelung, 17
Keng Ching-chung, 11
Keng Piao, 137, 140, 142, 194
Kennedy, John F., 173
Khrushchev, Nikita, 169, 170–71, 173
Kiangsi Province, 66
Kiangsu Province, 12, 37
Kirk, Alan G., 173
Kissinger, Henry, 179, 181, 206, 258
KMT (see Kuomintang)
Knowland, William F., 149
Kodama Gentarō, 22
Koo, Willington, 200
Korea, 18, 21, 25, 66, 152, 190, 236;

South Korea, 53, 84, 117, 158
Korean War (1950–53), 51, 150, 151,
    155, 157, 158, 179, 253; Mili-
    tary Armistice Agreement
    (1953), 158, 190
Koxinga (see Cheng Ch'eng-kung,
    Cheng government)
Kuo Ta-kai, 130
Kuomintang (Nationalist party), 25,
    27, 29, 31, 32, 38, 42, 44, 45,
    47–48, 49, 61, 62, 64, 65, 66,
    67, 70, 132, 134, 240; Central
    Committee, 47, 48, 70; Taiwan
    and Kuomingtang revolution (up
    to 1945), 30–33
Kurile Islands, 223
Kwangchow, 31
Kwangtung, 9, 15, 37

labor, 92, 94
land reform, 38, 50, 51
Laos, 190, 248
Lauterpacht, H., 162, 166–67
League of Nations, 29
Legal Status of Eastern Greenland
    Case (Permanent Court of Inter-
    national Justice, 1933), 163
legal system, 45, 126
Legislative Yuan, 44–45, 148
Lelyveld, Joseph, 209
Li Hung-chang, 18
liaison office (U.S.-PRC), 127, 181,
    183, 251
Liang Ch'i-ch'ao, 24–25
Liao Ch'eng-chih, 130, 134, 140
Liao Chih-kao, 137
liberation, peaceful (see reunification)
Lie, Trygve, 151
Lien Wen-ch'ing, 27, 28
Lin Hsiên-t'ang, 24, 27, 29
Lin Kung, 15
Lin Li-yun, 130, 134
Lin Piao, 176
Lin Shuang-wen, 15
Liu Ch'iu, case of aborigines' killing of
    shipwrecked sailors (1871–

About the Editor and
the Contributors

HUNGDAH CHIU is Professor of Law at University of Maryland School of Law, author of the *People's Republic of China and the Law of Treaties*, co-author of *People's China and International Law: A Documentary Study*, and author of eight other books on Chinese international law and relations. In 1976 he was awarded a certificate of merit by the American Society of International Law.

KING C. CHEN is Professor of Political Science at Rutgers University and author of *Vietnam and China, 1938-1954* and several other studies on Chinese foreign policy.

JOHN FRANKLIN COPPER is Associate Professor of International Studies at Southwestern at Memphis and author of *China's Foreign Aid: An Instrument of Peking's Foreign Policy* and several other studies on Chinese politics and foreign relations.

SHAO-CHUAN LENG is Doherty Foundation Professor of Government and Foreign Affairs at University of Virginia and author of *Justice in Communist China*, and four other books on Chinese politics and foreign relations.

JAN S. PRYBYLA is Professor of Economics at Pennsylvania State University and author of *The Chinese Economy, Problems and Policies* and several other studies on Chinese economy.

YU-MING SHAW is Assistant Professor of History at Notre Dame University and Associate at Center for Far Eastern Studies of the University of Chicago. He is now preparing a book on *Ambassador John Leighton Stuart in China*.